# ON YOUR OWN IN
# EL SALVADOR

## 2ND EDITION

# ON YOUR OWN IN
# EL SALVADOR

BY
HANK & BEA WEISS

EDITOR IN CHIEF
TIM BEWER

FIRST EDITION BY
JEFF BRAUER, VERONICA WILES,
AND JULIAN SMITH

ON YOUR OWN
PUBLICATIONS

## On Your Own in El Salvador, 2nd Edition

Copyright © 2001 by On Your Own Publications, LLC

All rights reserved under International and Pan-American Copyright Conventions. No maps, illustrations or other portions of this book may be reproduced in any form without written permission from the publisher.

### Published by

On Your Own Publications
Head Office: Bldg 120, Ste 207, Brooklyn Navy Yard, Brooklyn, NY 11205

### Photographs

CORSATUR, The Banco Agricola Comercial, Jeff Brauer, Veronica Wiles, and Julian Smith.
Front cover: Santa Ana Volcano and Lago de Coatepeque

### Previous Editions

English edition first published in November 1995
Spanish edition first published in September 1997

ISBN: 1-929377-06-1

Second edition, first printing

Cover and contents designed by Greg Evans & Paul Choi

Together the husband and wife team of **Hank and Bea Weiss** have had 40 years of real life adventure in El Salvador and have been first hand witnesses to the country's historic turn around over the past two decades. Hank is the product of two Midwesterners who had the vision to tell him to "learn a language because the world is getting smaller." He chose Spanish and has spent 14 of the past 20 years working in Latin America. Bea was born and raised in El Salvador and both now reside in San Salvador. Their work as engineers, directing rural and urban infrastructure projects, have taken them to the remotest corners of the country. Prior to this project Hank wrote three books on safety and training for the energy and transportation industries.

---

**Tim Bewer** gave up a career as a legislative assistant to become a freelance writer, editor, and photographer with a strong focus on travel. This vocational about face has taken him to over 30 countries. He has written or contributed to books on Wisconsin, Ecuador, and New York City, and his articles, covering topics ranging from autism to punk rock, have appeared in newspapers and magazines in the US, Canada, and the UK. He is currently at work on a guidebook to Minnesota and some day, if he can ever find the time, he will finish his novel.

**E**l Salvador, like much of Latin America, is in the middle of an historic period of transition. Prices will go up, restaurants and hotels will close and others will open. Bus schedules, government regulations and street names will change.

When you discover something newer, better, worse or just plain different from what we have reported, please write us and tell us about it. Your letters will be used to help us update the next edition of On Your Own in El Salvador.

We read every letter we receive, and especially appreciate those with practical information, travel tips, opinions and entertaining stories. The best correspondence will earn a free copy of one of our books. Drop us a line at OYO, Bldg 120, Ste 207, Brooklyn Navy Yard, Brooklyn, NY 11205, or email us at oyobooks@yahoo.com

Also, we always welcome inquiries from young, experienced writers interested in helping to compile a book to another destination. It's hard work, but we'd love to hear from you.

# Muchas Gracias

Pablo Garcia of Aventours
Julia Andino
Lena Johannessen of Ximena's and Lisa's Guest houses
Zulema Tovar of CORSATUR
Reynaldo Avalos
Patricia Aguilar
Loli de Melendez
Hank and Dorothy Weiss
Reynaldo and Carmen Avalos
and last but not least our sons Hanko and Franko Weiss

Special thanks for the use of photos to:

# CONTENTS

# San Salvador . . . . . .93

# To the West . . . . . .137

# To the North . . . . . . .205

# To the East . . . . . . . .225

# Spanish Phrasebook...281

# Index . . . . . . . . . . . . . . .283

# Culture Boxes

### Introduction

### Background

## Timelines

## Charts & Graphs

# Map Key

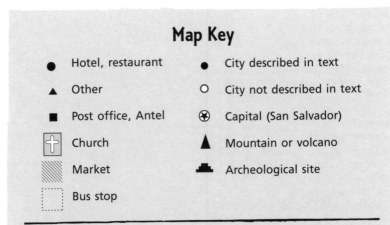

- ● Hotel, restaurant
- ▲ Other
- ■ Post office, Antel
- ✚ Church
- ▨ Market
- ⬚ Bus stop

- ● City described in text
- ○ City not described in text
- ✪ Capital (San Salvador)
- ▲ Mountain or volcano
- 🏛 Archeological site

**Avenidas:** Even numbers increase to east
Odd numbers increase to west
**Calles:** Even numbers increase to south
Odd numbers increase to north

**Map Abbreviations**
Av    Avenida (avenue)
C     Calle (street)
Nte   Norte (north)
Sur   (south)
Ote   Oriente (east)
Pte   Poniente (west)
Col   Colonia (suburb)
Bo    Barrio (neighborhood)

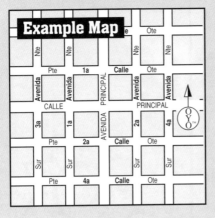

**Other General Notes**
- Hotels and restaurants not reviewed in text are italicized on maps.
- City population figures refer to entire municipalities, so actual city populations may be smaller.
- All prices are in US dollars ($).
- Festival dates in parentheses are main day(s) of festival.

# STOP PRESS

On January 13 a 7.6-magnitude earthquake shook El Salvador killing around 850 people and injuring another 8,000. Exactly one month later a 6.6-magnitude quake killed another 400 people and injured over 3,000. These two massive earthquakes caused extensive damage (estimated at $1.6 billion) throughout the country, particularly in rural areas, and left over half a million people homeless.

These two quakes have been named The Earthquakes of the Poor because most damage occurred to older bamboo, artisan brick, and adobe houses (the types that the poor generally live in) while modern buildings with proper foundations and steel reinforcements were for the most part unaffected. Most of the places detailed in this guide are back to normal though some of the areas hardest hit were the towns of Alegría, Santiago de Maria, Usulután, Tacuba (the Hotel La Cabaña got through with little damage and remains open), parts of San Vicente and Santa Tecla. Despite the widespread destruction roads, electricity, water, and other infrastructure are, for the most part, totally intact and tourists will have no problems visiting.

For hundreds of thousands of Salvadorans, however, it will take years for the nightmare to end. The best way to help out is to offer your time or money to charities involved in rebuilding some of the 325,000 houses that were damaged. We recommend you contact the Cooperative Housing Foundation, which is detailed in the Basics chapter, or any of the major international relief organizations such as CARE, Catholic Relief Services, and Habitat for Humanity. If you are in El Salvador ask your embassy or the Union Church in San Salvador for recommended organizations that are active in the rebuilding efforts.

# INTRODUCTION

E ven though we have lived in El Salvador for nearly 15 years, when we walk from our home in San Salvador or get out to the countryside the sights and experiences of this wonderful country still amaze us. Visits to the quiet colonial towns, volcanoes, cloud forests, and beaches still leave us in awe of the beauty of El Salvador's people and places. El Rincón Magico (The Magic Corner), as the country is lovingly known by Salvadorans, is one of Latin America's best keep secrets.

The preconceptions most Westerners have about El Salvador are based on sound bites and snatches of newspaper articles: "There was a war there, right?" There was a war, but it was a decade ago and visitors will see little evidence from that time outside the FMLN museum in Perquín.

Traveling in El Salvador used to be a questionable proposition. Scattered gunfire, suspicious soldiers asking what you were doing in the country and an atmosphere of tension almost thick enough to bump into made traveling there unforgettable but nerve-racking. Today, things aren't perfect—crime is a problem—but all in all life is back to normal. The complete turnaround in this little country is one of Latin America's major success stories.

So many things about El Salvador make it a fascinating and enjoyable place to explore. The food is tasty and cheap, and hotels are inexpensive. The tropical climate makes travel possible year-round, and you can get just about anywhere in the country in a few hours on the famously decorated busses. Whichever direction you choose, you're bound to run into an ancient volcano, a deserted beach, a beautiful mountain village or a serene colonial city. El Salvador has it all—you just have to know where to look.

That's where this book comes in. *On Your Own in El Salvador*, the first travel guide devoted exclusively to the country, has a twofold purpose. First, by providing extensive background information on the country, *On Your Own in El Salvador* enables you to fully experience El Salvador by helping you understand the country's history and culture. Our **Background** section covers El Salvador from its pre-Columbian roots to the results of its latest elections, touching on topics such as its people, traditions, food and politics along the way. Historical information is provided on almost every city, and

**culture boxes** throughout the book offer interesting glimpses into many aspects of Salvadoran life.

Second, *On Your Own in El Salvador* gives you practical travel information to let you devise your own itinerary to explore the country. Our **Basics** section tells you all you need to know to prepare for your trip and to make it as enjoyable and hassle-free as possible once you're there. Our **detailed maps** show you where to go, and we provide specific travel information on each city and sight, from hotel prices and restaurant hours to hiking distances and bus schedules. After all, background without practical information is only a history book, and a Must-See list without a historical framework is just a travel brochure. *On Your Own in El Salvador* gives you both, and we know it's enough to make a trip to El Salvador easy and rewarding.

We have always had a wonderful time in the Magic Corner and with this guide you will too. Maybe, like us, you will fall in love with it during your brief visit and decide to stay.

# El Salvador's Best  ~  El Salvador's Worst
(In no particular order)

## BEST
- **Fantastic seafood and great surfing** (El Tunco, El Sunzal and El Zonte beaches)
- **Mountain villages along the Flower Route**
- **Parque Nacional El Imposible**
- **Volcanoes and volcanic lakes**
- **Bosque Montecristo**
- **Beautiful children and friendly hard-working people**
- **Delicious fruit**
- ***Pupusas***
- **FMLN Museum and the Peace Route**
- **Archaeological finds at San Andrés and the David J. Guzmán National Museum**
- **Arts and crafts towns** (Suchitoto, Las Palmas and Ilobasco)
- **Great beaches like Playa El Espino**
- **Restaurante Doña Pema** (San Miguel)
- **Isla Meanguera**

## WORST
- **Crazy bus drivers**
- ***Manteca*** (lard)
- **Air Pollution**
- **The large number of orphans**
- **Urban gangs** *(maras)*
- **Mid-day drunks** *(bolos)*
- **Corrupt politicians**
- **Car accidents** *(choques)*
- **Litter**
- **Rural poverty**
- **The chaos and disorder of San Salvador's historic center**

# BACKGROUND

## El Salvador Yesterday

### PRE-COLUMBIAN HISTORY

Nearly 40,000 years after the first nomadic tribes crossed into the Americas, the cultures of North and South America met in the lowlands of Central America and gave rise to the flourishing civilizations of Meso-America. The most advanced of these cultures were the Aztec and the Maya, both of which had reached their peak long before the "New" World was discovered by the "Old."

■ **The Maya.** Of the two, the Maya were the most successful and had the greatest impact on the early peoples of what would become El Salvador. The Mayan world spread from central Mexico to Nicaragua, flourished while Europe endured the Dark Ages and survived six times as long as the Roman Empire. El Salvador sits on the southern fringe of this vast territory but bears traces of its influence even today.

The **Formative Period** of the Maya (1800 BC to 200 AD) saw the gradual development of many large, competitive city-states that were tied to cultures from Mexico to Panama by extensive trade and communication networks. Most of the Mayan accomplishments, though, came during the **Classic Period** (200 to 800 AD). During that era, complex agricultural bureaucracies supported large populations and Mayan thinkers predicted eclipses, "discovered" the zero in mathematics and developed a highly effective system of hieroglyphics. Their incredibly accurate "Long Count" calendar tracked the days while Mayan architects constructed the huge ceremonial centers that still stand throughout Latin America.

During the **Terminal Classic Period** (800 to 1000 AD) Mayan civ-

## Cuscatlán's "Children"

The Pipil spoke Nahuat, a dialect of the Nahuatl language spoken by the Aztecs of Mexico. When the Spanish arrived in El Salvador, the Aztecs that accompanied them recognized that the indigenous language was similar to their own, although the intonation was completely different. The Aztecs believed that the original Salvadorans spoke like children, and dubbed them the "Pipil", Nahuatl for "children."

ilization mysteriously collapsed. Historians disagree on the cause, but many now believe that the urban population became too large to support and city resources were stretched to a breaking point.

Mayan culture enjoyed a brief revival during the **Post-Classic Period** (1000 to 1520 AD). Commerce replaced religion as the dominant social force and an incredible nautical trade network coordinated as many as 4,000 boats on the sea at one time. Mayan cities throughout Central America shipped goods to one another this way.

By the 14th century, provincial revolt in many cities toppled the central social authority and Mayan civilization declined again. Mayan city-states battled each other for the next two centuries, and by the time the Spanish arrived, many of the cities of this once-great civilization had been deserted.

By the 16th century, five main tribes had made their way into El Salvador. The three earliest arrivals, the Pok'omáme, the Chorti and the Lenca, were concentrated in the country's eastern regions. The Lenca were the largest group, settling in what would become Usulután, San Miguel and La Unión departments, and spreading as far north as Chalatenango. They spoke the Potón language, and left behind many of their words in the names of Salvadoran towns. A group known as the Ulúa arrived later and established a few smaller settlements in the same region.

■ **The Pipil.** El Salvador's largest indigenous group arrived from Mexico around 900 AD, just as the Maya reign was coming to an end, and quickly became the largest group in the region. Pipil populations were concentrated in the central and western areas of El Salvador, in the region bordered by the Río Lempa and the Río Paz.

More warlike but less scientifically advanced than their Mayan forebearers, the Pipil lived within a society organized into city-states that resembled Mayan city-states. Cuscatlán (which means "Land of the Jewel" but is most often translated as "Land of Happiness"), located where the city of Antiguo Cuscatlán is today, was the largest of these and served as the Pipil capital. Sonsonate and Ahuachapán are two other modern Salvadoran towns that began as large Pipil city-states. The ruins of Tazumal, San Andrés and Joya de Cerén are all remnants of the Pipil civilization.

The Pipil operated within a corn-based agricultural economy and grew beans, tobacco, cocoa, pumpkins and gourds in communally owned fields known as *calpullis*. All of these crops were cultivated without the use of the wheel, the plow or domesticated cattle. The Pipil were among the first Meso-American groups to abolish human sacrifice, and they limited use of the death penalty to punishment for murder, adultery and sacrilege.

## CONTACT AND CONQUEST

Ever since 1513, when Vasco de Balboa gazed west from Panama and became the first European to see the Pacific Ocean, the influence of the Spanish and the conquistadors has been ingrained in the history of the Americas. The Spanish approached Central

# In the Beginning

They say the earth was spinning in space, humming in the silence. Darkness penetrated the borders of everything. All was black; black earth and black sky. The cold stretched throughout the frigid caverns of the Nothing.

Emptiness.

Death blanketed the world. Nothing flew, nothing floated, nothing moved. No rivers, no valleys, no mountains. There was only the sea.

One day Teotl rubbed two *achiote* branches together and produced fire. With his hands he sprinkled fistfuls of sparks that scattered themselves throughout the emptiness, forming stars. The mystery was populated with dots of light.

Suddenly in the highest reaches of the heavens appeared Teopantli, the Reformer who rules the universe. He emerged smiling, enveloped in a cascade of light.

Teotl threw a final handful of fire, which condensed down below into a ball of light: that was Tónal, the good father Sun.

But among the noise of the cocoons of life bursting open, of the worlds being engulfed in their orbits, of the explosions of light, Teopantli cried.

And his tear fell, remaining suspended. It turned white and began to spin. That was Metzti, the good mother Moon. And so she is sad. She projected her light onto the earth and it was no longer empty. The seas were pounding against the coasts. There were mountains and canyons. Wild beasts bellowed from the barren mountaintops. The moon's pale light shone upon two lions in combat. Lizards scurried among the ponds and vines. The rivers writhed like giant white serpents.

Life was singing.

—Pipil Creation Myth

America both from the south across the Panamanian isthmus, and from the north in Mexico, where Hernán Cortés conquered the Aztecs in 1521. In 1522, four ships piloted by Andrés Niño sailed into the Gulf of Fonseca. The sailors who disembarked on the island of Meanguera became the first Europeans to set foot in what would one day become El Salvador.

■ **De Alvarado's Campaign.** In 1523, Cortés sent Pedro de Alvarado, one of his principal commanders, to investigate rumors about civilizations in Central America that were said to be as rich as the Aztec. De Alvarado left Mexico with 100 cavalry, 150 foot soldiers, several thousand indigenous allies and strict instructions to conquer the area peacefully, if at all possible.

After overrunning the Maya-Quiché of Guatemala and establishing a capital there, de Alvarado began his invasion of El Salvador. He crossed the Río Paz near La Hachadura in Ahuachapán department in 1524. By the time his army arrived, many towns had already been deserted, either because their inhabitants had died from European diseases or because they had scattered into the countryside in fear of de Alvarado's already well established reputation for ruthlessness. When de Alvarado's troops finally faced off

## "A Good Four Fingers"

In the first battle between the Spanish and indigenous warriors, a Pipil archer named Atonatl fired an arrow through Pedro de Alvarado's left knee. The wound left the Spanish commander limping on a leg that was shorter than his other by "a good four fingers," according to a letter he wrote to Cortés. Atonatl became a national hero.

against Pipil warriors near Acajutla, the Pipil emerged victorious. Soon thereafter, a demoralized Pedro handed over leadership of his forces to his brother and left for Mexico, where he died fifteen years later and 40,000 *pesos* in debt.

In 1525, the Spanish moved into the Pipil capital of Cuscatlán, which had been left empty by its 10,000 inhabitants. Native tribes continued to resist the Spanish, though, and soon forced the evacuation of the newly established villa of San Salvador.

Before long, the momentum shifted again. The Spanish exploited the lack of unity that plagued native forces in El Salvador, just as they had when they battled the Aztec in Mexico. Each small tribe confronted the Spanish independently, rather than joining together into a unified front. By 1540, the Spanish gained complete domination over what is today El Salvador and incorporated it into the Spanish Captaincy-General of Guatemala.

## THE COLONIAL STATE

Realizing that El Salvador's wealth lay in its incredibly fertile volcanic soil, the Spanish quickly set up an agricultural society in El Salvador that was typical of its colonies in the New World. Throughout the land, they constructed plantations to grow cotton, balsam, cacao and indigo.

Good fortune for the Spanish brought misery for the indigenous populations. The Spanish settlers enslaved natives to work on plantations and instituted brutal labor systems. One system, a Caribbean import known as the *encomienda*, gave a Spaniard the right to demand labor and tribute from indigenous people in exchange for "educating" them and converting them to Christianity.

Indigenous laborers succumbed by the thousands to overwork, undernourishment and European diseases. Only 77,000 of El Salvador's original 500,000 inhabitants survived a plague in 1578, and by the end of the 16th century fewer than 10,000 indigenous people were left alive in El Salvador. Since there wasn't enough of a labor force left to work the *encomiendas*, the Spanish experimented with other labor systems. They eventually settled on *haciendas*, large plantations in which workers quickly became indebted to rich landowners.

■ **Colonial Society.** The early plantation culture was split into distinct social classes based on race. At the top of the cultural ladder sat the pure Europeans, either *peninsulares* (born in Spain) or *criollos* (born in the New World). Next came the Spanish-indigenous *mestizos*, who were allowed some administrative duties but could not own land, horses or guns in order to prevent them from rebelling. Next to the bottom were the *zambos*, with black and indigenous parents. The bottom class was reserved for purely native blood and the handful of blacks imported from Africa and the Caribbean.

Catholic clergy were partners in the process of "Europeanizing" the natives. The church preached humility and subservience to the natives, telling them to bear the burdens of this life while holding out for a future paradise. Native religions were destroyed, old celebrations forbidden, temples toppled and gods replaced. Ironically, the indigenous peoples' few defenders in this era were also representatives of the religious orders. Father Bartolomé de las Casas spent most of his 92 years in the 16th and 17th centuries defending the native tribes of El Salvador. "I prefer someone not baptized," he once said, "than dead and Christian."

At first, trade in cacao boomed when the Spanish replaced the chili peppers and corn in the original recipe for chocolate with sugar. It soon faltered, though, when so many indigenous workers died that there weren't enough left to work the cacao plantations. An economic depression that lasted for most of the 17th century was replaced by an agricultural boom in the 18th century, spurred by European demand for indigo. At one point, more than 90 percent of all indigo exported from Central America came from El Salvador.

Salvadoran nationalism is considered to have begun in 1786 when the Intendancy of San Salvador, separate from Guatemala, was established, though the Salvadoran clergy did not get their demand of a separate diocese until 1842. This nascent nationalism was fueled by mounting tensions between the Old and New Worlds which occurred for a variety of reasons. Many inhabitants of Central America felt that the colonies were run exclusively for the benefit of Spain. The Spanish Crown imposed high taxes, restricted sea trade to royal ships and demanded tribute. In addition, the abuse of indigenous peoples ran contrary to the orders of the Crown, adding fuel to the political fire.

By the end of the 18th century, many patterns were already in place that would haunt El Salvador for centuries to come. A wealthy, Europeanized elite ruled society and looked down on a mixed-blood majority that it viewed as almost sub-human. The economy was expanding rapidly but depended on exports for its wealth. As a result, land

## Blacks in El Salvador

**Y**ou don't see many blacks in El Salvador today because no more than 10,000 black slaves were imported to El Salvador during the colonial period. The long sea journey made African slaves expensive to import just to harvest indigo during its two-month season. Also, a planned slave rebellion in San Salvador in 1625 that was narrowly averted made authorities wary of importing any more slaves than was absolutely necessary.

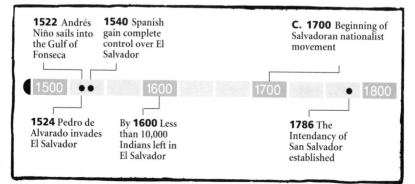

**1522** Andrés Niño sails into the Gulf of Fonseca

**1540** Spanish gain complete control over El Salvador

**C. 1700** Beginning of Salvadoran nationalist movement

1500  1600  1700  1800

**1524** Pedro de Alvarado invades El Salvador

**By 1600** Less than 10,000 Indians left in El Salvador

**1786** The Intendancy of San Salvador established

BACKGROUND

became El Salvador's most valuable commodity, rather than something used to benefit everyone. The Church supported the status quo as native populations were decimated through disease and abuse. Finally, the military was well on its way to becoming an autonomous, privileged class; a law called the *fuero militar* was enacted to exempt members of the armed forces from the jurisdiction of Spanish courts.

## INDEPENDENCE

Colonial resentment against Spain and Guatemala City, the Crown's appendage in the New World, continued to grow into the 19th century. A plunge in indigo profits, due in part to high taxes imposed by Spain, only made matters worse. When Napoleon invaded Spain in 1808, the Crown demanded huge sums from its colonies to fund its battles and to help return the deposed Ferdinand VII to the throne.

Spain's decision to rely upon its colonies to support a war on the other side of the sea infuriated the people of Central America, and eventually led to the collapse of the Spanish Empire. In 1811, Father José Mathías Delgado led El Salvador's first uprising against Spanish rule. The insurrection shook cities throughout the country, but ultimately failed. Delgado succeeded in setting the revolutionary machinery in motion, however. In 1814, Pedro Pablo Castillo, vice-mayor of San Salvador, led a second unsuccessful revolt against the Crown.

Soon after Napoleon's abdication in 1814, King Ferdinand VII returned to the throne and proceeded to persecute anyone in Central America who was suspected of advocating independence. But the revolutionary spirit lived on and Mexico, inspired by the success of the French and American revolutions, declared its independence from Spain in February 1821. On September 15 of that year, representatives of every Central American nation met in Guatemala City to sign the Declaration of Independence from Spain. September 15 is still celebrated as a national holiday throughout Central America.

The countries of Central America initially aligned together under Mexico, in what was known as the Mexican Empire. The Empire was short-lived, however, as the people of

**1811** José Mathías Delgado leads first uprising against Spanish

**1824** Anastasio Aquino leads peasant rebellion in El Salvador

**1879** Introduction of synthetic dyes in Europe ruins indigo market

1800      1850

**1821** Central American Declaration of Independence signed

**1823** Central American Federation formed

**1841** El Salvador withdraws from Central American Federation, becomes independent

**1882** Last Indian communal lands abolished in El Salvador

Central America discovered that life was just as unbearable whether Spain or Mexico was giving the orders. When many of the allied countries decided to break free from the empire, Mexico sent troops to El Salvador and laid siege to San Salvador. Soon, however, the empire collapsed entirely.

■ **The Central American Federation.** The Central American Federation, signed on July 1, 1823, was the next attempt at regional solidarity. Manuel José Arce, a creole who had helped settle Delgado's uprising peacefully, was appointed president of an alliance that included El Salvador, Guatemala, Honduras, Nicaragua and Costa Rica. José Mathías Delgado wrote the federation's constitution which made the Central American Federation the first nation in the New World to abolish slavery.

Despite the revolutions, the plight of ordinary peasants changed little through the first part of the 19th century, and El Salvador suffered frequent uprisings. In 1824, a *campesino* named Anastasio Aquino led a peasant rebellion near Zacatecoluca. Rallying under the cry "Land for those who work it!" Aquino's hastily-assembled army of 4,000 managed to capture Zacatecoluca and San Vicente. The ragtag troops, mostly peasants from local *haciendas*, were quickly subdued, and Aquino's head was displayed in a tree near San Vicente as a warning to other potential revolutionaries.

Civil unrest, among other things, led El Salvador to withdraw from the Central American Federation in 1841. By 1842, the Central American Federation collapsed under the combined weight of cultural disunity and political differences. From then on, each small Central American nation was on its own.

## EARLY NATIONHOOD

El Salvador was constituted as a "free, independent and sovereign nation" in 1841. Its early years were marked by struggles for political power and numerous short wars with its neighbors, including battles with Honduras in 1845 and Guatemala in 1844, 1851 and 1863. Many Salvadoran presidents, including Francisco Malespín and General Gerardo Barrios, came to power through coups or invasions from neighboring countries. Meanwhile, the Salvadoran population and economy grew slowly through the end of the 19th century, until coffee arrived on the country's plantations.

■ **Coffee.** The introduction of synthetic dyes in Europe in 1879 caused indigo prices to plummet. Coffee arrived just in time, though, and demand had just begun to skyrocket. The impact of this unremarkable bean on Salvadoran culture can't be overestimated; the

BACKGROUND

## A Clean Slate

The four main tasks of the National Truth Commission, created as part of the peace process, were to investigate the worst human rights abuses by both sides, study the issue of military immunity, make legal and political recommendations to prevent a repeat of abuses, and stimulate national reconciliation. In preparing their report they took direct testimony from over 2000 sources relating to 7,000 victims. The commission's work was seen by most segments of society as a great success. By wiping the slate clean some involved in murders did not receive the degree of justice they deserved, but the country was able to do what few Latin American nations have done in similar positions—focus on the future and not waste scarce development resources in revenge or digging up the past.

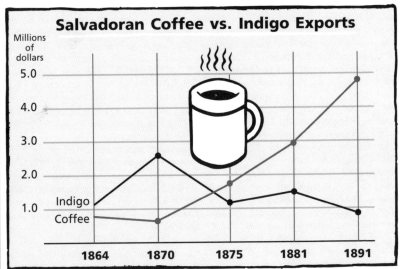

Salvadoran Coffee vs. Indigo Exports

coffee industry was and still is almost single-handedly responsible for many of the country's economic and social imbalances.

Coffee caused land ownership to be concentrated in the hands of the country's elite even faster than had occurred with indigo. Coffee couldn't be cultivated where indigo was grown; it flourished on the high, cool hillsides where the country's few indigenous people still happened to live and own land.

The government supported the coffee growers' ravenous appetite for more and more land, and in 1882 it passed a law abolishing the last vestiges of indigenous communal landholdings. Displaced peasants were forced to choose between working on coffee plantations for extremely low wages or migrating to neighboring countries such as Honduras.

The Salvadoran economy soon became dangerously dependent on the growth and export of coffee, to the exclusion of all other crops. Domestic manufacturing and food production fell sharply as coffee production rose, from 50 percent of El Salvador's exports in 1882 to 76 percent by the turn of the century.

For their part, the coffee growers saw themselves as the economic saviors of El Salvador. After all, they did bring enormous wealth into the country. Most of this money, however, was reinvested in the coffee industry or taken abroad. Little was paid in taxes or redistributed to benefit the other sectors of the Salvadoran economy. There was no incentive to pay coffee workers any more than bare survival rations, since the peasants couldn't afford the crop they grew anyway. Peasant resentment toward the unequal distribution of wealth grew steadily, and the government responded by increasing the size and strength of its police force.

By the end of the 19th century, an enormously unequal distribution of wealth had developed in El Salvador. While landowning *cafetaleros* earned upwards of $200,000 each year, their workers toiled for barely $2.50 per week. In 1890, one-half of one percent of the Salvadoran population controlled 90 percent of the country's wealth.

## INTO THE 20TH CENTURY

■ **Development and Unrest.** Urban development in El Salvador took off in the early 20th century, thanks in part to the emerging urban middle and working classes—in the 1920s El Salvador was the largest importer of structural steel in Central America. Around the same time, the first *sindicatos*, or workers' unions, began to appear in the cities. Displaced peasants strongly supported these urban leagues.

Rural areas, on the other hand, remained underdeveloped. The government built just enough infrastructure in the countryside to grow and extract coffee, and didn't spend much money on educating the populace. Schools weren't considered necessary, for example, since literacy wasn't a prerequisite for coffee-harvesting. In response, urban college students often traveled into the countryside to set up schools where they tutored *campesinos* in everything from mathematics to politics.

The government felt threatened by actions to organize peasants and it soon declared labor organizations illegal. Peasants who attempted to organize unions were imprisoned, tortured and killed. The National Guard, founded in 1912 for the purpose of keeping order in the countryside, was seen as an avenue to power and prestige by the emerging urban middle and lower classes.

BACKGROUND

# The History of Coffee

Coffee's crucial role in Salvadoran history is made more interesting by the plant's own unusual history. The word coffee is said to come from Kaffa, the province in southern Ethiopia where the intoxicating plant was discovered. According to legend, in 850 AD a goat herder named Kaldi was tending his flock near the Red Sea. He noticed that after his goats ate the red beans off a certain bush, they romped especially playfully. He tried the beans himself, and soon became the world's first caffeine addict.

Regardless of its source, coffee became popular throughout Ethiopia, although it was used mostly as a food—people would chew the leaves and fruit for a buzz of energy and to dull hunger pangs. Arabs began importing the beans more than 1,000 years ago and are credited with inventing the brewing process. Coffeehouses all over Mecca were decried by priests who said that coffee, as an intoxicating beverage, was prohibited by the Koran. Soon coffee made its way to Europe when a Dutch trader stole a single plant and brought it to Holland in 1616. London's first coffeehouses were open by 1652.

Less than a century later the valuable plant was smuggled yet again, this time to the New World. In the 1720s, a French naval officer stole a single coffee seedling from a bush in the Jardín de Plantes, the royal gardens of Paris, and took it with him on a boat to the Caribbean. When drinking water on the voyage ran low the officer was forced to share his ration with the seedling, which survived and went on to spawn the islands' coffee industry.

Coffee's final journey was to the South American mainland. When a Brazilian soldier visited French Guiana, he was given a bouquet as a farewell present from the governor's wife. One wonders just how fond a farewell it was, because inside the bouquet the wife had hidden a single, priceless coffee plant. Thus the Brazilian coffee industry—today the world's largest—was born. Coffee eventually made its way north to El Salvador, and was being cultivated in earnest by the middle of the 19th century.

The world economic depression in the 1920s reduced demand for luxury items like coffee, and exports fell sharply. In El Salvador, where coffee exports accounted for 95 percent of the country's revenue, almost half of the rural work force was suddenly unemployed. Support for leftist causes increased, sparked by earlier land grabs and recent layoffs. Militant unions in the western coffee-producing areas claimed 80,000 members, and in 1930 the Salvadoran Communist Party was founded. The government responded to the "communist threat" with more arrests, beatings, tortures and killings.

■ **Araujo's Short Tenure.** The presidential election of 1931 was won by Arturo Araujo, a little-known *haciendado* who paid his workers twice the going rate and who had established a worker's clinic on his hacienda. The surprise victor discovered that it was easier to make campaign promises to improve the lot of the common man than it was to fulfill them, and he was ousted in a coup the same year by his vice president, General Maximiliano Martínez. The military stayed in control until 1979.

## LA MATANZA

Civil unrest grew after Araujo's deposition. The Martínez regime violently repressed strikes and demonstrations and perpetrated enormous electoral fraud in the 1932 election to ensure its own victory.

All the while, the Salvadoran Communist Party quietly gathered support and planned an armed uprising for January 22, 1932. The government learned about the uprising ahead of time, though, and newspaper headlines warned the country of the planned rebellion days before it was to take place. Following an informant's tip-off, the government arrested three leaders of the uprising, including Faribundo Martí. However, many communist sympathizers continued their preparations for the uprising anyway.

On January 20, the Izalco Volcano lit up the skies as machete-wielding peasants occupied towns in the western coffee-growing highlands near Ahuachapán, Sonsonate and Santa Ana. The uprising was centered around indigenous villages and set loose decades of rage and resentment. About 100 local government officials and wealthy landowners were dragged out of their homes and offices and killed by peasant rebels, who looted shops and began to celebrate their "victory" almost immediately.

Soon, however, the government struck back. Soldiers and paramilitary organizations like the *cafetalero*-organized "White Guards" retook towns within days, inflicting heavy

Late **1920**s World economic depression, coffee prices plunge

**1931** Arturo Araujo elected president, deposed by General Martínez

**1940**s Economy begins to improve

1900 ● 1925 ●●

**1912** National Guard Founded

**1930** Salvadoran Communist Party founded

**1932** Indigenous uprising in western El Salvador, sparks La Matanza

**1950** Constitution written

## Uncle Sam Takes an Interest

The United States replaced Great Britain as the premiere world power in the early 20th century, and began investing heavily in El Salvador. The United States saw all of Central America as an important region in which to gain a foothold, since this was the best location for building a canal between the Atlantic and Pacific Oceans, as well as a source of cheap labor. US investment in El Salvador rose from $1.8 million in 1908 to $34 million by 1930.

losses on the poorly organized rebel troops. Although the government controlled the region within a week of the initial uprising, it continued to attack peasants with astonishing and calculated brutality, with the full support of the oligarchy. The Church remained silent.

■ **Backlash.** Soldiers executed anyone suspected of having links to the uprising, starting with the leaders. José Feliciano Ama, a rebel leader from Izalco, was hanged in front of an assembly of local schoolchildren. Soon, government troops targeted anyone who had indigenous features, dressed like a *campesino* or carried a machete. All were shot on the spot.

In Juayúa, the headquarters of the uprising, government troops killed all the men, women, children and dogs. Peasants, guilty or not, were forced to dig their own graves in the town plaza, lined up with their thumbs tied behind their backs and shot with machine guns mounted on the backs of trucks. In all, tens of thousands of peasants were slaughtered over the next week in an event that came to be known as *La Matanza* ("The Massacre").

In fact, nobody knows exactly how many people died in *La Matanza*; estimates vary from 10,000 to 50,000. Some sources claim that the army simply didn't have enough ammunition to kill more than 10,000 people. Most historians estimate the total was close to 30,000—nearly two percent of the Salvadoran population at the time.

Through the decades, the events of 1932 have fallen prey to selective memory. Regardless, its effects are still felt in modern-day El Salvador. Nearly an entire rural generation was wiped out, and El Salvador's indigenous population has never really recovered. Since then, indigenous Salvadorans have found it difficult to escape the mindset that being of native descent is somehow inherently dangerous. Aside from certain special occasions, they rarely wear their traditional dress or speak their native languages. Finally, *La Matanza* set in place a model for dealing with popular unrest that would be followed for decades to come.

"The Red Horse of the Apocalypse appears to signify the sinister glitterings of World Communism, which with the roars of indomitable fiends, with the din of violent torment, with the rage of merciless flames and the vapor of human blood brandishes its many arms, crazily seeking to topple the ancient structure of Civilization."

-Church edict, 1932

### AUGUSTIN FARIBUNDO MARTÍ (1893-1932)

# The Original Revolutionary

The man whose name was adopted by the FMLN was an early Salvadoran revolutionary who struggled to bring socialism to his country. Augustín Faribundo Martí was raised in an upper middle class family in the early 20th century and became a lawyer. He became involved in politics early on, and for the duration of his short life Martí was jailed and exiled repeatedly in his struggles against the conservative forces of the Salvadoran government.

In the late 1920s, Martí went to Nicaragua to fight alongside César Augusto Sandino, who was struggling to expel the US Marines who had occupied the country. Though the two were fighting for different causes—Martí for socialism and Sandino for nationalism—Martí came to admire the Nicaraguan leader, calling him the "world's greatest patriot."

When it became clear to Martí that Sandino would not embrace socialism, he returned to El Salvador in the early 1930s during a period of great civil unrest. Martí was thrown in jail just before *La Matanza* for his role in plotting the uprising. As the army combed the countryside and killed thousands of suspected communist sympathizers, Martí was executed by a firing squad for sedition and rebellion. When asked by a priest just before his execution whether he had any sins to confess, Martí answered no.

## AFTERMATH

Reeling from the twin blows of the Depression and *La Matanza*, El Salvador entered a decade-long Dark Age in the 1940s under General Martínez. The government declared a national state of siege and halted the few political freedoms that it had granted in the previous two decades. Union and political opposition activity was suspended; anyone who opposed the status quo was persecuted as a communist. The government instituted a national ID card system, shut down the independent press and gave the National Guard the right to search without a warrant. Coffee prices plunged in 1932, causing many unemployed peasants to flee into the northern departments and over the border into Honduras.

■ **Life Under the General.** Martínez, who discovered early on that a facade of democracy was sufficient to keep the United States content, kept power through the 1930s by rigging elections. Ironically, his success in eliminating the threat of a peasant uprising ultimately led to his own downfall. Without a common enemy to unite the government and the country's aristocracy, Martínez and his former supporters bickered over the pace of industrialization and economic diversification.

Before long, university students and laborers called renewed strikes. In a show of strength by El Salvador's emerging middle class, the strikes soon brought the country to a halt. When Martínez finally resigned in 1944, he left behind a legacy of centralized political power and a powerful military apparatus that was better at policing internal "threats" than it was at defending against external forces.

When the Depression ended with the 1930s, the Salvadoran economy began to pull out of its tailspin. Modernization efforts forged ahead and roads, including the Panamerican Highway, were built across the country. The Salvadoran government managed the economy more closely, but mostly for the benefit of the rich. US economic influence grew as well, in spite of Roosevelt's non-interventionist "Good Neighbor" policy. As El Salvador passed into the 1940s, many sectors of its economy were finally beginning to thrive.

## MODERNIZATION

The Salvadoran economy continued to grow through the middle of the 20th century in a surge of "progress" that masked festering social ills. Wealthy Salvadoran investors developed roads, factories and an electrical network. Much of the development was meant to reduce the country's dependence on the growth and export of coffee. The elite, perfectly content with coffee revenues, were divided on how best to proceed, although few were pleased at the prospect of being taxed to finance the change.

Many new jobs, mostly in San Salvador, provided work for a growing middle class. Despite this, the country's distribution of income became even more skewed, since most Salvadorans were still too poor to participate in the rising consumer economy.

■ **Cotton and Sugar.** New crops were planted on what little land remained uncultivated. Cotton was grown in coastal areas cleared in the 1950s. From 1935 to 1965, 110,000 hectares had been converted to the production of cotton. Sugarcane was planted in valleys that were too low for coffee and too high for cotton. Cultivation of sugarcane increased from 8,500 hectares in 1960 to 33,200 hectares in 1975.

The surge in production of these crops were the final two nails in the coffins of small landowners, who were forced off what little land they had left. Staple food crops were

MAXIMILIANO HERNÁNDEZ MARTÍNEZ (1882-1966)

# El Brujo

**M**aximiliano Hernández Martínez was the iron-fisted general known as the author of *La Matanza* in 1932. He is also remembered as El Brujo ("The Sorcerer") for his often outlandish "scientific" beliefs that he occasionally forced upon the Salvadoran populace.

Martínez received some training as a lawyer in El Salvador near the turn of the century, but soon left for a military education in Guatemala. After assuming the presidency, Martínez presided over the killing of thousands of peasants in 1932. Martínez justified his actions by explaining that "In El Salvador, I am God."

Martínez was also interested in the occult, believed in sorcery and held seances in his home. He had strange remedies for everything. Once, when the country was in the throes of a smallpox epidemic, Martínez ordered that red cellophane be placed on all the street lights in the city, since he believed that colored light would cleanse the air and stop the disease from spreading.

"It's good for children to go barefoot," he remarked. "That way they can better receive the beneficial emanations of the planet. Plants and animals don't use shoes." Another time he was overheard saying "it's a much greater crime to kill an ant than a man. While the man has an eternal soul, the ant is dead forever."

Twelve years after *La Matanza*, Martínez resigned the presidency and went into exile in Honduras, where he lived on a farm. At the age of 88, El Brujo was stabbed to death by his chauffeur.

pushed aside in favor of cotton and sugar, and the country became more dependent on imported food. With better machinery and larger farms the new crops required fewer workers during harvest season, and unemployment increased.

The new constitution of 1950 promised "liberty, health, economic well-being and social justice" to every Salvadoran. It provided for some reforms, including a 48-hour workweek, an 8-hour day and the right to vote for the country's women. However, the constitution promised more than the government was able to deliver. At the same time the Cuban Revolution of 1959 struck fear into the hearts of oligarchies everywhere and boosted hopes of leftist revolutionaries.

Some political opposition was allowed during this period, and urban labor organizations enjoyed some measure of freedom. But politics in the countryside was repressed by the National Guard, which had become a private army of the *cafetaleros*.

■ **The Christian Democrats.** The middle class gained a new voice with the founding of the Christian Democratic Party (PDC) in 1960, filling in the political void between the communists and the right-wing Party of National Conciliation (PCN). The PDCs sought social change through agrarian reform, and were frequently the target of government repression during their early years. Two years after the boycotted 1962 elections (in which university students nominated a donkey for president), the PDCs won the first-ever opposition seats in the National Assembly. PDC candidate José Napoleon Duarte was elected mayor of San Salvador and was twice reelected.

Through the 1960s and early 1970s, fear of another uprising grew among the elite and more money was funneled to the military. With money and political influence, the military was evolving into an independent political force, increasingly immune to the normal rules and values that guided the rest of society.

In the late 1960s the National Democratic Organization (ORDEN), a paramilitary civilian vigilante group, was founded and supported by elements of the military and aristocracy. Trained by the National Guard, ORDEN set out to combat the "growing specter of communism," in the process showing just how frightened El Salvador's elite had become.

## THE SOCCER WAR

In 1969, an old rivalry between El Salvador and Honduras erupted into a brief war, momentarily shifting attention from El Salvador's deteriorating political situation. The battle was caused by a number of issues, including a long-standing dispute over the exact location of a border between the two countries and the huge numbers of Salvadorans who had migrated into Honduras.

By the late 1960s, more than 300,000 Salvadorans had settled in Honduras, and many Hondurans resented losing their jobs to the hard-working immigrants. In addition, the two countries differed on how to apply rules relating to the emerging Central American Common Market. Salvadoran companies competed strongly against their Honduran counterparts, which slowed Honduran efforts to industrialize. Finally, rich Honduran landowners sought a scapegoat for land imbalances in their own country, and focused attention on the easiest target: Salvadoran immigrants.

## JOSÉ NAPOLEÓN DUARTE (1926-1990)
# JFK, the Pope and Duarte

José Napoleón Duarte is one of El Salvador's most recognizable political figure and was, for a time, its most popular. His political career made him a legend among Salvadorans through his efforts to slow military growth and to moderate political extremism. But by the end of his term as president, Duarte's administration had lost popular support and his efforts were generally perceived as a failure.

Duarte hailed from simple roots. His mother, who didn't have enough money to send José to a good school, convinced priests at Catholic schools to provide scholarships for Duarte and his brother. His father later won a fortune in the national lottery and used the proceeds to send Duarte to the US to study at the University of Notre Dame in Indiana.

When he returned to El Salvador, Duarte became active in domestic politics at a time when scant political opposition was allowed by the government. After helping found the Christian Democrat Party (PDC) in the early 1960s, Duarte was elected mayor of San Salvador. His popularity soared when his administration managed to install streetlights in the capital. The most popular photos in Salvadoran homes at the time were portraits of JFK, the Pope and Duarte.

In 1972 Duarte ran for president of El Salvador against a military leader. When it became clear that Duarte had won a majority of the votes, the military imposed a three-day blackout and clamped down on all opposition. Duarte was beaten and sent into exile, where he remained until the end of the decade.

After his return to El Salvador in the early 1980s, Duarte served with members of the military on two juntas. Since the death squads remained active during this time, many felt that Duarte undermined his claims to moderation by participating in a government that allowed such activities.

Duarte ran for president in 1984 against ARENA party candidate Roberto d'Aubuisson, and won in a close vote. He promised to end the civil war and to quash paramilitary groups that operated throughout the country. Though Duarte brought the rebels briefly to the negotiating table for peace talks in La Palma, his administration soon became corrupt and ineffective and in the end accomplished almost nothing.

Towards the end of his term as president, Duarte was diagnosed with terminal cancer. He promised to survive the duration of his term, which he did, and to write a sequel to his autobiography when the war was over. After Duarte's death in 1990, though, the war continued and the sequel was left unwritten.

Honduras began to expel Salvadorans in the late 1960s, causing the Salvadoran press to trumpet allegations of mistreatment at the hands of Honduran authorities. Tensions peaked around the June 1969 World Cup playoffs between the two countries, and erupted into war on July 14. Throughout the four-day war, the only organized call for peace was a rally staged by the Salvadoran Communist Party in San Salvador. Begun under the pretense of "protecting the human rights of Salvadoran settlers," the war ended when the Organization of American States arranged a cease-fire. By August,

Salvadoran troops returned home to a "victory celebration" staged in the capital in an official attempt to salvage some national pride.

■ **Who Won?** The "Soccer War," as it came to be known, left 3,000 dead, 6,000 wounded and caused $50 million in damage. Relations between the countries worsened and Honduras closed its borders to Salvadorans, blocked shipments of Salvadoran goods and stopped buying Salvadoran products. As Salvadoran emigrants returned home, land pressures and unemployment increased.

In the end, the Salvadoran military was the only group that benefited from the war. The "effectiveness" of the armed forces had been demonstrated, and Colonel Sanchez Hernández rode a wave of nationalistic fervor into the presidency in the 1970 elections. The military-allied PCN received 60 percent of the vote versus 28 percent for the PDCs. Nonetheless, repression, torture and disappearances of dissidents continued.

## THE TURBULENT 1970S

The United National Opposition, a coalition of the Christian Democrats and other leftist groups, nominated Duarte for president in the 1972 elections. The coalition fought governmental harassment in an uphill campaign battle and was stunned when the official vote count signaled that Duarte had been elected president. The government's Federal Election Board, however, announced that PCN candidate Colonel Arturo Molina had won.

This blatant fraud sparked a coup attempt on March 25 by young military officers who had lost patience with the corrupt government. Duarte called upon his supporters to confront the troops of the entrenched military who were advancing on the younger officers, but few responded. The coup failed and Molina assumed the presidency. Duarte, meanwhile, was hunted down by the military, beaten and exiled to Venezuela for his role. As a result of the loss, support for the Christian Democrats faded in the 1970s, and the best opportunity for political moderates to take power in years was lost.

■ **Social Chaos.** A rising tide of government-sponsored violence and intimidation in the 1970s was countered with attempts by the left to organize and retaliate. The opposition increasingly saw revolution as the only way to affect change in the country, as they formed numerous clandestine paramilitary groups which would eventually unite into a guerrilla army in the early 1980s. Arms from Nicaragua and Cuba began to filter into the hands of various resistance groups, including some which financed their

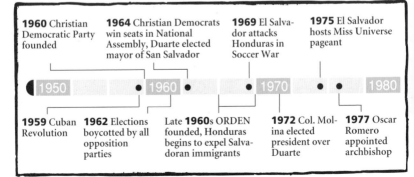

**1960** Christian Democratic Party founded

**1964** Christian Democrats win seats in National Assembly, Duarte elected mayor of San Salvador

**1969** El Salvador attacks Honduras in Soccer War

**1975** El Salvador hosts Miss Universe pageant

1950 • 1960 • • 1970 • • 1980

**1959** Cuban Revolution

**1962** Elections boycotted by all opposition parties

Late **1960**s ORDEN founded, Honduras begins to expel Salvadoran immigrants

**1972** Col. Molina elected president over Duarte

**1977** Oscar Romero appointed archbishop

Steep street, Chalatenango

Waterfall located near Perquín

## Missed Universe

In 1975 the Salvadoran government spent more than one million dollars preparing to host the Miss Universe pageant at the Los Chorros Turicentro just outside the capital. Peaceful student demonstrations in the streets of San Salvador, attended by as many as 50,000 people, were staged in protest of the decision to host the event. Police opened fire on the marchers, killing dozens and wounding many more.

operations by kidnapping and ransoming rich Salvadorans. By 1979, the left was responsible for as much as ten percent of all political killings and their followers demanded millions of dollars in ransom. Underground left-wing political groups also sprang up, replacing older leftist parties silenced since the 1972 election fraud.

Since legitimate political opposition was all but impossible, the left began a grass-roots effort to organize peasants. Trade unions, *campesino* organizations and student groups staged strikes, marches, rallies and sit-ins. Radical student groups at the National University prompted Molina to close down the campus in 1972 with tanks and planes. When the university re-opened a year later, it was run by a Molina-appointed rector. By the end of the decade, the country's economy had become paralyzed by unrest and foreign investment had dried up.

By 1975, members of the oligarchy had become terrified for their safety and looked for ways to protect their livelihood. Soldiers, ex-soldiers and rural landowners joined together into pro-government paramilitary groups similar to ORDEN, such as the White Warrior's Union (UGB) and FALANGE. They responded to the Church's increasingly leftist stance with pamphlets bearing messages like "Be a patriot! Kill a priest!"

Reform efforts by the government were continually undermined by the right. Molina met fierce resistance from landowners when he attempted to limit landholdings in San Miguel and La Unión departments to 86 acres, which would have required the government to break up many large farms. Eventually, the government relented and made the land reform voluntary. A 1973 cartoon in El Salvador showed one grade-school student leaning over to another and whispering, "El Salvador must be the largest country in the world because they've been carrying out agrarian reform for ten years and it's still not finished!"

■ **The Church Changes its Stance.** In the midst of the growing political turmoil, members of the Catholic Church were agitating for change as well. Under the guidance of Archbishop Oscar Romero and the Liberation Theology he espoused, the Church became involved in the political struggle, usually on behalf of the left. Priests went into the countryside to educate *campesinos* and to organize them into cooperatives and unions. For their efforts, members of the Catholic clergy were targeted by right-wing groups, and dozens of priests were killed. Many later joined rebel groups in frustration.

General Carlos Humberto Romero, a conservative functionary of the right (no relation to the archbishop), was elected president in 1977. Thousands of dead people were counted as having voted for Romero, and some villages registered more voters than their entire populations. Many in the country interpreted the elections as a sign that the oligarchy was digging in and tightening its hold on power.

Soon after the election results were announced, protestors occupied the Plaza Libertad in San Salvador to call for new elections. Thousands camped out. Day by day the crowds grew, until 60,000 sat facing the Metropolitan Cathedral. The scene was a carnival of protest with political speeches, live music and food for sale.

On February 28, the army surrounded the plaza and ordered the crowd to disperse within ten minutes. In response, protestors sang the national anthem. Soldiers opened fire and sent volleys of tear gas into the plaza. Dozens of protesters were killed, including many who fell trying to seek shelter in the Metropolitan Cathedral. Foreign news crews captured the event, and Oliver Stone used the stunning footage in the opening credits of his movie Salvador. In all, between 80 and 300 people died around the plaza. In the days following the attack, enraged crowds burned cars and government offices in the capital.

■ **Revolution in Nicaragua.** The Sandinista revolution against the US-backed Somoza dictatorship in Nicaragua in 1979 is often credited as one of the major sparks that ignited the Salvadoran civil war. Crowds in San Salvador supported the left, cheering "Romero y Somoza, son la misma cosa!" ("Romero and Somoza are the same thing!") The Salvadoran army, meanwhile, shifted its allegiance between the center and the right and was uncomfortable siding too strongly with either side. With a communist insurgency around the corner and Reagan at the helm, the US government soon

OSCAR ARNULFO ROMERO Y GALDAMES (1917-1980)

# The Voice of the Voiceless

**E**l Salvador's archbishop in the late 1970s, Oscar Arnulfo Romero was a revolutionary advocate for the dispossessed and repressed. He spoke out frequently against the army's blatant disregard for human rights and was criticized for aligning himself too closly with the political left. When the country's right felt that Romero's weekly homilies threatened their own interests, he was assassinated.

Romero was considered a political conservative when chosen in 1977 by Rome to serve as archbishop of El Salvador, the country's highest position in the Catholic Church. He had been groomed by the oligarchy, it was understood, and was expected to keep quiet. Romero replaced Archbishop Chávez, a politically liberal leader who had moved the Church toward the political left.

But soon after Romero's ordination, Father Rutilio Grande, Romero s friend and a well-known advocate of peasant rights, was gunned down on a country road. Despite a request from Romero, the government refused to investigate. This incident, along with Romero's frequent interaction with peasants whose families had been affected by army campaigns, caused him to reconsider his political views.

Romero soon gained the support of the country's underclass. His sermons were broadcast throughout the country and as many as 75 percent of all Salvadorans would tune in every week to hear him speak. Rightist forces felt threatened by Romero's growing influence and repeatedly bombed the radio station that broadcast Romero's words.

Many of Romero's homilies were directed against the army's violence and human rights abuses. Romero believed that the Church had an obligation to speak up for those who were otherwise silenced. "When a dictatorship seriously

took a particular interest in El Salvador's internal affairs.

General Romero eventually lost support from all sides. The oligarchy and the US considered him incompetent in the face of opposition, and the army didn't see him as useful any longer. On October 15 1979 Romero was deposed in a coup by army officers.

## CIVIL WAR

A civilian-military junta was appointed to replace General Romero. This group of army officers and prominent civilians was perceived as the country's best hope of avoiding an imminent civil war. The junta attempted some reforms, promised democratic elections and invited the nascent guerrilla movement to join in talks with the government. But few reforms were initiated and the paramilitary violence continued. Soon, the civilian members of the junta resigned in frustration. Although other juntas followed (including one with Duarte, who had returned from exile in 1980), none were able to affect change.

On January 22, 1980, the streets of the capital were filled with the largest peaceful protest march in El Salvador's history. Over 220,000 people demonstrated against the death squads, disappearances and killings. Suddenly, in the middle of the march, shots rang out from above the Presidential Palace. Dozens of protestors were gunned down as

violates human rights and attacks the common good of the nation," he explained, "when it becomes unbearable and closes all channels of dialogue, of understanding, of rationality—when this happens, the Church speaks of the legitimate right of insurrectional violence."

When the right accused Romero of directing the Church to undermine the government, Romero disagreed and responded, "the Church is not against the government. The truth is that the government is against the people and we are with the people."

Romero also denied that he was a leftist himself, as the government contended, although he did agree with much of what the left advocated. "I don t call them the forces of the left, but the forces of the people," he said. "Their voice is the voice of anger resulting from social injustice. What is called the left is the people. It is the people organized, and its cry is the cry of the people."

A day before he was killed, Romero addressed his sermon to the country's soldiers and called on them to reconsider their role in society: "I issue a special entreaty to the army, the National Guard, police and military. Do not kill your fellow peasants, your brothers and sisters. No soldier is obliged to obey an order which is against the law of God."

This address, seen by the armed forces as a direct call to mutiny, sealed Romero's fate. As he was giving mass in the Divine Providence Cancer Hospital on March 24, 1980, Romero was shot in the heart in front of the entire congregation. Soon afterward, Roberto d'Aubuisson, founder of the ARENA political party and one-time presidential candidate, was implicated in the murder.

More than 100,000 people attended Romero's funeral. As mourners moved across the Plaza Gerardo Barrios in front of the San Salvador Cathedral, army snipers atop the Presidential Palace opened fire, killing dozens. Many consider Romero's assassination and the tragedy at his funeral to be the real beginning of the civil war.

the crowd scattered. Most witnesses blamed government soldiers for opening fire without provocation.

■ **The Final Straw.** Two months later, on a Sunday afternoon in the middle of mass, Archbishop Romero was shot and killed by a lone gunman. Leftist supporters felt that if even the archbishop wasn't safe in El Salvador, all hope for a negotiated peace was lost.

By October, five guerrilla groups had united under the banner of the Faribundo Martí National Liberation Front (FMLN) and the civil war began in earnest. A handful of leftist political parties withdrew from the political process and formed the Democratic Revolutionary Front (FDR), which became the political wing of the FMLN. At roughly the same time, Duarte was sworn in as president with the support of the US government.

On December 2, four US churchwomen who had come to El Salvador to work with victims of the war disappeared on the road from the airport. Their car was found the next morning near Zacatecoluca, burned and without license plates. The bodies of the women, who had been raped and shot to death, were discovered in a shallow grave nearby.

Suddenly the civil war was more than just a Salvadoran problem. Despite a suggestion by then-US Secretary of State Alexander Haig that the nuns were killed when they tried to run a roadblock, the US suspended $25 million in military and economic aid pending an official investigation. The aid was resumed barely two months later, though, when the FMLN launched a series of major attacks.

The FMLN's "final offensive" in January 1981 helped the rebel movement gain credibility as a fighting force. The rebels made initial advances in northern and eastern El Salvador, forcing the government to abandon talk of reform and to focus its efforts on fighting.

When Ronald Reagan became president of the United States, a zealous fear of communism gaining a foothold in Central America spurred the US to pump millions of dollars of aid to El Salvador. US loans to the Salvadoran government jumped from $5.9 million in 1980 to $533 million in 1985. By 1985, when Congress threatened to block aid to El Salvador in response to its failure to control the activities of the death squads, Reagan declared that the government had made "good progress" in stopping human rights abuses. That same year the Salvadoran Catholic Church announced that government troops were responsible for 3,059 political assassinations during the first six months.

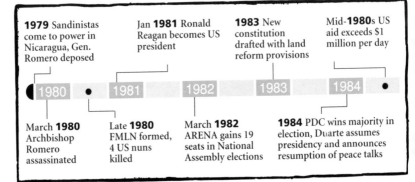

**1979** Sandinistas come to power in Nicaragua, Gen. Romero deposed

Jan **1981** Ronald Reagan becomes US president

**1983** New constitution drafted with land reform provisions

Mid-**1980s** US aid exceeds $1 million per day

1980   1981   1982   1983   1984

March **1980** Archbishop Romero assassinated

Late **1980** FMLN formed, 4 US nuns killed

March **1982** ARENA gains 19 seats in National Assembly elections

**1984** PDC wins majority in election, Duarte assumes presidency and announces resumption of peace talks

## Old Fears

**T**he 50th anniversary of La Matanza in early 1982 prompted 1,000 police to conduct a house-to-house search in San Salvador in fear of a memorial uprising.

■ **Rise of the Right.** The elections for the National Constituent Assembly in March 1982 were proclaimed a success for Salvadoran democracy and used by the US to justify its decision to provide more aid. But others maintained that the elections were merely a media event, and blamed the results on voting inflation and transparent ballot boxes. As then-US Ambassador Robert White said, "No power on earth can convince a poor unlettered *campesino* with a numbered ballot in his hand that the military commander of his district will not know for whom the vote was cast."

The recently founded Republican National Alliance (ARENA) gained a surprising 19 seats in the assembly. ARENA, representative of the radical right just as the FMLN represented the radical left, had paid a US advertising firm $200,000 to run its campaign. The investment paid off. Roberto d'Aubuisson, the party's founder, was elected president of the assembly, reflecting El Salvador's recent shift to the right in the face of the leftist insurgency. In 1982, the assembly appointed Dr. Alvaro Magaña, a banker, temporary president of El Salvador, although he was more of a figurehead than a legitimate leader. A year later the assembly drafted a new constitution.

■ **Failed Land Reform.** A key issue in the new constitution was land reform, a three-phase program initiated in 1983, supported by the US and written by the same US law professor who had drafted South Vietnam's land-reform program during the Vietnam War. The first phase, in which farms over 1,250 acres (15 percent of El Salvador's farmland) were to be turned into cooperatives, ultimately created large farms that were less productive than the private farms they replaced. The second phase, which would have redistributed holdings between 500 and 1,250 acres, was never implemented. The third phase was designed to give peasants ownership of small parcels of land that they had previously rented or sharecropped. By that point, 150,000 people were supposed to have benefited from the land reform program. In fact, less than 1,000 land titles were ever handed out.

When land reform was begun, right-wing landowners were enraged. Many peasants who applied for land titles were murdered or disappeared. Rodolf Viera, head of the Salvadoran Land Reform Institute, was gunned down after speaking out against the right-wing backlash. Before the land reform program totally collapsed, the assembly voted to allow landowners to own up to 262 hectares each. ARENA claimed victory for having stifled the program.

■ **Guerrilla Tactics and the Army's Response.** Through the early 1980s the FMLN continued to strengthen its control over northern and eastern El Salvador. Berlín and San Miguel were both occupied by guerrilla forces in 1983. The rebels, numbering 10,000 in 1984 compared with 50,000 government troops, staged successful attacks on military garrisons and important economic targets. The guerrillas destroyed the enormous Cuscatlán Bridge over the Lempa River in January 1984, despite 400 government soldiers on duty to protect it. Soon FMLN attacks in western El Salvador threatened the country's all-important coffee industry.

Guerrilla attacks on the country's infrastructure were an attempt to undermine the government by demolishing the country's basic economic lifelines. In the end, though, these attacks damaged the FMLN's reputation almost as much as they damaged El

### ROBERTO D' AUBUISSON (1943-1992)

# Man of the Right

**R**oberto d'Aubuisson, who died from cancer in 1992 at age 45, was a man of great contradictions. He was both a populist and an extremist, a presidential candidate and a disgraced co-conspirator in the assassination of Archbishop Romero. Above all, though, the founder of the ARENA party was the country's premier anticommunist throughout the war, as well as one of the chief organizers and supporters of El Salvador's death squads.

D'Aubuisson was raised in a lower-middle-class family, entered military school at 15 and was sent abroad to Taiwan and the US to learn how to combat communist insurgencies. At one point d'Aubuisson worked under General José Medrán, founder of ORDEN, El Salvador's first organized death squad.

Throughout his career, d'Aubuisson was almost as fiercely xenophobic as he was anticommunist. In his campaign against Duarte's moderate politics and the administration's close association with the US, d'Aubuisson alleged that Duarte and US President Carter had conspired to turn the country over to communism just like in Nicaragua. When evidence emerged that Nicaragua was supporting the Salvadoran guerrillas, d'Aubuisson advocated a retaliatory attack against El Salvador's larger southern neighbor.

Despite his extreme views, d'Aubuisson was also an effective campaigner and public speaker. He was an imposing figure, too, with a bulletproof vest, high-heeled boots, jeans and a pistol always tucked into his waistband. His short, muscular frame was surrounded by a constant entourage of bodyguards. The vest and bodyguards accompanied him everywhere after a sniper's bullet grazed him in 1982.

But d'Aubuisson is most remembered for his fiery rhetoric. In a deep voice, with jaws clenched and r's rolling hard, he would refer to then-President Duarte as "El Loco Duarte," and repeatedly curse US politicians and the foreign press.

In one of his better-known campaign tactics, d'Aubuisson would take a watermelon (whose color represented the PDC's official green) and chop it in half

Salvador's roads, bridges, buses, dams and power lines.

The army was fortunate that public confidence in the FMLN declined as the war progressed, because even with the help of US-trained quick-reaction battalions and surveillance photos showing the location of guerrilla troops, efforts to contain the revolution were often half-hearted and never very successful. When the army launched indiscriminate attacks against civilians whom it believed supported the guerrillas, they undermined confidence in both the government and the US policy of providing arms.

As early as 1981, more than 300,000 Salvadorans had fled to neighboring countries or to the US. Large parts of Chalatenango, Morazán, and Cabañas departments were left nearly deserted.

■ **Duarte's Return.** Salvadorans attached considerably less hope for peace to the 1984 elections than they had to the elections two years earlier. The FMLN refused to participate and hampered voting in areas under its control, and owners of radio stations were repeatedly threatened by paramilitary groups which warned them against broadcasting

with a single blow of a machete to show how like the watermelon the PDC was "green on the outside, but red [communist] on the inside." When d'Aubuisson began his campaign for the presidency, he continued to express his extremist political views by threatening to napalm villages and vowing to free the army of any human rights restrictions.

D'Aubuisson's legacy is tied to his involvement in the assassination of Archbishop Romero in 1980, his constant efforts to undermine any moderate political force in the country and his ARENA party. When the army broke in on d'Aubuisson and others plotting to assassinate Romero, d'Aubuisson tried to eat certain incriminating papers. After being sent briefly into exile, he was allowed to return in part because the US government at the time was more concerned with the threat of a communist takeover than they were with state-sponsored terrorism. D'Aubuisson was so closely tied to the death squads that then-US Ambassador Robert White described him to Congress as a "pathological killer."

Despite ARENA's shady beginnings, d'Aubuisson's political party has prospered. D'Aubuisson began the party after

failing to spur a coup to overthrow the 1980 military junta which included Duarte. Initially, he became known for television appearances in which he would hold up photos of suspected terrorists. Not coincidentally, the appearances would be followed by death squad attacks.

When ARENA came to power in the Constituent Assembly in 1982, his shadowy paramilitary friends resurfaced in the assembly building. In his 1984 campaign for the presidency, d'Aubuisson promised to exterminate guerrillas within three months of convening a new National Constituent Assembly, and promised to seize Duarte and try him for treason.

D'Aubuisson's political views mellowed shortly before his death, just months after the government and rebels agreed to the peace accords. He seemed to realize that, in the long run, his extreme views could actually harm his party's popularity, and moved himself more behind the scenes. President Cristiani later credited d'Aubuisson with making the agreements possible, and said that without his support radical elements in ARENA would never have allowed the talks to take place.

advertisements for the Christian Democrats. The US, which feared ARENA's virulently conservative platform, supported Duarte. Duarte won in a run-off with just over half the vote and became El Salvador's first freely-elected president in over 50 years. At the same time, the Christian Democrats won a majority in the assembly and announced plans to initiate social reforms.

With the momentum of a resounding victory, Duarte soon announced the resumption of peace talks with the guerrillas, to be held in the small town of La Palma in Chalatenango department. But after two rounds of talks no agreement could be reached, and each side accused the other of being unwillin  to compromise. In the remaining years of his presidency, Du  rte repeatedly clashed with the radical right and the military  and was unable to bring about the end of the war or any meaningful reforms.

## VOICES FROM THE WAR

"You know, let whoever wins, win. But let this war be over."
-Elderly man, overheard during a gun battle in his small town.

"It is almost odd to die of natural causes in this country."
-Salvadoran church leader, 1983

■ **The War Continues.** By the mid-1980s, the enormous US military funding began to show results as the army gradually regained control of areas once dominated by guerrillas. US-supplied jets gave El Salvador the most powerful air force in Central America and allowed the army to strafe and bomb large parts of guerrilla territory. When US aid to El Salvador peaked in the late 1980s, more than $1 million a day was being funneled to the Salvadoran government, and most of it was re-channeled to fight the war. Such enormous sums made El Salvador the fifth-largest recipient of US aid in the world. As fighting between the army and the FMLN dragged on, many Salvadorans came to believe that victory for either side was unlikely to come anytime soon.

The FMLN expressed a desire to participate in elections scheduled for late 1989, the same year George Bush became president of the US. The rebels asked that voting be postponed for six months, in order for them to have sufficient time to prepare for an election, and that both sides agree to an immediate 60-day cease-fire. The government refused to postpone the elections. In response, the FMLN killed more than 40 people in an election-day attack on the National Guard headquarters in San Salvador.

Despite a law that made voting mandatory, a combination of voter apathy and fear kept more than half of all Salvadorans away from the polls. For the first time in a decade, the FMLN didn't attack polling stations, although they did bomb power stations and black out 90 percent of the country. Rubén Zamora, a leftist leader recently returned from self-imposed exile, ran for president as the candidate of the Democratic Convergence Party (PDC).

ARENA candidate Alfredo Cristiani, a wealthy businessman raised on one of the country's largest coffee plantations and educated at Georgetown University in the US, was elected president. It was the first time in El Salvador's history that executive authority was passed peacefully from one freely elected civilian president to another. The US perceived Cristiani, who had a cleaner record than did his mentor d'Aubuisson, as a political moderate. ARENA hoped he would be able to help the party shed its rabidly conservative image acquired when d'Aubuisson was at the helm.

■ **A Chance at Peace.** In September 1989, the government and the FMLN began another round of peace talks at the collective request of other Central American nations. In October, negotiations were cut short when a bomb ripped through the headquarters of the Salvadoran Workers' National Union Federation (FENESTRAS), killing ten and wounding 29. The FMLN blamed the army and refused to return to the bargaining table. Within a month the guerrillas had launched a new offensive that reached the streets of the capital.

This "last offensive" of the FMLN was one of the most spectacular displays of guerilla tactics in Latin American history. Thousands of FMLN fighters entered the capital in all types of disguises from fake funeral processions to produce trucks with false beds lined with weapons. At one point the head of the Organization of American States was nearly captured in his hotel room but was saved by an air attack and a spectacular James Bond-style rescue. The guerillas managed to occupy several major areas of the capital, but their success resulted in a high degree of human suffering.

The government declared a national state of siege as it launched a counter-offensive in the capital. When the situation seemed as bad as it could get, six Jesuit priests were killed on the campus of the University of Central America on the morning of November 16, 1989. Their bodies, along with those of their housekeeper and her young daughter, were found riddled with bullets in their dormitory. The audacious murders, immediately pinned on the army, were reminiscent of Archbishop Romero's assassination almost a decade earlier. Many people wondered whether the cycle of violence would start all over again. Most Salvadorans will tell you that there was little joy during the Christmas of 1989.

Despite the turmoil, peace negotiations began again in early 1990. This time the UN mediated the talks, but was unable to help the two sides agree on the accountability and future role of the country's military. By the end of the year fighting had resumed. The FMLN shot down a government plane with a Soviet surface-to-air missile in late 1990 and, in January 1991, rebels downed a US military helicopter on its way to Honduras. Two US servicemen who survived the crash were subsequently executed by the FMLN, prompting the US to resume military aid.

## The Jesuit Case

**F**ive soldiers, three lieutenants and Colonel Guillermo Benavides, then head of the military academy, were charged with the Jesuit murders. There were rumors that higher-ranking officers had participated in the plot, but no hard evidence was available to prosecute them.

The prosecution fought a long battle to bring the case to trial. Even President Cristiani was frustrated at the embarrassing lack of progress, and asked Britain's Scotland Yard and the Spanish police to help in the investigation. In May 1990, important evidence disappeared, including Benavides diary. By January 1991, two state prosecutors had resigned to protest interference by the army and the Attorney General.

When the case reached the Supreme Court in April of that year, two lieutenants and all five soldiers were acquitted for having followed orders. Benavides and the other lieutenant were found guilty of the killings and sentenced to 30 years in jail, the maximum penalty allowable. Fourteen months later, in March 1993, both were set free under the government's General Amnesty law.

## PEACE

By the beginning of the 1990s, leaders and supporters of both sides were exhausted by the endless fighting. The turning point in negotiations came when the government accepted demands that it purge the armed forces. On September 25, 1991, representatives of the Salvadoran Government and the FMLN signed the New York City Accords at the United Nations headquarters, under the auspices of the UN and the Catholic Church. In this preliminary agreement, the FMLN secured the rights for peasants to permanently occupy land controlled by the guerrillas, and a bipartisan National Commission for the Consolidation of Peace (COPAZ) was organized to oversee the peace process and the FMLN's formal introduction to the political process.

The final peace agreements, known as the Accords of Chapultepec, were signed on January 16, 1992 in Mexico. A two-year timetable was established to implement a long list of reforms and changes in both the government and the FMLN. The government agreed to reduce the size of its 30,000-strong active forces by one-half, and to disband its 17,000-member rapid-deployment battalions. The notorious National Guard and Treasury Police, both implicated in death squad activities, were also to be disbanded. Intelligence services were transferred to civilian control, forced army recruitment was ended and entrance requirements for military service were made stricter.

Most importantly, the accords required the government to purge officers and judicial officials accused of human rights abuses and corruption, and to enact constitutional amendments that redirected the mission of the military toward defending the country from external threats instead of internal ones. A National Council of the Judiciary (CNJ) was created to evaluate the competency of all judges.

Land reform provisions required a transfer of all holdings over 245 hectares, with preference for land to be given to over 35,000 ex-guerrillas and soldiers. A new civilian police force, the National Civil Police (PNC), was created to replace the old, discredited National Police. An Office of the Counsel for the Defense of Human Rights was to take over monitoring of the human-rights situation after the United Nations Mission to El Salvador (ONUSAL) left the country. A National Truth Commission (see A Clean Slate) was established to investigate past human rights abuses by both sides to propose a list of recommended actions which the government agreed to adopt. The FMLN, for its part, agreed to lay down its arms in a five-stage demilitarization process and to be reborn as a political party.

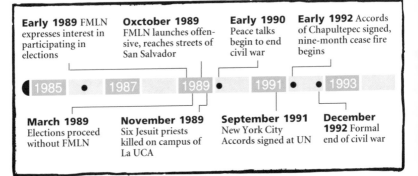

**Early 1989** FMLN expresses interest in participating in elections

**Oxctober 1989** FMLN launches offensive, reaches streets of San Salvador

**Early 1990** Peace talks begin to end civil war

**Early 1992** Accords of Chapultepec signed, nine-month cease fire begins

1985 • 1987 • 1989 • 1991 • 1993

**March 1989** Elections proceed without FMLN

**November 1989** Six Jesuit priests killed on campus of La UCA

**September 1991** New York City Accords signed at UN

**December 1992** Formal end of civil war

■ **Cease-fire.** A nine-month cease-fire between government and rebel forces, mandated by the peace accords, began on February 1, 1992, under the supervision of 1,000 UN troops. A crowd of 30,000 leftist supporters gathered in the Plaza Gerardo Barrios to celebrate the first day without fighting while Radio

## Making Up for Lost Time

**A**fter 13 years of strict rules forbidding rebels from drinking any alcohol, former FMLN troops celebrated for four days straight in San Antonio, near the Guazapa Volcano, and drank the town dry.

Venceremos, the clandestine wartime voice of the FMLN, broadcast freely from the roof of the Metropolitan Cathedral. A 40-foot FMLN banner hung across the entrance to the cathedral. Two blocks away, meanwhile, government supporters welcomed Cristiani back from the peace talks, watched a fireworks display and danced until dawn.

On December 15, a formal ceremony marking the end of the war was attended by Cristiani, FMLN leaders, the UN Secretary-General and Central American heads of state. That same day, the FMLN was registered as an official political party. After more than a decade of bloodshed which killed one percent of the Salvadoran population, left countless more wounded or indigent and drove nearly 15 percent of the population abroad, the civil war was over. The Salvadoran peace process is heralded as one the United Nation's greatest successes.

■ **The Elections of the Century.** March 1994 saw the first presidential, legislative and municipal elections in El Salvador since the end of the conflict. Two thousand election observers watched as campaign rhetoric flew. ARENA warned landowners that the FMLN wanted to nationalize all their holdings and claimed that an El Salvador run by the left would end up with food-rationing books like Cuba. The FMLN countered by pointing out how they had been putting their lives on the line for the sake of their country for the duration of the war, while ARENA seemed to discover voters only at election time.

The presidential election pitted Rubén Zamora of the Center-Left Coalition, representing the FMLN and other left-wing groups, against Armando Calderón Sol, a conservative lawyer, co-founder of ARENA and two-time mayor of San Salvador who had been linked to death squad activities while working with d'Aubuisson.

A light turnout tarnished the elections and the Supreme Electoral Tribunal was

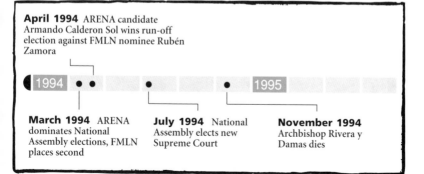

**April 1994** ARENA candidate Armando Calderon Sol wins run-off election against FMLN nominee Rubén Zamora

1994 • • • • 1995

**March 1994** ARENA dominates National Assembly elections, FMLN places second

**July 1994** National Assembly elects new Supreme Court

**November 1994** Archbishop Rivera y Damas dies

accused of making voting difficult for rural voters. *Campesinos* were required to vote in departmental capitals rather than in municipalities closer to home. Registration was particularly difficult since many rural records had been destroyed during the war. More than 70,000 people were unable to vote because their birth certificates could not be located.

## TRANSITION TO DEMOCRACY

Close results in the first round of voting required a run-off between ARENA and FMLN presidential candidates. In the end, pervasive distrust of the new FMLN political party and the lingering specter of communism convinced the electorate to side with ARENA, despite its links to the death squads. When the second round of voting was complete, Calderón Sol emerged with 68 percent of the vote and became El Salvador's new president. ARENA won 39 seats in the Legislative Assembly, groups sympathetic to the FMLN won 21 seats, the PDC won 18 and other groups took the remaining six seats. UN observers declared the election free of fraud, but some watchdog groups claimed otherwise.

In July 1994, a new Supreme Court was elected by the assembly, and no members of the previous court were returned to office, fulfilling the recommendations of the UN-sponsored Truth Commission. In late September, former soldiers stormed the Legislative Assembly demanding severance pay for 30,000 of their comrades out of work as a result of the peace process.

As 1994 progressed, internal squabbling soon threatened to split up the groups comprising the FMLN political party. By late 1994, the political left was in complete disarray as extremist elements broke from former rebel leader Joaquín Villalobos, who tried to toe a moderate political line. Supporters from all sides encouraged Villalobos to dissolve the FMLN once and for all. Villalobos, meanwhile, had other concerns as he was sent to jail on charges of libeling a prominent businessman. The Supreme Court later dismissed the charges and ordered his release.

In November, Archbishop Arturo Rivera y Damas, one of the late Archbishop Romero's strongest supporters, died of natural causes. Rivera y Damas followed in the footsteps of Romero by giving regular homilies that denounced human rights abuses and played a major role in bringing the government and rebels together to sign the 1992 peace accords. President Sol attended the wake for the archbishop, but said that he did not agree with all that Rivera y Damas stood for.

Disappearances in El Salvador had completely come to an end by the close of 1994,

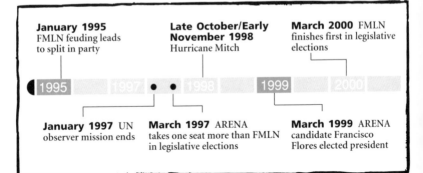

**January 1995** FMLN feuding leads to split in party

**Late October/Early November 1998** Hurricane Mitch

**March 2000** FMLN finishes first in legislative elections

1995   1997 ● ● 1998   1999   2000

**January 1997** UN observer mission ends

**March 1997** ARENA takes one seat more than FMLN in legislative elections

**March 1999** ARENA candidate Francisco Flores elected president

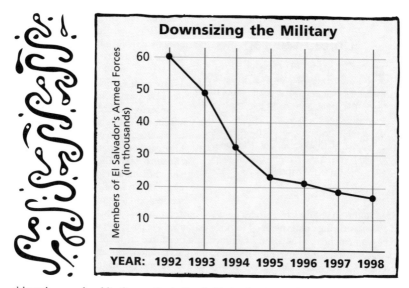

**Downsizing the Military**

Members of El Salvador's Armed Forces (in thousands)

YEAR: 1992 1993 1994 1995 1996 1997 1998

although several public figures (including leftist leaders) were killed under suspicious circumstances. The UN announced that the country's security forces continued to commit human rights abuses, but that their efforts to control such abuses had improved. All of this diverted attention from President Calderón Sol, who had an otherwise unremarkable beginning in his struggle to end corruption and crime.

In May 1994, the United Nations Security Council extended the ONUSAL observer mission in El Salvador for an additional six months to oversee the further implementation of the terms of the Peace Accords. The international community was particularly concerned with delays in judicial and land reform, and the integration of the new National Police Force (PNC) since escalating crime could cause social unrest.

In the end, ONUSAL remained in El Salvador until the end of April 1995 and left behind a smaller contingent of UN Observers (MINUSAL) that remained through 1996. In January 1997, the UN mission was formally terminated, even though the Peace Accords had not yet been fully implemented.

■ **Ups and Downs for the FMLN.** In January 1995, two of the five members of the FMLN coalition, the Resistencia Nacional (RN) previously known as the Fuerzas Armadas de la Resistencia, and the Expresión Renovadora del Pueblo (ERP), once known as the Ejercito Revolucionario Popular, withdrew. In March of that year, Joaquín Villalobos, then Secretary-General of the ERP, announced a new alliance between the RN, the ERP, the Movimiento Nacional Revolucionario (MNS) and splintered factions of the Partido Demócrata Cristiano (PDC). Organizing as the Partido Demócrata (PD), this new center-left party immediately cooperated with President Calderón Sol in securing Legislative Assembly approval for a controversial increase in the Value Added Tax to 13%.

Amidst protest from both left- and right-wing political parties as well as opposition from business leaders, this tax increase was deemed necessary by the coalition to finance recon-

## United We Tan

**F**rom 1991 to 1997 the United Nations Observer Mission in El Salvador (ONUSAL) monitored the peace process. Since the transition went better than most expected the observers had little to do during the last two years so locals dubbed this United Nations (Naciones Unidas in Spanish) group Vacaciones Unidas or United Vacations.

struction. The International Monetary Fund (IMF) signaled its support for the move by providing the government with additional credit.

In 1996 the PD withdrew from its alliance with ARENA and charged that the government had failed to keep promises to increase spending on health and education or provide job security to the state employees whose jobs were threatened by privatization.

■ **Recent Past.** The increase in violent crime became one of El Salvador's primary concerns following the war. One hundred and ten police offices had been killed in the line of duty by the end of 1996 (the total would rise to over 500 by the end of 1998). Growing public demand for firm action led the government, in that same year to pass an emergency law against common and organized crime. Shortly after the law's passage, however, the Government's Human Rights Ombudsman and other critics filed several constitutional challenges against it and it was never put into law. Other laws, however, have been passed to deal with crime, including tougher laws against organized crime, longer maximum sentences and stiffer penalties for possession of illegal arms.

January 16, 1997 marked the fifth anniversary of the signing of the Peace Accords. The municipal and legislative elections held in March under the scrutiny of international observers presented a stunning setback for the ruling ARENA party. FMLN swept to victory in 53 municipalities, including San Salvador, and it won reelection in all eleven towns where it had governed since 1994. On the national level the FMLN nearly doubled its representation in the Legislative Assembly and fell just one seat short of matching ARENA's total. ARENA and the FMLN each won about a third of the 84 Assembly seats with seven other parties splitting the remaining third.

The Presidential elections in March 1999 followed on the heels of destruction caused by Hurricane Mitch (see Hurricane Mitch). Thanks to strong divisions between "orthodox" and "reformist" wings of the FMLN, ARENA recovered from its 1997 setback and their candidate, Francisco Flores, emerged victorious with a 51.4 percent majority, though only 39 percent of the eligible public voted. The Harvard-educated

## Hurricane Mitch

**T**he Atlantic basin's fourth strongest hurricane ever hit Central America at the end of October 1998. Sustained winds of 180 mph and severe rainfall left 10,000 dead and caused billions of dollars in damage. Though Honduras and Nicaragua were the hardest hit, El Salvador suffered widespread flooding and landslides that resulted in 374 people dead and 56,000 homeless. The nation's road network was particularly hard hit and 15 bridges, including the three major bridges crossing the Lempa River, were damaged or destroyed.

Flores became the youngest president in Latin America at age 39. The 2000 legislative elections saw the FMLN regain their cohesion and take 31 seats in the Assembly to ARENA's 29, but combined with the PCN's 14 seats the right-wing still holds a slim voting majority.

Though peace and stability have replaced war, El Salvador remains socially polarized. Business and government are still dominated by the elite and large numbers of Salvadoran's remain impoverished.

# Geography

El Salvador is the smallest country in Central America—roughly the size of Massachusetts. It is 260 kilometers long east to west, 100 kilometers wide north to south and has 320 kilometers of Pacific coastline. It's conceivable to drive the length of the country in a day. El Salvador's size and shape has earned it the affectionate nickname *El Pulgarcito* ("The Little Thumb") of Central America.

El Salvador is divided roughly into three geographical regions running east to west. The Sierra Madre mountain chain fills the **interior highlands** bordering Honduras and Guatemala. The mountains are low and old, and are sparsely populated. The **central region** consists of high valleys separated by mountains and volcanoes. Most of El Salvador's major cities, 75 percent of its population and its best farmland, including many coffee plantations on the lower volcanic slopes, are located here. The **coastal plain** is narrow, extending just 10 to 20 miles inland, but fertile, dotted with a few port cities and farms and lined with beaches. The coastal mountain range borders it to the north.

■ **Earthquakes & Volcanoes.** El Salvador's hyperactive geography is a direct result of its location along the Cinturón del Fuego ("Belt of Fire"), a ring of volcanoes and fault zones that encircles the Pacific Ocean. According to historical records, there have been at least 50 destructive earthquakes in Central America since 1520, caused by shifting of the earth's plates and volcanic eruptions. Earthquakes are most frequent in the central highlands, which unfortunately is where most of the country's largest cities are located. There are 25 volcanoes (and another eight lakes of volcanic origin) in the country, although only Santa Ana, Izalco, San Salvador, El Playón, San Vicente, San Miguel, Conchagua, and Islas Quemadas (which is actually under Lake Ilopango) are active. The largest are Santa Ana (2,365m), San Vicente (2,181m) and San Miguel (2,129m). Periodic eruptions over the centuries have covered the country in ash, and usually coincide with earthquakes.

About 90 percent of El Salvador is blessed with incredibly fertile volcanic soil. The Río Lempa, the country's only large river, was formed by volcanic eruptions and has created a 24-kilometer wide alluvial plain in southeast El Salvador. The landscape

## A Limb for a Limb

The Guazapa Volcano, a guerilla stronghold devastated by fighting, has been partially reforested in memory of the 75,000 Salvadorans killed during the war. The plan is to plant one tree in this "reconciliation forest" for each victim, though they have not yet reached the intended total.

is dotted by a few large lakes including the Lago de Ilopango, just east of San Salvador. The dazzlingly blue Lago de Coatepeque lies next to Cerro Verde and the Izalco and Santa Ana Volcanoes west of San Salvador. Geysers are scattered throughout the country and provide nearly 20 percent of the the country's electricity.

El Salvador's Tallest Volcanoes

■ **Political Divisions.** El Salvador is divided into 14 **departments**, each with its own capital. Departmental capitals are usually the largest city in the department, and often share the department's name. **San Salvador**, the nation's capital, sits in the middle of the country in the department of the same name.

The rest of the country (as well as this book) is divided into three main regions. The **western region** contains Ahuachapán, Santa Ana, Sonsonate and La Libertad departments. The **northern region** contains Chalatenango, Cabañas and Cuscatlán departments. The **eastern region** is made up of San Vicente, La Paz, Usulután, San Miguel, Morazán and La Unión departments.

# Climate

El Salvador is situated in the tropics, where the climate remains more or less constant throughout the year but rainfall changes greatly with the seasons. In fact, the temperature changes more from day to night than it does from season to season. Altitude is the primary determinant of the climate and El Salvador spans three different weather zones. The agreeable climate in the central zone is one of the reasons most people live there.

The **rainy season**, known as *invierno* ("winter"), runs from mid-May to mid-October. Rain comes in predictable spurts, usually in late afternoon, and drenches some parts of the country more than others, but the sun still shines nearly everyday. The rains bring out the

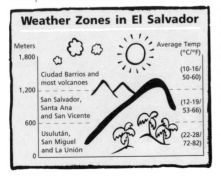

Weather Zones in El Salvador

best of the country's foliage—the greens are especially green—but many backcountry roads become impassable. They are also accompanied by some spectacular lightning displays. The **dry season**, or *verano* ("summer"), begins in mid-November and continues through mid-April. Flowers bloom across the country, but the weather is still hot. The short periods in between summer and winter are transitional seasons, similar to spring and autumn in zones farther from the equator.

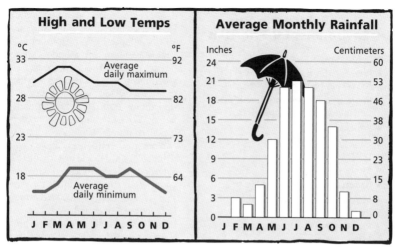

# Environment

El Salvador's incredible natural beauty is threatened by pollution and deforestation. Thankfully things are changing. The media takes an active role in increasing awareness of ecological issues and there is a new commitment by the Salvadoran government to address these concerns.

■ **What Little is Left.** El Salvador's environment has been under attack from the moment Europeans set foot in the country. The UN estimates that El Salvador has already lost an astronomical 95 percent of its natural forests. The country's virgin forest has been so thoroughly depleted that the remaining five percent is no longer sufficient to meet domestic demand, so wood for construction is now imported from Honduras. Many animals that once thrived in the forests, especially wild cats and monkeys, are now extinct. The country's rich and ultra-productive volcanic soil is one of its strongest economic assets, but erosion is a significant concern.

Limited access to fresh water is also a problem. During the 1980s, the water table in San Salvador dropped more than one meter per year. To meet demand, water was redirected from a river 130 kilometers away. Eventually, though, that source turned out to be polluted.

■ **Public Health.** It's occasionally taken public health

## TO GET INVOLVED

**Appropriate Technology Studies Center (CESTA)**
Carretera a San Marcos Km 4 1/2 #392
San Salvador
Tel 220-3006, 220-0046
E-mail cesta@es.com.sv

**The Salvadoran Association for Conservation of the Environment (ASACMA)**
1 Calle Pte y 87 Av Nte #4444
Colonia Escalón
San Salvador
Tel 263-7279
E-mail asacma@yahoo.com
asacma.webjump.com

**SalvaNATURA**
33 Av Sur #640
Colonia Flor Blanca
San Salvador
Tel 279-1515
E-mail salnatura@saltel.net
www.salvanatura.org

**Environment Foundation of El Salvador (FONAES)**
Calle Gabriela Mistral y 29 Av Nte #1013
San Salvador
Tel 226-3000, 226-3022

## El Salvador's Top Environmental Priorities

- Reforestation.
- Promote the use of gas or solar cookers in place of firewood.
- Improve soil conservation and sustainable agricultural practices.
- Protect biodiversity
- Stop the illegal disposal of toxic wastes.
- Modernize landfills.
- Reduce water and air pollution.
- Increase recycling and decrease littering.
- Promote water and energy conservation.

disasters to focus attention on El Salvador's environment. In November 1990, sulfuric acid explosions in Soyapango, near San Salvador, burned through tin-roofed homes in the area. The government said nothing, but reporters discovered that toxic waste was "stored" in steel drums scattered around a nearby facility. The government responded by handing out antihistamines.

Foreign companies have contributed to the debacle by looking to El Salvador and other Central American countries as storage facilities for waste that would need special treatment back home. A Texas-based company tried to ship toxic ash to La Unión, claiming that the material was harmless and would make good housing foundations. This attempt to "help" the people of La Unión would have brought enough heavy metal to make anyone living on it deathly sick.

Finally, the difficulty in enforcing environmental regulations contributes to the losses. Some rivers are polluted with pesticides that are used excessively or illegally, including many which are banned in the USA. Forests are destroyed for fuel, since high tariffs have made oil difficult to import for many years, and skyrocketing populations further strain resources that are already stretched to the breaking point.

## Environmental Statistics

- A mere one-quarter of one percent of El Salvador's land area is under government protection.
- Ninety-five percent of the urban population but only sixteen percent of the rural population have access to potable water.
- Over 200 varieties of orchids grow here and over 400 different bird species have been observed throughout the country.
- Five types of fresh water fish, three kinds of amphibians, 21 reptiles, 68 birds and 18 mammals have become extinct in El Salvador.
- Ninety percent of the rivers in the country are polluted.

■ **New Awareness.** As bleak as it may seem, there is still hope for El Salvador's battered environment. The Laguna El Jocotal in San Miguel department has been established as a wildlife restoration project. The area around Trifinio, at the juncture of El Salvador, Honduras and Guatemala, will be further developed with money from the Inter-American Development Bank and the blossoming El Imposible National Park will help protect what is left of the country's natural heritage. The Rio Sapo Ecological Reserve near Perquín is another ambitious project that is just getting started.

Politicians from both the left and right are beginning to agree that the environment can't wait much longer. In 1997, the government established a new Ministry of Environment and Natural Resources (MARN), but it is hindered by a lack of resources and environmental know-how. A wide range of new environmental laws encouraging pollution controls and reforestation were passed in 1998, but enforcement is slack. Unlike many developing countries El Salvador has managed to reduce their greenhouse gas emissions over the past several years.

The international community is also active on this issue. USAID's Green Project is providing training in sustainable development, funding reforestation and promoting the adoption of energy-saving stoves. GreenCOM, also supported by USAID, promotes composting as a method for turning coffee pulp into usable waste. Organic agriculture is a rapidly growing segment of the economy in El Salvador and several organizations are assisting farmers in this new and very lucrative endeavor.

Perhaps the most promising development is that Earth Day is celebrated by children in public schools across the country.

# People

El Salvador is a small but crowded country. Almost everyone speaks Spanish, and little of the original indigenous culture survives. Of approximately 6.2 million Salvadorans, about 58 percent live in or around the cities, which are crowded and growing quickly. The incredible population density—293 people per square kilometer—is made worse by a 2 percent annual growth rate, though that figure has fallen in recent years. Life expectancy is about 67 years for men and 74 years for women. Infant mortality has dropped considerably over the last decade to 28 per 1,000 (1999).

■ **Cultural Groups.** El Salvador can be roughly divided into three ethnic groups, which also tend to correspond to social classes. Salvadorans who claim pure European descent comprise about nine percent of the population but most of the country's upper class. *Mestizos*, who make up 90 percent of the population, are of mixed European and indigenous descent, and form part of all the social classes. Native Salvadorans (meaning those of indigenous descent) comprise just one percent of the population, are almost invariably poor and limited to rural parts of the southwest and southeast where they often make earn less money than other agricultural laborers doing similar work.

■ **Indigenous Inhabitants.** El Salvador's indigenous population is mostly descended from the Pipil tribe though Lenca and Maya have held on too. Since the Spanish arrived, they have frequently been repressed for raising their political voice and for resisting the appropriation of their lands (which has often meant siding with the left). They became increasingly isolated as the country adopted the language and customs of the Spanish. Native Salvadorans aren't easy to spot on the streets, partly because *La Matanza* in 1932 killed much of El Salvador's indigenous population. After the massacre, native people learned to dress in European clothes, cut their hair and speak Spanish in public. Many fear that by reasserting their traditional culture they will be inviting another crackdown.

These days it is generally safe for El Salvador's indigenous communities to

## TO GET INVOLVED

### INDIGENOUS ORGANIZATIONS

**Asociación Nacional Indígena
Salvadoreña (ANIS)**
Calle Obispo Marroquín
Oficina Antigua Aduana Férrea 5-1
Sonsonate
Tel 451-1721
ANIS, the largest and best-known indigenous
organization, represents the cultural, politi-
cal and economic interests of Nahuat-speak-
ing communities of Western El Salvador.

**Consejo Coordinador Nacional
Indígena Salvadoreño (CCNIS)**
Apartado Postal "MAIS"/10
San Salvador
Tel 222-2139
CCNIS represents some 10 community-
based organizations. Their staff of lawyers
assist with formal demands against the government for improving conditions for all
native Salvadorans. Their main success has
been uniting groups that in the past have
competed against each other for the same
limited resources.

**Miguel Amaya Amaya**
Comunidad Indígena Lenca
de Cacaopera
Domicilio Conocido
Cacaopera, Morazán
Under the tireless leadership of Miguel
Amaya Amaya, the Lenca community is
experiencing a revival of traditional cultural
practices including language, religion and
medicine. Plans are underway to develop a
community center with a health clinic, housing for elders, artisan workshops, a sweat
lodge, and visitor quarters.

### WOMEN'S ORGANIZATIONS

**Las Dignas**
Calle Gabriela Mistral #224
San Salvador
Tel 225-4457
E-mail dignas@vianet.com.sv
Las Dignas offers emotional support and
judicial consultants to women affected
by violence.

organize and the remaining populations struggle to protect their cultures from
extinction. In recent years, there's even been a limited revival of indigenous culture, due in part to the sale of native handicrafts. The government has established
an office to bridge communication between local indigenous groups and the state
thereby allowing demands for improved social and economic conditions to be

heard. By specifically incorporating indigenous
communities into budgets for post-war reconstruction, international organizations (such as
UNESCO's Culture of Peace Program) have also
lent a hand.

■ **Women.** Most women in El Salvador lead a difficult life that hasn't changed for centuries.
Salvadoran women have more difficulty finding
employment, struggle against abusive and legally-
sanctioned traditions and frequently bear children at such a young age that they are too busy
raising families to strive for change. Only recently
has their situation begun to improve.

Widespread discrimination means that women struggle to find work throughout the country. Sixty-five percent of *Salvadoreñas* who work do so in the informal economy—selling fruit and making *pupusas* on the street—while those with formal jobs are often paid less than men for equal work. One of the bright spots for women has been the growth of *maquiladoras*, foreign-owned assembly factories, where women make up 85-90 percent of the work force, though few hold management positions. Concerns about working conditions in these factories spurred a new level of women's labor activism. In 1996 the legislature responded to union demands for proper compensation for extra hours, an easing of bathroom-visit restrictions and prohibitions on physical abuse.

The country's upper class, including many Salvadorans educated abroad, now includes more women professionals than ever before. Nearly 30 percent of the country's doctors and attorneys, and an even larger percentage of dentists and high school teachers, are women.

Women have increased their presence in the government too. Women make up about one third of San Salvador's municipal council, ten percent of the National Assembly and President Flores has appointed a number of women to high posts, including the heads of the Foreign Affairs, Education, and Environment ministries. The FMLN even chose a woman, Maria Marta Valladares, as their vice presidential candidate.

Marital violence and the treatment of women as second-rate citizens, although evident in every country, is a particular problem in Latin America. There is also a history of sexual abuse in the countryside, where young, uneducated women work for wealthy landowners who control their pay and their lives. Reports of sexual assault have increased in recent years, but this is most likely a result of more women coming forward now that the issue being is taken seriously. Previously, one of the main problems in combating sexual assaults was that the law did not allow rape victims to testify and thus the chance of convictions were slim. The 1998 Criminal Procedures Code changed this.

The war also scarred the lives of many women. The death of husbands and fathers left many women and girls to tend households—often filled with children—by themselves. Without a second income, these women struggle to find work to support their remaining family members. Surprisingly the war also had a plus side for women. Fighting alongside women in the guerrilla armies gave many men a new-found respect for their female companions.

Public hospitals in El Salvador, influenced by the Church, still refuse to give abortions and the nation's gynecological wards are filled with an alarming number of women injured during poorly performed back-room abortions. Contrary to the wishes of the church, the government has taken a strong and active position in favor of family planning. The pill is the country's most fre-

## Educational Statistics

- Education is free through the ninth grade (up to age 14), but only 82 percent of children attend this far.
- Six percent of children never attend any school.
- Thirty-three percent of children old enough for secondary school attend.
- The adult literacy is 79 percent for men, 73 percent for women.

(1999)

## Cash From the North

**M**oney sent from relatives, *hermanos lejanos* ("distant brothers") as they are affectionately known, working abroad has had a big impact on Salvadorans back home. While some families suffered through the war with barely the clothing on their backs, others prospered with funds sent to El Salvador from hardworking family members in the US. Nearly one-third of all Salvadorans have relatives in the United States. The exodus north began in the late 1960s, when the first emigrants realized they could earn much more working in the United States.

Each year nearly $1.5 billion is sent from family members in the US to relatives in El Salvador each year. Money travels back by couriers, who make the weekly trip in heavily guarded convoys. A good day in a medium-sized city can mean receipts of nearly $25,000. Near Christmas, the amount increases to more than $100,000 in the same towns.

The war dampened the flow of funds, not only because so many people were leaving, but because few businesses wanted to risk carrying such large sums of money into the country.

Though the money sent back is the product of hard labor, the extra cash doesn't always mean good things for El Salvador. The economy isn't benefiting much, since a generation of Salvadorans is learning to survive on the funds they receive rather than from the money they earn working local jobs. Nearly 80 percent of the money is spent on food, which is mostly imported from neighboring nations, and little is reinvested in the country.

Almost an entire generation, most aged 17-40, left in search of work abroad. Eldest sons, young husbands and hardworking housewives and mothers abandoned homes and tradition in search of a better life, but at the expense of their families. Schools closed for lack of students and marriages fell apart, sometimes from the strain of a long-distance separation and other times when the spouse abroad found someone new. In a few cases, the spouse left behind supported a lover who helped spend the money sent from abroad.

For most, however, the money has made life back in El Salvador better. Since many Salvadorans who emigrated had always scraped by with what little money was earned in the coffee fields, newfound wealth has conferred status on many people who once labored as peasants. Some use their money to buy luxuries like cars, furniture and stereos, while others fund elaborate weddings in El Salvador.

quently used contraceptive.

Finally, the legal system shows signs that the rights of women will be guarded more closely despite the fact that according to article 182 of El Salvador's civil code a wife is required to be obedient to her husband and the husband is required to protect his wife. The country's labor code protects pregnant women from performing dangerous jobs, although this is occasionally used as grounds for discrimination. The 1983 constitution includes a provision guaranteeing equality for men and women in the eyes of the law. Though as a practical matter many of these laws are not always enforced, but the government has finally begun to address many of the problems.

# Religion

The Catholic Church has always been extremely powerful in Latin America, and El Salvador, with a population more than 80 percent Roman Catholic (though Protestant groups are growing) is no exception. In recent decades, Liberation Theology (see Liberation Theology) has influenced the Church and has been at the basis of its struggle with the government and the army. Beginning in the late 1960s, the Church organized base communities throughout the country that brought people together to worship and to take political action. As these base communities became more and more revolutionary and threatened landowners and the oligarchy, community members were frequently repressed, jailed and killed.

■ **The Church Against the Army.** The army first began its campaign against the Church in the 1970s, just as Liberation Theology began to take hold. Jesuit priests were targeted from the beginning, but the frequency of terrorist acts rose sharply when Oscar Romero became archbishop and began preaching the new gospel in earnest. By the late 1970s, when the army raided towns to search for communists, soldiers frequently attacked peasants who were active in the Church.

The campaign continued throughout the civil war. When the FMLN attacked the capital in November 1989, the army rounded up hundreds of Church leaders and charged them with having sheltered guerrillas. Relations between the Church and the military deteriorated quickly, until six Jesuit priests were murdered at the University of Central America later in the month. The investigation which followed led to the historic decision to prosecute military officers. In all, some 600 priests or Church sympathizers were murdered during the war.

Today the Church operates various social programs, but most are less politically oriented than they once were. An arm of the Church distributes international aid, and another operates an orphanage. The Church's legal aid office investigates human rights abuses in the country, in spite of frequent threats by the army. The late Archbishop Arturo Rivera y Damas, a less charismatic leader than his fiery predecessor, moved the Church to

## Liberation Theology

For centuries the standard church doctrine had been a fatalistic position; that poverty and suffering were part of God's will. In the mid-1960s some members of the clergy, especially Catholic missionaries, starting embracing the new Liberation Theology movement by telling people that they were the captains of their own ship. The movement went to the countryside and the factory sites and began to tell people that the poverty they suffered was due to the system that exploited them and was manipulated by the rich. They were instructed to improve their lot during this life instead of waiting for a future paradise. Not only did this change make the poorer, working class more politically aware, but it also made Catholicism more relevant and accessible. Despite the effect it had across the world, the Vatican never made it an official doctrine preferring to remain apolitical.

the political center and eased away from its sponsorship of Liberation Theology. The army and the church may not yet see eye to eye, but they have achieved their own sort of peace.

## FESTIVALS

El Salvador's many festivals are religious and cultural events that bring communities together, providing a common occasion to preserve and participate in religious traditions, eat and dance in the streets. The most important festivals are the *fiestas patronales* ("patron festivals") dedicated to each town's patron saint.

The festivals originated when the Spanish arrived and imposed Catholicism on native tribes. Now many towns carry both a Catholic and an indigenous name, such as Concepción Quetzaltepeque. Most, but not all, festivals are celebrated during the dry season (November through April). Outside the major cities, few people go to work for the duration of the festival.

Festivals are exciting affairs. Preparations begin a full 15 days ahead of time to give people time to prepare food and drinks, including chicha, which has to ferment. Vendors sell local food specialties, including *tamales, pan de torta* (a sweet bread similar to pound cake), chicken soup and plenty of sweets. Groups play traditional music and religious icons are carried soberly through the streets. During most festivals a young "queen" is crowned to preside over the celebrations.

■ **Important Holidays.** Huge **Christmas** celebrations throughout the country typically include three additional activities. First, children dress up and sing at the church and various houses. Next an image of the Virgin Mary and the Christ child is carried house to house by people carrying candles and singing. Finally a mass known as the Misa de Gallo ("Rooster's Mass") is held at midnight on Christmas Eve.

## Union Church

The Union Church of San Salvador was founded in 1946 to serve the country's ex-patriot, Protestant community, but many English-speaking Salvadorans belong too. The term "Union" refers to both the interdenominational and international character of the congregation and the fact that the church provides a wide variety of programs for adults and children as well as providing material support for those in need across the country. The present church, built in 1974, is located in Colonia La Mascota and frequently serves as a meeting place. Whether you are religious or not, this is a good place to come if you fall on hard times during your stay in the country. For information call 263-8246 or e-mail unionchurch@amnetsal.com. You can reach Pastor Jeff Jacobson directly at 257-5884, e-mail Jacobson@amnetsal.com.

## Dance of the Historians

Of all the festival dances in El Salvador, you re most likely to see the Baile de Los Historiantes. The story told through the dance mixes themes from pre-Columbian religious life with scenes from Spain under Muslim domination. At one point God intervenes to help the Christians defeat the Moors.

San Salvador celebrates one of the country's biggest festivals, called the **Fiestas Agostinas**, from the last week of July through the first week of August.

Thursday and Friday during the week before Easter Sunday, or **Semana Santa**, are also popular times to celebrate. In some cities with especially large festivals, Salvadorans participate in the Procession of the Crosses by walking across the town to visit mock-ups of the "14 Stations of the Cross," tracing Jesus' route to the Crucifixion. Izalco and Texistepeque both have famous Semana Santa celebrations.

# Politics and Government

■ **Structure.** The Salvadoran government has a unicameral legislature elected every three years, with members eligible for re-election. A president serves one five-year term and cannot be re-elected. The Supreme Court is the third branch of government. Municipalities are governed by popularly elected mayors.

■ **Background.** Political power in El Salvador derives from various sources. The wealthy minority has traditionally supported right-wing politics and the military

## TO GET INVOLVED
### Human Rights Organizations

**M**any human rights organizations set up shop in El Salvador during the war, and their work is far from over. If you're interesting in helping out, contact:

**Tutela Legal del Arzobispado**
(Church office that deals with human rights)
Avenida de Las Américas
Col. Medica
San Salvador
Tel 225-2603

**University of Central America Human Rights Office (IDHUCA)**
Universidad Centroamericana
Autopista Sur
San Salvador
Tel 273-4400

**Human Rights Commission of El Salvador (CDHES)**
Pje. A #119
Col. Medica
San Salvador
Tel 225-9906, 225-1475
Fax 225-0086

**Committee of Families for the Liberation of Political Prisoners and the Disappeared**
Calle Gabriela Mistral
Casa 614
Col. Centroamerica
San Salvador

**Government Human Rights Commission**
Paseo General Escalón
87a Avenida Sur
Bloque 2 #226
San Salvador
Tel 223-7443

**Amnesty International USA**
322 8th Ave.
New York City, NY 10001
Tel 212/807-8400
Fax 212/627-1451

BACKGROUND

in undermining efforts at political reform. Although the country has always had an enormous underclass, it has never been able to organize effectively and has been repressed for decades.

The Salvadoran government has been traditionally right-wing and fiercely anti-socialist. Since coffee became the country's dominant crop and a few wealthy families gained control of most of the country's plantations, coffee money was funneled to right-wing political causes to curry favor with the military and to discourage the rise of leftist parties that advocated land reform.

El Salvador's left, backed by the peasants, has had few opportunities to gain political power. When the chances have appeared, as with Duarte's victories in 1972 and 1984, either the military stepped in or the right has made compromise impossible through its support of death squads.

In addition to the military and right-wing politicians, the US government, via its embassy, has been the other main player in Salvadoran politics. For the entire civil war, the US supplied arms to the once-backwards military and kept the government afloat with regular loans that were eventually forgiven. The army needed weapons and airplanes to fight the guerrillas, especially since soldiers were initially reluctant to fight outside of a nine-to-five, Monday through Friday schedule. The government, meanwhile, had steered most of its budget to the military and needed cash just to stay afloat.

■ **Recent Changes.** The last twenty years have seen a tremendous upheaval in Salvadoran politics. The rise of the Christian Democrats in the mid-60s was a partial victory for the left, since Duarte and his clique were moderate and represented the country's lower and upper-middle classes. The rise of the FMLN as a political party represents a further step in the democratization of Salvadoran politics.

The peace accords have opened the political process to moderate and leftist forces even more and have also reduced the influence of the military, the US embassy and the most strident right-wing politicians. Leftist leaders are now able to confront the government more easily and safely, although suspicious deaths have not completely disappeared. The US embassy, with much less aid to distribute, carries a smaller stick. And the military, stripped by the peace process of many of its most notorious generals and without a significant internal threat to confront, has had no choice but to support the political process.

Even though the political process has become free and fair since the end of the war, voter turn out is shockingly low. Only 35 percent of eligible voters showed up to cast their ballots during the 2000 legislative elections. The consensus among the public is that their vote doesn't matter because promises will always go unkept and corruption will always remain. Though it's not necessarily a valid excuse, they have a point.

## POLITICAL Q & A

### Q: How could ARENA stay in power after being connected with the death squads and the army during the civil war?

**A:** The guerrillas overestimated the sympathies of most Salvadorans. When the FMLN declared "Either we all eat or no one eats," and proceeded to sabotage the country's infrastructure, peasants were the first to feel the squeeze. When coffee plantations were bombed and *campesinos* left without work, their already difficult life became unbearable.

Second, although ARENA sympathizers were involved in death squad attacks, the targets affected only certain families. Other families, stung by guerrilla sabotage near their villages, were glad to see the army clear the area at almost any price.

Third, ARENA had money and a charismatic leader. Owners of the country's coffee plantations stood to lose everything if the guerrillas won the elections, so they poured money into right-wing causes. D'Aubuisson was a popular figure, in spite of his reputation, and many Salvadorans didn't associate his shady past with the party he represented.

ARENA's recent successes can be ascribed to a combination of the ruling party's political experience, financial advantage and a lingering distrust of the newly-legalized FMLN. This distrust was mostly thanks to ARENA's savvy campaign rhetoric, which presented the vote as a choice between a strong, albeit tarnished, political giant and a ragtag bunch of communist ex-terrorists.

**Q: Why didn't the FMLN succeed in overthrowing the government?**
**A:** The main reason the guerrillas were unable to achieve their goal of bringing the government to a standstill was the air power supplied by the US. For the guerrillas to instigate a general popular uprising, they had to present themselves as a reasonable alternative government to the one currently in power, which they were ultimately unable to do. As a result, their support among the masses fell below the level necessary to unseat the government.

In the early stages of the war, the FMLN was able to present itself as a viable political alternative by taking control of towns for days or even weeks at a time, as the government army struggled to figure out how to retaliate on a nine-to-five schedule. But when the US kicked in by providing the army with helicopters and jets which enabled the air force to bomb large targets like rebels control centers, everything changed.

From that point on the guerrillas were unable to operate in large groups, since these groups were easily spotted from the air. Where once they were able to seize entire towns, the best the FMLN could do now was to plant a bomb and run. Large-scale assaults and face-to-face confrontation with the army were out of the question.

The guerrillas, essentially, were reduced to roving bands of terrorists. To many, the FMLN's actions began to seem almost as unacceptable as the atrocities committed by the army and the death squads. As the majority of poor Salvadorans started to feel the effects of the FMLN's continued attempts to disrupt the things on which day-to-day life depended—such as buses, bridges and roads—popular support for the guerrilla movement waned.

## POLITICAL PARTIES

■ **Christian Democratic Party (PDC).** Moderate and reformist, opposed to class conflict, party of the middle class, pro-civilian control. The liberal PDC, founded in the mid-60s and led for many years by José Napoleon Duarte, lost support for not being able to bring peace to the country while it retained power and for being perceived as corrupt. During the mid-1980s, the PDC under Duarte aligned itself closely to the military to avoid being accused of sympathizing with the left. The PDC earned just five Assembly seats in the last election and is no longer a significant electoral force.

■ **Faribundo Martí Front for National Liberation (FMLN).** Both a political party and former military force, the FMLN was an umbrella organization for many leftist organizations that weren't large enough to stand on their own. For most of the civil war,

Joaquín Villalobos (now a Cambridge researcher and international political consultant) led the major rebel organizations. Early on, the FMLN joined with the Democratic Revolutionary Front (FDR), a collection of dissident leftist groups.

Four guerrilla groups forged an alliance with the FMLN and agreed to support Rubén Zamora in his campaign for president in 1994. Zamora shaved his beard for the election to appear more clean-cut. Prior to the campaign, Zamora made fund-raising trips to the United States, and discussed the economy and the social system, rather than the war, in advertisements. As the election approached, elements of the FMLN actually renounced Marxism.

The transition from warfare to politics was difficult for the FMLN and its supporters. Each of the leftist parties that comprised the FMLN backed a separate candidate in the 1994 San Salvador mayoral elections. After the election, in which the left placed second with 32 percent of the votes, the FMLN struggled to prevent its constituency from splintering off into separate political parties. Eventually, though, Marxist and moderate factions found it impossible to coexist under the same title, and two of the original five factions split in 1994. The party, however, carried on, though internal conflicts have continued to impede the party's electoral ambitions. Nevertheless, the FMLN remains the primary opposition to ARENA and captured 31 seats in the 2000 legislative elections, two more than its main rival.

■ **National Action Party (PAN).** A small right-wing party that was founded by disgruntled civilian members of paramilitary groups who fought for the government during the war, but were denied benefits when the conflict ended. Tomás Mejía, the party's main leader, holds one of PAN's two seats in the National Assembly. Though tiny, they sometimes hold the swing vote on issues that divide the congress.

■ **National Conciliation Party (PNC).** A right-wing party created by the military. Colonel Arturo Molina, the PNC candidate for president in 1972, was opposed by

Duarte of the Christian Democrats. Duarte was defrauded of the win and exiled. In the end, opposition to the military strengthened as opponents became convinced that an armed insurrection was the only way to achieve political change. The PNC was gradually replaced by ARENA as the main right wing voice in El Salvador.

■ **Republican National Alliance (ARENA).** Founded in 1982 by army major Roberto d'Aubuisson and Armando Calderón Sol, ARENA brought together right-wing politicians and the army. ARENA gained popularity when President Duarte was unable to bring an end to the war or reverse the country's economic decline. In 1988, ARENA gained control of the National Assembly and a year later Cristiani, a protege of d'Aubuisson's, became president. The party has moderated since its founding but still stands for its traditional platforms of nationalism and anti-communism. Their success in achieving a peace agreement and turning around the economy has kept them as El Salvador's leading party.

# Economy

In El Salvador, opportunities are few, pay is low and bloated government bureaucracies empty the treasury and raise barriers and rules that make it difficult to get things done. Since so much of the land is cultivated for coffee, the country doesn't produce enough food to feed people at home. So, while the rich profit from selling coffee abroad, the poor pay a high price to buy the foods they need to survive.

■ **Production in Reverse.** Salvadorans have a reputation as hard workers, but their skills are not so easily applied at home. Work is difficult to find, especially outside the capital, jobs on farms don't pay very much and the minimum wage is often ignored. Though the average Salvadoran earns around $2,013 a year, most peasants don't make even half that much.

The country's agricultural system has two main markets: foreign countries which buy coffee and a large Salvadoran population which needs food. Coffee plantations take up huge amounts of land, but most of the profits go to the coffers of the owners who pay their workers low wages and ignore tax requirements. Corn and other staple food crops are rarely farmed, since they are worth much less than coffee. As a result, El Salvador has imported beans, corns and wheat since  the 19th century. Ornamental flowers and specialty foods such as cashews have diversified the countries non-traditional agricultural exports, but the change does nothing to reduce the need to import staple foods.

■ **Effects of the War.** El Salvador's economy has traditionally been strong—as recently as 1970, El Salvador was the most industrialized nation in Central America, but the war devastated the economy. The gross national product per person diminished 25 percent from 1979 to 1989, inflation reached 24 percent, and the unemployment rate

## ECONOMIC STATISTICS

| | |
|---|---|
| **Gross Domestic Product** | $12.4 billion. |
| **Employment** | Agriculture, 25%; Commerce, 22%; Services, 21%; Manufacturing, 19%; Construction, 7%; Other, 6%. |
| **Unemployment** | The official unemployment rate is 8 percent. The rate of under-employment (less than full-time work or total income below minimum wage) is estimated at around 30 percent. |
| **Minimum Wage** | Industry, commerce & service: $4.40 per day. Agricultural workers from $3.05 per day up to $3.57 per day for coffee plantation workers. |
| **Exports** | $2.5 billion. Coffee, sugar, textiles, and shrimp are the main exports. |
| **Export Markets** | USA, 64%; Central American Common Market, 25%; European Union, 4%; Other, 7%;. |

exceeded 30 percent. The FMLN, fighting under the slogan "Either we all eat or no one eats," sabotaged the coffee industry and much of the country's infrastructure. In all, the rebels destroyed more than 70 bridges and 35 percent of the country's buses. Underproduction cost the economy $2 billion each year. The government responded by devoting up to half of its budget to battling the guerrillas.

■ **End of the War.** The end of fighting resulted in an immediate rebound to the economy. In 1992, the government, spurred on by the fiercely capitalistic ARENA party, launched a massive national reconstruction program and extensive reforms which opened the market to international investment and made Salvadoran companies more competitive. The Cristiani government eliminated price controls on many consumer products, made importation easier and removed controls on foreign currency exchanges.

The international community responded positively to the reform program. The United States wiped out nearly $500 million of the Salvadoran national debt and the International Monetary Fund and the World Bank have provided large loans. In addition, El Salvador and Guatemala recently established a free-trade zone.

All this led to an annual growth rate of 6.85 percent for the next four years. In 1996 growth plummeted to 1.7 percent and has averaged just three percent through 1999. Causes for the decline included an increase in the value added tax to 13% (VAT accounts for 51% of total tax revenue); low prices for El Salvador's main exports, including coffee; and the effects of Hurricane Mitch in 1998 which not only caused much damage internally but weakened exports to neighboring countries.

Free zone (*maquiladora*) manufacturing for export is an increasingly important element of the Salvadoran economy. Over 300 U.S. companies are now based in El Salvador, including many electrical and telecommunications companies who have jumped in the profit from El Salvador's policy of privatization. Agriculture has declined in importance, but the service sector has taken up the slack and the financial sector is now one of the strongest in Central America. Remittances from family-members living abroad (see Cash From the North) continue to play an important role in the national economy and account for as much as 10 percent of the country's GNP.

The financial markets are the most dynamic in Central America accounting for one third of the total credits and deposits in the Central America region north of Panama. The government has also got its finances somewhat in order. Average deficits of less than three percent mean that El Salvador is now one of the least indebted countries in all of Latin America.

Organized labor has been strengthened by the end of the government death squads. Approximately 150 unions, public employee associations, and peasant organizations

represent over 300,000 people, approximately 20 percent of the country's work force.
■ **The Other Side of the Coin.** While things have undoubtedly changed for the better in the last decade not everything is rosy. The level of inequality measured by income distribution has increased and while El Salvador has the lowest lending rates in Central America, they are still about fifty percent higher than in places like the United States or Canada. Poverty levels also remain high. From 1900 to 1998 "extreme urban poverty" was diminished by half from over 23 percent to 12 percent, but "extreme rural poverty" was only reduced by four percent and remains at about 30 percent. Rural poverty is one of El Salvador's most difficult challenges for the future.

☺ ☺ ☺ ☺ ☺

# El Salvador in the Arts

■ **MOVIES ABOUT EL SALVADOR.** *Salvador* (1986) depicts recent Salvadoran history through the eyes of an American journalist. Oliver Stone's movie is engrossing but fanciful, and at times crosses the line into utter fiction. Whatever its shortcomings, it does give a vivid picture of the chaos of life in El Salvador during the early 1980s. *Romero* (1989) stars Raul Julia as Archbishop Romero. The movie moves slowly but manages to show Romero's struggle and death in a straightforward, almost hypnotic way. In the end, it's more effective than *Salvador* at getting its point across, although less entertaining. Plus, bonus points if you can spot the same actor who plays a "bad guy" in *Salvador* but a "good guy" in *Romero*.
■ **DOCUMENTARIES.** Many documentaries have also been made about the Salvadoran civil war. *Making the News Fit* (Cinema Guild, 1984, 27min) uses El Salvador as an example of how media bias can alter public views of news events. *El Salvador: The Seeds of Liberty* (Maryknoll World Video Library, 1981, 24min) focuses on the murder of the American nuns, and includes interviews with famous Salvadoran figures. *Guazapa* (Northstar, 1984, 37min) shows how guerrillas lived and fought on the slopes of the Guazapa Volcano, through the eyes of a reporter who lived with them for six weeks. *Witness to War: An American Doctor in El Salvador* (First Run Features, 1985, 30min) began as American doctor Charlie Clements' book about his work with Salvadoran peasants during the war. The documentary is well-known but ends up being as much about Clements, a Quaker who finds his neutrality sorely tested, as it is about the guerrillas he treats.
■ **BOOKS ABOUT EL SALVADOR.** Most books on El Salvador published in English focus on the civil war and its historical framework. *Latin America: A Concise Interpretive History* (1972), by E. Bradford Burns, is a good introduction to Latin American history. Tina Rosenberg's *Children of Cain: Violence and the Violent in Latin America* (1991) is a well-written, chilling account of the author's first-hand experience with Latin American violence from Chile to Guatemala, with a great chapter on El Salvador. Liisa North's *Bitter Grounds: Roots of Revolt in El Salvador* (1985), Philip Russel's *El Salvador in Crisis* (1984) and Jenny Pearce's *Promised*

*Land: Peasant Rebellion in Chalatenango, El Salvador* (1986) all deal with the civil war and its causes in detail. *Rebel Radio: The Story of El Salvador's Radio Venceremos* (1994) by Jose Ignacio takes a look at a different side of the war. *Mirrors of War* (1985) is an excellent collection of poetry and prose excerpts by Salvadoran authors writing about the civil war. Jeremy Paxman's *Through the Volcanoes* (1985) and Patrick Marnham's *So Far From God* (1985) each have a chapter on the authors' travels through El Salvador. A more recent take on history can be found in *Peace without Justice: Obstacles to Building the Rule of Law in El Salvador* (2000) by Margaret Popkin. and *Militarization and Demilitarization in El Salvador's Transition to Democracy* (1998) by Philip J Williams. *Bitter Grounds* (1997) and *The Weight of All Things* (to be published in 2001), novels by Sandra Benitez, both deal with peasant's struggles in El Salvador. *From Grandmother to Granddaughter* (2000) by Michael Gorkin, Mara Pineda, and Gloria Leal looks at the life histories of nine Salvadoran women from different segments of society. *A Bear for Miguel* (1997), by Elaine Marie Alphin and *Magic Dogs of the Volcanoes* (1990) by Manlio Argueta are children's books that take place in El Salvador. Birdwatchers are taken care of by *A Field Guide to the Birds of Mexico and Adjacent Areas: Belize, Guatemala, and El Salvador* (1998), Ernest Preston Edwards.

■ **SALVADORAN AUTHORS.** Both *Curbstone Press* (321 Jackson St, Willimantic, CT, 06226; tel 860/423-5110) and the *Latin American Literary Review Press* (121 Edgewood Ave, Pittsburgh, PA 15218; tel 412/371-9023) offer books by Latin American authors in translation, including some by Salvadoran authors.

**Salvador Salazar Arrué**, writing under the pen name Salarué, was one of the founders of the modern Central American short-story genre. *Cuentos de barro* (Tales of Mud, 1934) is his most famous book. **Claudia Lars** was born in 1899 under the name Carmen Brannon de Samayoa. She went on to become one of Central America's out-

standing poets. Her works include *Poesía última 1970-1973* (Latest Poetry, 1970-1973, 1976) and *Canciones* (Songs, 1960).

**Claribel Alegría** was born in Nicaragua in 1924 but considers herself a Salvadoran. She has published many books of poetry dealing with daily life in Central America, including the celebrated collection *Sobrevivo* (I Survive, 1978). She has also written novels, including *Cenizas de Izalco* (Ashes of Izalco, 1966) and *Flores del volcán* (Flowers from the Volcano, 1982).

**Manlio Argueta** is one of El Salvador's most famous literary

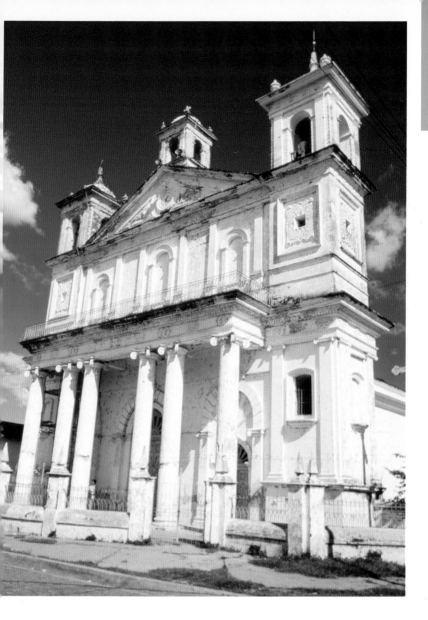

Colonial Church, Suchitoto

Colonial Church, Metapán

## ROQUE DALTON (1933-1975)
# The Pen and the Sword

Leftist writer Roque Dalton was a revolutionary and a prolific writer who joined the FMLN near its inception. Although Dalton escaped death and long-term imprisonment many times, he eventually died at the hands of his own comrades.

The son of a Salvadoran mother and an American father, Dalton received international acclaim for his writing. He wrote 15 books in all, most while in exile in Mexico, Cuba and Czechoslovakia. For much of Dalton's life, many of his books were banned in El Salvador for their leftist slant.

While still in El Salvador, Dalton was jailed repeatedly and earned a reputation for escaping under unusual circumstances. In 1960, the right-wing government of Colonel José Maria Lemus fell in a coup days before Dalton was to be executed. Later, an earthquake that rocked the capital opened a hole in Dalton's cell large enough for him to escape through.

Despite the acclaim his writing received, Dalton focused his attention on the revolution. In the early 1970s, he decided to return to his country and join the rebels in their struggle to overthrow the government. He joined a group called the People's Revolutionary Army (ERP) that included Joaquín Villalobos, future leader of the FMLN.

Dalton had difficulty adapting to the regimented rebel lifestyle and fell out of favor with the ERP. Soon, in a move the rebels would later regret, Villalobos and others accused Dalton of spying for the CIA and sentenced him to death. Dalton was executed along with another comrade by a firing squad on May 10, 1975. Their bodies were left at El Playón, the notorious death squad dumping ground. News of Dalton's death rocked the country's intellectuals, many of whom sympathized with the rebel cause but condemned the murder.

Years later, at the conclusion of the civil war, Villalobos discussed the situation more openly. He said that the rebel command made a mistake by killing Dalton, and thereafter preferred to incarcerate rather than execute its suspects. In a post-war interview about Dalton's death, Villalobos commented, "If there [was] one part of the history of our organization that I would like to erase, it would be this."

figures. The novelist and poet lived for a time in exile in Costa Rica because his works were so revolutionary and controversial. He is the author of *Un día en la vida* (One Day of Life, 1981) and *Cuscatlán, donde bate la mar del sur* (Cuscatlán, Where the South Sea Beats, 1983).

**Roque Dalton** was one of El Salvador's most famous and politically-aware poets. He was one of the founders of the left-wing People's Revolutionary Army (ERP) and was killed by his fellow revolutionaries after being fingered as a CIA spy. His books of poetry include *Poémas clandestinas* (Clandestine Poems, 1975) and *Las historias prohibidas del pulgarcito* (Prohibited Stories of the Little Thumb, 1975). *Poetry and Militancy in Latin America*, published by Curbstone Press, describes Dalton's views on the relationship between poetry and political participation.

# BASICS

## Getting There
### When to Go

A few factors to consider in planning a trip to El Salvador are airplane ticket prices, the timing of festivals and national holidays, and the climate. Ticket prices are much higher from December to mid-January and from July to mid-September, and empty seats are scarce. The big festivals are Semana Santa (the week before Easter), Christmas and the San Salvador city festival during the first week of August, which basically closes down the capital. Commerce grinds to a halt during these periods and everyone either celebrates or relaxes, so it's not a good time to cross a border or to have to deal with officialdom. Tourist spots and beaches are packed during holidays, and most hotel rooms are booked. Finally, since the timing of downpours are fairly predictable during the rainy season (mid-May through mid-October), they shouldn't make much of a difference if you plan your daily schedule accordingly.

## Packing

Two words: *pack light*. Heed the old correspondent's axiom: "Lay out everything you think you will need on the bed, then take half of that and twice as much money." Or, "Never take more than you could carry at a dead run for a kilometer." Besides, where will you put all your souvenirs if your bag is already stuffed?

■ **Carrying It All.** Internal-frame **backpacks,** the "soft" kind, are the choice of most long-term travelers. They're tough, flexible and usually more comfortable than external-frame packs. They don't protect your possessions as well, but smaller ones have the added benefit of being easy to cram under bus seats or in overhead racks. External-frame **backpacks** are more suited to the trail than the bus.

More outside pockets mean easier access and organization, but the exposed frames are easily bent or broken and are more awkward.

**Convertible packs**, the curious offspring of backpacks and suitcases, are a cheaper alternative to a full backpack. They're good if you don't plan to go far off the beaten track. Otherwise, you'll find that they resemble suitcases more than backpacks, since the shoulder straps and hip belt aren't meant for long hikes. Convertible packs usually travel better than backpacks, simply because they're designed with baggage handlers and luggage racks in mind. Take a **suitcase** only if you plan to stay in nicer hotels and have someone else carry your bags most of the time. **Day packs** are good for short trips when you don't want to carry all your stuff with you and for keeping your valuables close to you while on buses. Stuff a tough nylon knapsack into your bigger bag.

## CLOTHING

You don't need many clothes to travel. One set in addition to what you're wearing should be enough, plus a few extras:

- One **sweater**, **fleece** or **light jacket** for higher altitudes.
- One or two pairs of **long cotton pants**. Jeans are hot, heavy and take forever to dry.
- One pair of **shorts**. For men, a swimsuit that doubles as a pair of shorts is ideal.
- One or two **light long-sleeved shirts**, including one collared shirt that can pass as "dressed up" if the need arises.
- Two to four **T-shirts**.
- Plenty of **underwear** and **socks**.
- **Rain gear**. A poncho or waterproof jacket is essential during the rainy season.
- **Swim suit**.

## FOOTWEAR

If you plan to do a lot of walking, invest in a good pair of hiking boots. Make sure they fit well and break them in early. A pair of light sneakers or sandals are good for relaxing or exploring the beach.

## BEDDING

A sleeping sack (a dark-colored sheet folded lengthwise and sewn across the bottom and partway up the side) is the most versatile sleeping arrangement. A sleeping bag is necessary only if you plan to go camping at higher altitudes. You can also buy a hammock in San Salvador to string up on the beach. Bring your own pillowcase to store dirty clothes in during the day or to replace dirty ones in hotels.

## TOILETRIES

- **Toothbrush.**
- **Toothpaste.**
- **Dental floss.**
- **Soap.** A bar in a plastic container is better than liquid soap.

## Ready To Wear

Salvadoran fashion runs the spectrum from fancy Western styles to purely functional work clothing. Most men wear long pants and an unbuttoned long shirt, even if it's hot outside. Women often wear heels, skirts and blouses. Hats are pretty much standard gear in the midday sun and any time in the countryside. Everyone occasionally wears jeans, but pretty much only children wear shorts.

- **Shampoo/conditioner.** Seal inside a zip-lock bag—these things seemed to be designed to come open inside backpacks.
- **Nail clippers/file.**
- **Personal medicines/prescriptions.** Try to keep medications in their original, labeled containers to avoid border hassles ("But officer, I swear they're for headaches!"). Carry copies of the prescriptions for each medicine you are carrying, along with the dosage and the generic name in case you need a refill. Diabetics should take their own sterile needles plus certification of their condition.
- **Contraceptives.**
- **Tampons.**
- **Towel.**

## What Makes a Good Gift?

If you want to offer a token of thanks to someone who was especially helpful or friendly, small, unpretentious gifts are best, especially ones from back home such as souvenir T-shirts from your city, state or university. Any other objects with characteristic logos or pictures are fine too, like postcards, buttons and photographs. Children appreciate pens and notebooks, especially if they can't easily afford them for school. Small gifts such as pens or candy shouldn't be just handed out at random though—parents do not appreciate having their children taught that begging is good. Salvadorans are known throughout Central America for their strong work ethic.

## FIRST AID KIT

Some kind of medical kit is essential for every traveler who plans to leave major cities. They can be purchased as a unit or assembled on your own. Preassembled kits are available at many outdoor recreation stores, are compact but expensive and usually contain instructions on using the contents. Their contents are geared more towards wilderness-related injuries, so if you buy one you'll probably still want to add some items of your own.

- A **brief personal medical history** that describes your blood type, any specific medical conditions, recent illnesses and prescriptions you are taking.
- **Diarrhea medications.** Take two: Pepto-Bismol and Immodium tablets.
- **Thermometer** in a hard case (some airlines prohibit mercury thermometers) or a few disposable ones.
- **Tweezers.**
- **Calamine lotion** for insect bites and rashes.
- **Anti-fungal powder** for athlete's foot.
- **Antibiotic cream** or salve.
- **Band-Aids** in different sizes.
- **Moleskin** for blisters.
- **Sterile gauze pads.**
- **Adhesive cloth tape.**
- **Elastic (Ace) bandage** for sprains, small or medium size.

● **Pills** for malaria (Chloroquine, etc.), pain (aspirin, Tylenol, Advil), motion sickness (Dramamine), colds (Sudafed, Actifed), antacid tablets (Maalox).

## ESSENTIALS

● **Glasses/contact lenses**, if needed, plus replacement pairs.

● **Insect repellent.**

● **Flashlight.**

● **Film.** Both slide and print film is available in San Salvador at a few photo shops. There are also plenty of places to process film, though slides may be a hassle. Even small towns have places that sell and develop film, but the stock may be stale and all photo finishing is shipped to the capital anyway. The best things to do, then, is to bring your own film and wait until you get home to develop it. The x-rays will not damage standard film in your carry-on bags, but never put film in checked luggage where the machines used are much stronger.

● **Locks.** One combination lock for cheap hotel-room doors, plus a few smaller pad-locks to secure your bags. Available cheap from many street vendors in the capital. A cable lock is also useful to lock your bag to something sturdy for short periods or at night.

● **Name tag** securely attached to your bag.

● **Photocopies** of your passport and plane ticket. Leave one set at home.

● **Repair kit** including duct tape (the ultimate repair tool—to avoid taking a whole roll, wrap some around a pencil or something else that's skinny); extra batteries for flashlight and camera; scissors (maybe on Swiss army knife); sewing kit or strong thread and a few needles; spare flashlight bulb.

● **Spanish-English dictionary/phrasebook.**

● Any **special equipment** you may need: camping equipment (tent, sleeping bag, compass, sleeping pad, cooking equipment); snorkeling equipment; a surfboard in a travel case.

● **Sunglasses.**

● **Waterproof sunscreen.**

● **Swiss army knife.** No traveler should be without one. They often include tweezers and scissors.

● **Toilet paper.** So it is always there when you need it, not something that can be taken for granted.

● **Travel alarm clock** or a digital watch with a loud alarm.

● Wallet-size **photos** of yourself, and pictures of your family.

● **Water bottle** for hiking and long bus trips. Camping water bottles (Nalgene) and bicycle water bottles both work well—just be sure they close securely.

● **Ziplock bags.** Great for storing just about anything.

## MAYBES

● **Books.** Thick paperbacks are lightest, last longest, and most sought after when trading.

● **Flip-flops** for dirty shower stalls.

● **Hand towel.**

- **Journal** plus pens, paper and envelopes to write letters.
- **Pack cover**. To protect your pack from rain and to discourage thieves.
- **Shortwave radio.**
- **Vitamin supplements.**
- **Walkman** with tapes and extra batteries.
- **Washing supplies**, including detergent, clothesline.
- **Water purification tablets** or a water filter.

# ID Cards

Student identification cards aren't likely to be helpful in finding deals in El Salvador, but some offer basic insurance and access to special plane fares that make them worthwhile. Entrance fees to museums and such are already inexpensive, so you'll find that your university ID is just as useful (or useless) in many situations.

The International Student Identity Card (ISIC), though, offers benefits that justify its $22 cost. These include an emergency toll-free hotline, limited medical coverage and access to low airplane fares through Council Travel, STA and others travel and educational organizations. The International Youth Card, available to anyone under 26, offers some of the same benefits as the ISIC card. An International Teacher Card is available to educators. For information on these cards contact Council Travel at 800/226-8624 in the US or see www.ciee.org.

# Health & Travel Insurance

Be sure to straighten out potential complications with health insurance before you leave. Your best bet is to go with your own insurance company, provided it covers you while

## INSURANCE CHECKLIST

**BEFORE GOING...**
- Make sure your insurance company covers travel abroad.
- Understand if and how you will be reimbursed for treatment abroad—most foreign doctors won't accept your insurance card and will require you to pay cash on the spot.
- See which activities, if any, are not covered under your policy. These tend to be more dangerous pursuits like rock climbing and motorcycling.
- Always carry your policy number, proof of insurance and the telephone number of your carrier.

**IF SOMETHING HAPPENS...**
- Keep all receipts.
- Report thefts and muggings to the police as soon as they occur and get a copy of the police report.
- Contact your embassy or consulate for more serious matters like surgery. They can give you the names of reputable doctors and help arrange payments of large bills from your insurance company or your relatives.

## TRAVEL AGENCIES AND TOUR GUIDES

### (All are based just outside San Salvador)

**Alligatours**
Paseo General Escalón #3658
Tel 211-0967
E-mail adventure@alligatour.com
www.alligatour.com
(Sea kayaking specialists)

**Amor Tours**
73a Av Sur y Av Olimpica
Edificio Olympic Plaza, Local 21
Tel 279-0364, 224-2529
E-mail amortour@gbm.net

**Aventours**
Pablo Garcia Km 11.5 Carretera a la
Puerta del Diablo
Planes de Renderos
Tel 230-0083

**Discovery Tours**
Res. Real Miramonte
Calle Los Sisimiles #7
Tel 260-4245
E-mail discovery@sal.gbm.net

**El Salvador Divers**
3a C Pte #5020
Col Escalón
Tel 264-0961
E-mail esdi@ejje.com
(SCUBA specialists, primarily crater dives)

**Inter Tours**
Paseo General Escalón #1-A
Col Escalón
Tel 263-6188
E-mail intertours@vianet.com.sv

**Punta Mango**
Villas Españolas, Local B-3, Paseo
General Escalón
Tel 264-3110
E-mail saltours@es.com.sv
www.puntamango.com.sv
(Surfing specialists)

**Salvador Tours**
Centro Comerical Villas Españolas,
Local 3-b
Paseo General Escalón
Tel 264-3110, 264-3111
E-mail saltours@es.com.sv

**SET de El Salvador**
Av Olimpica #3597
Tel 279-3470
E-mail autoaventura@es.com.sv
(Birdwatching specialists).

you're out of the country. The International Student Identity Card carries limited protection which is worth the price of the card. Also, some credit cards offer insurance packages. Finally, there are specialized travel insurance companies which cover just about everything that could possibly happen while traveling, from flight delay reimbursement and lost baggage protection to emergency medical evacuation and repatriation of remains. Their premiums tend to be more expensive, so shop around for the best deal.

# Pre-Travel Immunizations

Some of the medications on this list below are just recommended, but others are more certain to save you pain and suffering. Some contraindications (limitations) exist for pregnant women, young children and people with certain medical conditions, so ask your doctor if you're not sure. Record every vaccination you receive in an International Certificate of Vaccination (the "yellow health card"), which is available from most public health departments. Travelers' clinics, usually associated with universities or government health clinics, are excellent sources of information and most give vaccinations.

## REQUIRED VACCINATIONS/TESTS

**AIDS** A negative HIV test is required for anyone over 18 who is planning to move to El Salvador permanently. Contact a Salvadoran embassy for details.

**Yellow fever** A certificate of vaccination for yellow fever is required for anyone older than six months who is entering from an area considered infected, such as much of South America. (Single dose, good for ten years)

## RECOMMENDED VACCINATIONS

**Malaria** Chloroquine phosphate pills taste terrible, but since no Chloroquine-resistant mosquito strains have yet invaded El Salvador, they are your best source of protection. Chloroquine is available in its generic form or under the brand name Aralen. Malaria is found only in rural areas so visitors to large cities don't need the pills. Also, some recommend only taking them if you are visiting coastal mangroves and very remote areas during the rainy season, so you may want to ask your doc-tor about this. *(One 500mg pill per week, beginning one week before entering the country and continuing four weeks after returning home)*

**Cholera** The Cholera vaccine is only about 50 percent effective, and is considered by many to be more dangerous than the disease itself. Since it isn't required to enter the country, the vaccine is recommended only for people with weak stomachs or for those who plan to spend extended periods in rural areas. *(Single dose, good for six months)*

**Hepatitis A (Infectious Hepatitis)** A pair of new vaccines, HAVRIX and VAQTA, offers protection against Hepatitis A for as long as twenty years. It is a good idea for everybody, but especially those planning to spend time in rural areas with poor sanitary conditions. Protection does not begin until four weeks after the initial dose so plan ahead. Those with a high likelihood of having already had Hepatitis A, such as those over age 40 and those with clotting disorders may want to have a screening for HAV-antibodies so as not to take the vaccine unnecessarily. For those only needing short term protection or with a contraindication against the vaccine the old immune globulin shot is still available. *(Vaccines, two doses taken at least six months apart; immune globulin, single dose, good for three to six months depending on the dose, boosters are necessary for longer stays)*

**Typhoid** Vaccination with the oral vaccine Ty21a is recommended for people visiting rural areas, for those staying longer than three weeks and for adventurous eaters. An injected vaccination is also available. *(Four pills taken over one week, good for five years; two shots at least four weeks apart, good for three years)*

**Rabies** A pre-exposure vaccination with the human diploid cell rabies vaccine (HDCV) or the Rabies Vaccine Adsorbed (RVA) is only recommended for anyone anticipating frequent contact with wildlife. Speak with your doctor about this, since it is expensive. *(Two shots administered over one month)*

**Routine Immunizations** The standard sequence of childhood immunizations should all be updated before traveling anywhere in the developing world. Check with your doctor for any of these you might need, including tetanus/diphtheria, measles, mumps, rubella, influenza, pneumococcal, poliomyelitis (a booster dose of the oral polio vaccine OPV or inactivated polio vaccine IPV) and a measles booster for anyone born after 1956. Schedule doctors' visits early, since some of these immunizations can't be administered together or require follow-up shots.

# Volunteer Opportunities

El Salvador's turbulent political history has given rise to many grassroots volunteer groups who welcome volunteers from abroad.

**Christians for Peace in El Salvador (CRISPAZ)** have been sending volunteers to El Salvador to promote literacy and health care since 1984. CRISPAZ is ecumenical but open to anyone. They also publish a bimonthly news and analysis magazine called SAL-VANET. Positions last at least one year, but there are also 7-10 day encounter programs and summer immersion programs. *(319 Camden, San Antonio, TX 78215; tel 210/222-2018; e-mail crispaz@igc.apc.org; in El Salvador tel/fax 226-0829; www.crispaz.org)*

**Cooperative Housing Foundation (CHF)** helps communities build quality, affordable housing and develop health and sanitation facilities. Volunteers for the "Visiting International Professional" program must have five years technical experience in cooperative development, finance, and/or property management skills. If you don't have that background they can probably still find something for you to do. *(8601 Georgia Ave, Suite 800, Silver Spring, MD 20910; 301/587-4700; in El Salvador 65 Ave. Sur #132, Col. Escalón; tel 245-4827, 245-4861; e-mail mailbox@chfhq.org; www.chfhq.org)*

**The Cooperative League of the USA (CLUSA)** has promoted cooperative businesses since 1916. They provide assistance to community organizations trying to develop agricultural, credit, and market projects. In El Salvador they have been very active, and successful, in developing organic agriculture. *(National Cooperative Business Association, International Program Division, 1401 New York Ave, NW, Suite 1100, Washington DC 20005; tel 202/638-6222; tel 223-0304; e-mail ncba@ncba.org; www.cooperative.org)*

**The Committee for Solidarity with the People of El Salvador (CISPES)** began in 1980 in opposition to US involvement in El Salvador and has evolved into a sizable activist organization. They are very left-leaning and make no bones about their affiliations with the FMLN. They have various programs dealing with social justice and human rights. *(PO Box 1801, New York, NY 10159; tel 212/229-1290; e-mail cispes-natl@people-link.net; www.cispes.org)*

**Exchange and Solidarity Center (CIS)** in San Salvador houses the Mélida Montes Language School (see Studying in El Salvador) and acts as a "reference point for international solidarity." The center was started in part by CISPES and places volunteers throughout El Salvador working with grassroots organizations, marginal communities and special-interest groups. *(Blvd Universitario, Casa #4, San Salvador; tel 226-2623; e-mail cis@netcomsa.com)*

**The Fellowship on Reconciliation Task Force on Latin America and the Caribbean** offers a volunteer program on which you can work with poor communities on non-violence education and human rights efforts. Costs such as travel, food and lodging are not included, and applicants must be at least 21 years old. *(2017 Mission St. #305, San Francisco, CA 94110; tel 415/495-6334; e-mail volfor@irc.org; www.forusa.org/voluntar.htm)*

**Partners of the Americas** pairs US states with specific areas of Latin America to plan and carry out programs in rural development, health and education. Louisiana is paired with El Salvador, but the programs should be open to anyone who is interested.

*(1424 K St. NW #700, Washington DC 20005; tel 800/322-7844; e-mail info@partners.net; www.partners.net)*

**Salvadoran American Health Foundation (SAHF)** was founded in 1983 by Salvadorans living in the US. With their sister organization, the Fundación Salvadoreña para la Salud y el Desarrollo Social (FUSAL) based in El Salvador they distribute medical supplies and equipment to nearly 400 hospitals and clinics across El Salvador. They also develop programs to help communities better their health and welfare. *(SAHF, 2050 Coral Way, Suite 600, Miami, FL 33129; tel 800/992-8858; FUSAL Blvd Orden de Malta #10, Santa Elena; tel 289-1100; www.sahf.org)*

**SOS Orphanages** These well-run orphanages in San Salvador, Santa Tecla, Sonsonate and San Vicente offer one of the most rewarding ways for you to lend a helping hand. *(21 C Pte #1523, Col Buenos Aires; tel 228-5126)*

**The United States Agency for International Development (USAID)** at the US embassy can provide you with a list of the humanitarian organizations they have worked with in El Salvador. *(Tel 278-4444)*

# Studying in El Salvador

To study in a Salvadoran school or university you are required to produce a certified high school diploma, a passport, a copy of your birth certificate and a medical certificate. If you write well in advance of the time you plan to go and ensure that your university will accept transfer credits, you can save yourself some money. The University of Central America (UCA) is the best university in El Salvador.

## LANGUAGE SCHOOLS

For up-to-date information you can call the Peace Corps office in San Salvador (Tel 263-8517) which keeps a list of Spanish schools.

**Academia Europea** teaches Spanish, as well as a handful of other languages including Italian, German and French. Private lessons are $12/hr while a 30 hours in group classes is $50. They have centers in San Salvador, Santa Ana and San Miguel. *(99 Av Nte #639, Col Escalón, San Salvador; SS tel 263-4355; SA tel 440-2045; SM tel 661-1167)*

**AmeriSpan Unlimited** offers Spanish classes from around $500 for two weeks, which includes airport pickup, homestay and two meals a day. Classes have a maximum of four people and meet for four hours a day. Optional excursions cost extra. *(PO Box 40007, Philadelphia, PA 19106; tel 800/879-6640; e-mail info@amerispan.com; www.amerispan.com)*

**The Cihuatan Spanish School** operates out of the friendly and popular Ximena's Guest House in San Salvador. Twenty hours of language classes per week cost $75. *(C San Salvador #202; tel 260-2481, fax 260-2427, e-mail ximenas@navegante.com.sv)*

**The Mélida Anaya Montes Language School** is run by CIS. The language program is $160 per week including homestay and two meals a day. Political and cultural discussions and field trips are also available. *(Blvd Universitario, Casa #4, San Salvador; tel 226-2623; e-mail cis@netcomsa.com)*

You can also arrange Spanish lessons at the **Hotel Amacuilco** on Lago de Coatepeque and the **Casa de Huespedes Torogoz** in San Salvador.

## SALVADORAN UNIVERSITIES

**Universidad Americana**
(Private)
Centro Profesional Feria Rosa
San Salvador
Tel 279-0680, 223-9691

**Universidad Centroamericana
José Simeon Cañas (UCA)**
(Public)
Autopista Sur and Jardines de
Guadalupe
San Salvador
Tel 273-4400
www.uca.edu.sv

**Universidad de El Salvador**
(Public)
Ciudad Universitaria
San Salvador
Tel 225-8826
www.ues.edu.sv

**Universidad Francisco Gavidia**
(Private)
Alam Roosevelt #3031
San Salvador
Tel 224-5962, 223-9704
www.ufg.edu.sv

**Universidad Nueva San Salvador**
(Private)
C Arce y 23 Av Syr
San Salvador
Tel 260-8989

**Universidad Politecnica**
(Private)
Blvd Tutunichapa y 5a Av Nte
San Salvador
Tel 225-2491
www.upes.edu.sv

**Universidad Salvadoreña
Alberto Masferrer**
(Private)
19 Av Nte #1040
San Salvador
Tel 221-1136

**Universidad Salvadoreña
Issac Newton**
(Private)
Av España #703
San Salvador
Tel 221-1972

**Universidad Tecnologica**
(Private)
Calle Arce #1114
San Salvador
Tel 271-5990
www.utec.edu.sv

# Other Useful Organizations and Publications

## GENERAL RESOURCES

**South American Explorers** has a wealth of information on all of Latin America. Their humorous quarterly newsletter/catalog South American Explorer is filled with travel guide listings, trip reports and other goodies. Membership benefits include discounts on catalog items and travel assistance. They'll be glad to send you information on a particular destination. (*126 Indian Creek Rd, Ithaca, NY 14850; tel 800/274-0568; yearly membership $50; e-mail explorer@samexplo.org; www.samexplo.org*)

## TRAVELERS WITH DISABILITIES

**The Information Center for Individuals with Disabilities** assists disabled travelers with fact sheets, newsletters and disabled-friendly travel agent lists. (*PO Box 750119, Arlington Heights, MA 02475; tel 617/727-5540; e-mail contact@disability.net; www.disability.net*)

## INTERNET RESOURCES

There aren't a whole lot of El Salvador-related websites in English, but the following might be of interest.

### CORSATUR

www.elsalvadorturismo.gob.sv
The official homepage of the Salvadoran Tourism Corporation has some useful information about El Salvador in English, and even more in Spanish.

### Embassy of the United States in El Salvador

www.usinfo.org.sv
Up to date information for visitors to El Salvador including information about services available to US citizens.

### Library of Congress Country Studies

http://lcweb2.loc.gov/frd/cs/svtoc.html
In depth facts about the history, geography, economy, politics and government of El Salvador. Unfortunately it hasn't been updated since November 1988.

### Info El Salvador

www.infoelsalvador.com
A long list of El Salvador-related websites on just about any topic.

### Latin American Network Information Center

http://lanic.utexas.edu/la/ca/salvador
Another list of El Salvador related websites maintained by the University of Texas at Austin, though most are in Spanish.

### El Diario de Hoy

www.elsalvador.com/noticias

### La Prensa Gráfica

www.laprensa.com.sv
El Salvador's leading newspapers are both on the web. The news comes from a very conservative slant, but they are a good source of current information, if you read Spanish.

### Useful USENET groups

rec.travel.budget.backpack
rec.travel.latin-america
soc.culture.el-salvador (primarily in Spanish)

**Mobility International USA** provides information on handicapped travel around the world and has a list of publications and videos. It also offers exchange programs specifically for travelers with disabilities. *(PO Box 10767, Eugene, OR 97440; tel 541/343-1284; e-mail info@miusa.org; www.miusa.org)*

**The Society for the Advancement of Travel for the Handicapped** has a range of information geared to disabled travelers and publishes Open World magazine. (347 5th Ave, Suite 610, New York, NY 10016; tel 212/447-7284; e-mail sathtravel@aol.com; www.sath.org)

## OTHER

**The Diabetic Traveler** is a quarterly newsletter. *(Box 8223 RW, Stamford, CT, 06905; tel 203/327-5832; yearly subscription $18.95)*

**The International Gay Travel Association** can provide you with a list of member travel agencies. *(52 W. Oakland Park Blvd. #237, Wilton Manors, FL 33311; tel 800/448-8550; e-mail iglta@iglta.org; www.iglta.org)*

BASICS

# Coming and Going
## Visas & Embassies

To enter El Salvador, you need one of two documents. A **tourist visa**, available from Salvadoran embassies abroad, is good for the life of your passport minus one year. They're free to Americans but cost for some other nationalities, and require two photos, some background information and a few days' processing time. In El Salvador the Ministry of the Interior handles immigration issues efficiently, but not always rapidly. *(Centro de Gobierno, 9a C Pte y 15 Av Nte, first floor; Mon-Fri 8am-4pm; tel 222-3988)*

The new **tourist card** is a handy alternative. It's available for $10 at borders and the airport and is good for six months. Citizens of Great Britain and Germany don't need a visa or tourist card to enter. Citizens of the US, Canada and Australia do.

### VISAS FOR BORDERING COUNTRIES

Visa requirements change, so check with your embassy in El Salvador to see if you need a visa to enter any of the three neighboring countries. Most people will be able to get a tourist card at the border. If you do need a visa, most embassies require your passport, a few passport-sized photos, a small fee and a few days to process the paper work.

### TO GUATEMALA

**DON'T NEED VISA**: US, Canada, Central American countries, some European countries. A $5 tourist card available at the border is valid for three months.

**DO NEED VISA**: Australia, New Zealand, other Latin American countries, other European countries. The visa costs $10.

### TO HONDURAS

**DON'T NEED VISA**: US, UK, Canada, Australia, New Zealand, Japan, most Western European countries. If you're from one of these countries you can stay for 30 days without a visa. Then you can apply for an extension at an immigration office, and can stay up to 90 days before you have to leave and re-enter the country.

### TO NICARAGUA

**DON'T NEED VISA**: US, Spain, England, some European countries, some South American countries, Guatemala, El Salvador, Honduras. Residents of these countries will receive a 30-day tourist card.

**DO NEED VISA**: Canada, Australia, New Zealand, some European countries. The visa costs $25 and is valid to enter Nicaragua for 30 days. After you enter the country, it's good for a 30-day stay. Visas can be extended twice, for 30 days more each time, at the immigration office in Managua. After that you have to leave and re-enter the country.

# By Air

Comalpa International Airport is one of the biggest and safest in Central America and the Caribbean and is increasingly become a regional air hub.

■ **To and From the US.** The least expensive flights to El Salvador from the US are from the gateway cities of Miami, Houston, Los Angeles, New Orleans, Chicago, New York,

# FOREIGN EMABASSIES IN SAN SALVADOR

**Argentina**
79 Av Nte y C Pte # 704
Col Escalón
Tel 263-3674

**Belgium** (Consulate)
75 Av Nte y 3 C Pte #3951
Col Escalón
Tel 264-3920

**Belize**
Condominio Médico B
Local 5
Urb. La Esperanza, Blvd
Tutunichapa
Tel 226-3682

**Brazil**
Blvd del Hipódromo #305,
Col San Benito
Tel 224-0186

**Canada**
C Las Palmas #111
Col San Benito.
Tel 279-4659

**Chile**
9 C Pte, Pje Bella Vista
#121
Col Escalón
Tel 263-4346

**Colombia**
C El Mirador #5120
Col Escalón
Tel 263-1936

**Costa Rica**
Av Albert Einstein #11-A
Col Lomas de San
Francisco
Tel 273-3111

**Ecuador**
77 Av Nte #208
Col Escalón
Tel 263-5323

**France**
1 C Pte #3718
Col Escalón
Tel 298-4260

**Germany**
7 C Pte #3972 y 77 Av Nte
Col Escalón
Tel 263-2099

**Greece**
77 Av Nte #335
Tel 263-3402

**Guatemala**
15 Av Nte #135
Tel 271-2225

**Honduras**
3 C Pte #3697 entre 690 y
71 Av Nte
Col Escalón
Tel 223-4975

**Korea**
Pje. Unión y C Juan Santa
María # 330
Col Escalón
Tel 263-0810

**Israel**
85 Av Nte # 619
Col Escalón
Tel 263-3183

**Italy**
C La Reforma #158
Col San Benito
Tel 298-3050

**Japan**
C Loma Linda #258
Tel 224-4612

**Mexico**
C Circunvalación y Pje 12
Col San Benito
Tel 243-2037, 243-3458

**The Netherlands**
(Consulate)
1 C Pte #3519
Col Escalón
Tel 298-2185

**Nicaragua**
71 Av Nte 1 C Pte #164
Col Escalón
Tel 224-1223

**Panama**
Alameda Roosvelt y 55 Av
Nte #2838
Tel 260-5453

**Peru**
7 C Pte #4111
Col Escalón
Tel 263-3315

**Spain**
C La Reforma #164
Col San Benito
Tel 298-1188

**United Kingdom**
Paseo General Escalón
#4828
Tel 263-6527

**United States**
Blvd Sta. Elena
Antiguo Cuscatlán
Tel 278-4444

**Venezuela**
7 C Pte #3921
Col Escalón
Tel 263-3977

San Francisco and Washington DC. Prices for a round-trip ticket start around $400, but vary considerably depending on when you go and where you leave from. Prices during the high season (December to mid-January and July to mid-September) are up to 50 percent more expensive.

## Airline Offices in San Salvador

**Aerolineas Argentinas**
Alam Roosevelt
#3006 and 57a Av Nte
Tel 260-5450

**Air France**
Ed. Inlama #645
Blvd del Hippodromo
Tel 263-8101, 263-8103

**American Airlines**
Edificio La
   Centroamericana
Planta Principal
Alameda Roosevelt
#3107
Tel 298-9762

**Continental Airlines**
Centro Comercial
   Metrocentro
Edificio El Roble 9o
Nivel
Tel 260-2180, 260-3262

**COPA (Panama)**
Alameda Roosevelt and
   55a Av Nte #2838
Tel 260-3399, 260-5843

**Delta Airlines**
Blvd Santa Elena
Edificio Atrium Plaza
Local 12
Santa Tecla
Tel 289-4422

**Iberia**
Centro Commercial
Plaza Jardin, Edificio C
Tel 223-2600

**Japan Airlines**
Blvd Del Hippodromo
#645
Edificio Inlama
Tel 263-8101, 263-8170

**LACSA (Costa Rica)**
43 Av Nte #216
Between Alam
   Roosevelt and 1a C Pte
Tel 260-9933

**Mexicana**
Av La Revolución
Hotel Presidente
Tel 271-5936, 271-5950

**TACA International
Airlines**
Plaza Las Americas
Edif. Caribe
Tel 267-8222

**United Airlines**
Centro Comercial
Galerias, Local 14
Paseo General Escalón
Tel 279-3900

**VARIG** (Brazil)
Urb. La Esperanza
2nd Diagonal and Pje #5
Edificio Diagonal, 4th fl.
Tel 226-0840

You will rarely get the best price on a ticket by booking directly with the airlines. Some of the best deals are to be found in the Sunday travel sections of large newspapers like the *New York Times* and the *Chicago Tribune*. Some reputable budget travel agencies are **Educational Travel Centre** (800/747-5551, www.edtravel.com), **Council Travel** (800/226-8624, www.counciltravel.com) and **STA Travel** (800/781-4040, www.sta.com). The later two are large budget travel organizations with many regional offices throughout the US while the former is tiny but usually has tickets at the same price and with fewer restrictions. A local favorite in the eastern US for tickets to Central America is **Peace Frogs** (888-737-6472, 804-977-1415, http://peacefrongstravel.com).

■ **To and From Canada.** Flights from Canada to Central America are routed through the United States. **Travel CUTS** (416/614-2887, www.travelcuts.com) is Canada's budget travel giant, and you don't have to be a student to use their services.

■ **To and From the UK.** The cheapest flights from the United Kingdom originate in London. Many discount "bucket shops" advertise in papers like the *Sunday Times*, the *Evening Standard, Time Out* and *TNT*. Make sure the shop is bonded before you buy a ticket. Council, STA, and Travel CUTS all have offices in the UK. **Just the Ticket** (020/7291-8111, www.justtheticket.co.uk) has consistently low prices.

■ **To and From Continental Europe.** Your best bets for low-cost fares from the rest of Europe to Central America are from Amsterdam, Brussels, Frankfurt and Athens. But it may be cheaper if you travel through London. **USIT** (www.usitnow.com) is one of the biggest con-

## Public Holidays

| | |
|---|---|
| **January 1** | New Year's Day |
| **March, April** | Semana Santa (Holy Thursday, Good Friday, Easter) |
| **May 1** | Labor Day |
| **First week in June** | Corpus Christi |
| **June 29-30** | Bank Holiday |
| **August 1-6** | Festival of El Salvador del Mundo (San Salvador) |
| **September 15** | Independence Day |
| **October 12** | Columbus Day |
| **November 2** | All Souls' Day |
| **November 5** | First Call of Independence (1811) |
| **December 24-31** | Christmas |

tinent-wide travel agencies and has offices in France, Germany, Greece, and Spain among others. Council Travel and STA also have offices and partners throughout the continent.

■ **To and From Australia and Asia.** Coming from Australia and Asia, flights through Miami and Los Angeles are least expensive. STA has offices in Australia, China, Japan, Malaysia, New Zealand, Philippines, Singapore, Taiwan, and Thailand. Council has partners in Australia, China, India, Nepal, New Zealand, Singapore, Taiwan and Vanuatu while USIT has a branch in New Zealand.

■ **Around Central America.** Flying between the countries of Central America is easy and getting easier, since TACA, Copa, and Lacsa airlines have travel pass programs that offer big discounts if you make several flights. Regular fares to San José, Costa Rica start at about $350 while Managua, Nicaragua or Tegucigalpa, Honduras can go as low as $100.

■ **To and From South America and Mexico.** Flying to El Salvador from South America is a little more interesting. There are sometimes direct flights to major cities, but they are seasonal and subject to change. In almost all instances you need to make a connection in another Central American city such as San José, Costa Rica or Panama City, Panama and so you could save money by making those journeys by bus. There are direct flights to Mexico, but even here connecting flights are common and the prices are high.

■ **Airport Transportation.** The airport is located 44 kilometers from San Salvador, and getting to and from the city is a pain in the neck, even without traffic a ride in a taxi can take up to an hour. Taxis and microbuses run between the city and the airport and will

## Questions to Ask When Purchasing an Airplane Ticket

- Can I change my return date? What's the charge?
- If the ticket has an open-ended return date, how long is the ticket good for?
- Is there a special student or youth fare? How can I qualify?
- Is there a charge for stopping over in another city along the way? How long can I stay in the stopover city?
- Can I return from a different city than the one I traveled to originally?
- What do I do if my ticket is lost?

**BASICS**

be waiting for you just outside the terminal. Prices are inflated (taxi $11.50; microbus $2.50-$10), so the best option may be to split the cost of a taxi with others. Acacya microbuses run daily from San Salvador to the airport. *(3a C Pte and 19a Av Nte #1107; tel 271-4937/8; 6, 7, 10am, 2pm; $2.50 one way)*

■ **Departure Tax.** It will cost you a whopping $26.50 to leave El Salvador by plane.

# By Bus

Over half a dozen companies make the trip to Guatemala from San Salvador stopping to pick up passengers in Santa Ana. Most leave from either the International Bus Station or the Western Bus Terminal, but a few also leave from some of the fancier hotels. A smaller number of companies go to Honduras and on to Nicaragua, Costa Rica and Panama. Full details are given in the San Salvador chapter. A cheaper, but more time-consuming option to get to Guatemala and Honduras is to take a regular bus to the border where you can cross on foot and pick up another local bus on the other side. This may be the best option if you are departing from a city other than San Salvador or Santa Ana. However, if you do make the trip this way, cross early enough to ensure you will be able to find a bus on the other side.

# By Car

Driving to El Salvador from the US means passing through Mexico, which requires drivers to buy insurance and obtain a permit to return (both available at the border). If you drive straight through and use the toll roads you can make the trip from the US border in two days.

## El Salvador's Best Drives

Here are some of our favorites, in no particular order:

**Road from Panamerican Highway through San Jorge to Coastal Highway.** This paved road connects the Panamerican Highway just west of San Miguel to the Coastal Highway east of Usulután. Along the way it winds up and over the gently sloping base of the San Miguel Volcano. The volcanic soil turns the road maroon in parts, and fences made from piled lava rocks line rich coffee estates. If you come from the north, there's a stunning view of the southern coastal plains as you pass over the base of the volcano.

**Road from San Salvador west to Sonsonate.** Soon after you turn off the Panamerican Highway at El Poliedro, this road crosses a small river where people bathe and wash clothes. As it passes into wide, flat plains, the distinctive triple peaks of Cerro Verde and the Izalco and Santa Ana Volcanoes come into view on the right.

**Road from San Salvador to Playa El Palmarcito.** Heading south out of the capital you get some spectacular views of the not-so-distant Pacific Ocean. Then, west of La Libertad the Coastal Highway hugs the winding shore and passes through five tunnels. The scenery here is as stunning any along California's northern coastal highways.

**Panamerican Highway from San Salvador to Santa Ana.** The wide, divided highway is lined with overhanging trees, and passes through El Salvador's rich western farmlands. Notice on the right how even the hillsides are cultivated.

Foreigners are required to show a license and proof of ownership at the Salvadoran border, but you shouldn't have to pay anything at all. With these documents you're allowed 30 days in the country. To stay longer than that you need to go to the Ministry of Transit and pick up *a permiso de circunvalación al dentro del país*, ("permit for driving within the country"), good for another 30 days. Bring your documents, plus a photocopy of your license and $2.85. (*Departamento General de de Tránsito, Autopista Norte; tel 226-4840; Mon-Fri 8am-12pm, 2-4:30pm, Sat 8-11:30am*)

# By Sea

By the time you read this, the ferry from La Unión to Nicaragua might be running. The trip takes about 4 hours and actually cuts about 4 hours off the driving time from El Salvador to Managua. Check with ISTU or CORSATUR in San Salvador for details.

# Borders

There are seven land borders where you can enter and leave El Salvador. The dramatically improved immigration offices, the best in Central America, are open 24 hours and crossing is usually simple and straight forward. However you should still try to arrive at the border as early in the day as possible since the Honduran and Guatemalan border offices are not as well run. At the border, people will likely mob you with offers to change money or to help you with your paperwork, but since there are now banks and there isn't any paperwork to worry about with a tourist card, you can just ignore them. The immigration service has a help line (243-6383) in case you have any questions ahead of time.

**Road from Panamerican Highway northeast to Quetzaltepeque.** This road passes through an enormous dried lava flow that continues up the slopes of the San Salvador Volcano to the south. The blackened, jagged wasteland is striking in the middle of the surrounding green farmland.

**Panamerican Highway in front of San Vicente.** Terraced farms fill the valleys and stretch all the way up the volcano.

**Road to Cerro Verde.** For sheer oohs and ahhs, this steep road might just take the prize. In a few short kilometers up to the top of Cerro Verde you're treated to views of Lago de Coatepeque glittering to the east, the Izalco cone and Cerro Verde itself. The road is narrow and winding, but paved. There are a few places to pull over to admire the vistas.

**Road from Sonsonate to Ahuachapán.** Lovely mountain scenery anytime, but especially between October and February when the coffee plants are in bloom. See The Flower Route for more details.

The approaches to many Salvadoran cities and towns, especially those up in the mountains, are often as scenic as the towns themselves. Apaneca, La Palma, Santiago de María, Tacuba, Juayúa, Santiago Texacuangos, Suchitoto, Perquín, Metapán, and Ciudad Barrios have some of the most beautiful approaches.

**INTERNATIONAL BORDERS**

**GUATEMALA**
La Hachadura (Ahuachapán). a.k.a. Puente Arce.
Las Chinamas (Ahuachapán). a.k.a. Puente El Jobo.
San Cristóbal (Santa Ana).
Anguiatú (Santa Ana). a.k.a. Paso de la Ceiba.

**HONDURAS**
El Poy (Chalatenango).
Sabanetas (Morazán).
El Amatillo (La Unión). a.k.a. Puente Goascorán.

It may be tempting (and not particularly difficult) to slip across the border without going through all the proper channels. But you're just asking for trouble if you do that, since when you leave they'll look for the entrance stamp. Take the extra time to get all the right stamps and signatures or a tourist card.

# While There
## Business Hours

In Latin America business hours are flexible. During lunchtime (12-2pm) many shops and offices are closed, though the lunchtime siesta is slowly disappearing, especially in the capital. Here are some rough guidelines for when you can expect certain businesses to be open:

■ **Banks.** Mon-Fri 9am to 5pm, Sat 9am to 12pm.
■ **Government offices.** Mon-Fri 8am to 4pm.
■ **Post offices.** The main post office in the Centro de Gobierno is open Mon-Fri 8am to 4pm. The express-mail service in the same building is also open during these periods.
■ **Restaurants.** Since Salvadorans are early risers, breakfast usually starts around 6am. Lunch is served from 11am to 2pm and dinner from 5 to 9pm. When there's music and drinking, some restaurants will stay open much later.
■ **Shops.** Mon-Fri 8am to 12pm, 2 to 6pm, Sat 8am to 12pm. Department stores generally don't close for lunch.

## Time/Electricity/Measurements

El Salvador is one hour behind Eastern Standard Time and six hours behind Greenwich Mean Time. Since the country is along the equator it doesn't have daylight savings time.

The country runs on 120 volts, the same as Mexico and the US. You'll have trouble finding a third (grounding) hole, so bring a three-to-two prong converter if you have something important that needs to be plugged in.

El Salvador operates on the metric system, with a few exceptions. Fuel is sold by the gallon, and weights are occasionally measured in *libras* ("pounds," equal to 0.48kg) as well as in kilograms.

## Safety & Security

Although crime is certainly a problem in El Salvador, especially since the end of the war, you're unlikely to encounter any trouble if you take some simple precautions and stay alert. Youth gangs and bandits armed with guns from the civil war cause problems. However, a new and effective police force now patrols the streets of the country and is visible even in the smallest towns. Prepare yourself by learning about the dangers in advance and by taking extra precautions with how you carry your baggage and money.

Theft is the most common problem, especially in large cities where crowds fill the sidewalks, buses are packed and markets are teeming with people. Crowded public places are pickpocket hunting grounds. Beaches are another place where theft is common, since bags are often left unattended.

The new Tourism Police have the mission of assisting, advising, and helping visitors. Each of El Salvador's 14 departments has its own branch and those in San Salvador, at least, have some officers who speak English. For general questions the Tourism Police can be reached in San Salvador at 245-5448.

■ **Preparation.** The best source of information about the specific dangers in the country is your embassy in El Salvador. Contact them as soon as you arrive, or in advance if you're planning a long stay. If you are coming from Honduras or Guatemala your embassy there will also know the latest situation. The US State Department website (http://travel.state.gov/travel_warnings.html) provides security bulletins for every country and though they err on the side of caution it is a fantastic resource overall. Shortwave radios are also a convenient way to keep up to date with the big news once you're there.

■ **Staying Safe.** There are a few basic rules of action to keep in mind while traveling. When you arrive in San Salvador with your bags, take a cab to your hotel to avoid pickpockets on buses, who know that recently-arrived foreigners are often the easiest targets. If you're staying at a questionable hotel, try locking your bags to the frame of your bed when you leave your room. Needless to say, always lock your hotel door, even if you have to use your own lock.

Avoid unsafe parts of towns, parks, and bus and train stations, especially after dark, but also during the day. Ask the hotel manager where it is safe to walk in the city. Walk with authority and only peek at your map or guidebook when you're out of sight. If you need to put your bags down, watch them closely or lock them up to something solid. If you ever feel threatened, forget your inhibitions and howl. Attention is your best defense.

■ **Carrying Valuables.** How you carry your valuables is as important as watching where you go. You shouldn't wear any jewelry, but if you must, wear cheap stuff that nobody would want. Carry your most important things—travelers' checks, some cash, passports, and airplane tickets—in a money belt or a pouch that fits under the waistline of your pants. Split up the rest of your money—put some cash deep in your luggage and the remainder in another part of your clothing, such as under the insoles of your boots. That way, even if you're robbed of everything you're carrying, you'll still have some cash left.

Smart travelers often stick some cash in their socks, underwear, bra or into extra pockets sewn inside their clothing. Pockets closed with short strips of Velcro are more difficult (and noisy) to pick, and bags made of heavy nylon are harder to slash open.

## The New Good Guys

**E**l Salvador's new National Civilian Police (PNC) is one unquestionably positive consequence of the peace accords. The country's police were once so poorly trained, corrupt and violent that most Salvadorans routinely avoided them, even when they had nowhere else to turn.

The new National Police are an enormous change for the country. Unlike their predecessors, they are not under army command, and their composition—20 percent former guerrillas, 20 percent former police members and 60 percent civilians—helps ensure that they aren't partial to any particular political wing. Each member of the now 18,000-strong force are also required to undergo a psychological exam intended to weed out the most notorious offenders from both sides of the conflict.

The National Police are clean-cut, usually with navy pants and a blue or white shirt, and they carry pistols in contrast to the rifles used by the old police force. The government constructed a new police academy to train them, foreign governments are chipping in with funding for training and equipment (The US planned to give $1.5 million in 2000) and a reassuring one in ten are women.

■ **Dangers for Women.** El Salvador is as *macho* as much of the rest of Latin America, so women travelers face special problems and should take extra precautions. You're especially likely to be pestered if your hair is light and your complexion is fair, but wearing skimpy clothing will make any woman's life more difficult.

Latin men often hiss or proposition women as they pass on the street. Ignore them and avoid eye contact—any sort of response will be seen as a come-on. If you ever feel threatened, move away quickly and yell to attract attention. It is best not to go anywhere alone at night. Overall though, few women encounter anything more than an occasional annoyance.

■ **In the Water.** Though El Salvador's shores have a reputation for shark attacks, they don't happen often enough to worry about. Rip tides, though, are a real danger. These strong outward currents can quickly pull even strong swimmers away from the beach. You can't swim against them, but they don't pull you under the water and tend to fizzle out where the waves break, so don't worry about being pulled completely out to sea. If you get caught up in one, try not to panic—just remember to float and try to swim parallel to the beach. When the rip tide dies out, you can return to the beach by swimming at a 45-degree angle to the shore.

# Health

The best advice on staying healthy abroad is simply to pay attention to how you feel. You know your body better than anyone else; if anything feels out of whack, there is a good chance that it is. Always seek qualified medical help whenever possible. If this means going out of your way to get to a large city, do it. Most health hazards involve unsanitary food and water, so be careful about what you eat and drink. Beyond that, get your immunizations, cover yourself with bug spray and don't get too much sun, and you should be all right.

A medical kit is essential (see Packing). Cover any cut or scratch you receive immediately with a Band-Aid and antibiotic ointment, since a routine infection could become worse if it is ignored. For more serious problems, your embassy should have a list of recommended doctors, many of whom speak English and were trained in the West. Most medications are available at pharmacies without a prescription, but pharmacists have little training and can not be relied on for medical advice.

Some symptoms of disease don't show up for a while, so it may be difficult to associate something you picked up along the way with an illness that shows up after you return. Doctors routinely misdiagnose travel-related illnesses, since they rarely see many of them. So keep a close eye on your general state of health for about six months after you return and tell your doctor where you've been if you get ill during this time.

## GENERAL HEALTH CONCERNS

■ **Food and Drink** Remember the four keys to safe eating and drinking under unsanitary conditions: "Peel it, boil it, cook it or forget it."

Peel fruits and vegetables whenever possible. Drinking unpurified water is probably the easiest way to slip up and catch something nasty, so watch everything you drink. Don't drink anything that doesn't come in a sealed bottle opened in front of you, and steer clear of all ice except in the best restaurants. Don't hesitate to ask if the water in your drinks has been boiled. Carbonated and alcoholic drinks are safe if they are not mixed with any contaminated water or ice, as are yogurt and coffee or tea made with water that has been thoroughly boiled. Dairy products can be a problem if they were made with unpasteurized milk. Any fruit juice or ice cream product that uses unpurified water is also a potential problem.

If you're cooking your own food, you should boil questionable beverages for at least ten minutes, filter them through a specialized water filter (no T-shirts) or use purification tablets. Chlorine tablets like Puritabs or Steritabs and iodine tablets such as Potable Aqua all work well. Five drops of tincture of iodine (2%) per quart or liter of water will also kill just about everything in there within 30 minutes. Careful, though, since too much iodine can make you sick. Powdered drink mixes help the chemical taste go down more smoothly.

The food at many roadside stands may look tempting, but remember you're taking your health into your own hands. Sometimes, it comes down to a choice between eating questionable food or going hungry: the risk is yours.

■ **Travelers' Diarrhea** is a fact of life in the developing world. Since diarrhea robs your body of fluids and electrolytes, drinking lots of clean fluids at the first sign of gastric distress is the first step towards feeling better. Try weak tea with a little sugar or flat, watered-down soda. Bland soups go down reasonably well, too. Unspiced foods such as bananas, rice, beans and potatoes provide protein and vitamins. Avoid other solid foods and milk until you feel better.

SYMPTOMS: an intestinal tract that feels like it's full of club soda.

TREATMENT: Pepto-Bismol, Kaopectate, Lomotil, Immodium AD. If more severe, persistent symptoms develop like nausea, vomiting, stomach cramps, fever or bloody stool, you may have dysentery (see below). With any of these symptoms, the ingredients in Lomotil and Immodium are potentially dangerous (Pepto-Bismol is OK, though). Seek medical attention if you think you have something worse than diarrhea.

Studies have shown that a single 500mg dose of the prescription antibiotic ciprofloxacin decreases the length of bouts of travelers' diarrhea significantly. Some doctors advise travelers to carry ciprofloxacin or other quinoline-class antibiotics.

■ **Mosquitoes** The best strategy is to avoid being active at times during the day and in places where mosquitoes are most prevalent: dawn, dusk and night, and in the hot, damp regions along the coast and in the jungle. The greatest risk is below 600 meters during the rainy season. Mosquitoes almost never climb above 900 meters (though Global Warming will likely change this) and are less prevalent during the dry season. Wear long-sleeved shirts and long pants to cover as much skin surface as possible whenever you can.

Only buy repellents containing DEET, the most effective chemical repellent. A solution with a 12-30 percent concentration of DEET is recommended, since too little isn't effective and too much isn't particularly good for you. Lotions last longer and are more compact than sprays. Also, consider a personal mosquito net that can be slung over a hammock or a bed.

■ **Dehydration** is an excessive loss of body fluids that can be caused by strenuous activity, diarrhea or high altitude. If you are sweating and thirsty, chances are you're dehydrated already. The easiest way to stay hydrated is to drink almost continuously, usually more than you think you need.

SYMPTOMS: very little urination, dark yellow urine, dry mouth, headache.

TREATMENT: drink water or rehydration mixtures (see Travelers' Diarrhea).

■ **Heat Cramps** occur when you lose too much salt by perspiring, usually from strenuous activity in hot weather.

SYMPTOMS: muscle cramps, sweating.

TREATMENT: drink slightly salted water (one teaspoon of salt in one quart of water), rest.

■ **Heat Exhaustion**, also known as heat prostration, is an extreme case of dehydration. Body temperature is usually not much higher than normal at this stage, but without attention this may lead to heatstroke.

SYMPTOMS: pale, clammy skin, excessive sweating, rapid breathing and pulse rate, nausea, dizziness.

TREATMENT: administer fluids and salts (see Traveler's Diarrhea), lay person down in cool place, loosen tight clothing, raise feet slightly above head. Seek medical attention if condition does not improve.

■ **Heatstroke** is a potentially life-threatening condition which occurs when the body becomes unable to regulate its own temperature under extreme heat stress. Internal organs are threatened as body temperature rises and water and salt are depleted.

SYMPTOMS: body temperature in excess of 104 degrees Fahrenheit (40 degrees Celsius), hot, dry and flushed skin, lack of sweat, rapid and strong pulse, confusion, unconsciousness.

TREATMENT: move person to coolest place possible, remove clothing, apply cool water to skin, wipe with cool damp cloths, seek medical attention immediately.

■ **Sunburn** occurs amazingly fast when you're close to the equator. An hour or two near the middle of the day, even with sunscreen, can turn you into a living chili pepper. Gradually increase your exposure time to the sun over the course of a few weeks, starting with no more than half an hour. Always wear sunscreen (at least SPF 15) and don't forget to reapply it after sweating or swimming. Wear long sleeves, loose, light-colored clothing and a hat whenever possible.

SYMPTOMS: according to severity, redness, swelling, blisters.

TREATMENT: calamine lotion or other sunburn-relief gels, cold compresses and pain medication such as aspirin. More severe cases with blistering may require medical attention.

## INSECT-BORNE DISEASES

■ **Chagas' Disease** (American Trypanosomiasis) is transmitted by the nocturnal reduviid ("kissing") bug. Take care when sleeping in mud, adobe brick or palm thatch buildings, especially with cracks or crevices in the roof and walls. Lather on the DEET and string up the mosquito net.

SYMPTOMS: swelling of the eyelid, "pink eye," rash and fever.

TREATMENT: seek medical attention for testing as soon as possible. Past a certain point, Chagas' Disease becomes untreatable and may cause long-term damage to the heart and internal organs.

■ **Dengue Fever** (Breakbone or Dandy Fever) is transmitted by *aedes* mosquitoes. No vaccines are available, but luckily the disease tends to be relatively benign and to eventually run its course. It is more common than malaria and most prevalent around the Cerrón Grande Dam, north of San Salvador, than in other parts of the country.

SYMPTOMS: flu-like, including severe, sudden fever, headache and pain in muscles and joints. Often accompanied by vomiting, nausea, swollen lymph nodes and a pale rash or flushing of the face. The fever usually comes in two to three day cycles, separated by a daylong period of remission.

TREATMENT: stay hydrated, rest, seek medical attention.

## Power Line Blues

Rebel troops destroyed thousands of power lines during the war in an attempt to undermine El Salvador's infrastructure. Since the rebel army was a fraction of the size of the government army, attacks on the country's electrical system affected everyone and made the rebels seem bigger than life.

All of this made work as a Salvadoran power repairman no fun at all. Teams of electricians worked throughout the civil war to repair damaged power lines in huge, labor-intensive operations. Since rebels often booby-trapped the area around the downed lines, electricians frequently waited for hours while a team of explosive experts combed the area.

Electricians were flown throughout the country to work on downed lines, and labored under army helicopters which hovered overhead to defend against ambushes. If you keep an eye out for them, you'll spot telephone and electrical poles throughout the country that were knocked down by the FMLN and hastily clamped back together by power repairmen.

## Kitchen Cure for Montezuma's Revenge

**M**ix one cup of fruit juice (for potassium) with one teaspoon of honey or corn syrup (for glucose) and a pinch of table salt (for sodium). This mixture should be no more salty than tears. In a second glass dissolve one teaspoon of baking soda in eight ounces of water. Drink alternately from each glass until you aren't thirsty anymore or until both are empty, whichever comes last. Keep this up throughout the illness.

■ **Encephalitis** (Japanese Encephalitis) is a viral infection transmitted by mosquitoes. It occurs primarily in rural areas of the tropics during the rainy season. Most people who are infected show no symptoms, and symptoms that do appear resemble those of other insect-borne infections. If any of these occur suddenly or together, see a doctor.
SYMPTOMS: weakness, stiffness, muscle soreness, delirium, vomiting. Fever, chills and headache often begin suddenly. Convulsions, paralysis and coma may follow without treatment.
TREATMENT: stay hydrated, seek medical attention immediately.
■ **Leishmaniasis** (Dum-Dum fever or Kala Azar) is one of a number of tropical parasitic diseases transmitted through the bite of sandflies. More serious internal conditions may take months or even years to appear. Sandflies are most active at night.
SYMPTOMS: small (1-2 cm) sores on the face that won't heal, followed by fever and swelling of some internal organs.
TREATMENT: seek medical attention.
■ **Malaria** People used to think malaria was caused by breathing polluted air (hence the name, from Italian for "bad air"). We now know that the disease is caused by a parasitic protozoa carried by female mosquitoes. Four parasite species cause malaria. The *plasmodium vivax* species is the most common, and rarely fatal. *Plasmodium falciparum*, on the other hand, which accounts for only a small percentage of infections, can be deadly within hours. Keep in mind that even with prophylaxis, infection is still possible.
SYMPTOMS: chills and headache, followed by high fever, headache, nausea, diarrhea, stiffness, aching joints, brown urine, exhaustion, mental haziness and delirium. These symptoms, characterized by alternating hot and cold spells, usually recur in waves every two to three days.
TREATMENT: seek medical attention, even if a prophylaxis is being used.

## DISEASES OF SANITATION
■ **Cholera** Luckily, attacks of this acute intestinal infection are often mild and easily treated. To minimize your chances of catching it, avoid contaminated food and water.
SYMPTOMS: sudden acute diarrhea, vomiting, extreme weakness and muscle cramps.
TREATMENT: stay hydrated to offset effects of diarrhea, seek medical attention. (*Tetracyclene, two 250mg pills , 4 times a day*)
■ **Dysentery** usually follows a bad bout of travelers' diarrhea, and comes in two forms. Bacillary or bacterial dysentery is highly contagious but short-lived and will usually go away in a week. Amoebic dysentery, even though it is characterized by less severe symptoms, is more serious and can cause long-term damage. A stool analysis is necessary to determine the cause of the diarrhea.

SYMPTOMS: bloody diarrhea, stomach pain, headache (both types), fever, vomiting (bacillary only).

TREATMENT: immediate medical attention for prescribed antibiotics. *(Bacillary dysentery: tetracyclene, one 250mg capsule, 4 times a day for 7-10 days)*

■ **Giardia** (Giardiasis) is caused by ingesting an intestinal parasite through contaminated water or food, and occurs around the world.

SYMPTOMS: severe digestive system distress, diarrhea, fatigue and weight loss.

TREATMENT: eat, drink and rest as much as possible. *(Metronidazole or Flagyl, one 250mg pill, three times a day for five days)*

■ **Hepatitis A** (Infectious Hepatitis) is a disease which attacks the liver. It is transmitted through improper hygiene, contaminated food or sexual contact and is especially dangerous for pregnant women.

SYMPTOMS: nausea, headache, fever, vomiting and loss of appetite. Eventually, dark-colored urine, light-colored stool, a pain on the right side of the body near the liver. A yellowish tint to the skin and/or eyes may develop.

TREATMENT: rest, drink lots of fluids. Seek medical attention immediately.

■ **Typhoid Fever** is a dangerous infection of the stomach and intestines, transmitted through contaminated food or water. Immunization provides only limited protection.

SYMPTOMS: typhoid fever progresses through a detectable pattern beginning with flu-like symptoms—headache, sore throat, occasional diarrhea and vomiting, all during the first week. Fever rises while pulse rate drops. During the second week, trembling, delirium, weakness and weight loss set in and pink spots may appear on the body.

TREATMENT: drink lots of liquids, seek medical attention immediately.

# Other Health Concerns

■ **AIDS** is the final stage of infection with the human immunodeficiency virus (HIV). Unless you plan to indulge in intravenous drug use overseas, the greatest risk of contracting AIDS is through sexual contact or a tainted blood transfusion. Therefore don't share needles, and if you plan to exchange bodily fluids with anyone whose sexual history you aren't sure of, use a condom.

SYMPTOMS: fatigue, chills, fever, sudden weight loss, white or dark spots on the skin (usually the face), a persistent dry cough, constant diarrhea.

TREATMENT: Though several new antiviral therapies can prolong and improve the lives of those infected with HIV, there is still no cure for AIDS.

■ **Leeches** However disgusting they may be, leeches don't transmit disease and their bite is painless. Always check for these after passing through bodies of water and damp forests. If you get one, don't panic and don't yank it off. Apply insect repellent, salt, lemon juice or vinegar, or burn it with a lit cigarette. Cover the cut with a bandage and rub it with some antibiotic ointment.

■ **Ticks** Check for ticks after passing through dry vegetation. It's important to get both the tick's body and head, which can remain behind and cause infection. To get rid of one, apply alcohol, Vaseline or oil. Or light a match, blow it out, and apply it to the tick.

■ **Rabies** If you are bitten by an animal that is acting strangely, whether overly friendly or foaming at the mouth, there's a chance you could contract this horrific disease. Treatment for rabies must begin before the first symptoms appear, because once rabies takes hold there is nothing that can be done to save your life.

SYMPTOMS: restlessness, irritability, inability to eat or drink, foaming at the mouth, insanity. Symptoms may take from 10 days to two years to appear.

TREATMENT: wash the wound thoroughly with soap and water but don't close it up. If possible, capture or kill the animal for testing. Seek medical attention immediately.

■ **Transfusions** Much of the blood supply in developing countries has not been screened for AIDS. If you find yourself or someone you know in a situation where a blood transfusion is required, first make sure a transfusion is absolutely necessary; in some cases, colloid or crystal plasma expanders can be used instead of blood transfusions. If a transfusion is imminent, try at all costs to insure that the blood has been screened for the HIV virus, even if it means moving to a different hospital in another country. Evacuation to your home country is an expensive but potentially life-saving alternative.

## Other Medical Resources

**The International Association for Medical Assistance to Travelers (IAMAT)** seems almost too good to be true. For nothing at all (or a small donation), IAMAT will send you comprehensive pamphlets on many diseases. They also enclose a list of English-speaking doctors in almost every country around the world (including El Salvador), all of whom have agreed to a fixed-fee schedule and 24-hour availability. *(417 Center St., Lewiston, NY 14092; tel 716/754-4883; www.sentax.net/~iamat)*

**Traveling Healthy** is a bimonthly newsletter available for $45 a year. You can subscribe or see a sample issue on their website. *(Travel Medicine Inc., 369 Pleasant St., Northhampton, MA 01060; www.travelinghealthy.com)*

**The US Centers for Disease Control and Prevention** in Atlanta offers a wealth of continuously-updated information on health and disease issues around the world, including risk areas, treatments, and advice on staying healthy. *(International Travelers' Hotline 877/FYI-TRIP; www.cdc.gov/travel)*

### BOOKS ON HEALTHY TRAVELING

*International Travel Health Guide* by Stuart R. Rose, M.D., Travel Medicine, Inc.

*The Pocket Doctor: A Passport to Healthy Travel* by Stephen Bezruchka, M.D., Mountaineers Books.

*Staying Healthy in Asia, Africa and Latin America* by Dirk Schroeder, Avalon Travel Publishing. This is our personal favorite.

*Travelers' Medical Resource* by William Forgey, M.D., Globe Pequot Press

*Where There Is No Doctor* by David Werner, The Hesperian Foundation.

# Money

■ **Currency.** As of January 1, 2001 the US Dollar is the country's second official currency and is accepted everywhere. The *colon* or "*peso*" equals 100 *centavos*, and is circulated in ¢5, ¢10, ¢25, and ¢100 notes. *Centavos* are available in 5, 10, 25 and 50-*centavo* coins.

■ **Exchanging money.** Since the government initiated a free-market exchange system in 1990, a handful of *casas de cambio* (exchange houses) have sprung up to compete with banks so you won't have too hard a time getting rid of your Guatemalan *Quetzales* or Honduran *Lempiras*.

■ **Travelers' checks** are difficult to change everywhere in El Salvador, but you stand a better chance if you carry your receipt and passport with you. If you stop by American Express' office in San Salvador, they will stamp your checks and send you to the bank upstairs for a quick and easy exchange.

**Rates** for exchanging money vary from place to place, and travelers' checks get the highest rate. *Casas de cambio* and banks offer the best rates, while hotels are the worst—they occasionally won't let you exchange money at all unless you're a paying guest, however, if you are desperate late at night they may be your only option.

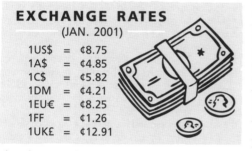

## EXCHANGE RATES
### (JAN. 2001)

| | | |
|---|---|---|
| 1US$ | = | ¢8.75 |
| 1A$ | = | ¢4.85 |
| 1C$ | = | ¢5.82 |
| 1DM | = | ¢4.21 |
| 1EU€ | = | ¢8.25 |
| 1FF | = | ¢1.26 |
| 1UK£ | = | ¢12.91 |

**Carrying money.** Despite the difficulty of exchanging them, you should carry most of your money in travelers' checks. American Express is the most recognized brand, and they have an office in San Salvador.

Though travelers' checks are replaceable, you should safeguard them like cash since a refund center may be far away or closed when you need it. Also, carry (separately from the checks, of course) a copy of your receipts, a list of refund centers and the phone numbers of refund centers and the home office, in case you have an emergency and need to call collect.

**Credit cards** are accepted at most big restaurants and stores in the major cities and are the best form of back-up funds. There's a problem with credit card numbers being "borrowed," though, so get in the habit of calling collect back to your credit card company every now and then to check the status of your account and to make sure that all charges on it are yours. If you plan to drive a car, most credit cards will cover the cost of insurance and eliminate the need for a cash deposit.

■ **Getting money.** There are various convenient and inexpensive ways to get money while abroad.

Easiest for most are the **Automatic Cash Machines** are found all over the country's main cities.

**Credit cards** will let you withdraw funds on the card, but most charge interest starting the day money is withdrawn. Check with your credit card company before you leave and find out how and where you can get money issued to you.

If you plan to use a credit card abroad and you'll be away for longer than a month, you'll have to deal with the monthly statement. With an American Express card, you can pay off your statement at any of its offices abroad. With other credit cards, you should be able to make a payment in advance and draw upon the funds as you use the card. The other option is to have someone at home handle everything. Whatever you do, stay in regular contact with your credit card company (most accept collect calls from abroad) and anyone else involved in keeping your finances straight.

**Direct money transfers** are generally the most expensive way to get money while abroad. In addition to its regular cardholder and traveler check services, American Express also has a Moneygram service that will transfer cash in ten minutes between any two of its offices, or from American Express in the US to a branch of some Salvadoran banks. The fee is based on how much you transfer, although it will usually be more expensive than cashing a personal check for cardholders.

Foreign banks will also transfer money to Salvadoran banks. Do this only as a last resort, since your local bank won't likely have much experience transferring money to El Salvador. If you decide to do this, first go to the receiving bank to get all the details, then call home. Ask what currency the money will be issued in, what will be the rate of exchange and how long the process takes. Even if you try to clear up everything in advance, the process could still take weeks for any of a number of beautiful bureaucratic reasons.

Finally, US citizens have an emergency service (for jail or medical reasons only) and can have money issued to them by the embassy.

■ **Spending Money.** Bargaining is expected in many small purchases. It takes skill and patience—merchants or fruit sellers aren't your enemies, but they want to sell something for a high price just as much as you want to buy it for a low price. Don't let yourself be ripped off; but please remember to keep things in perspective. A few *centavos* mean much more to most Salvadorans than they do to you.

Speak with a few people selling the same thing first, and learn what a fair value should be. Playing vendors off against each other often gets prices down fast ("but that woman said she'd sell it to me for ten!"). Also, know when to bargain. In some places, like the market or with vendors selling goods on the street (except food), you're expected to bargain. In other places, like hotels in the off-season, your chances of getting a better price this way are smaller. Cooked food prices are generally non-negotiable.

■ **Costs.** El Salvador can be an inexpensive place to travel—if you have to, you can get by on $10 or less per day. But you don't win a prize for living on the cheap, and a hot shower or dinner at a nice restaurant can turn a bad day around. Hotel prices (in dollars) start in the single digits and food on the street is very inexpensive, usually less than $2 per meal. Restaurants charge about half what a comparable place would charge in the US. Beers cost about $1 per bottle, and Cokes—available everywhere—are about $0.50 each. Public transportation is the best deal in El Salvador—the longest ride across the country will never cost more than $3, and most bus fares are under $1. Prices also vary from region to region. The east is slightly more expensive than the west, although La Unión is inexpensive. San Salvador, of course, is the most expensive place in the country.

# Mail

Sending and receiving mail in El Salvador is an imperfect science. To guarantee that your letter or package arrives you probably won't want to use the regular postal service, but then again, you're going to have to pay much more.

■ **Sending Mail.** When deciding how to send something, consider what it's worth and how much you're willing to pay to get it where it's going. The regular postal system has improved, but is still inefficient. There's even a slight chance that someone will go through your letter or package. Allow two weeks for a regular letter to arrive in El Salvador, and a little less for one to be sent home.

If you are going to send a package from the post office, bring it there opened but in its packaging and ready to be closed, so customs can inspect it. If it's important, consider using one of the private courier services. EMS has an office in the main post office and there is a list of other companies in the San Salvador chapter. They will deliver letters both to and from El Salvador, as well as between some other Central American countries.

Sending a letter outside of the country through the post office costs about $0.50. Packages cost more and take longer. Most courier services start at $0.65 for a letter while rates per pound vary wildly depending on destination and type of service.

■ **Receiving Mail.** To receive letters in El Salvador, you can either use the general delivery/poste restante system or have American Express hold your mail (see San Salvador). It's best to send general delivery/poste restante letters to San Salvador. For either of these two options, use dull stamps, underline your family name on everything and make sure the sender puts only your name—no "Mr." or "Mrs." which might confuse the person filing the letters. For general delivery/poste restante mail, write clearly in this format:

> [Your name]
> Lista de Correos
> Correo Central
> [City], El Salvador
> Centroamérica

# Telephones

Antel, the Salvadoran national telephone company, was recently sold off by the government to several private companies. This has resulted in a dramatic rise in quality and service and El Salvador now has one of the best telecom systems in Latin America. El Salvador's international country code is 503.

## USA DIRECT-DIAL NUMBERS

Call these numbers from any phone (no money is required) to speak to an operator:

| | |
|---|---|
| AT&T | 190 |
| Americatel | 158 |
| MCI | 195 |
| Sprint | 191 |
| Telecom | 155 |

Public telephones in El Salvador are a nice little surprise: they're everywhere and they work. To make **domestic calls** you'll need a calling card, which are sold in most pharmacies and neighborhood stores. Each company's phones only accepts its own cards. If you don't want to buy a phone card you can also make domestic calls from CTE Telecom offices in main towns. Other smaller companies, including Telefonica and Telemovil also have call centers in some towns.

For **overseas calls,** dial-direct services to the US, which can be made either from street phones or from call centers, cost anywhere from $0.50 to $1.75 per minute depending on the time, day and length of the call. These services also permit collect calls and AT&T, MCI and Sprint have bilingual operators who can help you out if you're in a bind. Most of the cyber cafes offer PC to Phone services which are cheaper, but the connections can range from pretty good to atrocious.

# Getting Around

■ **Buses.** El Salvador's buses are cheap, reliable and eye-catching. Whether you're traveling within a city or between cities, you'll be mixing with the masses, gazing out through colorful murals and speeding along at an alarming clip. And don't even consider standing out in the middle of any road in the country a moment longer than you absolutely have to, since these babies push their horns and engines to the limit but treat their brakes like fine china. The drivers, though still reckless, are improving thanks to new bus driver schools. Bus owners too are attending classes at "standards of conduct" schools.

Central America is where old US school buses go to die, although many of them seem to be doing quite well and are usually packed with passengers. Most Salvadorans travel on buses which get incredibly crowded and uncomfortable during peak hours. The government subsidizes the purchase of fuel for the bus system, so drivers are interested in getting as many passengers to squeeze on as they possibly can. Have your money ready.

Buses between cities offer a good panorama of the country. Life zooms by, but some of the same volcanoes sit on the horizon without moving for what seems like the entire trip. On the longer rides, stick your luggage somewhere secure and within sight. Vendors line the streets at transit points selling fruit and drinks. Some of the routes between major cities have express buses, which take less time than regular buses.

You'll sometimes find that it saves time to take two buses to a destination by switching at a transit point. Some non-commercial towns, like San Francisco Gotera in Morazán department, don't have many regular routes, so switching buses is the most convenient way to get there.

You can cross into neighboring countries by taking a local bus to the border, walking across and then taking another bus on the other side, or you can take an international bus from El Salvador to a neighboring country that brings you across the border. International direct buses are usually more comfortable and eliminate the need to search for transport on the other side. You will have to wait for everyone on your bus to clear

## Recipe for a Salvadoran Bus

1. Take one old US school bus.
2. Paint up like a Beatles cartoon.
3. Write name of girlfriend on windshield and patron saint on side.
4. Add air horn and crazy driver, mix well.
5. Start engine and don't stop for anything.

Top: Kayaking through a mangrove estuary
Bottom: Fishing boats on the Jiquilisco Estuary

Top: Isla Meanguera
Bottom: Lago de Coatepeque

# Driving in El Salvador

- Look out for cows in the road, especially at night.
- Beware of bus drivers—they don't slow down to let you pass. And, if you try to pass and they're coming in the opposite direction, they sometimes speed up.
- Check your oil, water and tires regularly.
- Always carry a supply of water, available at gas stations.
- Night driving can be harrowing. There are never lights on the road and rarely passing cars. This is also the time you're most at risk for being stopped and robbed. Don't drive at night if your car isn't working well or if you spook easily.
- Women should not drive alone in rural areas.
- People expect to pay a *colon* or two if you give them a lift—brighten their day by saying no thanks.
- With only two lanes on most roads, passing is dangerous. Learn to wave in—start waving your arm wildly on the passenger side to signal the person you are passing to slow down and let you pass. It feels ridiculous at first, but it just might save your life.
- Honk in advance when you pass through a town; children and animals often linger alongside roads.
- Drivers often disregard traffic lights, a habit learned during the war when cars were attacked at stoplights. So, be extra sure that cross traffic is stopped before moving on a green light.
- Many minor roads are impassable without a 4x4, and nobody for kilometers will have a phone. Don't bite off more than you can chew. Know when to turn around.
- Make sure you can see far ahead in the oncoming lane when passing. Don't pass behind another car.
- Most importantly, drive slowly enough so that you can avoid anything unexpected without going off the road.

customs, though, and that may take some time.

Domestic buses depart regularly—usually every few minutes between major cities and less frequently for smaller towns. They run from around 5am until dark, when service stops. It's usually easy to flag a bus down, and they'll even stop for you in the middle of traffic (wave to the cars that line up behind as you step on board).

*Estaciónes* (bus stations) are located in the centers of major towns, except in San Salvador where three are scattered on the outskirts of town. Bus stations are dirty, unsafe places that aren't great for hanging around. Taxis that sit inside bus stations and wait for passengers usually charge more than taxis which are passing out front.

■ **Taxis.** Salvadoran taxis are generally inexpensive and reliable, if dilapidated. Few have meters, so agree on a price before you leave the curb. Taxis are available in Santa Ana, San Miguel and San Salvador. In Santa Ana and San Miguel, don't pay more than $3 for a ride. In San Salvador, prices are a little higher, but you shouldn't pay much more than $3-5 for a trip with in the Western or Central parts or town and $10 to cross the whole city.

■ **Driving.** Driving your own car in El Salvador has some advantages and disadvantages,

# CAR RENTAL AGENCIES

**Avis Rent a Car**
43 Av Sur # 137
Col Flor Blanca
Tel 260-7456, 260-7157

**Colón Renta Autos**
Final Av Bernal Pol. C 1
Ciudad Satélite
Tel 274-1410

**Dollar Rent a Car**
Prolongación Calle Arce
# 2226
Col. Flor Blanca
Tel 260-2424

**E-Z Rent a Car**
Calle El Progreso # 1
Col Flor Blanca
Telefax 224-2749

**Henry Renta Autos**
3a C Pte. # 813 y Blvd
 Constitución
Tel 221-8852

**Kin's**
Residencial Sta. Teresa Pol.
 N 56
Av Santa Gertrudis
Ciudad Merliot
Tel 229-0991

**Metro Renta Autos**
Av Los Andes, # 2956
Col. Miramonte
Tel: 261-0603

Av El Boquerón y Calle
Libertad # 25
Ciudad Merliot
Telefax 289-0327

**Thrifty Car Rental**
Aeropuerto Internacional
Tel 339-9003

**Tropic Car Rental**
Av Olímpica #3597
Col. Escalón
Tel 223-7947, 279-3236

**Universal Rent a Car**
73 Av Nte # 239
Col Escalón
Tel 279-4767, 245-0192

**Uno Rent a Car**
Edif. Sunset Plaza L-10
Calle La Mascota y Av
 Jerusalén
Col.Maquilishuat
Tel 263-9366, 264-2958

Hotel Terraza
85 Av Sur y Paseo Gral.
Escalón
Tel 263-0044

San Miguel
Av Roosevelt, Edif. Plaza
Roosvelt L-1-4
Telefax 661-0344

# TIPS ON RENTING A CAR

- To get a good price, contact the rental agency as far in advance as possible.
- Small rental-car agencies are cheaper, but their cars may be less reliable—no deal is worth the hassle of being stuck in the middle of nowhere.
- Your credit card should cover the cost of insurance, and you can use it in place of a security deposit.
- Longer rental schedules are cheaper.
- Pick-up trucks are cheap, durable and not as big a target for thieves.
- Get unlimited mileage or you'll be limited to the city.
- Make sure the tires are almost new. Don't risk a flat.
- Make sure the spare fits correctly by trying it out before you leave.
- Get the phone number of someone to call in case of an emergency. Even with this number, don't expect that they'll pay much attention to you if you get stuck, though. They have your security deposit slip, so you're on your own as far as they are concerned.
- Consider renting a cellular phone along with the car.
- On the road, don't take chances. If something sounds funny, return the car immediately.

BASICS

but it will definitely change your experience of the country, for better and worse. With your own car you can stop where you want to take photos, turn on a whim down unexplored detours and travel to remote places that buses rarely see. With your bags in the trunk and your map in the back seat, pickpockets can't threaten you and somehow you'll always find a road to where you're going. The road system has been almost completely rebuilt, both in the cities and the countryside, so that is no longer much of a concern except in the most remote areas. But rental fees, gas and insurance make it expensive to travel by car and border crossing can be time-consuming and frustrating. You'll be in real trouble if the car dies kilometers from the nearest service station; El Salvador is not a place where you want to get stranded.

Foreign drivers in El Salvador are required to carry their licenses with them, although it wouldn't hurt to bring an international drivers' license too. Make sure your insurance applies for driving outside your own country. You won't have any problems finding gas, since even the smallest towns have gas stations that sell both diesel and unleaded fuel. Car repair shops line all the main roads, especially at the entrance to towns, and don't charge much. Make sure the mechanic knows what to fix and establish what it will cost before he starts.

■ **Car Rental.** Renting a car eliminates some but not all of the problems you'd have with your own car. Rentals can be a cheap way to go if you're traveling in a group and you have arranged a deal in advance. Also, rental cars eliminate the hassle of bringing your car across the border and through customs.

■ **Motorcycles.** If you plan to take your motorcycle through El Salvador, the rainy season is not the time to do it. Look out for crazy drivers and make sure you can repair everything yourself.

■ **Bicycles.** Although bicycle racing is popular in El Salvador and there are many cyclists on the road, we don't recommend it; Salvadoran drivers aren't known for their willingness to share the road.

■ **Hitchhiking.** Hitching is a way of life in rural El Salvador, where truck drivers cover costs by giving lifts to peasants along the way. Buses pass so frequently along major roads, though, that hitching is usually unnecessary. Remember, like anywhere in the world, you're always taking a big gamble by hopping into a stranger's vehicle. If you get a ride in the back of a pickup, offer to pay a few *colones* for gas when the ride is over.

# Accommodations

Lodging in towns beyond the capital has improved since the war and new hotels, B&Bs, and lodges are springing up all the time, though some towns still lack accommodation. Throughout the country you can still find a passable room with a private shower for less than $10. The lone exception is for the adventurous few who find their own spot on a secluded beach—at times the country's finest accommodations of all.

Places to stay in El Salvador have various names. Hotels are usually, but not always, the best. Other titles like *posada, pensión, hospedaje* and *casa de huéspedes* are for places which can be good, bad or somewhere in between. Motels, which charge by the hour, are the exception—try to avoid them.

Salvadorans expect to vacation with their entire family and to sleep with everyone in

a single room, so rates are occasionally bloated on the assumption that you'll squeeze in a few more people. Learn to live without hot water, because none but the best hotels and the odd mountain town will have it. Always ask to see a room first, since quality varies from one door to the next. Make sure that the sheets are clean, and ask for a fan if your room doesn't have one already.

If you have any general hotel questions try the **Salvadoran Hotel Association** (*Tel 298-3629, fax 298-3628, www.elsalhoteles.com*)

# Food & Drink

Salvadoran food is inexpensive, simple, occasionally unhealthy and sometimes delicious. *Pupusas* are the Salvadoran mainstay, although fast-food restaurants make hamburgers and pizza a competitive second. The country has tons of fresh, exotic fruit, its own soda and a few domestic beers. In the larger cities there are enough restaurants to satisfy any taste.

Lunch is the biggest meal of the day and can cost anywhere from about $1.50 on the street to a lot more in the capital's most exclusive restaurants. It's usually worth tracking down a restaurant instead of settling for street food, since restaurants can be inexpensive and the food is usually better (and better for you). Even the country's smallest towns have restaurants, and they're usually pretty good.

■ **Local Cuisine.** El Salvador has a variety of dishes and drinks, some traditional and others imported. The *plato típico*, served everywhere, consists of a cup of refried beans, a spoonful of cream, a fried plantain and a few cornmeal tortillas. *Mariscada* is a common cream-based seafood soup. It's usually best and freshest near the coast, naturally, but can be found just about anywhere. **Restaurante Doña Pema** in San Miguel serves the Mother of all *Mariscadas*, the one by which all others are judged.

*Pupusas*, the most distinctive Salvadoran food, are small, thick *tortillas* filled with soft, white cheese. They're often fried, and are great hot off the skillet. A special version of *pupusas*, made from rice, is sold in the town of Olocuilta. You'll probably want to put some *cortido de repollo*—pickled and chopped cabbage and carrots, often in a jar on the table—on top of your *pupusas* to add some crunch and cool them down, followed by a sprinkle of chili sauce to heat them back up. You also have a choice of what goes inside: *chicharrón* ("fried pork rinds"), *queso* ("cheese"), *frijoles* ("beans"), or *revuelta* ("everything"). *Tamales* are made from cornmeal and margarine boiled in a large leaf. They're deliciously doughy when made well, and can come with chicken or beef inside. Vendors sell them hot on the street for about $0.25.

■ **Restaurants.** There's every type and quality of restaurant in El Salvador. Decent restaurants are often not much more expensive than little holes in the wall. Crowds are usually a tip-off that a place serves good food, so head out to eat lunch at the same time as the rest of the country—around noon.

# Salvadoran Recipes

### Pupusas

Masa (a finely-ground corn meal available at many specialty food stores)
Soft white cheese, such as mozzarella
Tabasco sauce

Mix the masa with water and form the resulting dough into two thin tortillas, each about five inches in diameter and 1/2 inch thick. Place the cheese in the center of one tortilla and place the other on top, pressing the edges together to seal the filling inside. Place in a hot pan or on a griddle with a dash of vegetable oil and cook evenly on both sides. Serve with Tabasco sauce and *curtido de repollo* (see below). Other fillings can be substituted for or mixed with cheese, including cooked beans and meat.

### Curtido de Repollo

(Chopped cabbage in vinegar)
One cabbage
4-8 oz vinegar
1 carrot
1 onion
Oregano
Salt
Chili pepper

Slice the cabbage and vegetables into small strips, place in vinegar and add oregano, salt and chili pepper to taste. Allow the mixture to soak for approximately six hours before serving with *pupusas*.

### Sopa de Frijoles Rojos o Negros

(Red or Black Bean Soup)
2 cups red or black beans
1 onion
3 cloves of garlic
Salt

Soak beans in water overnight. Wash them off and place in a pot of boiling water. Add the onion, garlic and salt (to taste) then cook until they are soft. Yucca or a ham bone may also be added to the soup for additional flavor. Best when served with fried rice. If you wish, add cubed avocado pieces.

### Horchata

Rice
Milk, water, ice
Sugar, nutmeg, cinnamon
Pumpkin and gourd seeds (optional)

Toast uncooked rice (two teaspoons per glass, about 3/4 cup per pitcher) in an unoiled pan until slightly brown but not burnt. Grind up into a powder, using a food processor if you have one. Add sugar, nutmeg and cinnamon to taste. Mix in milk and water to fill glass or pitcher (two parts milk to one part water). Serve iced. You can also buy ready-made mixes in supermarkets.

### Totopostes

2 cups of toasted and milled corn (corn mass)
3 oz of butter
1/2 cup of sliced cheese

Mix all ingredients very well. With your hands, form balls in the size that you wish. Then put the balls in aluminum foil (you can also put it in a cornhusk). Baked at 350 F for 10 to 15 min or until they turn an attractive golden color.

### Empanadas de Platanos

Fried beans or white beans
3 cups of bananas
Butter

Cook the unpeeled bananas with sufficient water. When they are ready, peel and blend in food processor. Refrigerate. Make small balls with your hands and extend the balls with your fingers, making a small circle and then crush. Use beans to form the breading and then fry with the butter.

### Casamiento

1/2 lb of cooked rice
1/2 stick of butter
1 green hot pepper
1 red hot pepper
1 onion
4-6 oz tomato paste
1 cup of red beans

With the butter, fry the pepper, onion, >

BASICS

tomato and garlic clove. Add the juice formed and when it comes to a boil, mix the rice and beans and leave it until it has a good flavor.

### Tamal de Elote

(Corn Tamale)
  6 cups of toasted and milled
    corn (corn mass)
  1/2 lb of cheese butter
  1/2 lb of crisp pork rind
  3 oz of fried butter
  Salt
  Sugar
  Cornhusk to bundle up

In a food processor, mix the crisp pork rind, cheese and butter into a paste. Add this to the corn and mix well, flavor with salt and sugar to taste. Put the prepared mass in the cornhusks. Put the tamales in a kettle and then add fill about 1/4 full with water. Cook for 40min, at medium heat.

### Camarones a la Criolla

(Shrimp Creole)
  1 onion, chopped
  1 1/2 cans water
  2 tsp parsley, minced
  1 clove garlic, minced
  2 lbs shrimp raw and cleaned
  2 green peppers, chopped
  1 tsp salt
  1 tsp flour
  1 tsp pepper
  9oz tomato sauce

Sauté onions in oil until tender (about 6-8 minutes). Stir in garlic and green pepper; sauté 2 min. Blend in flour. Add tomato sauce and simmer 5min. Stir in water, parsley, raw shrimp, salt and pepper. Cover and simmer 30min. Serve over rice.

### Chiles Dulces Rellenos con Camarón

(Shrimp Stuffed Peppers)
  6 medium green peppers
  1/4 tsp Worcestershire sauce
  3 tsp butter
  1/2 cup chopped celery
  3 tsp flour
  1 lb Shrimp, cooked in salt water
  1 tsp salt
  3 oz cooked macaroni
  1/2 tsp crushed basil leaves (optional)
  2 oz Cheddar cheese, grated

Cut off top of peppers and remove seeds and membrane. Pre-cook in salted water for 5min. Melt butter in skillet; blend in flour, salt and basil. Add milk and Worcestershire all at once. Stirring continuously, until thick and bubbly. Add diced shrimp and macaroni to sauce. Fill peppers with shrimp mixture and stand upright in well-greased baking dish. Bake uncovered at 350 F for 20 to 25min. Sprinkle with grated cheese, and bake until cheese melts.

### Pastel de Piña Fresca

(Fresh Pineapple Pie)
  2 eggs
  1/8 tsp salt
  1 1/3 cups sugar
  2 cups fresh pineapple, cubed
  1 tsp lemon juice
  1 tsp butter
  1/3 cup flour

Beat eggs slightly, add sugar, lemon juice, flour and salt. Mix with cubed pineapple. Pour filling into baked pie shell, dot with butter and cover with top crust. Bake at 450 F for 10 min, then at 350 F for 35 min, or until pineapple is tender.

El Salvador, and especially San Salvador, is filled with US fast-food chains; there sometimes seems to be a Pizza Hut on every corner, and sometimes two. A McDonald's occupies a beautiful building two blocks from the central plaza and Burger King, Dunkin' Donuts and Wendy's are buying up some of the best real estate around. A few local fast-food chains, like Biggest, Sir Pizza and Toto's Pizza, thrive nationwide. Fried chicken is very popular, and Pollo Campero does it right by Salvadoran standards. You'll see many Salvadorans flying to the US carrying big boxes of drumsticks and thighs with them, at the request (or demand) of their families.

■ **Markets & Vendors.** Markets have the freshest fruit, which is the way to go if you have something to carry them in and can wash them off. The best fruit is available early in the day. Shop around for the best prices and buy in bulk.

Otherwise, the food stalls in the market serve up tasty—but not necessarily healthy—food. If you're going to eat there, or even at a restaurant, take a look around to see if it is clean. Also, ask a few people who work at the market where the best place to eat inside is; one or two places always have the best reputation.

■ **Drinks.** El Salvador has a large selection of native drinks for such a small country, including beer, liquor, soda and a surprisingly refreshing beverage made out of milk, rice and cinnamon called *horchata*. Five brands of beer—Pilsner, Premium, Suprema, Regia and Golden Light—are produced domestically. Pilsner is most popular

## A Beginner's Guide to Salvadoran Fruits

El Salvador's markets offer an amazing variety of fruit, including some you've never seen before—guaranteed. Many tasty fruits are also sold, sliced and bagged, on the street.

**Anona/Guanabana.** There are two types: One has a dark green, uneven skin and appears in January. Its flavor is slightly acidic and more pronounced than its sister fruit. The other type appears later in the dry season and has a greenish-gray, rough outer skin with white or pale pink meat.

**Granadilla.** Egg-shaped with a pulpy yellowish outer shell. It is eaten from the shell with a spoon, seeds and all, which gives the sweet juicy pulp a nut-like flavor.

**Jocote.** A grape-sized fruit with a red or green peel, orange flesh and a big seed. You bite through the peel into the fleshy inside, which tastes sweet, a little like a tart mango.

**Majoncho.** A short, stubby, triangular, tough-skinned banana used for cooking and in stews.

**Mamei.** Fleshy, orange and about eight inches long. It has many seeds and tastes tart like an apricot.

**Platano.** This large slender, tough skinned banana is used in cooking and almost never eaten raw. When green it is sliced and fried to make chips called *platanitos fritos*.

**Zapote.** Round, about five to six inches long and three inches around with a brown peel and orange inside. Tastes like a fruity, sweet potato. It makes a great flavoring to ice cream.

and has a vaguely Bohemian flavor, Premium is good enough to be exported, Golden Light tastes like water and Regia comes in big brown bottles popular with teenagers.

*Aguardiente* is a liquor produced by the government, distributed at *expendios* (government-licensed liquor stores where alcoholics tend to linger) in almost every little town. This stuff is made from sugar cane, tastes vaguely like rum and could strip paint. Tres Puentes is the national brand, Muñeco is made in San Salvador and Unidas is from Santa Ana, but they're all basically the same cheap firewater. Alcoholic *chicha* is made of ground cornmeal, fermented and mixed with brown sugar. It's been consumed for thousands of years—they found traces of it at San Andrés—and it's still going strong.

Sometimes soda seems more plentiful than purified water. Coca-Cola does an amazing job of shipping the magic liquid to towns that helicopters couldn't even locate. For some reason Pepsi is scarce, except in Pizza Huts and Texaco Starmarts. Kolachampán, the "national soda," is an incredibly sweet concoction that Salvadorans love but many foreigners can't seem to develop a taste for. A few other smaller brands are passable,

## Flower Power

**N**ot everyone making a purchase from the flower vendors in the markets is looking to add a beautiful floral arrangement for their home–some are just hungry. Flowers are a common ingredient in many Salvadoran dishes and chances are you'll munch some during your stay.

One of the most popular edible blossoms is the Laroco, which is a prized ingredient in cheese *pupusas* and a great pizza topping, among other things. The Madre Cacao ("Mother Chocolate") tree has a pretty pink, bell-shaped flower that is often mixed with eggs and string beans. The Pito is a long, beautiful, fire-orange tube that also finds its way into egg and bean dishes (such as *frijoles parados con pitos*) and is taken to help induce sleep. Even the national flower, the Izote, is not spared. "There are so many Salvadorans," a local saying goes, "that they eat their national flower!"

including Tropical's cream soda.

Mineral water is for sale across the country, including gas stations and supermarkets. It's a good idea to carry a bottle around with you, since the tap water can make you sick (see Health). Coffee, of course, is everywhere and is usually first-rate, even at tiny *cafeterías*.

■ **Vegetarian Food.** There are a handful of vegetarian restaurants in San Salvador and one in Santa Ana. Many peasants survive on beans, rice and tortillas since meat is too expensive, which makes a majority of Salvadorans default vegetarians anyway. Be warned that refried beans are often cooked in lard. You can ask for *frijoles parados* ("whole beans") as an alternative.

# Media

■ **Newspapers.** The Salvadoran press, historically very right-wing, has begun to spread its boundaries. Compared with the period during the civil war when the press was clearly under the grip of the military, Salvadoran newspapers are experiencing something of a liberal Renaissance, although they still have a long way to go. The nation's five dailies have a combined circulation of over 250,000. *La Prensa Gráfica*, El Salvador's biggest daily, is very conservative but good for daily news events and goings-on, and includes entertainment listings. Close on its heels is *El*

*Diario de Hoy*, just as popular and even more conservative. *El Mundo* and *El Diario Latino* are smaller papers that come out in the afternoon, and both have a more moderate stance. *Primera Plana* is a left-leaning weekly that caters to a younger audience. The weekly *Que Pasa* and the monthly *Revue*, published in English and Spanish, are free and cover both El Salvador and Guatemala.

■ **Radio.** There are around 160 licensed radio stations in the country. Radio Venceremos (100.5 FM) has evolved from the government-targeted, clandestine voice of the FMLN into one more Top-40 money-maker. The morning news at 7am is good, though, with occasional interviews of political and entertainment hot-shots. The station still has an FMLN slant but political ties have largely been severed. YSKL (101.4 FM) is another good source for news. Radio Feminina (112.5 FM) is a popular rock and top 40 music station. YSUCA (90.1 FM) is the radio station of the Universidad Centroamericana and has a variety of music and other interesting programming.

■ **TV.** Twelve TV stations operate in El Salvador. The four independent VHF stations cover most of the country while the government-run station has a weak signal that doesn't get beyond the capital. Seven UHF stations serve San Salvador and surrounding towns. High quality cable TV brings international programming to San Salvador, Santa Ana, and other large cities and even many cheap hotels offer it to guests.

# Out & Around

■ **Hiking, Camping and Climbing.** For such a small, densely populated country, El Salvador has a respectable range of places to enjoy the outdoors. El Imposible and Cerro Verde National Parks and Bosque Montecristo are the most obvious spots, but there are also great trails and views near Apaneca, Metapán, Perquín and Santiago de María. Any large volcano, particularly those near big cities, is good for a day's climb, with spectacular views almost guaranteed. Plenty of options even further off the beaten path, like hiking in the hilly regions of Morazán and Ahuachapán departments, await the more adventurous. If you're going to go hiking, drop by the Instituto Geográfico in San Salvador before you leave to purchase a good map of the area (see San Salvador).

■ **On the Water.** El Salvador has some superb beaches and, if you come at the right time, you'll find some pristine and deserted sections of coast. El Espino, San Diego, El Tunco, El Icacal, El Cuco and the Costa del Sol are all great beaches. Fishing villages line much of the coastline, and for a reasonable price you can hop aboard for a roller-coaster ride on the waves or bargain for a lift to a nearby destination. Take a trip from Playitas to the islands in the Gulf of Fonseca, crash into the waves off Playa San Marcelino or explore

## El Salvador's Best Breaks

**WESTERN SPOTS**
- Playa Barra de Santiago to Acajutla
- Playa Los Cóbanos
- Playa El Zonte

**NEAR LA LIBERTAD**
- Playa El Tunco
- Playa El Sunzal
- Playa Conchalío
- The Point (La Libertad)
- La Paz (La Libertad)
- Playa San Diego

**EASTERN SPOTS**
- Playa El Cuco
- Playa Las Tunas

## Turicentros

The *turicentro* concept is a bit like the state park system in the US. They are generally places of natural beauty preserved and maintained by the state for the enjoyment of all. Swimming is the main activity, but other facilities that you will find at various locations include hiking trails, outdoor theaters, and sports facilities. The reputation they once had for being filthy and run-down is no longer true. Most have been remodeled and the cafeteria service and garbage collection have all been improved.

Not only are *turicentros* fun, but it can be interesting to watch the average Salvadoran family at play. The key to enjoying them is to either go during the week or very early in the morning. On weekends and during holidays most of these parks become uncomfortably crowded–although that can be an interesting experience in itself.

the quiet inlet near Barrio Santiago in a dugout canoe.

■ **Surfing.** It's hard to believe a country only 260 kilometers long has some world-class waves, but El Salvador does. Most breaks are concentrated near La Libertad, with a few more good spots in either direction.

The surf season lasts roughly from late February until November. Things are less active between November and February, but offshore winds can still create good waves during that period. In general, the waves are usually one to two-meter right breaks. Often they'll climb to three meters, and occasionally as high as five.

■ **In Town.** A handful of cultural centers and galleries in the capital host art exhibits, plays and other events. Movie theaters in the larger cities show American films in English with Spanish subtitles (small-town theaters tend toward skin flicks and low-budget action-adventure movies). There are many options in San Salvador to enjoy live Latin or club music, provided you have the clothes and the cash, while La Luna and a few smaller cafés in the capital are considerably more relaxed and inexpensive. The national theaters in San Salvador, Santa Ana and San Miguel host concerts occasionally. If you'd rather relax at night, try the main plaza in a small town like Conchagua, where people gather to flirt, discuss the day's events and watch the stars come out.

# Shopping

The *artesanos* of El Salvador produce a number of crafts that make good gifts or souvenirs. There is nothing that can't be bought at one of the markets in **San Salvador**, but prices are generally higher. Another advantage to making your purchases in the villages is that the individual craftsmen will usually invite you into their workshop and let you see how the items are made.

Hammocks, most from the small village of **Concepción Quetzaltepeque** in Chalatenango department, are intricately woven and come in many different materials and designs. They make good traveling companions, especially if you plan to camp out on the beach.

Small wooden boxes and other pieces from **La Palma** in northern Chalatenango department are El Salvador's most recognizable craft. The wooden pieces are painted with simple, childlike designs of the Salvadoran countryside in bright colors and then lacquered. Any shop that sells Salvadoran crafts—in or out of El Salvador—will invariably include pieces from La Palma.

The western town of **Nahuizalco** is known for its wicker furniture. These pieces take an incredibly long time to make, and would be great souvenirs if only they weren't so hard to take home.

**Ilobasco** produces painted ceramics that are exported throughout Central America. Although some of the work is rather rudimentary, the ceramics studios make the city an interesting place to visit.

**San Sebastián** in San Vicente department produced some of the country's best textiles on big wooden looms. Now, you'll find more Chinese imports lining store shelves in El Salvador than textiles from San Sebastián, but the process is interesting to see.

Leather goods are another great souvenir of El Salvador. **Santa Ana** is the place to go to get leather belts, saddles, handbags, wallets, shoes, and the sharpest, most comfortable pair of cowboy boots you've ever worn.

# SAN SALVADOR

## San Salvador Then

In many ways the history of San Salvador is the history of El Salvador. The city's anguishes, disappointments, high hopes, promises and occasional blessings mirror the experiences of the entire country.

■ **Founding.** The Pipil capital of Cuscatlán, established in 1054, was the first major city settled in the vicinity of present-day San Salvador. This indigenous nucleus, situated in the nearby Zalcuatitán Valley, was wealthy and powerful, but the arrival of the Spanish quickly brought the prosperity of the Pipil culture to an end. Pedro Alvarado attacked the city when he entered El Salvador in 1524, but was soon defeated. He returned just as quickly to mount a second campaign against the Cuscatlecos, but soon realized that the only way to defeat the Pipils would be to establish a colony in the area.

Toward the end of March 1525, Gonzalo de Alvarado established the villa of San Salvador near Cuscatlán, naming it in honor of Christ, Divino Salvador del Mundo ("Divine Savior of the World"). Within a year, however, the new town was burned to the ground during a surprise Pipil uprising. The few Spanish who survived fled to Guatemala.

The Alvarado family's history with San Salvador wasn't through yet, though. In 1528, Jorge de Alvarado, in charge of the campaign to settle El Salvador in the absence of his brother Pedro, sent their cousin Diego to re-found the villa of San Salvador in its present-day location. Soon local tribes were subdued, and many settlers moved back into the area. San Salvador was declared a city in 1546, with the Parque Libertad, Iglesia El Rosario and El Cabildo (town hall) constituting the center of town.

■ **Independence.** In 1811, Father José Delgado sounded the call for Central American independence from San Salvador. Early in the morning of November 5, church bells rang out across the city to show that the struggle had begun. When news reached San Salvador in 1821 that the revolution had been a success, the streets filled with celebrations. Loyalist Spanish forces from neighboring countries were completely subdued in 1835,

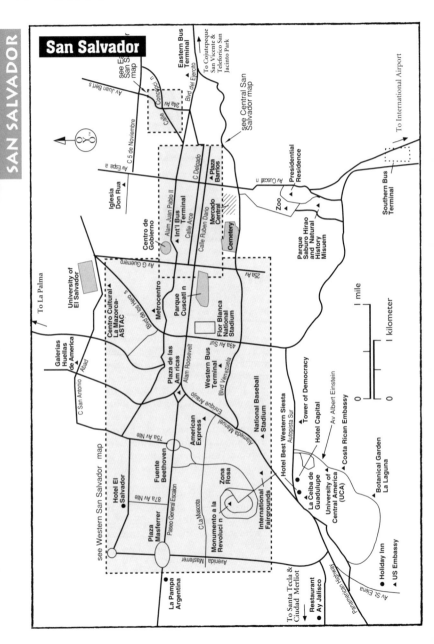

and San Salvador was declared capital of the short-lived Central American Republic. The city became El Salvador's capital when the republic collapsed four years later.

San Salvador expanded quickly from the 19th century into the 20th. Telephones and electricity arrived by the 1880s, and the nearby San Salvador Volcano erupted repeatedly over the years. In 1940, about 100,000 people lived in the capital. Fifty years later the figure stood at one million, due in large part to an influx of *campesinos* from the impoverished and war-ravaged countryside.

■ **Recent History.** During the early part of the war, the capital escaped much of the fighting, but in August 1981, the FMLN dynamited eight nearby power stations and left the city without power for ten days. Aside from the psychological effects of a countryside engulfed in war, though, the capital didn't suffer much direct damage during the first half of the 1980s.

Citizens of the capital tried to go on with their lives as usual, but the effects of the war couldn't be ignored. A ten o'clock curfew was imposed and strictly enforced; the Church documented hundreds of cases of people who were killed after being caught violating the curfew. San Salvador's social rhythms were changed as well. Hotels started offering "taps to taps" deals, in which guests who didn't want to venture out after dark paid one price for dinner, dancing and a room for the night. Some people braved the danger and lingered outside in the evenings, to jog, stroll or hold hands.

■ **Earthquake.** This uneasy peace was shattered on October 10, 1986, when an earthquake measuring 7.5 on the Richter scale destroyed buildings throughout the city and closed down most businesses. Hotels and office buildings collapsed, trapping and burying hundreds. The US embassy, the Ministry of Planning and the old Gran Hotel San Salvador were all leveled or badly damaged. Four of six major hospitals were damaged along with thousands of homes, mostly in impoverished neighborhoods where the houses were poorly constructed.

The death toll rose into the hundreds, with tens of thousands injured and hundreds of thousands left homeless. The Salvadoran government appealed to the international community for assistance as it struggled to find adequate sources of water, food and medicine. The army, meanwhile, concerned itself more with staving off a possible guerrilla attack than helping out with the rescue effort, and it declared the city center a restricted zone. Helicopters and army trucks patrolled the streets to prevent the guerrillas from taking advantage of the chaos. In response, the FMLN declared a cease-fire in the capital during the emergency.

■ **Fighting Reaches the Capital.** The FMLN succeeded in bringing the war to San Salvador in 1989. The rebels' original plans entailed simultaneous attacks on Usulután, San Miguel, Zacatecoluca, Santa Ana and San Salvador in an effort to instigate a popular uprising. They attacked on the eve of a holiday, when many soldiers were scheduled for weekend leave. The army found out ahead of time, however, canceled the leave and placed its units on alert.

As a result, the attacks on Santa Ana, Zacatecoluca and Usulután failed, and only San Miguel and San Salvador were jeopardized. In San Salvador, the guerrillas uncharacteristically stormed wealthy neighborhoods to tempt the army into bombing the homes of its major supporters, since earlier in the war the government had bombed poor neighborhoods occupied by the FMLN. President Cristiani's house in Colonia Escalón was one of the first attacked by the rebels.

The army didn't take the bait, however, and contented itself with driving the guerrillas out of the city slowly rather than trying to crush them outright. Only 200 soldiers were sent to fight and, when they failed, the army resorted to strategic air strikes. Although some wealthy residents later complained of air attacks on their neighborhoods, the northern and western sections of San Salvador suffered minimal damage during the occupation.

Though the guerrillas controlled as much as ten percent of the city at one point, they were driven out in part because they missed an opportunity to attack the Salvadoran Air Force at the nearby Ilopango airport. Also, San Salvador's population proved to be less than thrilled by the guerrillas' attempt to initiate a general uprising. City residents simply wanted the guerrillas to leave and to take the fighting elsewhere. In all, about 700 people died in the fighting in San Salvador, including almost 100 civilians. Two thousand people were wounded, half of them civilians, and emergency shelters were packed with more than 2,500 refugees.

# San Salvador Now

The geographic, economic and political heart of El Salvador is probably the dirtiest, most crowded and most dangerous place in the country, but it also offers things that you won't find anywhere else. With a little patience, you can find almost anything in San Salvador, and since you can't really avoid the capital anyway, you might as well make the best of it.

Most of the tremors that hit the area come courtesy of the San Salvador Volcano which towers to the west, though the political and sociological earthquakes are all homemade. It's reassuring to know that this concrete jungle is only 30 minutes from the beaches near La Libertad and the shores of nearby Lago de Ilopango, both or which are good places to escape to if you're in the city for a while.

San Salvador is Central America's most densely populated city, with an amazing 1.7 million residents if you count everyone in the middle-class suburbs and ragged shantytowns that surround the city. People from all over the country come to the capital in search of work. Now that the war is over, many have moved back to the countryside, but unemployment in the city is still high. People get by, though, and you'll find vendors hawking everything imaginable on most street corners.

First impressions of San Salvador aren't usually positive. The pollution, the noise, the chaos and the crowds can be overwhelming at times. Crime is a problem, especially downtown near the Plaza Barrios. You won't see many people out on the streets at night, which is unsettling in such a major city. Sometimes the city can be incredibly frustrating-try to stay calm when you find out that traffic is backed up for ten blocks because workmen are repairing a pothole in the busiest intersection of the city during rush hour. Even the more exclusive western neighborhoods, although clean, are more sterile than inviting. Colonia San Benito, for example, has high walls, wide, empty streets and few people in sight besides guards.

On the other hand, San Salvador is handily located right in the center of the country, within a day's travel of anywhere and conveniently close to the international airport. The city is packed with hotels, from five stars to no stars. You'll find almost every type of restaurant you could imagine here, including *pupuserías* and $20-a-plate gourmet eateries with piano bars and crystal glassware. San Salvador offers the best—some would say only—nightlife in

## Swinging in San Salvador

**W**hat the Pipils knew as Zalcuatitán, or "Valley of the Feathered Serpent," the Spanish renamed Valle de las Hamacas, or "Valley of the Hammocks." The more accurate (if less poetic) name came from the observation that the area swings like a hammock every time an earthquake or volcano strikes. San Salvador was first flattened by an earthquake in 1575, and averaged two or more each century for the next 300 years.

Soon after San Salvador was declared the capital of El Salvador, the quake of 1854 destroyed most of the city's buildings and stirred debate about whether the government should move its capital to a more stable location. In the end, the government decided to rebuild in the same area, although it restricted buildings to two stories. Even though buildings have been constructed taller than that since then, Salvadorans have learned that in the swinging confines of their capital, shorter buildings are safer buildings.

the country, with many places worth checking out after hours. Museums and galleries are good for quiet Sunday afternoons, and there are usually games being played in the city's various stadiums. You can even go hiking nearby, either along the paths of the botanical garden at La Caldera or on the slopes of the San Salvador Volcano (see Santa Tecla).

On the whole, although San Salvador's crowds, crime and pollution may make you tense, you'll find there's plenty to do. The city is a convenient base from which to explore the country and will keep you occupied for days—whether you want it to or not.

# Orientation

San Salvador can be a confusing concrete jungle at times. It does have enough of an order, though, that if you take a moment to learn what makes it tick—which way numbers go, what major roads cross and leave the city and where the major landmarks are situated—you'll find that getting around isn't too difficult after all.

■ **Landmarks.** If you ever get lost, you won't travel far before bumping into one of these, so it's a good idea to know where some of them are. On the West San Salvador map, west to east along the Paseo Escalón you'll find the Plaza Masferrer, the Fuente Beethoven and the Plaza de las Américas with the statue of El Salvador del Mundo. Metrocentro is north a few blocks on 49a Av/Blvd de los Héroes, and the Zona Rosa restaurant and nightlife district is tucked in between Paseo Escalón and Alameda Araujo to the southwest. If you ever want to know which way is west look for the volcano, unless you are in Santa Elena or Ciudad Merliot, in which case this rule doesn't work.

The Central San Salvador map contains most of the major sites of the city, with the Metropolitan Cathedral (which is the exact city center), National Palace, National Library, National Theater and central market squeezed within two blocks of the Plaza Barrios. The Centro de Gobierno is north off of Alameda Juan Pablo II. A handful of budget hotels and poorer sections of the city are contained in the eastern map. The full San Salvador map lists a few more sites not shown in the other maps, including the University of El Salvador in the north, the zoo and presidential palace to the south and the University of Central America (La UCA) to the southwest.

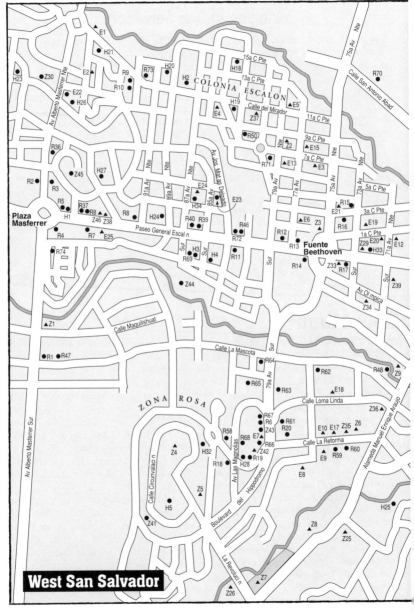

West San Salvador

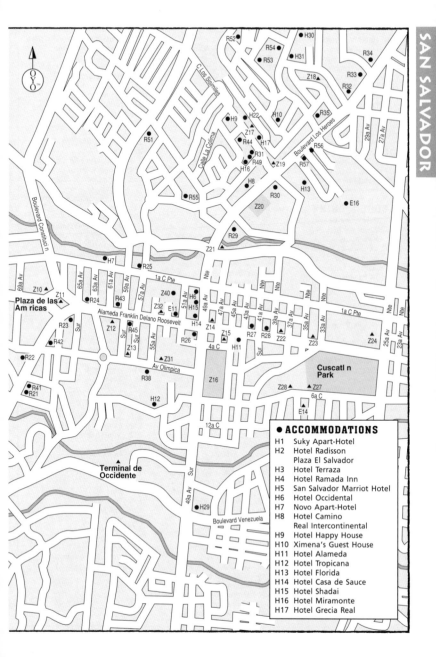

● **ACCOMMODATIONS**

H1  Suky Apart-Hotel
H2  Hotel Radisson
     Plaza El Salvador
H3  Hotel Terraza
H4  Hotel Ramada Inn
H5  San Salvador Marriot Hotel
H6  Hotel Occidental
H7  Novo Apart-Hotel
H8  Hotel Camino
     Real Intercontinental
H9  Hotel Happy House
H10  Ximena's Guest House
H11  Hotel Alameda
H12  Hotel Tropicana
H13  Hotel Florida
H14  Hotel Casa de Sauce
H15  Hotel Shadai
H16  Hotel Miramonte
H17  Hotel Grecia Real

**SAN SALVADOR**

H18  Hotel Mediterraneo Plaza
H19  Hostal Verona
H20  Hotel Casa Blanca
H21  Hostal Lonigo
H22  Villa Real Guest House
H23  Hotel Meyers Guest House
H24  Escalón Plaza Hotel
H25  Los Abetos 15 Hotel
H26  Hotel Nice & Easy
H27  Hotel Hacienda Santa Fe
H28  Hotel Princess
H29  Hotel Venecia
H30  Casa de Huéspedes Torogoz
H31  International Guest House
H32  Hotel Maria Jose
H33  Hotel Mariscal
H34  Hotel Posada del Rey

● **FOOD & DRINK**

R1   Restuarant Del Arbol/El
     Arbol del Diós
R2   Kalpatarú
R3   Cardisi's Ice Cream
R4   Burger King
R5   Daruma
R6   La Panetiere
R7   La Pampa Argentina
R8   China Town
R9   El Rosai
R10  Kamakura
R11  La Diligencia
R12  Jau Sin
R13  El Bodegón
R14  Las Carnitas de Don Carlos
R15  Restaurant China Inn
R16  Gino's Pizza
R17  Wendy's
R18  Restaurant Dynasty
R19  Basilea Restaurant
R20  Pizza Hut
R21  Pizza Boom
R22  Toto's Pizza
R23  Burger King
R24  Pizza Hut
R25  Chef's Restaurant and Bar
R26  China Palace
R27  La Fuente de Salud
R28  Cafe de Don Pedro
R29  Pueblo Viejo
R30  Restaurant Doña Mercedes
R31  Restaurant Asia
R32  Pupeseria Margot
R33  El Corral Steakhouse
R34  Rio Bravo
R35  Vesuvio Pizzeria
R36  Ultima Alucinacion
R37  Restaurant Hunan
R38  Port Restaurant
R39  Biggest
R40  Mr. Donut
R41  La Tablita
R42  Señor Tenedor

R43  Pollo Campero
R44  Restaurant Acajutla
R45  Pop's Ice Cream
R46  Chilis Burgers
R47  Tipicos Margot
R48  Texas Ranch
R49  La Hola Beto's
R50  La Carreta
R51  Neskazarra
R52  Salvatore's
R53  La Fajita
R54  El Establo
R55  Tipicos Miramonte
R56  El Sopon Tipico
R57  La Posada de Abilio
R58  Guadalajara Grill
R59  Porto Fino
R60  A lo Nuestro
R61  Paradise
R62  Los Ranchos
R63  La Media Concha
R64  Coconut Grove
R65  Ole Tasco
R66  La Cantineta Bar/El
     Arriero Steak House
R67  Cuatro Gatti
R68  Shaw's
R69  Capri
R70  La Ventana
R71  El Charrua
R72  Vittorios
R73  Plaza Seoul
R74  Piedras Calientes

▲ **OTHER**

Z1   Genesis 7 Curiosidades
Z2   Las Columnas Centro
     de Artes
Z3   Cines Gemelos Beethoven
Z4   Monument a la Revolucion
Z5   Galería 1-2-3
Z6   Plaza San Benito
Z7   International Fairgrounds
Z8   Mercado Nacional
     de Artesanias
Z9   American Express office
Z10  TACA Airlines headquar-
     ters, Cines Caribe
Z11  El Salvador del Mundo
Z12  American Airlines office
Z13  El Laberinto Gallery
Z14  Esso Automarket
Z15  Laundromat
Z16  Flor Blanca National
     Stadium
Z17  Laundromat
Z18  La Luna Casa y Arte
Z19  El Mundo Feliz
     Amusement Park
Z20  Metrocentro/Continental
     Airlines office
Z21  Metrosur shopping center

Z22  Artisans of El Salvador store
Z23  Military Compound
Z24  Hospital
Z25  National Baseball Stadium
Z26  David J Guzmán
     National Museum
Z27  Tin Marin Museum
Z28  National Gymnasium
Z29  Galerias
Z30  Societa Dante Alighieri
Z31  Credomatic
Z32  Copa Airlines
Z33  Casino
Z34  Fundacion Maria de Nunez
Z35  Centro Cultural de España
Z36  Loma Linda Shopping
     Center
Z37  Antiguedades Rosenthal
Z38  Casino Tropicana
Z39  Patronato Pro
     Patrimonio Cultural
Z40  La Alianza Francesca
Z41  CORSATUR
Z42  Punto Literario
Z43  Rinconcito's
Z44  Centro de Estudios
     Brasileños
Z45  Academia Europa
Z46  British Club

▲ **EMBASSIES**

E1   Columbia
E2   Chile
E3   Venezuela
E4   Mexico
E5   Argentina
E6   Ecuador
E7   Brazil
E8   Canada
E9   Uruguay
E10  Spain
E11  Panama
E12  Nicaragua
E13  Peru
E14  Honduras
E15  Germany
E16  Belize
E17  Italy
E18  Japan
E19  France
E20  The Netherlands
E21  Belgium
E22  Korea
E23  Greece
E24  Israel
E25  United Kingdom

■ **Streets and Avenues.** San Salvador's streets are laid out in a somewhat logical, generally grid-like fashion; the only real problem is that many of the city's main roads keep switching names every few dozen blocks. Like most Salvadoran cities, San Salvador has *avenidas* ("avenues") which run north to south. Avenida Cuscatlán/España is the main avenue, and consequently it has two different names; one each for its northern and southern halves. Even-numbered *avenidas* increase east of Avenida Cuscatlán/España. West of Avenida Cuscatlán/España, *avenidas* are numbered with increasing odd numbers. The unofficial outer routes of San Salvador are Avenida Masferrer to the west and the Terminal Occidente to the east, while 49a Avenida divides the city roughly in half.

Likewise, *calles* ("streets") run east to west. Calle Delgado/Arce divides all even (to the south) and odd (to the north) *calles*. The unofficial northern and southern limits of the city are Autopista Sur to the south and Calle San Antonio Abad to the north. The busiest *calle* has three different names: it starts out as Calle Rubén Darío in the city center, then changes to Alameda Franklin Delano Roosevelt near 25a Av as it heads west, and finally becomes Paseo General Escalón as it passes the Plaza de las Américas heading towards the Plaza Masferrer. Calle Delgado/Arce, one block north of Calle Darío/Alameda FDR/Paseo Escalón, is named Delgado in the city center, and changes to Calle Arce as it passes Avenida Cuscatlán/España heading west. Boulevard Venezuela, which has recently been reconstructed with several overpasses to speed traffic along, is another important east-west artery.

Really, it's simple once you get the hang of it. Avenida Cuscatlán/España and Calle Delgado/Arce bisect the city, meeting one block north of the Plaza Barrios in the heart of the city. Paseo General Escalón with its nice houses, Boulevard de los Héroes with its restaurants, nightlife and malls and Avenida Juan Pablo II in front of the Centro de Gobierno are the city's other main roads.

■ **Leaving San Salvador.** Many roads lead out of San Salvador in every direction. Leading out of the city to the north is 24a Av/Calle Concepción (which becomes the Troncal del Norte), which heads first to Apopa and then on to the departments of Cuscatlán and Cabañas and eventually the Honduran border. The Boulevard del Ejército runs east out of the city and joins the Panamerican Highway, before continuing on to San Vicente. Avenida Cuscatlán (which turns into Avenida de los Diplomáticos but is usually referred to as the Comalapa Highway by locals) and 49a Av head southeast out of the city towards the airport and the Costa del Sol.

You'll find another route south if you're heading west and you make a left (to the south) at the Plaza de las Américas and El Salvador del Mundo, toward Santa Tecla along Alameda Manuel Enrique Araujo. Once you leave the city you can either turn off to the south toward La Libertad or continue to the west towards Santa Ana.

■ **Bus Terminals.** The Terminal de Occidente (western terminal) on Boulevard Venezuela is south of the Plaza de las Américas. The Terminal de Oriente (eastern terminal) is on the Boulevard del Ejército on the north side of the notoriously congested Plaza Arce. A big factory sits like a fort between the terminal and Boulevard del Ejército. The Terminal del Sur is south of the center in the suburb of San Marcos. International bus stops are scattered around town with the main activity at the Puerto Bus terminal across from the Centro de Gobierno.

■ **Neighborhoods.** The city is basically divided into the richer west, up near the volcano, and the poorer east. The small streets around Paseo General Escalón west of the Plaza de las Américas and Colonia San Benito near the Zona Rosa are filled with some of the city's fanciest houses plus some of the best restaurants and nightlife. Here, empty

**SAN SALVADOR**

## Gang Trouble

**G**ang violence in cities like Los Angeles and New York has spurred the US government to deport many of its worst offenders back to their native countries. For some Salvadorans with a history of violence and arrests, that means a return trip to El Salvador.

This forced repatriation is difficult both for the deportees and for their country. El Salvador isn't equipped to deal with gangs, and the deportees find that life back in their native country isn't so easy. To ease the transition, many of the members do what comes naturally to them to survive: they form new gangs in El Salvador.

Many young Salvadorans view gang members with a mixture of fear, awe and admiration. With their foreign clothes and confident swagger, gang members are easily able to find recruits among the country's undereducated and unemployed youth. As Salvadoran gangs become larger and their tactics more violent, the cycle of violence begun to the north gradually returns home.

streets are lined with trees, flowers, high walls, security cameras and barbed wire. Less wealthy areas of San Salvador, especially near the Terminal Oriente and around the central market, can be dangerous (this is where most of the gang activity takes place) so take a taxi at night, try to travel in a group during the day, and keep your guard up all the time. In recent years, the National Advisory Board for Culture and the Arts (CONCUL-TURA) along with the municipality of San Salvador has been working to spruce up the city's historic center. It is still pretty run down, but this could be a turning point.

The capital has grown considerably over the past five years, especially to the southwest where the thriving Ciudad Merliot fills in what used to be a gap between San Salvador and Santa Tecla. Also, the Santa Elena area, around the US Embassy, has become thoroughly suburbanized with wide streets surrounded by trees, parks and new businesses.

Inexpensive restaurants are scattered throughout central San Salvador, while more pricey ones sit along the Paseo General Escalón and in the Zona Rosa. Others, including many steak houses and restaurants with nightly entertainment, are set along the Boulevard de los Héroes. You'll find inexpensive and medium-priced hotels in the center and in the east, while the most expensive hotels are scattered throughout the city.

😊 😊 😊 😊 😊

# Accommodations
## LUXURY HOTELS

**Holiday Inn** (Full San Salvador map) This modern 132-room hotel is just north of the US embassy in Santa Elena and has all the facilities you would expect for this price including a pool, gym, restaurant/bar, and business center. Probably your best choice if you are travelling by helicopter since they have not one, but two heliports. Best value in this category. (*Tel 241-4000, 247-7000, fax 247-7070, e-mail holisal@saltel.net; 128 rooms, S $75, D $85, 4 suites, $115; all with private bath, hot water; AC, cable TV; phone; laundry; pool; restaurant; bar*)

**Hotel Best Western Siesta** (Full San Salvador map) This small luxury hotel next to the Ceiba de Guadalupe has a small pool with an interesting fountain. It's pleasant, but for what they're asking you'd expect a little more. *(Tel 278-5266, 243-8858; 88 rooms, S $76, D $82, suits $98, all with private bath, hot water, AC, cable TV, phone; laundry; pool; casino; restaurant, bar)*

**Hotel Camino Real Intercontinental** (West San Salvador map) Same class as the Hotel Radisson Plaza El Salvador, just a bit older, although many rooms and furnishings are new. It is a popular spot for foreigners here on business. You can enjoy live music at the bar every night, and *mariachi* music and a buffet by the pool on Wednesday and Friday evenings. *(Tel 211-3333, fax 211-4444, e-mail camino.ventas@salnet.net; 228 rooms, S/D $130, 6 suites $250, all with private bath, hot water, AC, cable TV, phone; laundry; pool; sauna; gym; restaurant, café, bar)*

**Hotel Princess** (West San Salvador map) A new hotel aimed at businessmen with a good location in the Zona Rosa. Service and facilities are all high class, as you would expect at this price. *(Tel 298-4550, fax 298-4500, e-mail hotelprincess@ejje.com; 210 rooms, D $130, 6 suite, $185, all with private bath, hot water, AC, cable TV, phone; laundry; pool; spa; gym; restaurant, café, bar)*

**Hotel Radisson Plaza El Salvador** (West San Salvador map) The poshest hotel in El Salvador sits right next to the World Trade Center. All the rooms in the new tower have top-rate facilities, with electronic key cards and the country's only fire extinguisher system that meets US standards. Rooms on the north side have great views of the San Salvador Volcano and all have original Salvadoran art on the walls. Guests have access to the swimming pool; tennis, squash and racquetball courts, gym and business center. *(Tel 257-0777, fax 257-0777; 240 rooms D $130, 15 suites $185, all with private bath, hot water, AC, cable TV, phone; laundry; pool; four restaurants, bar)*

**Hotel Terraza** (West San Salvador map) This hotel's long-term overhaul was finally completed in 1999 and it is now no longer so overpriced for what you get. The restaurants are both quite good too and the price includes a full buffet breakfast. *(Tel 263-0044; 80 rooms, S $74, D $80, all with private bath, hot water; laundry; pool; 2 restaurants; bar)*

**San Salvador Marriot Hotel** (West San Salvador map) Much improved since being privatized and taken over by the Marriot chain. It has a very good view out over the pool. *(Tel 283-4000, fax 283-4040, e-mail sansalvador.marriot@salnet.net; 226 rooms S $99, D $110, 8 suites $253; all with private bath, hot water, AC, cable TV, phone; laundry; pool; sauna; massage parlor; 3 restaurants, bar)*

## HOTELS IN WESTERN SAN SALVADOR

**Casa de Huéspedes Torogoz** A pleasant and reasonably cheap hotel that is often full. They offer internet access and Spanish classes. *(Tel 225-1656, 235-4173, e-mail eltorogoz@vianet.com.sv; 5 rooms, D $13 with shared bath, $18 with private bath, cable TV; laundry; restaurant)*

**Escalón Plaza Hotel** This is a classy, yet cozy B&B in a good location and the service is impeccable. *(Tel 263-7480, 263-7482, fax 263-7464, e-mail aimee@sal.gbm.net; 15 rooms, S $56.50, D $67.80, including continental breakfast, private bath, hot water, AC, cable TV; laundry; restaurant; bar)*

SAN SALVADOR

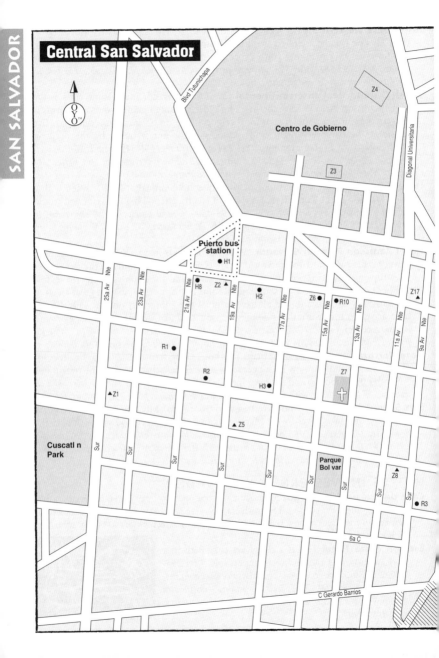

**Central San Salvador**

Centro de Gobierno

Z4

Z3

Blvrd Tutunichapa

Diagonal Universitaria

Puerto bus station

● H1

25a Av

23a Av Nte

21a Av Nte

19a Av Nte

17a Av Nte

15a Av Nte

13a Av Nte

11a Av Nte

9a Av Nte

● H8    Z2 ▲

● H2

Z6 ●

● R10

Z17 ▲

R1 ●

R2 ●

H3 ●

▲ Z1

Z7 ✝

▲ Z5

Cuscatln Park

Sur    Sur    Sur    Sur    Sur

Parque Bol var

Sur

▲ Z8

Sur

● R3

6a C

C Gerardo Barrios

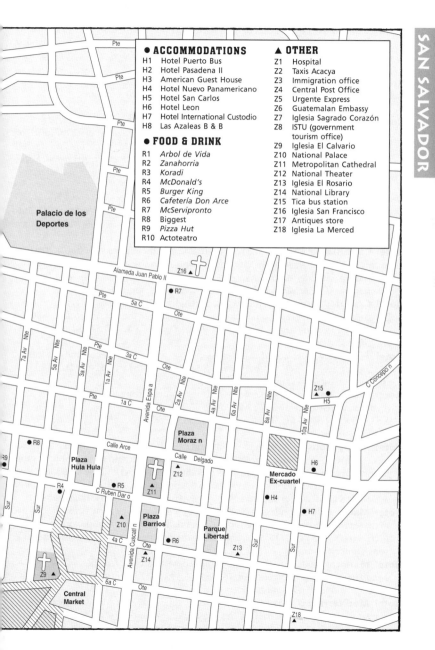

## ● ACCOMMODATIONS

H1  Hotel Puerto Bus
H2  Hotel Pasadena II
H3  American Guest House
H4  Hotel Nuevo Panamericano
H5  Hotel San Carlos
H6  Hotel Leon
H7  Hotel International Custodio
H8  Las Azaleas B & B

## ● FOOD & DRINK

R1  *Arbol de Vida*
R2  *Zanahorria*
R3  *Koradi*
R4  *McDonald's*
R5  *Burger King*
R6  *Cafetería Don Arce*
R7  *McServipronto*
R8  *Biggest*
R9  *Pizza Hut*
R10 Actoteatro

## ▲ OTHER

Z1  Hospital
Z2  Taxis Acacya
Z3  Immigration office
Z4  Central Post Office
Z5  Urgente Express
Z6  Guatemalan Embassy
Z7  Iglesia Sagrado Corazón
Z8  ISTU (government tourism office)
Z9  Iglesia El Calvario
Z10 National Palace
Z11 Metropolitan Cathedral
Z12 National Theater
Z13 Iglesia El Rosario
Z14 National Library
Z15 Tica bus station
Z16 Iglesia San Francisco
Z17 Antiques store
Z18 Iglesia La Merced

**Hostal Lonigo** This quiet hotel defines itself with personalized service. Reservations must be made at least two days in advance and discounts are available for extended stays. *(Tel 264-4193, e-mail hotellonigo@vianet.com.sv; 19 rooms, S $56.50, D $68 with private bath, hot water, AC, cable TV; pool; laundry)*

**Hostal Verona** A quiet hotel with good service. *(Tel 264-6035, e-mail hostalverona@tel-sal.net; 14 rooms, S $50.85, D $62.15, T $73.45, private bath, hot water, AC, cable TV; internet service; laundry; cafe)*

**Hotel Alameda** Once an old, crumbling overpriced hotel it has been completely modernized into a good place to stay. La Mansion restaurant is a good place for lunch or dinner (or take room service) and the Cavalier bar has dancing on Fridays and Saturdays. *(Tel 260-0299, 260-1199, e-mail hotelalameda@salnet.net; 105 rooms, S $65, D $70, T$79, all with private bath, hot water, AC, cable TV; laundry; pool; sauna; restaurant 6:30am-10:30pm, bar)*

**Hotel Capital** (Full San Salvador map) A new and reasonably priced (for what you get) hotel aimed at business people. The rooftop pool perched atop the eight-story building is a nice touch. *(Tel 247-7100; 60 rooms, S $58.50, D $67.80, private bath, hot water, AC, cable TV; pool; laundry; restaurant; bar)*

**Hotel Casa Blanca** Although the rooms are fine and the service good the best aspect of this hotel is the view of the city and volcano from the balcony and sitting room. Prices drop with long-term stays. *(Tel 263-2545; 8 rooms, S $40, D $45 including continental breakfast, private bath, hot water, AC, cable TV; laundry; restaurant)*

**Hotel Casa del Sauce** Large rooms and a friendly staff make this hotel a good mid-range choice. Try to get a room in the back though, since those in the front tend to be a bit noisy. Prices are negotiable. *(Tel 260-6192; 8 rooms, S $24, D $28.50; private bath, AC, cable TV; laundry)*

**Hotel Florida** A hotel aimed at business people with small rooms and a pleasant rooftop terrace. *(Tel 260-2540; 20 rooms, S $20 D $25 with fan, S $24.50 D $30.50 with shared bath, cable TV; laundry; café)*

**Hotel Grecia Real** Parents take note—this new hotel distinguishes itself with a children's play area. *(Telefax 260-1820, 261-0577, e-mail hotelgr@telemovil.net; 45 rooms, S $33, D $38, plus $5 for AC, all with private bath, hot water, cable TV, phone; laundry; pool; restaurant; bar)*

**Hotel Happy House** A step up in quality and price from the bargain hotels, this place seems to live up to its name. The little green garden, furniture and stereo are out of some happy 1970s home. The management is friendly (even happy) and the rooms are large, but the beds and bathrooms could stand to be modernized. *(Tel 260-8633; 15 rooms S $28.50, D $30, all with private bath, hot water, AC, cable TV; laundry; restaurant)*

**Hotel Maria Jose** A spotless, new B&B with a comfortable sitting area. The owner manages the place and pays attention to the smallest details when providing service. *(Tel 263-4790; 8S $49, 3D $59, includes breakfast, private bath, hot water, AC, cable TV; pool; laundry; restaurant; bar)*

**Hotel Mariscal** Modern rooms come equipped with kitchen facilities. *(Tel 298-2844, e-mail hotelmariscal@hotmail.com; 16 rooms, S $40, D $73, private bath, hot water, AC, cable TV; laundry; restaurant; bar)*

**Hotel Mediterraneo Plaza** Combining the architecture of a Mediterranean coastal mansion with all the modern facilities you could want and personal service makes for a great place to stay. Taking your meals in the tropical garden beneath the shade of coconut palms and mango trees is another great touch. *(Tel 264-2444, e-mail mediplaz@salnet.net; 16 rooms S $62, D $68, 2 suites $90, all with private bath, hot water, AC, cable TV; pool; sauna, Jacuzzi; gym; laundry; restaurant; bar)*

**Hotel Miramonte** All of the rooms are large and comfortable but you should try to get one with a balcony to fully enjoy the quiet neighborhood. *(Tel 260-1880, 261-0536; 17 rooms S $31.50 D $39 with fan, S $34.50 D $44 with AC, all have private bath, hot water, cable TV; laundry)*

**Hotel Myers Guest House** A spacious old home with a beautiful garden has been converted to a B&B. The price includes a continental breakfast and 15 minutes of free internet. *(Tel 264-6725; 10 rooms, S $45, D $50; private bath, hot water, AC, cable TV; laundry; restaurant; bar)*

**Hotel Nice & Easy** This new hotel has clean simple rooms in a quiet neighborhood. *(Tel 263-4175; 8 rooms, S $50, D $60 includes breakfast, private bath, hot water, AC, cable TV; laundry; restaurant; bar)*

**Hotel Occidental** This homey place looks like...somebody's home, with patio, courtyard, knickknacks on the shelves and pictures on the walls. The rooms are spacious and clean with large bathrooms. *(Tel 260-5724; 10 rooms S $17.25, D $20, T $22.80, with private bath, cable TV, fan)*

**Hotel Posada del Rey** Designed in a colonial style with spacious rooms it has ample facilities for those in town on business. *(Tel 264-5244; 11 rooms, S $60, D $70 including breakfast, private bath, hot water, AC, cable TV; laundry; restaurant)*

**Hotel Shadai** A small establishment with clean rooms at a good price. *(Tel 260-5747; 8 rooms, S $17, D $19.50, private bath, fans, cable TV; café)*

**Hotel Tropicana** A new hotel offering comfortable rooms in a quiet neighborhood. The large patio surrounded by tropical plants. *(Tel 223-7625, 224-4379; 18 rooms, S $23, D $34, T $51, all with private bath, hot water, cable TV, AC; pool; laundry; restaurant; bar)*

**International Guest House** Very similar in price and quality to the nearby Casa de Huéspedes Torogoz plus the price includes breakfast. *(Tel 226-7343; 10 rooms, D $18 with private bath, cable TV, phone)*

## An Organic Experience

The same friendly people who run Ximena's Guest House in the capital also operate the 25-hectare Finca Organica Las Termopilas ("Hot Springs Organic Farm") in the countryside just 25 minutes to the north of San Salvador. The farm produces some 40 different fruits and vegetables, honey, and coffee, plus they make the traditional adobe bricks. Nature lovers will also appreciate the wildlife that makes its home in this reforested oasis.

In the midst of a large, exotic garden is the rustic Hotel Lisa Guest House. The spacious double rooms with private baths are $22 per couple while a bed in the dorm is just $5 per person. Both have hot showers. Much of the food produced here is destined for the farm's La Posada de John Paul restaurant.

If you want a fully organic experience you have the option of working on the farm to cover the cost of your room and board. Whether you want to work, or just relax this, is a fantastic place to get away from the hectic pace of the capital. Contact Ximena's Guest House in San Salvador for reservations and information.

**Las Azaleas B&B** Small, clean, quiet, and friendly; just about everything you could want. Plus, the garden is full of its namesake flower. *(Tel 225-7616; 6 rooms from $20, private bath, hot water, cable TV; laundry; café)*

**Los Abetos 15 Hotel** The quiet neighborhood and pleasant garden are a nice touch on top of the clean and airy rooms. *(Tel 298-4420; 9 rooms, S $35, D $45 includes buffet breakfast, private bath, hot water, cable TV; restaurant)*

**Novo Apart-Hotel** A decent, well-kept, long-term place to stay. The staff is very helpful and the sculptures out by the kidney-shaped pool are worth a look. Hammocks swing next to the pleasant grassy courtyard. If you just want a short stay there are big discounts on weekends. *(Tel 260-2288, fax 260-5053, e-mail informacion@novoapart-hotel.com; 50 rooms, S $55, D $60, all with private bath, hot water, AC, kitchenettes)*

**Ramada Inn** The Ramada offers a back home feel and rooms with balconies. *(Tel 263-0033, fax 263-4099; 21 rooms S $62, D $68.50, all with private bath, hot water, AC, TV, telephone; laundry; pool; restaurant, bar, café)*

**Suky Apart-Hotel** Fully-furnished apartments with small kitchens and full baths intended for rent by the week, but they take short term rental too. *(Tel 263-6218; 10D $66, all with private bath, hot water, kitchen, cable TV; laundry)*

**Villa Real Guest House** An old home converted into a hotel with large rooms and friendly owners. *(Tel 260-1579; e-mail villarealsv@netscape.net; 10 rooms S $26, D $40 all with private bath, hot water, cable TV; pool)*

**Ximena's Guest House** This revitalized place is a favorite with American and European backpackers for its relaxed atmosphere and friendly management. Guests have access to a large common room with cable TV and VCR plus they will store your luggage free of charge while you are exploring the rest of the country. Lisa, Lena and René are a wealth of knowledge about San Salvador and eco-tourism throughout El Salvador. The Spanish school Cihuatan operates out of here and you can get 20 hours of language classes for $75. *(Tel 260-2481, fax 260-2427, e-mail ximenas@navegante.com.sv; 15 rooms, dorm $4, S $22, D $30, T$45, with private bath, hot water, cable TV, AC; laundry; restaurant)*

## HOTELS IN SANTA ELENA

**Casa Austria Guest House** Just south of the embassy is this friendly and comfortable hotel where you will be made to feel right at home. *(Final Blvd Sta Elena, C Jucuarán Políg G #1; tel 278-3401, fax 263-7431; 16 rooms, S $50, D $60, T $70 including breakfast, private bath, hot water, AC, cable TV; internet access; laundry; restaurant; bar)*

**Hotel Berlin** This new European-style B&B, located just behind the US Embassy, has immaculate rooms and the owners speak English and German as well as Spanish. Guests can use the health center next door for a small fee. *(Av El Espino #62 y 64; tel 243-8877, fax 243-8872; 12 rooms S $60, D $70 including breakfast, private bath, hot water, AC, cable TV; internet access; laundry; restaurant; bar)*

## HOTELS IN CENTRAL SAN SALVADOR

**American Guest House** The classic backpacker's hotel in the center of town. This weird, groovy place has the atmosphere and odor of life at the turn of the century, with gold wallpaper and antique TVs. The managers are friendly and they have a storage room. *(Tel 271-0224; 11 rooms, S $11.50 with shared bath, S $17.25, D $20, with private bath, hot water; laundry; restaurant)*

**Hotel Internacional Custodio** Reasonably new, simple, clean, comfortable and just two blocks from the Tica Bus terminal. What more can a budget traveler ask for? *(Tel 221-5810; 13 rooms, S $4.50, D $5.75 with shared bath, D $9.25 with private bath; laundry; cafeteria)*

**Hotel Leon** Not as nice as the San Carlos or as comfy as the Panamericano, but cheaper than either and this is one of the few places where the higher your room is the lower the price. *(Tel 222-0951; 38 rooms $4/$5.25/$6.90 for 1/2/3 people without fan, +$1 for fan, +$2 to be on first floor; laundry)*

**Hotel Nuevo Panamericano** Well-run and comfortable, but a little pricey for the quality of the rooms. *(Tel 221-1199; 27 rooms $8.80-$11.50 depending on size, location and TV, with private bath, fan, AC; laundry)*

**Hotel Pasadena II** This clean, inexpensive hotel just south of the Puerto Bus terminal, surrounds a tiny concrete courtyard. *(Tel 221-4786; 16 rooms, S $10.50, D $15, T$18.30, all with private bath, fan)*

**Hotel Puerto Bus** On the second floor of the Puerto Bus terminal, this hotel is spotless, convenient, impersonal, and overpriced. It's a good choice if you need to catch an early morning bus to Honduras, Nicaragua or Costa Rica or arrive by bus late at night. However, you can take a cab across town to a similar place and still save money overall. *(Tel 221-1000; 7S $30, 20D $40, 7T $50, all with private bath, hot water, TV, phone, AC; restaurant)*

**Hotel San Carlos** The rooms are a little old and basic but a good deal for the price. Doña Rivera, the owner, runs a tight ship. *(Tel 222-4808; 27 rooms $9.20 per person; laundry)*

## HOTELS IN EASTERN SAN SALVADOR

**Hospedaje Figueroa** Sofas, hammocks and flowering bushes give this place a comfy atmosphere. The rooms are clean and completely bare, and they lock the doors at 10pm. *(Tel 222-1541; 4S $2.85, 17D $4.60, 5D with private bath and fan $6.90-$8)*

**Hospedaje Izalco** A big place that extends back off the street forever. An extra $2.30 will get you cable TV. *(Tel 221-7214; 49 rooms, S $9, D $12, T $17, all with private bath, TV; laundry)*

**Hospedaje Santa Rosa** Clean enough, and a better deal than the Hospedaje Izalco. Grab a beer with the locals next door at Ara's Beer or a bite at the Comedor Centroamerica in front. *(Tel 222-9290; 15D $4.75 with private bath, fan)*

**Hotel Imperial** Big, old, run-down rooms are nonetheless a good bargain. *(Tel 226-7343, 222-4920; 13*

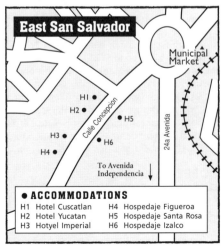

**East San Salvador**

Municipal Market

Calle Concepcion

24a Avenida

H1
H2
H3
H4
H5
H6

To Avenida
Independencia

● **ACCOMMODATIONS**

| H1 Hotel Cuscatlan | H4 Hospedaje Figueroa |
| H2 Hotel Yucatan | H5 Hospedaje Santa Rosa |
| H3 Hotyel Imperial | H6 Hospedaje Izalco |

*rooms with shared bath, 25 rooms with private bath, prices are negotiable, but cheap; laundry; restaurant)*

**Hotel Yucatán** Run by a friendly family that enjoys talking with foreigners. *(Tel 221-2585, 11S $2.85 with private bath, 9D $5.75 with private bath, less for shared bath)*

# Food & Drink

## BELGIAN

**Ultima Alucinacion** A couple from Belgium run this elegant and artsy place with a focus on middle European cuisine. All of the food, from the mushrooms on toast to meat and seafood entrees, are delicious and impeccably presented. Salads go from $4.80 to $7.50 and entrees from $8.50 to $13.25. The small bar offers a large selection of Belgian beers. *(Tel 263-1320; Mon-Sat 12-3pm, 5:30-10pm)*

## BREAKFAST

**Hotel La Terraza Cafe** This covered, open-air dining area is a good choice for breakfast. The menu is pretty standard, but the mushroom omelet is amazing. Prices are much lower than the other large hotels. *(Mon-Sat 7-10am, 12-3pm, 6-10pm)*

See also **Pueblo Viejo** under Salvadoran.

## CHINESE

**Jau Sin** In a big, old house with a few Chinese wooden dividers and wooden chandeliers. Chow mein costs $4.50 and seafood starts at $7. *(Tue-Sun 11am-3pm, 6-11pm)*

**Restaurant China Inn** Another of the city's decent Chinese options. All the usual dishes start at $5. *(12-2:30pm, 5:30-10pm)*

**Restaurant Dynasty** Red neon borders the walls above the tall black screen at this swank Chinese restaurant. You can enjoy sweet and sour shrimp, lemon chicken, or eggplant with chicken inside or outside on the terrace overlooking the Zona Rosa. Main dishes run from $7.50 up to $12.50. *(Tel 263-9955; 12-3pm, 6-11pm except Sun closes 10pm)*

**Restaurant Hunan** Many consider this one of the best Chinese restaurants in Central America. The Hunan Chicken (served with a special wine and spicy pepper sauce), Peking Duck (served with tortillas and eaten like a taco), Mushroom Pork, Cashew Pork, and Orange Chicken are all excellent. Main dishes range from $5 to $16.50 and the all-u-can eat lunch buffet is a steal at $4.50. The dining room, filled with traditional Chinese decoration, has a panoramic view to the south. *(Tel 263-9989; Mon-Fri, 12-3pm, 6-10pm, Sat, 12-3pm, 6-11pm, Sun, 12-4pm)*

## COFFEE/SNACKS

**Cardisi's Ice Cream** Some truly delicious custards and ice creams. Expensive, but worth it. *(11:30am-9pm)*

**La Panetiere** A great sidewalk café with tasty desserts, coffees, crepes, gelatos and sandwiches. The chilled cappuccino comes in various flavors with both high-test and decaf coffee. *(Mon-Sat 10am-6pm)*

**Shaw's** One of the best places in the capital for a coffee or a snack. The coffee cakes, carrot cakes, cheese cakes, blackberry pie, and croissants are all superb. Shaw's also has branches in the Galerias Mall and Metrocentro. *(11am-8pm)*

**Sweets** Light snacks and meals, deserts, and a fantastic orange espresso. *(Locations throughout the city; 9am-6pm)*

## FAST FOOD

**Biggest** A hamburger chain that undercuts the competition with full meal combos from $2. *(Locations throughout the city; 7-10pm)*

**Metrocentro Food Court** This gigantic mall has over 30 fast food joints.

**Pollo Campero** This fried and roasted chicken specialist is one of the country's most popular fast food restaurants. They have many combos which include chicken, french fries, and a beverage for $2.50 or you can buy a whole chicken for about $7. *(Locations throughout the city; 6am-10pm)*

**Pollo Real** A good place for roasted chicken and other typical Salvadoran foods. Two people can share a bird with all the trimmings and drinks for under $10. *(Locations throughout the city; 12-9:30pm)*

## FRENCH

**Neskazarra** As good as Basque food gets outside of France. Main dishes run from $7 to $10.50. *(Tel 260-1106; 12-3pm, 6-10pm)*

## GERMAN

**Piedras Calientes (Hot Rocks) Restaurant** A typical German menu with meat, meat, and more meat. German sausages (Munich and Frankfurt wursts with potato salad) are $4.50 and weinerschnitzel, huntsmen style roast pork, and steaks start at $8. Of course there is also German beer and wine. The service is slow but the food is excellent. *(Tel 263-8778; 12-3pm, 5-9:30pm)*

## GREEK

**Mykonos, La Casa Del Gyro** If you need a gyro fix, Mykonos is there for you. The chicken and beef gyros with *tzatziki* (yogurt and garlic sauce) are served on regular or whole-grain pitas. Their Greek salad, *Kataifi* and *baklava* are also good. A meal here goes for about $5. *(Located in the Galerias Mall; 12-10pm)*

## INTERNATIONAL

**Basilea Restaurant** A comfortable and classy restaurant set on the second floor with a lushly-bordered patio overlooking the Zona Rosa. The menu is renewed periodically with many favorites like the best pepper steak in town and a divine fish almandine plus some pastas and Southwest grill items all of which run from $6 to $16. *(Tel 223-6818; 11am-11pm)*

**La Ventana** A German journalist and a Salvadoran dancer run this popular bistro. A great reading room with a wide selection of newspapers and magazines complements the varied European meals ($6-$8), coffees, wines, and beers. *(Tel 226-5129; Tue-Thur, 8am-1am, Fri-Sat, 8am-2am, Sun 10am-midnight)*

**Paradise Restaurant** One of the most popular but pricier Zona Rosa restaurants.

Mains, like the excellent cheese fondue, start at $10, with shrimp and lobster dishes topping out at $24.50. The interior is decorated with pictures of movie stars and movie posters, but you won't be able to see them clearly since the lights are kept so dim. *(Tel 224-4201; Mon-Sat 12-3pm, 6-11pm)*

## ITALIAN

**Capri**  Good, cheap Italian food. What more could you want. Entrees start at $5.25. *(Mon-Sat 12-2:30pm, 6-10pm)*

**Cuatro Gatti Restaurant**  Located in an old mansion with an elegant, old world décor. The menu is traditional Italian/European with a large selection of pastas (try the gnocchi) running from $7.50 to $16.50. Reservations are essential. *(Tel 223-6027; Mon-Sat 12-3pm, 6-11pm)*

**El Rosal**  In a corner house with a small balcony area overlooking its patio garden, this informal Italian restaurant, now in it's third generation, is packed with simple wooden tables. Lasagna *tres quesos* ("three-cheese lasagna"), spaghetti with meat sauce, and pizzas, all from $4, are cooked fresh to order. *(Mon-Sat 12-9pm)*

**Porto Fino**  A seafood restaurant and an Italian restaurant side by side separated by a nightclub bar. Both get good reviews. *(Tel 223-7289; Mon-Sat 12-3pm, 6-10pm)*

**Salvatore's**  An Italian owner serves up combos from $4 and personal pizzas from $2.85. *(11am-2:30pm, 5:30-10pm)*

**Vesuvio Pizzeria**  Individual wood-fired pizzas for about $4.50 and pastas for $5.50. *(Locations throughout the city; 11:30am-10:30pm)*

## Hash House Harriers

The Hash House Harriers ("a beer drinking club with a running problem") got its start in 1938 in Kuala Lumpur, Malaysia with British rubber plantation workers who added copious beer drinking to the old English sport of the "Hares and Hounds." Today over 1500 clubs in just about every major city in the world have been formed and the Salvadoran chapter has run off and on since 1984. The mixed gender group of hounds follows a roughly seven-kilometer trail in or around San Salvador, or occasionally elsewhere in the country, laid out with flour and chalk by the hares.

Most hashers come from El Salvador's transient European and North American community and because of the beer/cost ratio this is a favorite of many Peace Corp volunteers. The biweekly gathering is a great way to see some different parts of the country and is one of the best ways for a newcomer to meet others and find out what is going on here. The hashers gather every other Saturday at the British Club, usually at noon, and depart to points unknown at 12:30. Six dollars gets you transportation to and from the club and all the beer you can drink. Bring a whistle.

*(For more information check out the SHHH bulletin board at the British Club or the SHHH website (http://webhash.nstemp.com)*

**Vittorios  Restaurant** The fettuccine Alfredo is sinfully rich and altogether too tasty and the spinach stuffed ravioli is simply delicious. Vittorios has both a very pleasant interior, and a lovely covered patio area. Main dishes run from $6.40 to $12.50. *(Tel 263-6267; Mon-Sat 12-2:30pm, 6-10pm)*

## JAPANESE
**Daruma** This Japanese restaurant in the same complex as the Suky Hotel is about as close as El Salvador will get to Japan, apart from some financial aid packages to fix bridges. Sushi dishes average $5.50. *(12-3pm, 6-11pm)*

**Kamakura  Restaurant** This Japanese restaurant welcomes you with sliding wooden doors and offers a small *sushi* bar with fish from $1.85 a piece. Prices for plates like *tempura, yakitori, terkiyaki,* and *sashimi* start at $9 and go way, way up. The Japanese woman who owns Kamakura learned her Spanish back in Japan, then came here to assist in building the international airport and decided to stay. If you can, get one of the tables on the patio where there is a waterfall. *(Tel 223-1274; Mon-Sat 12-3pm, 6-10:30pm)*

## KOREAN
**Plaza Seoul** The only Korean restaurant in the country is also one of the most adventurous dining options. There are over 30 choices on the menu, but it is written in Korean characters with Spanish descriptions of the dish so, unless you are fluent in Spanish choosing from the menu can be a bit of a crapshoot. Thankfully the friendly staff will do their best to help. *Kalbi* and *bulgolgi* go for $9 while sushi tops out at $23. The food is milder than traditional Korean food, but excellent nonetheless. Your choice of where to dine is almost as varied as the menu. Choose traditional tables and chairs indoors, rough-hewn log-tables next to a beautiful garden outdoors and a large, squat table with cushions for sitting on your knees. *(Tel 263-1053; 12-10pm)*

## MEXICAN/TEX-MEX
**Restaurant  Ay  Jalisco** The friendly Ay Jalisco has a large menu of Mexican dishes between $2.25 and $8.50, though if you want it hot, be sure to tell the waiter. They also have premium Mexican beers, *café de olla* (traditional Mexican coffee, hot and sweet with a touch of vanilla and cinnamon), and a wicked margarita. *(Located at the Metrocentro mall and they have another location on C Principal in Colonia Merliot; 12-3pm, 6-10pm)*

**Chili's  Burgers** This aptly named place, popular with local teenagers, serves up Tex-Mex food and a variety of charcoal-grilled hamburgers from $5. *(Mon-Sat 12-3pm, 5:30-10pm)*

**Guadalajara  Grill** Both the food and decorations come from Guadalajara, Mexico. Main courses, including an excellent mole chicken and the Tampiqueña plate, are large and go for around $7. The two outdoor dining areas have good views and are a pleasant place to spend an evening. The dance floor can get quite lively on weekends. *(Tel 263-8413; 12-3pm, 6-11pm)*

**La  Fajita** A good Mexican restaurant with reasonable prices. A quesadilla costs $1.75 and a taco is $3. *(12-3pm, 6-10pm)*

**La  Tablita** All your favorite Mexican dishes cost around $2.50. *(12-3pm, 5:30-10pm)*

**Las Carnitas de Don Carlos** Stylish but traditional, they claim to be the first Tex-Mex restaurant to open in El Salvador. There's a big oven in the center to grill the dishes, which are served by waiters in colorful outfits. Munchies like tacos and fajitas go for about $4. *(Noon-late)*

**Shagul Authentic** Mexican flavor and budget prices. Most items are around $2. *(Metrocentro, 11:30am-8pm)*

## SALVADORAN

**A Lo Nuestro** Gourmet Salvadoran cuisine served in a splendid atmosphere. Any notions that Central America food is always simple will be shattered after just one bite. With prices from $5.25 it's also a good value. *(Tel 223-5116; 12-3pm, 6-10pm)*

**Actoteatro** This new branch of La Luna is one of the best lunch spots in the center. They have simple Salvadoran dishes like chicken platters from $2.50 in an artistic setting often accompanied by live music. *(Open daily for lunch, and for dinner when there is a show on in the adjacent theater)*

**Café de Don Pedro** This open-air restaurant looks like a 1950s drive-up and is a San Salvador classic. It has a wide-open, everyone-knows-everyone feel, with a varied menu that includes everything from inexpensive omelets and soups to filet mignon for $7. Six bottles of beer in a bucket of ice will run you $5.14. Old-timers, mostly men, come here to have coffee and listen to the roaming *mariachi* bands. *(7-10am, 12-2:30pm, 6-9pm)*

**El Establo** A student hangout with typical Salvadoran fare. A bowl of *mondongo* soup, a Salvadoran hangover cure, is $2.90, shrimp goes for $3.15 and the specialty of the house, *cabrito horneado en su salsa* ("young baked goat with sauce"), is $5.90. *(12-3pm, 6-10:30pm)*

**La Carreta Restaurant** This newly renovated restaurant serves above average Salvadoran dishes in a pleasant outdoor dining area. *Tamales*, *enchiladas*, and *pupusas* (both rice and corn) bursting with various fixings start at $1 while steak platters top out at $8.50. *(12-3pm, 6-10pm)*

**La Diligencia** A classic Salvadoran place decorated with stained glass windows and staffed by friendly waiters. Some of their nightly promotions include all-u-can-eat shrimp on Wednesday and 2-for-1 beer and cocktails on Saturday and Sunday. Steaks start at $5, though some entrees go for under $2. *(Tel 264-3160; Mon-Sat 7am-11pm)*

**Pueblo Viejo** Rusted rifles and old photos on the stucco walls give this restaurant an old-world feel in every respect but the price. This place can get loud for such a nice restaurant, especially when soccer games are shown on the big screen TV, but it is always quiet for the excellent $3 breakfast buffet featuring fruit, juices, *platano*, beans, breads, and cooked-to-order omelets. *(Metrocentro; Mon-Sat 6:30am-11pm, except Sat closes 1am)*

**Tipicos Margoth** A popular chain featuring typical Salvadoran dishes like *pupusas*, *chilate*, *nuegados*, *yuca frita*, *enchiladas*, *empanadas*, *platano frito*, *quesadillas*, *tamales de elote*, etc. *(Locations throughout the city; 12-10pm)*

**Tipicos Miramonte** Good food, a varied menu, and low prices; everything you

Top: El Imposible National Park
Bottom: Tazumal

Top: Jaltepeque estuary
Bottom: Traditional farming near San Vicente

need for an enjoyable meal: Basic chicken and fish plates are about $2.50. *(12-2:30pm, 6-10pm)*

## SEAFOOD

**Coconut Groove** Seafood cocktails (conch, crab, octopus, shrimp) are generous and run $5 to $11 and *ceviche* is $4.25 to $6.25. All is served under thatch roofs. *(Tel 264-4914; 12-3pm, 6-10pm except Sat closes 11pm)*

**La Hola Beto's** Hanging nautical artifacts give this crowded seafood and pasta joint a slightly salty air. Prices are a little less than other similar seafood places. A full seafood dinner under the big red awning will be under $10. *(Tel 263-7304; Mon-Sat 12-3pm, 6-11pm)*

**Restaurant Acajutla** Seafood of all varieties is made fresh the moment that you order. Entrees start at $5. *(Tel 263-1722; 12-3pm, 6-10pm except Saturday until 11pm)*

Also see **Porto Fino** under Italian.

## SOUP

**El Sopon Tipico** A typical Salvadoran soup place. Try the bean or the *gallo en chicha* ("chicken in corn beer") soups from $4.25 and up. *(12-3pm, 6-9:30pm)*

## SPANISH

**El Bodegón** Formal, expensive, elegant, and uptight, but undeniably one of the best restaurants in the country. The attention to detail ranges from wooden tables out of some museum to the quiet removal of bread-crumbs. Chef Angel García serves up a constantly changing continental menu with a Spanish flare. Prices, as you would guess, are high with many dishes over $15. Reservations are advisable. *(Tel 264-5143; Mon-Sat 12-3pm, 6-11pm)*

**La Posada de Abilio** Another of the city's pricey Spanish restaurants. Their specialty is *paella valencia*, a rice dish with chicken and shrimp, but the shrimp with garlic is good too. Main dishes average $10. *(Tel 243-1260; 11:30am-11pm)*

**Ole Tasco Restaurant** The Spanish owner-manager serves up a dinner that's the next best thing to a trip to Madrid. Start out with a plate of olives and *tapas* before trying old standbys like *paella* or lamb and *callos a la Madrileña*. Entrees start at $5.70. The outdoor terrace, with its tiled fountain and dark-wood bar all add to the experience. *(Tel 263-7877; 12-3pm, 6-11pm, except Sun closes 10pm)*

## STEAKS

**El Charrua** An Argentinean restaurant with original recipes for such creatures as goat, rabbit, suckling pig, shrimp, and local cuts like *puyaso*. Prices start at around $5 per plate. *(Tel 260-2674; 12-2:30pm, 6-10pm)*

**La Cantineta Bar/El Arriero Steak House** A sidewalk café/bar with an Argentinean steakhouse out back. The *bife de chorizo* ("steak with sausage") costs $10, but is really good. *(Mon-Sat, noon-midnight)*

**La Media Cancha** Get your Central America BBQ starting at about $3. *(Mon-Sat 12-3pm, 6-11pm)*

**La Pampa Argentina** An Argentinean grill that would be right at home on the pampa, aside from the waiters in tuxedos. The rough wood theme is carried over from sign to ceiling to walls, tables and benches. Some of the best steaks in Central America, according to some, start at $5. They also have another branch in Santa Elena just south of the US Embassy. *(Tel 264-0892; Mon-Thur 12-2:30pm, 6-10:30pm, Fri-Sat 12-2:30pm, 6-11pm, 12-3:30pm, 6-9:30pm)*

**Los Ranchos** One of the country's best steak houses, the owners also have restaurants in New York, Miami, and Nicaragua. Nicaraguan cuts of beef are served to perfection. *(Tel 264-5858; 12-3pm, 6-10pm)*

**Rio Bravo** Over 100 rough wood tables fill this steak house which hosts live *salsa* and *merengue* groups on weekends for a $2.85 cover. Tacos are $2.30 and other dishes run from $3.50 to $5.75. *(6pm-2am)*

**Texas Ranch** Barbecued meats (as the name suggests) and shellfish (well, why not). Adding to the mix are exotic international drinks. Prices run from $5.70 to about $11. *(Tel 279-0737; 12-11pm, bar opens at 5pm)*

## VEGETARIAN

**Kalpatarú** Enjoy the same famous coffee, tea and vegetarian food in their new and improved location which combines a health food store and book store. The lunch buffet runs $5.25, and the salad bar goes for half that. Natural fruit juices and daily specials are served. *(Tel 263-1204; 12-9:30pm)*

**Koradi** This health food store/restaurant serves vegetarian meals like soy burgers and whole-wheat pizzas from $4 It's a nice change from the usual Salvadoran and fast food in the center. *(Tel 221-2545; Mon-Fri 8am-5:30pm, Sat 8am-3pm)*

**La Fuente de Salud** Delicious and nutritious, this vegetarian cafeteria is popular with the lunch crowd. A plate of food at the "Fountain of Health" includes rice, tortas and soy beef and costs $1.75. A big fruit salad is $1.15. *(12-3pm, 6-9pm)*

😊 😊 😊 😊 😊

# Sights

## MUSEUMS AND GALLERIES

**David J. Guzmán National Museum** (West San Salvador map) Founded in 1883 and recently reopened after an extensive and impressive renovation, this is the best museum in the country. The collection covers the country's pre-Colombian cultures, with an impressive Mayan collection, and has a wide selection of colonial relics. A visit here gives you a chance to learn about the cultural origins of the people and towns that you will see or have

just visited in El Salvador. One of the highlights is the 12th or 13th century statue of Xipe Totec ("Our Lord of the Flayed Hide") found near Tazumal. Xipe Totec was the Maya/Toltec god of fertility and penitential torture and is represented by a life-size figure of a Mayan priest wearing the skins that were killed in sacrifice. The liberty bell from La Merced church, an important Salvadoran icon, is held here too. *(Tel 243-3750; Tue-Sun, 9am-12pm, 2pm-5pm)*

**Tin Marin Museum** (West San Salvador map) This brightly colored museum at the north end of Cuscatlán Park specializes in children, though the adults who accompany them will likely enjoy themselves too. The ten or so attractions inside the museum change regularly, but recent displays have included a five-meter-tall erupting volcano, a rainforest, Computerland, a lesson on oral hygiene inside a giant mouth, and a TV production studio. In all cases the children get to play games so that they have so much fun they don't even realize they are learning. To see the museum you must join a 90-minute tour with a knowledgeable and enthusiastic guide. *(Tel 271-5110; Tue-Fri, 9am-1pm, 2pm-5pm, Sat-Sun 10am-1pm, 2pm-6pm; admission $1.25)*

**Patronato Pro Patrimonio Cultural** (West San Salvador map) This converted colonial house shows off the history of Salvadoran art from the beginnings of art in El Salvador up to the modern day, including such local notables as Valero, Lecha, and Salarraue. The work of new local designers is also shown here. *(Tel 223-9464; Mon-Fri 8am-12pm, 2pm-5pm)*

**Galería 1-2-3** (West San Salvador map) Features works by artists from throughout Central America. *(Tel 223-1624; Mon-Fri 8:30am-12:30pm, 2:30-6pm, Sun 8:30am-12:30pm)*

**El Laberinto** (West San Salvador map) Has a permanent collection of local and international artists. *(Tel 223-1115; Mon-Fri 9am-12:30pm, 3-6:30pm, Sat 9am-1pm)*

## PARKS

**Teleferico San Jacinto Park** This beautiful park east of San Salvador is known as El Reino del Pajaro y la Nube ("The Home of the Bird and the Cloud") and is one of the top attractions in the capital. Perched atop San Jacinto Mountain (aka Amatepec) are an amusement park, restaurants, and shops. The panoramic views of San Salvador, Lago de Ilopango and the San Vicente volcano are worthy attractions all their own. But even if none of that interests you the approach to the park alone makes a visit worthwhile You ascend the 1,350 meters to the park via a 15-minute gondola ride. To get there you can take bus #9 which goes to Ciudud Credisa. *(Mon-Sun 9am-7pm, admission $2.85)*

**Zoo** (Full San Salvador map) Around 650 species calls this respectable 17-acre zoo home. It is often packed with families on weekends. *(Take city bus 2 and transfer to city bus 10; tel 270-0828; Wed-Sun 8am-5pm; admission $0.60)*

**Parque Saburo Hirao and Natural History Museum** (Full San Salvador map) If the zoo isn't enough to entertain the little tykes, follow the signs half a block south to the Parque Saburo Hirao, named after the Japanese philanthropist who built it. This children's park has playgrounds and an adult area where parents can watch their kids. The small Natural History Museum/botanical garden has a few exhibits on different kinds of plants and animals, geology, and paleontology. *(Wed-Sun 8am-4pm; admission $0.60)*

**La Laguna Botanical Garden** (Full San Salvador map) Escape the hubbub of the capital to spend an afternoon wandering along the cool, quiet paths of La Laguna. Located at the bottom of the crater of an extinct volcano, the garden shelters hundreds of different plants and flowers from around the world. The petrified lava and other volcanic remains are interesting too. *(Take city bus 44 towards Santa Tecla, garden is to the south of the road leading back toward San Salvador, get off at the sign, walk 1 kilometer downhill to park; tel 243-2012; Tue-Sun 9am-5pm; admission $0.45 per person)*

**Parque Cuscatlán** (West San Salvador map) This tree-filled oasis is the largest park in the center of San Salvador and one of the best places to take refuge from the smog and noise produced by the city buses. The recently reopened National Exhibition Hall *(tel 222-4959)* displays fine arts.

## CHURCHES

**Metropolitan Cathedral** (Central San Salvador map) This massive structure was built to replace a wooden church that burned down in 1951, only to be badly damaged itself in the 1956 earthquake. There is a shrine to Archbishop Romero at his burial site inside. Shortly before his death, Romero declared that Church funds would not be used to rebuild the cathedral until more pressing needs, like feeding people, were satisfied first. It was on the steps of the cathedral that civilians were filmed being gunned down by the army during his funeral.

Years later Archbishop Monseñor Fernando Saénz Lacalle, worked to rally the support of the parishioners, private enterprises and government to complete this work of art and in March 1999 it finally reopened. The floor is laid out in the form of a Grecian cross and the impressive dome is supported by 15 columns. Also notice the side altars where you will see the open confessionals, a style that dates back to early Christians.

**Iglesia Don Rua** (Full San Salvador map) A short distance from the city center stands the tallest church in the city. The plain white and yellow walls contrast with two levels of ornate stained glass. One series of windows tell the story of Don Bosco, a 19th-century Italian saint known throughout El Salvador for his work with children. There's a painting of him to the right of the altar. Directly overhead in front of the altar are four triangular mosaics of Ezekiel, Daniel, Isaiah and Jeremiah. If you can wrangle permission to climb the huge bell tower, the view of the city and the valley can't be beat.

**La Ceiba de Guadalupe** (Full San Salvador map) The prettiest church in the capital sits a stone's throw away from the fumes and horns of the Panamerican Highway on the road to Santa Tecla. But pass through the intricately carved wooden doors on the blinding white exterior, and the highway sounds quickly fade. Inside, you'll find an incredible wood ceiling, paintings of the Virgin and angels over the altar, and interesting round stained glass windows that rotate to let in outside air. The church is at its busiest on December 12th as Salvadorans honor the Virgen de Guadalupe.

## OTHER INTERESTING CHURCHES IN THE CENTER

**Iglesia El Calvario** This peaceful and beautiful Gothic church stands in stark contrast to the chaos of the central market which surrounds it.

**Iglesia El Rosario** This air-polluttion stained church was once the setting for El Salvador's high society weddings. Father José Matías Delgado, the father of Central American independence, is buried here.

**Iglesia La Merced** Father Matías Delgado rang the bells of this church at dawn on November 5th, 1811 beginning the fight for Independence from Spain.

**Iglesia Sagrado Corazón** Most impressive for the interior woodworking, particularly on the roof.

**Iglesia San Francisco** Also has a lovely interior.

## MONUMENTS

**El Salvador del Mundo** (West San Salvador map) The national symbol of El Salvador—Christ on top of the globe—stands tall in the Plaza de las Américas. The original version of this famous monument was sculpted in 1777 by a Franciscan, Silvestre García. This one was erected in 1990.

**Monumento de la Revolución** (West San Salvador map) The entrance to the wealthy neighborhood of San Benito is the unlikely location of this towering image made out of a mosaic of colored stones. The naked Orwellian figure with its arms thrown upwards and head back is an impressive sight, making the monument look a little like a place to perform ritual sacrifice at night. It was supposedly erected to commemorate the "revolutionary movement of 1948," but it could just as easily have been built to commemorate recent events instead.

# Other Sights

**National Palace** (Central San Salvador map) The entrance to this grand old building is flanked by statues of Christopher Columbus and Queen Isabel, donated in 1924 by the king of Spain. Formerly the presidential residence, the palace was rebuilt in 1921 replacing the original 1870 building which was destroyed by an earthquake. It has since fallen into disrepair and is currently undergoing a (relative) whirlwind of restoration. The old tile floors, plaster columns and black iron grillwork surrounding the expansive, tree-filled courtyard inside come from another era, as do the old carved wooden doorways and cracked marble staircases that lead to one of the palace's 104 rooms.

The National Archives are stored in the basement and contain documents that date back to the 1600s. During the war, documents were collected from city halls across the country to protect them from the guerrillas. While restoration continues you can visit for free during normal working hours.

**National Theater** (Central San Salvador map) An ornate opera house seems as out of place in the middle of downtown San Salvador as a nine-hole golf course, but go a block east of the Metropolitan Cathedral and you'll find this 1917 building filled with plush red seats and marble floors. Thick carpeting and ornate scrollwork muffle the traffic noises and make you feel as if you've stepped into another century. There are different rooms representing various art styles and the bathrooms are probably the best in the city. The chandeliers are from Austria and a famous 230-square-meter mural covers the ceiling.

A variety of productions, from theater to poetry readings are presented and the National Orchestra plays about every two weeks for $2.85. All the seats in the three levels are the same price, but the second floor gives you the best angle over the stage. The box office opens shortly before showtime.

**National Library** (Central San Salvador map) Relocated in 1993, the National Library continues to suffer the effects of the 1986 earthquake that destroyed 40 percent of its collection. Today, this monolith seems sadly empty inside the huge building formerly occupied by a bank. The first floor houses the reference section and international works. Up the broken escalator on the second floor are Salvadoran and Central American books and the card catalog. There's also a large painting upstairs which depicts all the past presidents of El Salvador, life-size, up to Cristiani. *(Mon-Fri 8am-4pm, Sat 8am-12pm)*

**University of Central America** (Full San Salvador map) The shaded campus of La UCA, as this university is usually called, is a good place to relax and meet Salvadoran college students. The university has seen a great deal of the country's history and there is a shrine at the graves of the seven Jesuit priests who were assassinated by the Salvadoran army at the end of the war while working here. There's a decent bookstore, an eatery with food resembling what you'd find at US college campuses and plenty of stores outside the doors to the campus that make a brisk business out of photocopying textbooks and notes. There is usually some art exhibit, concert or seminar going on here. Check www.uca.com.sv or call 273-4400 for details. *(Take bus 101)*

**Parque Libertad** (Central San Salvador map) This stark, concrete square, dominated by the El Rosario church, is where the city began. Inside the park is an impressive statue of the winged Liberty, but even more spectacular is the view of the cathedral with the volcano in the background at sunset. However, for safety sake, this view should be admired as part of a group.

**National Baseball Stadium** (West San Salvador map) Players from all over Latin America and the Caribbean, even a few Japanese and Gringos, play in the winter league here. The season runs from November to March with games played on weekends and Tuesday and Thursday nights. Box seats are $2.25 to $3.50 and bleachers are just $1.25. *(Tel 224-5669)*

😁 😁 😁 😁 😁

# Shopping
## MARKETS

**Mercado Central** (Central San Salvador map) This two-story concrete building surrounding the Iglesia El Calvario resembles a massive parking garage. Inside is a maze of stalls with seafood, veggies, swinging beef and poultry carcasses strung up all around. The market is a mob scene by 6am with locals snapping up the freshest fruits and vegetables. Food is the main commodity on sale here but the armadillo skins, furniture and used clothing are available all day long. Traders spill over on to streets and shoppers laden with bags block the pavements. You'll notice some vendors selling neat bundles of medicinal herbs. Ask them what each is for and you'll be amazed at the homemade remedies that are available for every conceivable ailment—don't expect most of them to work though.

**Mercado Nacional de Artesanías** (West San Salvador map) Every type of Salvadoran craft is available from one of the 50-plus stores in this clean, well laid out market. Goodies from Guatemala and other Central American countries are also for sale. Though items will be cheaper in the village where they are made, prices are reasonable.

**Mercado Ex-Cuartel** (Central San Salvador map) The majority of the stalls at this large market sell crafts, including hammocks, leather goods, textiles, pottery, etc. from all over the country. Prices are generally lower than in the Mercado Nacional de Artesanías and the variety is impressive.

## ARTS AND CRAFTS

Quality is high in these shops, and in general, so are the prices.

**Genesis 7 Curiosidades** This small shop sells a quirky selection of crafts and knick-knacks from all over Central America. You can browse through paper flowers, wood-carvings and new-age literature, or rent a compact disc. Check out the bead curtains made of dried seeds. *(Av Alberto Masferrer Sur and C Maquilishuat; tel 261-1262; Mon-Sat 8:30am-7:30pm)*

**Galería Huellas de América** (Full San Salvador map) Everything at the gallery "Footprints of America" is made out of finely-worked cow and snake skin. Crafts are made on the premises, so ask to take a peek in back to see how it's done. *(Tel 284-1617; Mon-Fri 9am-9pm)*

**Galería El Arbol del Díos** (West San Salvador map) You'll recognize this gallery by Fernando Llort's distinctive childlike figures on the white front wall. A pricey gift shop sells Salvadoran crafts, and the gallery sells hundreds of Llort's colorful, cubist originals and prints that make some of the most beautiful, if expensive, souvenirs from El Salvador. A 20x30cm print sells for $58-$115 and originals start in the hundreds. If you have any money left, stop off for a bite at the Restaurant del Arbol next door. *(Tel 263-9206; Mon-Thur 12-10pm, Fri-Sat 12-11pm)*

**La Carte** A popular stop for ceramics, wall decorations and wooden objects. La Carte has an especially good collection of Christmas items around the holidays, including hand-embroidered tree skirts, ceramic angels and Christmas stockings. *(3a C Pte #5331; tel 263-1429; Mon-Fri 9am-12:30pm, 2:30-6pm)*

**Union Church Gift Shop** A large assortment of quality local handicrafts, including pottery, woven and stitched items, hammocks, wooden goods and a large variety of T-shirts—all at good prices. The also have a large Christmas selection. *(Final C #4, Col La Mascota; tel 263-8246; Wed-Sat, 9am-12pm, 2pm-5pm, Sun 10:45am-12pm)*

## Señora Luck

**T**wo types of lottery tickets are sold on nearly every street corner in El Salvador. You scratch the silver tickets to see if you've won instantly. The others, on white paper with a row of numbers, give you a shot at the weekly national lottery—the winning numbers are announced in the daily newspapers. Tickets for the one million *colon* ($114,286) prize cost $1.14 and the two million *colon* ($228,571) prize are $2.29. Buying a few lottery tickets is the easiest way to lend a helping hand to El Salvador's less fortunate since not only are the people who sell the tickets are invariably poor, but all the proceeds go to charity.

**SAN SALVADOR**

**Exclusiva** This shop in the Basilea Mall in the Zona Rosa has quality crafts from across Central America. *(Next to Shaw's; tel 279-0061; 9am-12:30pm, 2:30-6pm)*

**Arte y Madera** This shop features fine handicrafts, gifts and sculpture made from exotic woods though the store's English-speaking staff are very knowledgeable about all styles of Central American crafts. The owner has written a Central America cookbook called *Sabor!* which is on sale here as well. *(3a C Pte #4440; tel 263-7328; Mon-Sat, 9am-6pm)*

**Bello Hogar** A small shop with a lovely selection of ceramics (including the famous Talavera style of brightly painted pottery), glassware, and wrought-iron work. The staff is very helpful. *(C El Mirador and 99a Av Nte; tel 263-1945; 9am-12:30pm, 2:30-6pm)*

**Piñata Minerva** Choose from a large selection of pre-made *piñatas* or have one custom made from your picture. A large custom job costs about $11.50 and usually takes a week (they can do rush orders if you ask). Their work is fantastic. *(Paseo General Escalón #3916, at Fuente Beethoven; tel 263-5636; Mon-Sat 9am-6pm)*

## OTHER

**Metrocentro** (West San Salvador map) Metrocentro, a gigantic shopping mall is the largest shopping center in Central America. The hundreds of stores include everything you would expect including supermarkets, department stores, clothing stores, restaurants, banks, and a post office. There are also three food courts.

**Galerias** (West San Salvador map) This exclusive shopping center is home to large department stores, several clothing and accessory shops, a movie theater, ice skating rink, carousel, and the Plaza Gourmet dining area with many fast food places and cafes. If you are nearby it is worth a quick peek for the mall's unique design. It was built around a beautiful old mansion that now serves as a sort of cultural center. Note, as these are some of the top stores in the country, prices are generally high.

**La Despensa de Don Juan** This is the largest and most modern supermarket in the country. The shelves are stocked with a large selection of Latin American, Spanish and US products and the bakery, meat counter, and pharmacy are all excellent. *(They have stores in Escalón, San Benito and Zona Rosa)*

# La Luna Casa y Arte

**A** group of artists turned this house in San Salvador's European Zone into a spot to give people a place to come, relax and enjoy the arts. Set in the middle of a residential neighborhood, its painted walls and hip, college-age-and-up crowd make it look straight out of Greenwich Village. The menu is heavy on vegetarian and typical Salvadoran meals with prices starting at about $5. Lunches are accompanied by various activities such as films, poetry, or yoga amongst other things. Come by and grab a schedule at the front door. Nightly music ranges from Latin to jazz to rock. An attached store called El Ropero sells left-leaning reading material, clothing and jewelry. Entry is free before 9pm, and about $3 (more for special events) per person after that. They recently added a second branch called Actoteatro in the city's historic center at 1a C Pte #822. Stop by while you are out seeing the sights. *(Tel 260-2921, e-mail info@lalunacasayarte.com; Mon-Sat 10am-12pm, 4pm-1am)*

# Entertainment

For listing of plays, movies, art exhibits and similar events check the "El Salvador" section of the monthly *Revue* magazine (in English and Spanish), the weekly *Que Pasa* entertainment guide (also in English and Spanish) or the "Tiempo Libre" entertainment guide (Spanish) published every Friday in *El Diario de Hoy* newspaper.

## NIGHTLIFE

The **Zona Real**, a group of about 25 clubs, bars, cafes and restaurants located behind the Hotel Camino Real Intercontinental, is the closest place to the center of the city to grab a bite, tie one on and hit the dance floor. A wee bit further up from the Zona Real is the **European Zone** where you will find bistros, cafes and bars like the casual Bar Café Les 3 Diables, the restaurant/bar/book store/art gallery La Ventana and if your tastes are a bit more bohemian La Luna Casa y Arte (see below). La Barra Irlandesa has live Irish music and Guinness beer. Rio Bravo and El Corral Steakhouse also have live music on weekends for a modest cover.

For years the **Zona Rosa** has been San Salvador's most popular locale for late-night entertainment. This collection of open-air restaurants, chic clothing stores, cafes and ritzy discos spreads out over eight square blocks in Colonia San Benito from the intersection of Boulevard del Hipódromo and Calle La Reforma. If you feel like dancing, come well-dressed and expect to pay as much as $10 cover. Some of the most popular places for a drink are Mario's, The Guadalajara Grill and Paradise while dancers can't do better than the Underground, Studio 225, and Señor Frog's discotecs. Rinconcito's, a restaurant/bar/art gallery/internet café, is a good place to start, end, or spend the night.

With nearly 50 watering holes along **Paseo General Escalón** you are sure to find something for an evening's entertainment. The names and owners change frequently though the gin mills at the Galerias Mall, Chili's Burgers and The Sports Bar are old standbys for ex-pats. Near the Parque Beethoven, at 75a Av, there are a few discos, restaurants and movie theaters.

At the end of Escalón at the intersection with Avenida Masferrer, you'll find the **Plaza Masferrer**, a mellower alternative to the high-priced, exclusive nightclubs at the Zona Rosa and Boulevard de los Héroes. If you want to dance try Padrisimo's Discotec and the British Club on the weekends or head uphill from Plaza Masferrer where you can hear all types of music.

# Cultural Centers

There is a bit of a cultural renaissance currently sweeping the country and new places are opening all the time. If nothing on this list catches your eye look up "Centro de Cultura" in the phone book and see what's new.

## SALVADORAN

**Centro Cultural La Mazorca—ASTAC** (Full San Salvador map) Look for the bright murals on the front wall of the building, then come inside to see the art gallery filled with the work of local artists or watch some educational videos. The small store next door, La Cosecha, sells handicrafts and offers art lessons. *(Tel 226-5219; Mon-Fri 8am-12pm, 1:30-6pm)*

**Las Columnas Centro de Arte/Academia de Teatro y Arte "William Shakespeare"** (West San Salvador map) Offers theater, art and music productions and courses for children and adults. Schedules are posted on the door.

**Fundación Maria Escalón de Nuñez** (West San Salvador map) Has an active schedule of art and cultural events. *(Tel 298-1603)*

## OTHER CULTURES

Salvadoran culture isn't the only one celebrated in the capital. Each of these offers relevant language courses if you have an interest. **La Alianza Francesa** *(Tel 260-5807)* covers all things French. **The Centro Cultural de España** *(Tel 279-0323)* is associated with the Spanish Embassy. For a taste of Italian there is the **Societa Dante Alighieri** *(Tel 263-5311)*. The growing popularity of Brazilian culture and the Portuguese language is represented by the **Centro de Estudios Brasileños** *(Tel 264-3856)*. **The Academia Europea** *(Tel 263-4355)* offers a wide variety from across Europe.

# Festivals

■ **The August Festivals.** The Fiestas Agostinas began in the 16th century with a simple parade. By the 18th century they had grown, thanks to the sponsorship of local aristocrats. A wooden image of El Salvador del Mundo, El Salvador's patron saint, was carved and carried through the town. Soon images were carved for each of the city's patron saints. Today, when the float bearing the image of El Salvador del Mundo passes, everyone kneels. On the last day of the festival, a carved image of Christ is carried through the city in front of enormous crowds.

The signing of the **Peace Accords** is celebrated on January 16 and November 1 is the **Día de los Muertos** ("Day of the Dead").

# Buses

## URBAN BUSES

San Salvador city buses are numbered under 100, except 101 which goes to Santa Tecla. All cost $0.20, except buses that go outside the city proper. Microbuses also run roughly the same routes much more quickly—albeit much more crazily—and cost $0.34.

Many of the buses are dreadfully maintained and drivers will often take big risks to make a fare. There are more than twice the number of buses needed to meet passenger demand and the pollution they cause is a form of cruel and unusual punishment for the city, but little is being done about it because no one has to courage to stand up to the country's strong bus company owners. Also, bus routes are sold, and it is widely believed that politicians and military officers have vested interests in maintaining the status quo.

■ **MAJOR DESTINATIONS: National University (3, 9, 30)** from central market and

# The British Club

**O**pened back in 1959, the British Club, just off the Plaza Masferrer, is one of the friendliest and most dynamic places in the country. The British Club features all the best from the British Isles including quiz nights, darts tournaments, fish and chips, and one of the few snooker tables in Central America. However, American football takes over the TVs all day Sunday and on Monday nights for half the year. Other diversions include a swimming pool, poker tournaments, and live music on Friday nights. This is a member-owned club, but everyone is welcome and they'll give you a free one-month membership if you ask. (Tel 263-6765; e-mail britishclub@email.com; 5-11pm)

Metrocentro; **(33b)** from eastern San Salvador. **Planes de Renderos (12pr, 12mc)** from central market. **Lago de Ilopango and Turicentro Apulo (15)** from central San Salvador ("Hula Hula" bus stop). **Panchimalco (17p, 17r)** from central market. **Ciudad Merliot toward Santa Tecla (42). La UCA (44)** from Zacamil. **Plaza Masferrer (52)** from Reloj de Flores. **US embassy and Santa Tecla (101)** from city center past Plaza de Las Américas.

■ **MAJOR DEPARTURE POINTS: Western bus terminal (4cd)** to northeastern San Salvador; **(34)** to the Zona Rosa and central market; **(42)** toward Ciudad Merliot and Santa Tecla. **Eastern bus terminal (5, 21)** to southern San Salvador; **(7)** to southeastern San Salvador; **(8)** to southeastern San Salvador; **(23, 24)** to north central San Salvador; **(29)** to Metrocentro. **(6)** to Plaza Las Americas via C Arce. **Southern bus terminal (Ruta A)** to central San Salvador. **Central San Salvador market (6)** to north-central San Salvador; **(16)** to southeastern San Salvador, then north to C San Antonio Abad; **(20)** to northeastern San Salvador; **(30)** to central market, Metrocentro and National University; **(34)** to western bus terminal and the Zona Rosa. **Plaza Masferrer (Ruta A)** to southern bus terminal. **Metrocentro (29)** to eastern bus terminal; **(30)** to central market and National University; **(44)** to La UCA; **(52)** to Plaza Masferrer; **(Ruta B)** to Centro de Gobierno. **Centro de Gobierno (31)** to southeastern San Salvador; **(Ruta B)** to Metrocentro. **Zona Rosa (34)** to western bus terminal and central market.

## NATIONAL BUSES

There are plans to move the Eastern and Western bus terminals to better sites, as the government did with the Southern terminal. Unfortunately the bus business is notoriously corrupt and so the moving process will probably not occur anytime soon.

## EASTERN BUS TERMINAL

Call 222-0315 for information. **Berlín (303)**, infrequently, 109km, 3hr. **Chalatenango (125)**, every 10 min until 5:30pm, 69km, 2hr 20min. **El Poy (119)**, every 30 min until 4pm, 92km, 4hr 30min. **Ilobasco (111)**, every 15 min until 5pm, 54km, 1hr 40min. **La Palma (119)**, every 30 min until 4pm, 81km, 4hr. **La Unión (304)**, every 40 min until 4pm, 183km, 4hr. **San Francisco Gotera (305)**, infrequent service, 170km, 3hr 30min. **San Miguel (301)**, every 5 min until 4:30pm, 136km, 3hr. Direct is 2hr 30min. **San Sebastián (110)**, every 30 min until 5pm, 50km, 1hr 30min. **San Vicente (116)**, every 10 min until 6:30pm, 58km, 1hr 30min. **Santa Rosa de Lima (306)**, every 30 min until

3pm, 176km, 4hr. **Santiago de María (310)**, every 20 min until 4pm, 118km, 2hr 30min. **Sensuntepeque (112)**, every 15 min until 4:30pm, 84km, 2hr. **Suchitoto (129)**, every 15 min until 5pm, 44km, 1hr 30min. **Usulután (302)**, every 10 min until 4:15pm, 112km, 2hr 30min.

## WESTERN BUS TERMINAL

Call 223-3784 for information. **Ahuachapán (204)**, every 10 min until 5pm, 100km, 3hr 30min. **Apaneca (206a)**, infrequently, 91km, 2hr 30min. **Chalchuapa (202)**, every 7 min until 5:30pm, 78km, 90min. **La Libertad (102)**, every 15 min until 5:30pm, 36km, 1hr. **San Juan Opico (108)**, every 10 min until 6:45pm, 40km, 1hr 10min. **Santa Ana (201)**, every 5 min until 8pm, 63km, 2hr, direct bus is 90min. **Sonsonate (205)**, every 5 min until 6:20pm, 65km, 1hr.

## SOUTHERN BUS TERMINAL (aka Rutas del Pacifico)

Call 279-3548 for information. **Costa del Sol (494, 513)**, every 30 min until 5pm, 60km, 2hr. **La Herradura (495)**, every 15 min until 6pm, 60km, 2hr. **Puerto El Triunfo (185)**, every 30 min until 2:30pm, 107km, 2hr 30min. **Usulután (302)**, every 10 min until 4:15pm, 112km, 2hr 30min. **Zacatecoluca (133)**, every 8 min until 6pm, 55km, 1hr.

## INTERNATIONAL BUSES

■ **FROM THE WESTERN TERMINAL: Mermex** (Tel 279-3484) sends buses to Guatemala City at 4:15am and 8:30am, 5hr, $4.60. **El Condor** (Tel 224-6548) sends buses to the **Mexican border** at Tecunumán and Talisman (via Sonsonate and La Hachadura) at 7am, 9pm, 9hr, $10.

■ **FROM THE INTERNATIONAL BUS STATION: Puerto Bus** sends buses to Guatemala, Honduras and Nicaragua. Same day ticket purchases only. *(Tel 222-2158)* **Guatemala** roughly every hour from 7am to 4:30pm, $8, 5hr 30min. **Honduras**, 6am, 7:30am, 1:30pm daily, 6hr 30min, $16. **Nicaragua**, 5:30am, 11hr, $20. **Cruceros del Golfo** *(Tel 222-2138, 222-3224)* sends one bus a day to Tegucigalpa at 6am, 7hr, $25. **Comfort Line** *(Tel 279-0060)* leaves twice a day for Guatemala City at 8am and 2pm, 5hr, $18.75.

■ **FROM OTHER LOCATIONS: Tica Bus** has been around for a long time and runs buses to most Central American countries. You can buy tickets here during office hours. Buses pass by the office shortly before departure. *(Tel 222-4808; Mon-Fri 9am-12pm, 2-7pm, Sat 9am-12pm)* **Guatemala City**, 6am, 5hr, $8. **Tegucigalpa**, 7:30am, 7hr, $16. **Managua**, 5am, 11hr, $25. **San José**, 5am, 24hr, $35. Stops for the night in Nicaragua. **Panama**, 5am, 40hr, $60. Stops in Nicaragua and Costa Rica. **King Quality** has daily buses leaving for Guatemala and Honduras from the Hotel Siesta and the Hotel Marriott in the Zona Rosa. The buses leave from the Hotel Siesta and then pass the Hotel Marriott. *(Alam Juan Pablo II y 19a Av Nte; tel 222-2158, 271-3330)* Tegucigalpa, 12:45/1pm, 7hr, $30. Guatemala City, 6/6:15am, 1:30/1:45pm, 5hr, $22. **Pullman Tours** *(Tel 243-1300, 243-2405, e-mail pullmantour@salnet.net)* leave twice a day for Guatemala City from the Hotel Marriott in the Zona Rosa at 6:30am, 3pm, 4hr, $45.

# Details

■ **AMERICAN EXPRESS:** *(Centro Commercial La Mascota, local #1; tel 279-3844; Mon-Fri 8am-12pm, 2-5pm).*

■ **BOOKSTORES:** San Salvador has several high quality bookstores that stock titles in English, some of the biggest selections are at: **The Book Shop** *(Located in both the Metrocentro and Galerias malls; tel 245-0879; Mon-Sat 10am-7:30pm),* **Eutopia** *(Located at Galeria 123; tel 243-5335; Mon-Fri 10am-7pm, Sat 10am-3pm),* **Punto Literario**

## Love Under the Volcano

Time passes. Towering *ceiba* trees grow from seedlings and fall to the ground. Young children become parents, grandparents and then pass away. But Cipitín is still beautiful. His eyes are still black, his skin is the color of cinnamon and he carries a sweet-smelling stick so he can leap over streams.

Time passes, but the son of the Siguanaba remains forever ten years old, his eternal youth a gift of the gods. Always elusive, he steals about, hiding among the foliage and playing among the petals of wild irises.

Cipitín is the god of young love. They say the young women of the town always go, in the chill of the early dawn, to leave him flowers so he will play on the banks of the river. From high in the treetops he spies on them, and when a girl passed below he shakes flowers free from the branches.

But you should know that Cipitín already has a sweetheart—a girl, small and beautiful, just like him. Her name is Tenáncin.

One day Cipitín had fallen asleep on the petal of a large flower. Tenáncin was wandering in the forest picking tiny flowers when she lost her way. Running, lost, she stumbled through the brambles and came to the flower where Cipitín was sleeping. She saw him.

The rustling of the bushes awakened Cipitín, and he fled leaping over the bushes. He ran from flower to flower, singing sweetly. Tenáncin followed him. After a long time, Cipitín came to a rock on the side of a volcano. Tenáncin's feet and hands were scratched and bleeding from the thorns.

Cipitín touched the rock with a *shilca* and a door of moss gave way. Holding hands, the two entered—first Cipitín, then Tenáncin. The moss door closed behind them.

And Tenáncin was never seen again.

Her father searched the forest and hills, and several days later died from the pain caused by the loss. They say the cavern where Cipitín and Tenáncin disappeared is on the Sihuatepeque Volcano in the department of San Vicente.

Time has passed. The world has changed, rivers have run dry and mountains have been born. Yet the son of the Siguanaba remains forever ten years old. It's not unusual for him to perch on an iris or hide in the treetops, spying on the girls that laugh down by the river.

*–Salvadoran Folk Tale*

*(Blvd Del Hippodromo #330; tel 245-1472; Mon-Sat 10am)*. For books in Spanish you best bets are **Libreria UCA** *(Tel 210-6699; Mon-Fri 8am-7:30pm, Sat 8am-12:30pm)* and **Clásicos Roxsil** (see Santa Tecla)

■ **COURIER SERVICES: DHL** *(47 Agenda Nte y Pasaje Las Terrazas #104; tel 260-7722, 260-4486)*. **Federal Express** *(Av El Espino #68; tel 243-7222)*. **Gigante Express** *(Col Escalón, 11 C Pte #3971; tel 254-2121 - Centro, Blvd Distrito Comercial Central 1 C Ote; tel 222-6454)*. **Trans Express** *(Km 5, Carretera a Santa Tecla, Plantel Cía General de Equipas; tel 279-1511)*. **UPS** *(Col Roma, C El Progresso #3139; tel 245-0400)*. **Urgente Express** *(C Rubén Darío #1056 and 19a Av Sur, Edif Bolívar #2-1; tel 222-0664, 226-0085)*.

■ **EMERGENCEY NUMBER:** 911.

■ **ENGLISH-LANGUAGE CHURCH SERVICES:** Union Church of San Salvador has "Expatriate Christian Services" on Sunday 10am. *(Final C #4, Col La Mascota; tel 263-8246; Pastor Jeff Jacobson)*. Jewish Temple services in Hebrew, Fridays at 6:30pm. *(Blvd Del Hipódromo #626 in front of Finata; tel 223-6124)*. There is Catholic mass in English on Sunday at 4pm at the San Benito Chapel in the Zona Rosa. *(One block up hill from the Princess Hotel; tel 264-3698)*.

■ **HOSPITALS:** The best hospital in the country is the Hospital del Diagnostico *(21 C Pte y 2a Diag; tel 226-8878)*. Ask your embassy for recommendations for specialized treatment.

■ **INTERNET CAFES:** You won't have much problem checking your e-mail while in San Salvador. The going rate is about $1/hr. **Cibercom** *(Centro Comercial Villas Españolas, Local D-2, Col Escalón; 8am-8pm)*. **Cyber Café** *(Col Jardines de Guadalupe, Av Rio Lempa #18; 8am-8pm)*. **Cyber Café Punto Azul** *(Alameda Roosevelt, #3022; 8am-9pm)*. **Cybermannia** *(Paseo Gen Escalón #3949; 8am-7pm)*.

■ **LAUNDRY:** San Salvador has a few laundromats that let you wash clothes for about $1.75 per load. **Lavanderia Deluxe** *(Centro Comercial Metrópolis Edificio B Local 3; 8am-6pm)*. **Lavanderia El Rosal** *(Calle El Progreso, Centro Commercial El Rosal; 7am-7pm)*. **Lavandería Lavapronto** *(Av Los Sisimiles #2924, Col Miramonte; Mon-Sat 7am-8pm)*.

■ **MAIL:** The **central post office** is in a sketchy area on the north end of the Centro Gobierno. They have fax, internet, and telegraph service, the latter is still used in some of the country's most remote villages. There's another branch at Metrocentro. *(Mon-Fri 8am-4pm)*

■ **MAPS:** The **Instituto Geográfico Nacional** is the place to pick up all maps of El Salvador, especially if you plan to go hiking or will be in the country for a while and need a good map to get around. Prices are $5 and up. Theoretically you can order maps online at www.cnr.gob.sv/ign/ign2000.htm, but the website is a real mess so you probably will be better off going to their office. *(1a C Pte y 43a Ave Nte, #2310; tel 260-8000, 260-6417; Mon-Fri 8am-12pm, 2-5pm)*

■ **TAXIS:** Two reputable companies are **Radio Taxis** *(Tel 263-2001)* and **Acontaxis** *(Tel 237-2531)*

■ **TOURIST INFORMATION:** The government-run **Salvadoran Tourism Institute** (ISTU) can provide you with information about traveling in El Salvador and passes for visiting some of the national parks. A lot of the information is fluff, but the people who work there are friendly. There's also an ISTU office at the airport *(C Rubén Darío #619,*

*tel 222-8000; Mon-Fri 8am-4pm)* The **Salvadoran Tourism Corporation** (COR-SATUR) is a more up to date source of overall information about the country. *(Blvd del Hipodromo #508, tel 243-7835, e-mail corsatur@salnet.com; Mon-Fri, 8am-12pm, 2-5pm)*
■ **VISA EXTENSIONS:** The Ministry of the Interior handles immigration issues very efficiently, although you might have to wait in line for a while. *(Centro de Gobierno, 9a C Pte y 15a Av Nte, first floor; Mon-Fri 8am-4pm; tel 222-3988)*

# Near San Salvador
## Planes de Renderos

South of San Salvador is the well known Planes de Renderos, a favorite excursion from the capital for both locals and foreigners. The curving highway there is lined with some of the best restaurants in the area that opened here to take advantage of the views over the city (best in the early evening). The scenic road winds through lush vegetation with broad vistas seemingly around every bend before reaching several popular parks.

### FOOD & DRINK

**Restaurant Bella Vista** This formal restaurant has an amazing view of the city, best in the early evening. It's decorated inside with some impressive cut-glass scenes made from photos of El Salvador in the 1920s. The "Beautiful View" Restaurant, around since 1945, was handed over to Ana Palomo, the current manager, and her sister Lorena by their parents. Exquisite pasta dishes start at $7 while *camarones* Oscar, one of the house specialties, is $15, and worth every penny. There is live jazz on Friday and Saturday nights from 8:30-11:30pm. *(Km 6; tel 370-0144; Mon-Fri 12-3pm, 6-11:30pm, Sat noon-midnight, Sun noon-4pm)*

**Placita Grill** This brightly decorated, little restaurant is a good choice for Mexican. Tasty tacos with all the trimmings cost just $2.50. The staff have both an eye for detail and a sense of humor which rounds out a great dining experience. *(Km 6.5; 12-3pm, 6-11pm)*

**Restaurant Casa de Piedra** Located in an old hacienda style house, the informal "House of Stone" is a favorite with the younger set. The varied menu features mostly Salvadoran meals such as *pupusas* and seafood with dishes ranging from $4-$7. Weekends see live music or karaoke. *(Turn right at km 8.5 and then after one block turn right again and follow the winding driveway for 800 meters; noon-midnight)*

**Pupuseria Paty** Many locals regard Paty's *pupusas* as some of the best in the country. True fanatics can order them *gigante*, which are twice the normal size. Logically, *pupusas* are the specialty but the menu also has other typical plates like *platano* and bean dishes, chicken, soups, *loroco* (a spice made from flowers), *tamales* and cheese *quesadillas*—all at budget prices. *(Km 10, where the road forks to Panchimalco, they have a second location near the entrance to Parque Balboa; 12-10pm)*

**Pandora Galeria Gourmet** An art gallery/restaurant with a bohemian touch inside and a beautiful garden and mountain views outside. A great place to stop for coffee and deserts though if you want a proper meal they have a limited menu of Noveau Couisine. *(Located at the entrance to Parque Balboa; 12-10pm)*

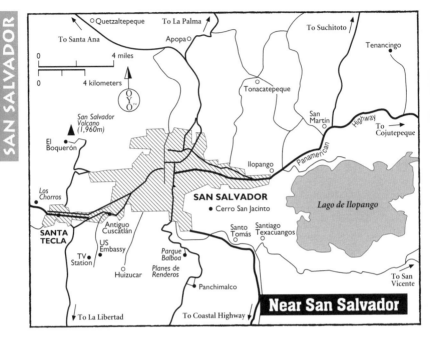

**Near San Salvador**

## SIGHTS

**Parque Balboa** This large municipal park sits high up in the Planes de Renderos district. It's one of the most popular weekend day trips from the city for Salvadorans and thankfully has been cleaned up and reforested over the past few years. The football field sees some heavy use, as do the bike paths, skate park, and children's play area. Birdwatchers will also find a visit rewarding. A handful of private *pupuserías* and outdoor cafés cater to Salvadorans on a romantic getaway. Security is tight, nevertheless it is not advisable to remain here after 6pm. *(Km 12)*

**El Parque de la Familia** The new Family Park has an arts and crafts area, roller skating, skateboarding, playgrounds, and cafeterias. On weekends there are various cultural events in a small amphitheater set in the midst of an old orange grove. *(Km 13; Tue-Sun 8am-8pm; admission $0.60)*

**Puerto del Diablo** An enormous boulder split in half here long ago, leaving behind a curious formation known as the "Devil's Door" at the summit of Cerro Chulo. From the top of these two boulders there's a great view of the coast, Lago de Ilopango, countless volcanoes, and on the clearest days you can see all the way to Honduras. The red roofs of Panchimalco rest at the foot of the precipice.

During the civil war Puerto del Diablo's beauty was marred by death squads who dumped the bodies of their victims over the edge. Now the only thing that's dumped here is trash; the trail to the top is littered with 25 years of bottle caps. It begins at a clearing between the two large rocks off to the right. *(Km 14)*

## DETAILS
■ **BUSES: San Salvador (12)** from the Mercado Central will take you to these parks and restaurants, every 15 min until 7pm.

# Panchimalco
Nahuat, "Place of Shields and Banners"
Pop. 33,500
17km from San Salvador

## PANCHIMALCO THEN
According to legend, a natural catastrophe in the 11th century forced people living in the Planes de Renderos, which today looks out over the city of San Salvador, to seek refuge in what is now Panchimalco. In recent years, archeological evidence has surfaced which confirms that there actually was a migration to Panchimalco at that time, and that the town's population quickly expanded across two square kilometers in the aftermath.

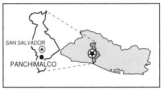

During the Spanish invasion, Panchimalco earned the alternate translation of its name: "The Fort." The concave shape of the land around the city provided a natural barrier which allowed the inhabitants to stave off attacks by Spanish troops longer than most other indigenous villages.

## PANCHIMALCO NOW
A dusty, quiet town, Panchimalco's location in a geological concavity leaves it surrounded by towering mountains on all sides. It's within seven kilometers of the Planes de Renderos and beside the Parque Balboa, with the Puerto del Diablo visible to the north. Pigs, dogs and children compete for space and attention along the hilly cobblestone streets, while other youngsters play ball in front of the old white church.

Panchimalco is still inhabited by many Pancho Indians, descendants of the Pipils who take pains to maintain their traditions and distinguish their culture from that of mainstream El Salvador. This is one of the few places in El Salvador where fabrics are still made by hand on Prehispanic waist looms.

A more famous tradition, however, are the Antiguas Cofradias, quasi-religious fraternal groups who preserve the customs of the feast days of the local patron saints. These colorful celebrations are a combination of Prehispanic pagan rituals and Catholic celebrations and involve processions, rituals and social meetings where *chicha* (a fermented corn drink), *tamales* and the traditional rice with pork are served. There's not much going on here outside of the festivals, but Panchimalco still makes for an interesting side trip from San Salvador.

## FOOD & DRINK
There are several basic cafeterias in the park in front of the Church of Santa Cruz. You can get a breakfast for $1.50 while a full lunch or dinner will just set you back $2.50.

## SIGHTS

**Church of Santa Cruz** This national monument built in 1725 lost three arched gables and an organ to the 1854 earthquake that destroyed much of San Salvador. The altar and the carved ceiling above it are worth a peek, and the room to the right houses some of the holy icons (including one depicting the burial of Jesus—notice His indigenous features) that are carried around during the town's festivals.

**Calvary Church** Inside this small chapel are two interesting images of Christ. On one side is the Black Christ of Esquipulas and across from it is the contrasting Dulce Nombre de Jesus (the White Christ). The feast days of both the black and white Christs take place in January.

**Centro de Arte** Tonatiu Arts and Crafts are made and sold at this school on the town's main street. One of the more interesting selections are the paintings made on the orange clay Spanish roof tiles (*tejas*). There are also several Prehispanic musical instruments on display. They don't keep regular hours, but are usually open normal business hours during the week. If they are closed during the day and the caretaker isn't in ask a neighbor to call someone to open up for you.

## DETAILS

■ **BUSES: San Salvador (17)**, every 15 min until 7pm, 17km, 40min. A microbus also leaves for Panchimalco from the southern side of the central market in San Salvador, in front of the Banco Cuscatlán. It's also #17 and takes less time. The last microbus returns to San Salvador at 8:30pm

■ **FESTIVALS:** The Cofradias carry out celebrations for different saints every month of the year. ISTU or CORSATUR in San Salvador will have details on the dates. **Second Sunday in May and September 13-15** Señor de la Santa Cruz de Roma. These famous festivals, both in honor of the same saint, are best known for the Procesión de las Palmas on the second Sunday afternoon in May, in which the Virgin Mary is paraded through the streets by men in traditional dress accompanied by large palm fronds. This is one of the most important cultural events in El Salvador and attracts tourists from around the world. In September, the colonial drama Los Chapetones is the highlight. Both festivals used to be a much bigger affair. Today the fairs are more general entertainment than indigenous festival, and the one in May is larger. Both feature the sale of traditional weavings and pottery, along with dances, music, speeches, marathons and fireworks.

# Santiago Texacuangos

Nahuat, "Fence of Big Stones"
18km from San Salvador

Santiago Texacuangos, is a pleasant, picturesque town perched on a volcanic peak. From the central plaza you can enjoy a meal or a drink with a beautiful view of Lago de Ilopango and the Chichontepec and San Salvador volcanoes. If the old Church of Santiago the Apostle fronting the Central Plaza is open and your Spanish is good you might be able to convince the caretaker or the parish priest to let you climb the steeple where the views are even better.

The views aren't the only thing Santiago Texacuangos has going for it. The town has active arts and crafts cottage industries and you might see textiles being woven on pedal looms that were introduced in colonial times. The town's most unique products, however, are the cornhusk dolls and you will have ample opportunity to purchase some. Strangely, Santiago Texacuangos is not a common destination for travelers, but considering it's proximity to the capital it should be.

## ACCOMMODATIONS

**Santa Rosa Inn** If you want to get away from everything, you can take refuge in these two peaceful, hidden cabins. It's so laid-back, in fact, that many local residents don't even know it exists. María Mezear, the manager, will go out of her way to make your stay enjoyable and to make you feel welcome. She will serve up breakfast or lunch (you are on you own for dinner), point out some great walks through the surrounding hills and coffee farms, and will turn on the satellite TV, if you insist. Although you won't have much trouble getting a room, it is often empty during the week, you do need to make reservations in advance. *(Located 1 km before town; tel 263-9044, 263-9019; 6 rooms, $20 per person with shared bath, $30 per person with private bath)*

## SIGHTS

**Casa de Cultura** The making of traditional crafts is taught here and you can watch young artisans working, then buy the finished products. The paintings by local artists of the town and surrounding area are also worth a look. *(Located next to the Municipal Government building; Mon-Fri 8am-4pm)*

**Union Coffee Cooperative** The Union Coffee Cooperative, made up of approximately 100 small coffee growers and headed by the dynamic and innovative Alicia Palacios, has won many environmental awards. Their shade-grown Café Texacuango is one of the best beans money can buy. If you call ahead you can arrange a tour. The best time to visit is between December and April when the coffee is being harvested. *(Located about 3 km west of town on La Ruta Panoramica, the highway that leads past Lago de Ilopango; tel 220-8326)*

## DETAILS

■ **BUSES: San Salvador (21),** every 30 minutes until 7pm, 18km, 30 min. You can catch this bus at the Parque Libertad.

■ **FESTIVALS: July 25-26** Santiago the Apostle. September 20-21 San Mateo.

# Lago de Ilopango
### Nahuat, "Goddess of Maize"
### 16km from San Salvador

The placid Lake Ilopango straddles the borders of the provinces of San Salvador, La Paz and Cuscatlán, and is surrounded by volcanoes and mountains. This volcanic lake is the country's largest and one of El Salvador's most popular tourist sites, especially since it's so close to the capital. Dramatic cliffs overlook the green waters of the lake and in the early morning mist the area resembles a scene from a traditional Chinese painting. Ilopango is one of

**Lago de Ilopango Region**

C Roosevelt • Soyapango
Eastern Bus Terminal
Blvd del Ejercito Nacional
**SAN SALVADOR**
Panamerican Highway
Apulo
Corinto
San Agustín
Club Salvadoreño
Turicentro Apulo
Hotel Vista de Lago
Mirador 70
• Amatitán
**Lago de Ilopango**
Rio El Desagüe
To International Airport

the country's favorite destinations for aquatic sports like windsurfing, kayaking, diving, water-skiing and jet-skiing, but it is large enough not to be overrun by the powerboats.

Ilopango is an immense volcanic crater that resulted from a massive eruption around the year 250 AD. This was one of the largest seismic events in the planet's history and the resulting ash was flung over much of the country. The eruption is as of much interest to historians as it is to volcanologists. The volcanic findings provided an important link in the explanation of the migrations of Mayan communities that then inhabited the western region of El Salvador toward the north. This migration contributed to the establishment of the great Mayan civilizations at places like Copán in Honduras. More recent volcanic activity resulted in the emergence of two islands, known as Los Cerros Quemados ("The Burnt Hills"), during the 19th century.

## ACCOMMODATIONS

**Hotel Vista de Lago** The private cabins are nothing fancy and the facilities are a little run down, but the view from up here is spectacular. The restaurant sits out on the ridge overlooking the lake, and has a fair variety of entrees starting at $4. Try the specialty of the house, a local deboned lake fish called *guapote deshuezado*. (*Carretera Apulo km 12.5, 2 km before the lake; tel 295-0532; 30 double cabins $25-35, all with private bath, hot water, AC; laundry; pool; 10am checkout; restaurant Tue-Sun 9am-5pm, bar*)

## FOOD & DRINK

**Mirador 70** Like the restaurant at the Hotel Vista de Lago, this place also enjoys an excellent view of the lake and that's the main reason to dine or snack here. Their specialty is the *mojarra rellena*, lake fish stuffed with shrimp and a full meal will range from $8 to $14. (*Located 2 blocks after Hotel Vista de Lago; 12-7pm*)

## RECREATION

**Club Salvadoreño** This sprawling club at the end of the road around Lago de Ilopango boasts one of the few golf courses ($28 for 18 holes) within easy reach of the capital. Palm trees dot the posh, manicured facilities, next to rows of polished cars and small private boats. If golf isn't your game, there are also tennis courts, pools, a soccer field and a volleyball court. Choose among two bars and two restaurants where a full meal will cost about $10. If you want to stay the night, five 6-person cabañas are a good deal at just $8 each. Although access is restricted to members, they offer temporary membership cards for visitors for $35 for 15 days. For membership info, call the central office in San Salvador at 225-1634 or 225-1654. *(At end of lake road; Wed-Sun 8am-4pm, Thur-Sun 8am-6pm)*

**Turicentro Apulo** The closest *turicentro* to San Salvador is one of the most popular in the country, with large pools, tall trees and restaurants on the shore of the lake. It has seen extensive renovations over recent years, but when the crowds pour in from San Salvador the beach is not very inviting. Cabañas rent for $4.50 per day.

A better idea than swimming is to climb aboard one of the boats that make trips around the lake. A short ride of 30 minutes or so is only $3.50 for person and the boatman will take you to some interesting sites nearby. A trip all around the lake takes about 3 hours and costs around $30 per boat. The 3-hour trip includes enough time to see all the major points of interest around the lake, including Amatitán (a private part of the lake with extravagant houses), Rio El Desagüe, Corinto (where the Club Salvadoreño is located) and some of the lakeside villages. *(8am-5pm; admission $0.80)*

## DETAILS

■ **BUSES: San Salvador (15)**, every 15 min until 5pm, 16km, 55min. Leaves from the "Hula Hula" bus stop in front of the National Palace in San Salvador.

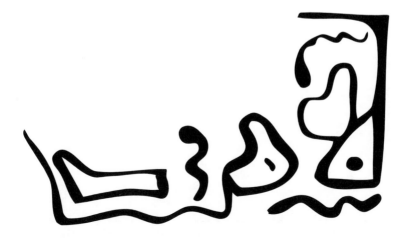

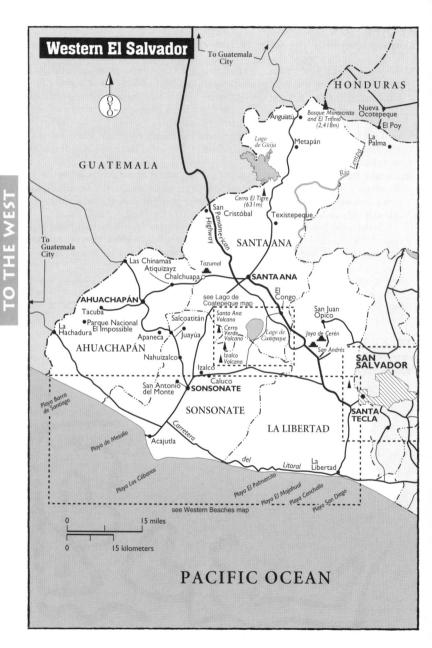

# Western El Salvador

To Guatemala City

HONDURAS

Nueva Ocotepeque

El Poy

La Palma

Anguiatú

Bosque Montecristo and El Trifinio (2,418m)

Lago de Güija

Metapán

GUATEMALA

Río Lempa

Cerro El Tigre (631m)

San Cristóbal

Texistepeque

San Panamerican Highway

SANTA ANA

To Guatemala City

Las Chinamas

Atiquizayz

Chalchuapa

Tazumal

SANTA ANA

El Congo

AHUACHAPÁN

Tacuba

Parque Nacional El Impossible

La Hachadura

Apaneca

AHUACHAPÁN

Nahuizalco

see Lago de Coatepeque map

Salcoatitán

Juayúa

Santa Ana Volcano

Cerro Verde Volcano

Izalco Volcano

Lago de Coatepeque

San Juan Opico

Joya de Cerén

San Andrés

SAN SALVADOR

Izalco

Caluco

SONSONATE

San Antonio del Monte

SONSONATE

LA LIBERTAD

SANTA TECLA

Playa Barra de Santiago

Carretera

del

Litoral

La Libertad

Playa de Metalío

Acajutla

Playa Los Cóbanos

Playa El Palmarcito

Playa El Majahual

Playa Conchalio

Playa San Diego

see Western Beaches map

0     15 miles

0     15 kilometers

PACIFIC OCEAN

# TO THE WEST

Western El Salvador, with its beaches, forests, volcanoes and mountain towns, seems straight out of a tourist brochure. It has some of the most dramatic volcanoes and mountains in the country, from Cerro Verde, Izalco and the Santa Ana Volcanoes, clustered near the Lago de Coatepeque, to the cloud forests of Montecristo in the northern reaches of Santa Ana department. In the other direction, flat coastal plains slide into the beaches of Santiago and Metalío.

The cities of the west are as diverse as its geography. The coffee city of Santa Ana, the second-largest city in the country, is one of the most enjoyable places to spend time in El Salvador, while the cloudy mountain towns of Juayúa and Apaneca are about the most relaxing.

Finally, the west is packed with things to do. Spend some time climbing the mountains near Lago de Coatepeque or hiking in the Montecristo Reserve. Splurge on a fine pair of boots in Santa Ana and strut like a real *vaquero* or explore the beaches and inlets south of Ahuachapán.

The sights of western El Salvador are close to the capital. A day's travelling, with or without a car, will get you anywhere and back to San Salvador if you leave early in the morning. Many buses run between San Salvador, Sonsonate and Santa Ana, and even small towns like Apaneca and Juayúa are easy to get to. Public transportation is more difficult to find along the Coastal Highway and north toward Montecristo.

Heavy rains douse the west from July to October, so don't be surprised if many dirt roads become impassable during that time. You can cross into Guatemala at La Hachadura and Las Chinamas in Ahuachapán department and at San Cristóbal and Anguiatú in Santa Ana department.

■ **EMERGENCY POLICE NUMBERS (PNC): La Libertad department:** 346-0705, 335-3121. **Sonsonate department:** 450-2791, 451-1099, 451-5447, 451-6944.

**Ahuachapán department:** 443-1048, 443-1373. **Santa Ana department:** 440-4273, 440-4255, 440-4271, 440-4193.

# Santa Tecla

(Nueva San Salvador)
Pop. 135,000
12km from San Salvador

## SANTA TECLA THEN

Santa Tecla, also known as Nueva San Salvador, is located next to San Salvador in the earthquake-prone Zalcuatitán Valley. By the 19th century, at least two quakes every 100 years led many people in the area to suggest that it might be better to relo-cate the Salvadoran capital to what was believed (incorrectly, time would prove) to be a more stable
spot. It took the destructive quake of 1854, though, to convince the government to move, and the ranch of Santa Tecla was chosen as the new location. Somehow, though, the switch was never made, and San Salvador still "swings" every few decades.

## SANTA TECLA NOW

Sandwiched between the San Salvador Volcano and the coastal mountain range in the Uliman Plane (from the Nahuat, meaning "Place Where Rubber is Harvested"), Santa Tecla is ringed by mountains that keep it cool. Towering palm trees fill a broad main plaza and a market chokes many streets, including the highway, in the center of town. One interesting aspect of the city is the 19th century architecture. Many of Santa Tecla's structures have an interesting Neoclassical-influenced colonial design. Some good exam-ples are the Hospicio Guirola, Iglesia del Carmen, Iglesia El Señor del Calvario and the City Hall. The two new ring roads that now carry traffic around instead of through the town have made the Santa Tecla more peaceful.

Aside from many commercial centers and mini-malls, Santa Tecla is quiet, essentially just a glorified suburb of San Salvador. It does offer one of the best bookstores in the country and some interesting places to eat. It also serves as the handiest departure point for climbing the San Salvador Volcano.

## FOOD & DRINK

**Cafetería Terraza** A dark place in one of the city's oldest buildings with good sand-wiches and hamburgers from $2.50. *(8am-8pm)*

**Pip's Carymar** A large *pupusería*/restaurant/pastry shop with all the atmosphere (and noise) of a truck stop, but they are famous for the bakery and cakes they make–try the *torta chilena*. A glass of *horchata* costs $0.70 and *pupusas* are served from 3:30pm on. *(8am-9pm)*

**Meson de Goya** A great place run by college students. The Central American Technical Institute (ITCA) built this Meson as a training ground for the future chefs

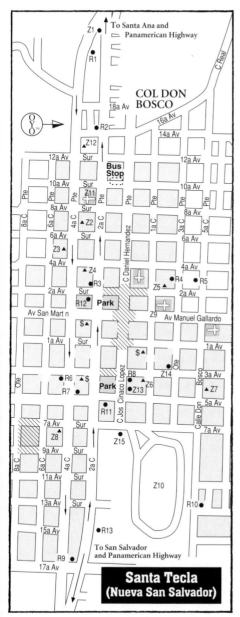

● **FOOD & DRINK**

R1  *Mariscos Las Delicias*
R2  Pip's Carymar
R3  *Ice Cream*
R4  Pizzeria Italia
R5  *Pupuseria*
R6  *Restaurant OK*
R7  *Elsy's Cakes*
R8  *Toto's Pizza*
R9  *Restaurant La Marea*
R10  Restaurant La Cueva
R11  Merendero Tecleño
R12  Cafetería Terraza
R13  Meson de Goya

▲ **OTHER**

Z1  Shell gas station
Z2  Supermarket
Z3  FMLN sign
Z4  Clásicos Roxsil
Z5  City Hall
Z6  Shopping Center
Z7  Club Tecleño
Z8  Shell gas station
Z9  Iglesia del Carmen
Z10  Sports fields
Z11  Iglesia Señor del Calvario
Z12  Talabartería El Alazan
Z13  Casa de la Cultura
Z14  Artesanias Dulces Albanes
Z15  La Casa Guirola

and hotel managers. The food and service are first class and the prices are reasonable. The *a la carte* menu ranges from $4.50 to $11.25. *(Tel 228-9302; Tue-Sun 7am-8pm)*

**Pizzeria Italia** Enjoy a large cheese pizza for $6 in this festive place filled with music, beer posters and bright colors. Just so things don't get out of hand, though, there's a three-beer limit per person. *(Thur-Tue 10am-2pm, 4-9pm)*

**Restaurant La Cueva** This restaurant is one of the classier places in town, set up on the second floor over the owner's house. Meat and seafood dishes run $7.50-$11.50, while a big bowl of *mariscada* costs $8.60. Their special is a Cuban meat dish with cheese, onions, cilantro and a special tomato sauce, all for $2.85. (*Mon-Thur 11am-9pm, Fri-Sat 11am-10:30pm*)

**Merendero Tecleño** This is a very traditional Salvadoran place that has been around for decades. Try the *chilate con nuegados*, a desert that is eaten after the *pupusas*. (*Thur-Tue 10am-9pm*)

## SIGHTS

**Casa de la Cultura** A small museum displaying handicrafts, paintings and photography. The information center can also answer all your questions about the area. (*Mon-Fri 8am-4pm*)

## HIKING

**San Salvador Volcano** The crater of this looming giant is a beautiful place to hike and to view the surrounding landscape, including San Salvador, Santa Tecla, the San Vicente Volcano, the green waters of the Lago de Ilopango and the Puerto del Diablo. Quezaltepeque, as the San Salvador Volcano is also known, actually has two peaks. The higher peak, Pichaco (1,890m), is about three kilometers east of the lower peak, El Boquerón ("The Big Mouth"), which makes for a good climb. The three kilometers around the lip of El Boquerón take about two hours to hike. Near the crater, a local TV station has established a small botanic garden; it makes a beautiful vista point as well.

The hike down the 400 meters to the bottom of the crater is difficult and takes about 90 minutes. Inside the crater you'll find a second, smaller cone formed in the 1917 eruption that flattened most of San Salvador. Flowers are grown in the crater and it is not unusual for women in their 50s walking barefoot and with baskets of flowers on their head to pass you like greased lightning.

To get there, take bus 103 from 4a Av Sur and C Hernandez in Santa Tecla (departures every two hours) to the pueblo of Boquerón near the top of the volcano. From there, it's about one kilometer more to the rim. For those driving on their own, access to the volcano is easy during the dry season but may require a 4 x 4 during the rainy months. There have been cases of robberies reported by people climbing here, so it is recommended that the Tourist Police (298-6005) joins hiking groups. (*See Near San Salvador map*)

## SHOPPING

**Plaza Merliot** El Salvador's newest shopping center is located at the border of Santa Tecla and New San Salvador, an area known as Ciudad Merliot. It is complete with supermarkets, movies, boutiques, children's play areas, etc. They go all out decorating the food court for Christmas so you may want to stop by in December.

**Artesanías Dulces Albanes** This place is famous for its selection of sweets and pastries typical to El Salvador including *mazapanes* (sweets made of cashews and fruit), as well as other tropical fruit sweets like *nance* and *guayaba*. (*10am-6pm*)

**Talabartería El Alazan** Here two old leather crafters make excellent custom products including belts ($26) and saddles ($300). *(Tel 228-2783; 8am-5pm)*

## DETAILS

■ **BOOKSTORES: Clásicos Roxsil** The friendly López family—mother, father and two daughters—has been publishing books in El Salvador for 25 years, and runs one of the country's best bookstores to boot. They carry an extensive collection of Salvadoran authors and other Latin American and Spanish literature, as well as large and small color maps of El Salvador. Plus, they can order you almost anything from anywhere else in the country. Tell them you heard it here. *(Mon-Fri 8am-12:30pm, 2:30-6pm, Sat 8am-12pm)*

■ **BUSES:** All buses that leave San Salvador's western terminal pass through Santa Tecla on their way west (see San Salvador). Also, bus **101** runs between Santa Tecla and San Salvador, passing near El Salvador del Mundo.

■ **ENTERTAINMENT:** The local theater **Adalberto Guirola** hosts plays by local organizations from time to time.

■ **FESTIVALS: September 13** Santa Tecla. **December 16-25 (24)** Natividad del Señor.

■ **SPORTS: Club Tecleño** If you're going to be in the country for a while, you can use this private club's tennis courts, pools, basketballs court and restaurant for $35 per month, payable every three months. They have two locations in town. Short term passes are now available, call for details. *(Tel 228-3468, Tue-Sun 10am-9pm).*
**Polideportivo** This group of buildings, pools and tennis courts was constructed for the Pan-American Olympic games on a beautiful site about halfway up the Volcano. Now it is used by students and locals to practice for local and international sporting event. The tennis counts and Olympic swimming pool are first class with a great view. You can use the facilities for next to nothing. Call to find out the schedule. *(Tel 289-1093)*

# Near Santa Tecla

**Los Chorros Turicentro** It's a *turicentro* and it's near San Salvador, but it's still surprisingly pleasant. Four natural pools are filled by water cascading down thickly vegetated slopes—almost like a Hawaiian jungle paradise, except for the crowds. The highest pool seems to have the cleanest water, and the entire *turicentro* is surrounded by ferns, flowers and dripping moss. If you didn't bring a picnic you can grab a bite at one of the small *comedores* at the bottom.

This is the busiest *turicentro* in the country so, even more than with the others, a weekday visit is recommended. Whenever you come, bring flip-flops for the changing rooms and leave your valuables somewhere else, since there's nowhere to put them; the changing rooms will only hold your clothing. Smaller side paths up the mountain may look tempting, but we advise against it—robberies have been reported there. *(18km west of San Salvador, on the Panamerican Highway just west of Santa Tecla; bus 79 from San Salvador from 11a Av Sur and C Rubén Darío toward Lourdes, every 15 min until 5pm, or from* *the Western Terminal take bus 108 for San Juan Opico or 109 for Quetzaltepeque and tell the driver you are going to Los Chorros; $0.80 per person, seniors free; 8am-5:30pm)*

😑 😑 😑 😑 😑

# San Andrés

32km from San Salvador

These ancient ruins lie in the Zapotitán Valley to the west of San Salvador, in the middle of the beautiful, rolling countryside along the Panamerican Highway. The setting is as interesting as the ruins themselves, making San Andrés enjoyable as well as educational.

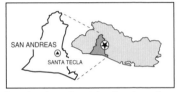

During the last five years, the park has been completely remodeled, making it one of the best day trips from San Salvador. A modern museum built at the site entrance contains a scale model of the complex plus collections of eccentric flints (a symbol of power for the Maya), painted ceramics, tools and the famous archaeologist Stanley Boggs' original notes. The museum also has a new media center with films that provide some information about the people who built the city and lived here.

The Maya, Aztec and Pipil all built their campfires here at one time or another. Evidence has been found that indicates that the region had been inhabited since 200 BC, although most construction occurred after 600 AD.

The ruins were first explored in 1940, but it wasn't until 1977 that a formal excavation was begun. Archeologists have found an abundance of painted pottery nearby along with two *metates* (stone implements used for grinding grains) which indicate that families once lived here.

The partially unearthed ruins cover three and a half kilometers of what would otherwise be prime farmland in the department of La Libertad. The rest remains hidden under smooth, rolling grassland dotted with signs that warn against playing soccer on the site. Like Tazumal, the low step pyramids are mostly covered in smooth concrete, leaving little of the original structures visible.

One main tower and two smaller towers surround a main plaza area. The largest, a double-terraced pyramid with a staircase on its western side, is made mostly of blocks of compacted volcanic ash. A structure to the west may have been an altar for rituals performed by priests or nobles. (The sign at the far end of the site simply explains why that section of San Andrés is closed off.)

During the process of remodeling San Andrés, a complete 17th-century indigo mill was discovered. The excellent state of preservation of the mill is thanks to the eruption of the volcano El Playón in 1658 which covered the area with a thick layer of ash. According to archaeologist Paul Amaroli, it is the best example in the world of an existing colonial indigo mill. When this mill operated El Salvador was the world's leading exporter of indigo and the museum has an interesting display of the importance of this product during colonial days.

Artistic and cultural events are hosted from time to time at the amphitheater. There is also a small arts and crafts store and a bookstore with a decent collection of literature about the Maya, however, some of the books are less expensive in the bookstores of San Salvador. Although there is enough information available at the museum to guide you around the complex, most of it is in Spanish so you may wish to have a bilingual guide accompany you around the site.

Since it's so close to the capital, San Andrés receives over a quarter of a million visitors a year—enough to cause heavy traffic at times. Come on a sunny weekday to avoid the crowds and to enjoy the stark, simple lines of the ruins and the surrounding scenery. To the east, you can watch clouds roll up the base of the San Salvador Volcano which makes this a pleasant picnic area. *(Northwest of San Salvador on the Panamerican Highway, just past the Río Sucio and the military base with two tanks out front. Take any bus west from San Salvador towards Santa Ana and get off at the sign for San Andrés, then walk 200m down the dirt road to the ruins. Tue-Sun 9am-4pm; admission $2.85 per person and $1.15 per vehicle. The service of the guides is free, however, we recommend that you tip them well)*

# Near San Andrés
## ACCOMMODATIONS

**Restaurante and Hotel La Conacaste** If you want to stay near the site and visit for a few days, this is your only option. The hotel has 12 basic single rooms with private bathroom and fans for $23 per night which includes use of the pool; a nice feature if you've been walking around the ruins all day. The meat and shellfish plates, ranging between $3 and $11, are quite good. *(Located at km 24 on the Highway from Santa Ana in front of the free zone known as Exposalva or Zona Franca; tel 318-0642; restaurant open 8am-8pm)*

## FOOD & DRINK

**Restaurant Joya de Cerén** Located at the fork in road that leads to San Juan Opico this restaurant is one of the best dining options in the area. Besides the tasty food you can siesta in a hammock or refresh yourselves in the pool. The wide menu ranges from shrimp for $6.30, to an economical chicken or beef dish for $3.50. Use of the pool costs $1 and to rent one of the cabins for the day is $3. *(8am-8pm)*

**Restaurant The Curve** The Curve is part of a famous local chain of restaurants specializing in beef dishes. The price, quality and quantity of the meat they serve make this carnivore heaven. An 8-oz. beef plate costs $3.50, while the 16 oz. is $5. *(5 km after San Andrés Archaeological Park on the Panamerican Highway; Tue-Sun 12pm-6pm)*

**Restaurant Las Carnitas** Very popular with locals they specialize in typical plates of meats and shellfish. Try the *mondongo* soup made with tripe and seasoned with many spices like *achiote* and oregano. It costs $3 and is said to cure hangovers–appropriately it is usually served on Saturdays and the days after holidays. *(Located at km 24 marker in the city of Lourdes about 8 km from San Andrés; 11am-7pm)*

## SIGHTS

**Hilasal Towel Factory** At the factory store, located right next to the entrance to San Andrés, you can buy the artistic, world-renowned Hilasal towels and other high quality cotton products at good prices. Some will tell you they are the best towels in the world. They also have a mini zoo with some species native to El Salvador and Central America, but it's hardly worth going out of your way to see it.

**The National School of Agriculture** If you are interested in agriculture this is one of the best options in Central America. Here, you can observe some of the research work that is carried out in the experimental plots. The bamboo and other tropical plants including new varieties of papayas, coconuts and avocados that have been introduced in El Salvador are interesting. You can also see the school, fish farm and livestock on the grounds. There is a restructuring going on now, so call the MAG (Tel 228-4443 or 295-0328) for current details. *(A few km north of San Andrés on the opposite side of the Panamerican Highway)*

**Chanmico Lagoon** Follow the street that takes you to Quezaltepeque for approximately 2 km, and there is a sign that says *A Laguna Chanmico* ("To Chanmico Lagoon"). Although not especially attractive for swimming this is a paradise for birdwatchers. During the months of November to January many migratory birds nest in here and there are a great variety of aquatic birds year-round.

**San Andrés Horse Park** Equestrian sports are very popular in El Salvador and there are regular international horse and polo competitions here. This is also used for the famous Peruvian *paso fino* horse exhibitions as well as for dog shows. Times and dates are published in the local press. If you want to ride you will also find some excellent horses for rent. *(Located next to the Fort of the Cavalry regiment on the left side of the Panamerican Highway coming from San Salvador, shortly before arriving at the Joya de Cerén turnoff)*

# Joya de Cerén
### 25km from San Salvador

Unlike most Central American ruins, which are the remains of fancy religious centers and royal residences, Joya de Cerén is the best-preserved domestic archeological site in the Americas. The ruins, near San Juan Opico, are spread over a small area and none are particularly stellar, but the site and the museum next door are both good places to learn what everyday life in El Salvador was like 1,500 years ago. UNESCO declared Joya de Cerén a World Heritage Site in 1993.

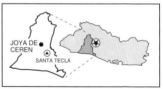

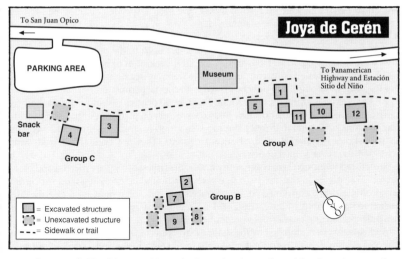

■ **Background.** The history of Joya de Cerén has been shaped by the volcanoes that loom (and loomed) menacingly on the horizon. The Ilopango Volcano, which stood where the Lago de Ilopango is today, erupted in 260 AD and smothered the surrounding Zapotitán valley under one meter of volcanic ash.

Over the next three centuries, people gradually drifted back into the area, bringing with them a complex culture which in many ways allowed them to live better than many Salvadorans do today. Archeological evidence indicates that Joya de Cerén's inhabitants ate deer and dog meat, corn, three varieties of beans, squash, chili peppers, cacao, avocados and nuts. Farmers fought erosion in their small cornfields with low soil ridges to divert water runoff, and vegetable, flower and fruit gardens surrounded their houses. Residents traded with civilizations in Honduras, Guatemala and perhaps others as far away as Costa Rica.

But just as the region was completely resettled by the end of the 6th century, the Laguna Caldera Volcano erupted and buried part of the valley again, this time under three meters of ash. Though nobody could have possibly survived the eruption and the 1,000-degree ash that blanketed the area, no human remains have been found at the site, leading archeologists to theorize that the inhabitants had advance warning and left in time.

At such extreme temperatures vegetable remains were instantly carbonized, preserving the plants that were part of the daily lives of Joya de Cerén's inhabitants. So much rock and dust accumulated, in fact—14 layers at last count—that the site became a small time capsule on the order of Pompeii in Italy.

The ruins were discovered in 1976 when a bulldozer clearing land for grain silos overturned part of an ancient wall. The discovery was initially ignored—the grain silos were constructed and still operate side by side with tourists and archeologists. In time, though, archeologists realized that something important was waiting just beneath the surface, and ground radar was used to locate other buildings deep beneath the clay and ash. Since 1997 large-scale excavation works have been suspended because the site was growing faster than it could be maintained.

■ **The Site.** The entire excavation is no more than 100 meters from end to end, and only two of the three groups of ruins (A and C) are open to the public. These sections are visible from the path, set back inside large steel enclosures to protect them from the weather and overzealous souvenir hunters. The walkway begins at group A and continues to group C. Group B can only be visited with special permission.

All the buildings at the site were found lined up 30 degrees east of north, possibly to catch a crosswind for ventilation. The houses were built on platforms of baked clay, with clay columns, walls, and thatched palm roofs. In group A, structures 10 and 12 were for shamanistic or communal use by healers or priests. They are distinctly shaped, with restricted access via a small doorway.

Structure 3 in group C is a community house, the largest (40 square meters) and best-preserved structure in the site. Two large vases were found here holding traces of *chicha* an alcoholic drink consumed at group meetings and still popular in El Salvador. Structure 4, probably a house, contained a sleeping mat and plant seeds. Remains of henequen, cacao and guava trees were found nearby.

Archeologists were stumped by the shape of structure 7 in group B before figuring out it served as a steam bath, with solid mud walls lined with a bench and a small round hole in the domed ceiling. The ceiling is important in that it proves the indigenous inhabitants of the Americas already used the arch in construction before the Spanish arrived (it was previously thought that they had learned it from the Europeans). The bath was used for both medicinal and ceremonial purifications. Structure 9 is a warehouse.

Joya de Cerén's inhabitants left few things behind in their hasty departure. On the floor

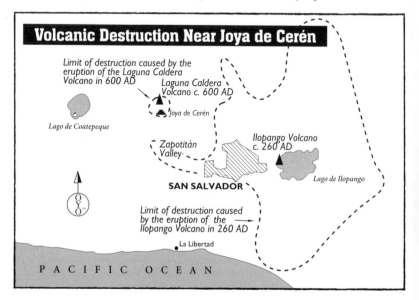

**Volcanic Destruction Near Joya de Cerén**

Limit of destruction caused by the eruption of the Laguna Caldera Volcano in 600 AD

Laguna Caldera Volcano c. 600 AD

Joya de Cerén

Lago de Coatepeque

Zapotitán Valley

Ilopango Volcano c. 260 AD

Lago de Ilopango

**SAN SALVADOR**

Limit of destruction caused by the eruption of the Ilopango Volcano in 260 AD

La Libertad

PACIFIC    OCEAN

Top: Wharf, La Libertad
Bottom Left: Fruit seller, Juayúa
Bottom Right: Izote, the national flower

Top:     Suchitoto and Lago de Suchitlán
Bottom:  Buses, San Salvador

## To Get Involved

If you're interested in participating in an archaeological dig, try contacting María Isaura Arauz at CONCULTURA, the Salvadoran organization that coordinates the work. *(Blvd Distrito Comercial, Centro de Gobierno; tel 221-4367)*

of one house researchers found a lump of hematite used to paint pottery. Some ceremonial pottery was also discovered, including a sculpture with an alligator head.

The museum next to the site is very well-done and clearly organized, with explanations of the history of the site in Spanish, examples of beautifully painted pottery and the fossilized footprint of an early resident. There are usually some enthusiastic young archeology students around—identified by their Joya de Cerén T-shirts—who will be glad to give you a free (though a tip is welcome) guided tour of the museum and site. A small cafeteria serves snacks and drinks.

There's a lot to learn here if archaeology is your thing. If, on the other hand, you prefer impressive masonry and lingering vistas, you'll probably be disappointed. You can't actually walk in and around the delicate ruins, since they are closed off inside cages and below ground level. The museum is informative and is small enough so that you can take your time poring over the exhibits and still have time to visit the site. The whole thing can be done in about two hours and you can squeeze Joya de Cerén and San Andrés into a long afternoon. It's only about 5 km between the two sites and if you ask around at San Andrés there are guides who will take you between them on horseback. The area is often packed with schoolchildren on field trips for the day. *(8km south of San Juan Opico, just north of the steel bridge; take bus 108 from San Salvador to San Juan Opico, get off at "ruinas" stop; Tue-Sun 9am-4pm; admission is $3 per person and $1.15 per vehicle)*

# La Libertad

Pop. 36,000
36km from San Salvador

## LA LIBERTAD THEN

The port city of La Libertad (The Freedom) is situated south of San Salvador in an area known to ancient tribes as "Oak Mountain." La Libertad was first used for international shipping in the 18th century, but didn't expand until the 19th century. In 1854, the city hosted the first steam boat ever to ply the coastal waters of El

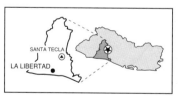

Salvador. Three years later, a multi-national force of 1,200 left from here to boot meddling US filibuster William Walker out of Nicaragua once and for all.

## LA LIBERTAD NOW

La Libertad is a commercial and fishing port somewhat smaller than Acajutla, and is a popular weekend beach getaway from San Salvador. Stores sell beach balls and practi-

TO THE WEST

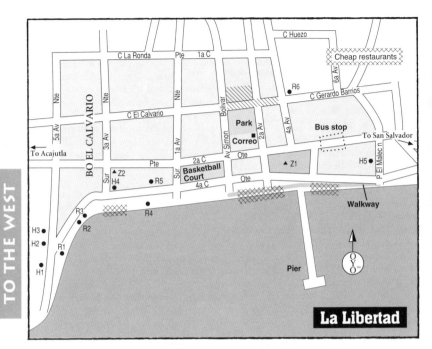

La Libertad

cally every restaurant in town serves fresh seafood. The streets teem with all types of people, from wealthy weekenders from the capital to old expatriate surfers. Every afternoon the city comes even more alive as fishermen return to sell their catch on the wharf which is controlled by a handful of fishing cooperatives.

The pier is usually filled with an interesting combination of fish merchants, boat keepers and tourists who come to ogle the day's catch and to watch the boats being hauled up. You'll find a real maritime zoo here with countless varieties of fresh shellfish, seashell, fish and other sea creatures sold at low prices, especially if you remember to bargain. Also on sale are some interesting arts and crafts made with elaborate seashells. Another unique find is shark liver oil which the locals believe can cure many illnesses.

La Libertad isn't beautiful, but it certainly is happening. Stay here to travel to the surrounding beaches during the day or to cruise along the Coastal Highway and enjoy the view. The beach, where Oliver Stone filmed part of *Salvador,* is black with volcanic sand, and kids wander up and down it peddling shells. While it has good waves it is too rocky. Besides, all the fishermen throw their fish guts and other junk right off the wharf. Other beaches a few kilometers in either direction are good, but the best surf

● **ACCOMMODATIONS**

H1 Hacienda Don Rigo
H2 La Posada de Don Lito
H3 Hotel Rick
H4 La Posada Familiar
H5 El Malecón Don Lito

● **FOOD & DRINK**

R1 El Delfin
R2 Restaurant Punta Roca
R3 *El Nuevo Altamar*
R4 *Sandra Restaurant*
R5 *Restaurant Alta Mar*
R6 *Ice cream*

▲ **OTHER**

Z1 Turicentro La Libertad
Z2 Hospital de Tablas

is a few hundred meters to the right of the wharf on a rocky corner of the beach called Punta Roca.

Great effort has been made to develop and improve tourism. Among the achievements has been the establishment of the Tourist Police force. The delinquency that ports are known for has diminished considerably here. The number of visitors and new start up businesses is on the rise. There are also plans to refurbish the deteriorated seaside walk.

## ACCOMMODATIONS

**El Malecón Don Lito** Clean, jungle decor and a good pool. The restaurant serves seafood dishes for $5-$10. Room prices double for 24 hours. *(Tel 335-3201; 16S $19.50, 4D $20.25, all with private bath, AC; restaurant)*

**La Posada de Don Lito** Owned by guess who, so wave to him as you walk by. There's a restaurant across the street. Prices double for 24 hours. *(Tel 335-3166; 10 D $23 with fan or $27.50 with AC, all with private bath)*

**La Hacienda de Don Rodrigo** The third site in the Lito Empire has a pool and a good view. *(Tel 335-3166; 20D $17.25 with fan, $19.50 with AC, all with private bath)*

**Hotel Rick** The rooms are simple but clean and popular with surfers due in part to its location near Punta Roca. Deep sea fishing can be arranged here. *(Tel 335-3033; S $11.75 D $17.25, all with private bath)*

**Hotel La Posada Familiar** Simple, clean little rooms and a great interior patio. The restaurant serves a variety of chicken dishes from $2.50 and fish platters from $4. *(Tel 335-3252; 8S 4D, $9-$14.25, some with private bath; the rate is for 12 hours; laundry; restaurant)*

## FOOD & DRINK

One of the most entertaining things to do in La Libertad is eat during *Lunadas* (nights of the full moon) where the many seaside restaurants offer all types of special dinners by the light of the moon.

**Restaurant Punta Roca** Probably the best place on the beach to have a beer and relax. Bob Rotherhan, a Miami native, runs the place with two floors and great views. Bob came to La Libertad in 1974 and was the first in the area to open a restaurant. During the war, most of his business came from Salvadorans escaping from the city. Bob can also arrange for a half or full day of deep sea or sport fishing. *(11am-8:30pm)*

**El Delfín** A pleasant place with a patio overlooking the waves and a parrot to liven up the atmosphere. Manager Ricardo Guardado has been around for 11 years and likes

## The Don of La Libertad

**D**on Lito is the most famous character in town. Give him credit for running some pretty spiffy, clean hotels that cater to El Salvador's emerging middle class. He'll roll every one of his r's describing to you how he engineered everything himself and built his mini-empire from scratch. Salvadorans flooded to La Libertad during the civil war in search of a psychological escape from the terror, and a night's stay at one of Don Lito's hotels was a good break. He also has a lot to do with the emergence of La Libertad as an international tourist attraction.

to talk (in Spanish) about the local scene. They serve a great variety of shellfish and fish plates–a tasty lobster *reina* costs $12. *(11am-8pm)*

**La Dolce Vita** The menu at this award-winning restaurant is a unique combination of Italian and Salvadoran seafood recipes with such specialties as *dolce vita* lobster for $15, shellfish pasta *a la marinera* for $8 and some great shrimps dishes for $10. The three floors are well decorated with a great view of blue sky against the Salvadoran coastline. *(1.5 km east of La Libertad along the Coastal Highway; tel 335-3592; 11am-late)*

**La Curva de Don Jere (The Curve of Don Jere)** A popular local hangout specializing in *mariscada* (seafood soup) starting at $8 plus a good variety of shellfish and fish dishes. *(1.5 km east of La Libertad along the Coastal Highway 100 meters before La Dolce Vita; 9am-10pm)*

**Merendero Doña Paulina (Paulina's Lunchroom)** If you can't wait to get to La Libertad to eat, stop here. Prices range from $1.70 to $3 and you can eat in or get it to go. The typical Salvadoran fare served in the afternoons is especially good. If you want to stick around awhile you can use their pool. *(Km 33 on the Highway from San Salvador to La Libertad; tel 335-3325; 6:30am-9pm)*

## SIGHTS

**Turicentro La Libertad** The Antiguo Puerto de La Libertad ("Old Port of La Libertad") has been converted into a *turicentro*. As usual, admission includes access to bathrooms and changing rooms. *(8am-5pm; $0.80 per person)*

## RECREATION

**Fisherman's Restaurant and Beach Club** Located just east of La Libertad at Las Flores Beach this club offers 3 pools, a good restaurant, dressing rooms, tennis courts, ping pong tables, and games for the kids. Although it is a membership club, if you pay $5.75 per person and consume a minimum of $11.50 per person in the restaurant, they will let you use the facilities. The restaurant is complete with a pleasant view and an international bar. *(Located about 100 meters down the beach from La Dolce Vita restaurant. On weekends call 264-3110 or 335-3272 to be sure they have room)*

**Hospital de Tablas (Surf Board Hospital)** Located next to the Hotel Posada Familiar, this small shop rents and repairs surfboards and associated gear. A 12-hour board rental costs $8.60. *(8am-6pm)*

## DETAILS

■ **BUSES:** The **80** bus serves all the beaches west of town, every 15 min (often more on weekends) until sunset. **Playa San Diego (82)**, every 15 min (often more on

## Surf's Up, Again

**W**est of La Libertad are some of the best surfing beaches in Central America. Playa El Tunco, Playa El Sunzal, and Playa El Zonte became world famous with surfers in the 1960s due to their steady but varied breaks, and by the mid-70s there was a large surfing community here. Not surprisingly the flow of surfers fell to a trickle during the 80s thanks to the war. Since the peace agreement, however, the world's surfers have returned and so have the surf shops, lodges, and cafes that support their obsession.

Weekends) until sunset, 5km, 20min. **San Salvador (102)**, every 15 min until 5:30pm, 36km, 1hr.

■ **FESTIVALS: October 22-24 (23)** San Rafael and San Miguel. **December 7-8 (7)** Virgen de Concepción.

■ **VISITOR'S INFORMATION:** You can get tourist information at the Caseta Touristica at the entrance to the old pier. A tourist-focussed newspaper called the Zona Azul gives you the local events, attractions and news in Spanish.

# Playa San Diego

A long stretch of white sand with soft waves, this beach, one of the loveliest in Central America, is practically uninhabited during the week. Along the beach are a mixture of cheap *comedores* and dream houses built by people who are never around to use them. Bamboo shack restaurants along the beach charge about $3.50 for a plate of fresh fish. Look for signs for the Villa San Diego or the Villa del Pacífico beach resort about five kilometers east of La Libertad off the Coastal Highway. Your best bet is to drive down and find a passage in between the brick walls to a good section of the beach.

## ACCOMMODATIONS

**Las Cabañas de Don Lito** The suites and cabins each hold two people. Prices double for 24 hrs. *(On the highway outside the entrance to the beach; tel 335-3216, 4 suites $27.50 with cable TV, AC, 12 cabins $12.60, all with private bath)*

**Via del Pacífico** A clean, well-kept hotel with a swimming pool, ocean side dining and a great view of La Libertad and the bay. It is also a good place to eat (service from 8am-8pm). A main dish goes from $5.50 for chicken to an exquisite giant shrimp or lobster for $17.50. Breakfast costs between $3.50 and $5. *(About 100 meters off the road; tel 345-5681; 12D $31.50)*

## DETAILS

■ **BUSES: La Libertad (82)**, every 15 min (often more on Weekends) until sunset, 5km, 20min.

# Walter Deininger National Park

Just across the Coastal Highway turnoff to San Diego Beach is the newest coastal botanical park in Central America. The reserve's 732-hectares of arid tropical forest, donated by the Salvadoran philanthropist Walter T. Deininger, is surprisingly diverse, offering a good lesson in arid land ecology.

Even though the terrain surrounding the park is quite dry, there are numerous waterfalls, wells and oasis here and as you walk around you'll notice the variety of coastal microclimates that they create. This is a good birdwatching area too with over 87 species recorded including falcons and toucans. Several mammals at risk of extinction make their home in the park such as anteaters, coyotes, and *tepescuintle* which is like a tropical raccoon. Also along the trails are some lookout points with stunning views of the Pacific Ocean and an archaeological site.

In order to visit you must contact the contact the Salvadoran Tourism Institute

## San Antonio Waterfall and Cave

**N**ear Walter Deininger National Park, on the Coastal highway before the road to the San Diego Beach, you'll see various signs referring to the San Antonio Falls and a cave called "la Cueva de la Curva." The local advice is not to visit these sights alone since delinquents frequent them and there have been several assaults on tourists. If you wish to visit you should have one of the tourism police available in La Libertad go along with your group.

*(Rubén Darío #619, tel 222-8000)* in San Salvador ahead of time to arrange a guide. You will need to bring your own water and to eat you can either choose one of the open-air *comedores* right next to the park or take the short road down to Playa San Diego where there is a little more to choose from. *(7am-3:30pm; $3, seniors free)*

# Western Beaches

The times to reach these beaches are only estimates, but since the buses stop for person, sack of rice and chicken along the road they are realistic. If you are in a consider taking a taxi or hitching a ride to your destination.

## Playa Conchalío

When the tide is low, Playa Conchalío is enormous—a nice place to relax in relativ tude except on weekends and holidays when it can be very crowded. A kiosk entrance called "Champa Las Brisas" serves oysters, clams and beer. The beach in front is rocky, but 20 meters to the right is a sandy area backed by countless palm trees and many more places to eat.

To get there turn left about three kilometers west of La Libertad, right after the old Hotel Los Arcos. Make the first left onto a dirt road, turn right at Rancho Tabosa after about 100 meters, then go through the little neighborhood straight ahead to the beach. Or, tell the bus driver to let you off in front of the old Hotel Los Arcos. From there it's a five or ten-minute walk.

### DETAILS
■**BUSES: La Libertad (80)**, every 15 min (more often on weekends) until sunset, 3km, 30 min.

## Playa El Majahual

El Majahual is a grimy, active beach filled with Salvadorans looking for business or a good time. On weekends and holidays there are so many buses and people here that you can hardly find the sand.

The beach here has soft, shiny black sand, medium waves and no rocks. As soon as you walk in you're mobbed by people begging you to stop at their hotel or *rancho.* Not surprisingly, the cheap accommodations and *comedores* seem to go on forever—look around, because some are better than others. People on the beach sell pony rides, coconuts and drinks.

## ACCOMMODATIONS

Many *ranchos* offer food, parking, changing facilities and rooms for the night. Prices vary from $5 for a weeknight to $12.50 for a weekend night for a tiny room with a single bed and light. Bring bug repellent.

**Hotel El Pacífico** A jukebox makes this place loud and lively. Most people just come here for the day, and no wonder—the rooms are stark and small, with just a bed, fan and table. Rates are for 12 hours. *(Along the road to beach; 45 rooms $7 with common bath, $8 with private bath; pool; restaurant)*

**Hotel Solimar** Turn left before the Hotel Pacífico, and go down the dirt road about 100 meters to find the hotel in a grassy enclosed area, with a small pool and so-so rooms. Again, usually just a day hangout, so the prices are for 12 hours only. Singles will fit two people. A seafood plate at the restaurant runs around $5. *(16S $7 for 12 hours, all with private bath; pool; restaurant)*

**Club Tecleño** Lots of grass and breezes, coconut trees and benches. You need to get permission (in the form of a courtesy card) from the main office to use the private beach area. Or just drive in, since there's usually no one at the gate. To stay overnight, reservations are usually required about a week in advance. Small rooms fit four people, large rooms eight, and the restaurant serves breakfast and lunch. *(Past El Majahual beach across from the Cerro Mar Resort; tel 328-3468, small room $5.75, large room $9.25, all with kitchen, private bath and furniture; restaurant)*

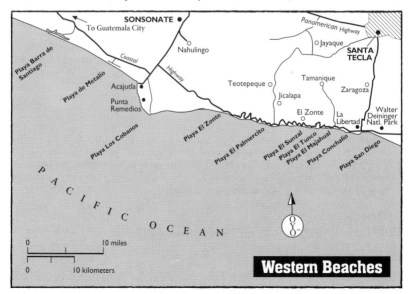

Western Beaches

### FOOD & DRINK
Numerous *comedores* serve fish, shrimp, chicken and meat. Most close around 10pm, but some are open all night. Try a *mariscada* for $6.50 or a fish plate for about $3.

### DETAILS
■ **BUSES: La Libertad (80)**, every 15 min (more often on weekends) until sunset, 5km, 45 min.

## Playa El Tunco
This surfer's hangout has a bigger selection of lodging than other area beaches so it makes a good choice if you are looking to ride the long left break or just relax under the sun. El Tunco's primary landmark is a large volcanic rock that resembles a pig, hence the name which means "hog" in English.

### ACCOMMODATIONS
**Hotel Los Surfeadores** The original surf hut on the beach. The rooms are simple, two beds and a fan with a shared bathroom. They rent more surf boards than anything else. *(At the end of the Playa El Tunco, one km down the road at the turn off at Km 42 of the Coastal Highway; 4 rooms, $7)*

**Tienda Erika (Erika's Store)** Erika has two small rooms for rent on the second floor of her store. It's similar to the Hotel Los Surfeadores next door but with a view and a breeze. It would be a good idea to call ahead to book a room on weekends *(Tel 827-5349; 2 rooms, $5.75)*

**El Tubo Surf Shop** El Tubo's owner Jaime Alonso runs a full service surf shop, but has some clean rooms for rent as well. *(Tel 826-6084, 826-7610; 4 rooms, $8 to $9 per room depending on size and view; restaurant)*

**Tortuga Surf Lodge** The Tortuga, opened in April 2000 by the friendly and helpful Roberto Gallardo, is another decent place to lay your head. Prices are negotiable for long stays and transportation can be arranged to the airport and other surf spots. *(Tel 298-2986, e-mail rob.gal@vianet.com.sv; 4 rooms, $12 with shared bath, $16 with private bath, $5 to put a third person in a room)*

### FOOD & DRINK
**Restaurante La Bocana** Those on a surfer's budget will appreciate La Bocana's fresh food. The menu runs from $1 sandwiches and hamburgers to fish for $3.50 though some seafood specialties top out at $12.50. The second floor has a great view and a sea breeze and owner Luis Alonso (Jaime, of El Tubo, is his brother) often lets customers hang out a hammock for the night. *(7am to 8pm)*

### DETAILS
■ **BUSES: La Libertad (80)**, every 15 min (more often on weekends) until sunset, 7km, 1hr.

## Playa El Sunzal
This is fast becoming one of the favorite beaches west of La Libertad for many visitors. Only 13 km from the port city of La Libertad, this Salvadoran beach is one of the most

famous with surfers and surfing movies have been shot on the long right break. If you are into surfing or just watching surfers then this is the place, but the fantastic coastal views will compete for your attention.

The public beach at El Sunzal can get crowded on weekends so you may want to take a short stroll to Playa El Tunco or the beach next to Club Salvadoreño. Both are less than 1 km away.

## ACCOMMODATIONS

There are no formal hotels at El Sunzal, just a few surfer-friendly beach houses that hang out "Rooms for Rent" signs, including the Sleep Surf right next to Café Sunzal.

## FOOD & DRINK

**Café Sunzal** Opened in January 2000 this is, without a doubt, one of the best restaurants around and has one of the best beach views in El Salvador. The décor, the surf and exquisite food all blend into a great romantic ambience and the prices are reasonable considering the quality and location. The blue-plate specials are a three-course meal and go for about $12.50 and the shrimp with oyster and mushroom sauce is recommended. If you're not in the mood for seafood the stuffed chicken breast is a good choice for about $8. *(Km 43.5 of the coastal highway; tel 328-0132, 328-0098; Tue-Sun 11am-5pm)*

## RECREATION

**Club Salvadoreño** This is a second location of this exclusive country club with similar facilities. See Lago de Ilopango for details.

## DETAILS

■ **BUSES: La Libertad (80)**, every 15 min (more often on weekends) until sunset, 8km, 75 min.

# Playa El Palmarcito
## ACCOMMODATIONS

**Club Atami** This stylish grassy resort with thatched huts, pools, and well-kept picnic areas is farther down the coast near Playa El Palmarcito. The view from the garden over the ocean is magnificent. This place makes a great secluded getaway, even if there isn't any service at night. If you'd like a room, reservations are recommended (their office is at 69 Av Sur #164 in San Salvador; tel 223-9000) and due to the resort's popularity you should call as far in advance as possible. You can also spend the day here if you have a passport; just explain at the gate that you're a tourist. *(Coastal Highway; tel 274-6206, 886-2260, e-mail shangrila@pro.com.sv; $5.25 per person per day, hut $2.25 with 4 hammocks, doubles and quads $15 per person per night, the Oasis Shangri-La Guesthouse sleeps ten for about $75; all with private bath; checkout 3pm; restaurant 8:30am-9pm)*

**TO THE WEST**

## DETAILS
■ **BUSES: La Libertad (80)**, every 15 min (more often on weekends) until sunset, 13 km, 90min.

# Playa El Zonte

In the 1970's a Japanese visitor fell in love with El Salvador, and a native girl. Their son, Saburo bought a piece of land on this black-sand beach, started the **Horizonte Surf Camp** and the rest is history. The laid back, but well run Horizonte has a restaurant, bar, cabins, campground, and swimming pool. You can also take surfing lessons. Like with most of the surfer's lodges the price is negotiable depending on how long you stay. (*e-mail saburosurf-camp@hotmail.com; prices start at $5 per bed and $3 per hammock or you can pitch your own tent for $1.75*) Two friendly women run the artsy surf hotel **La Casa Del Fria**. A meal at the restaurant, where the menu depends on their mood, starts at about $2.25. (*4 rooms, D/S $8*)

## DETAILS
■ **BUSES: La Libertad (80)**, every 15 min (more often on weekends) until sunset, 17 km, 1hr 45min.

# Playa Los Cóbanos

Fifteen kilometers south of Sonsonate near Acajutla lies Los Cóbanos, one of El Salvador's most popular beaches. The section right where the road ends is rocky and not too impressive, but wider, flatter expanses await a moderate walk in either direction. It will cost you $1.15 to park on weekdays and $1.75 on weekends and $1.15 to enter through a private gate with a changing room and picnic tables.

Los Cóbanos has some of El Salvador's best coral formations so diving and snorkeling is quite popular here. Several dive shops in San Salvador run trips to the area.

Two hotels, the Solimar and the Mar de Plata, are available if you want to spend the night, but it's better to stay in Sonsonate and come here for the day. Many restaurants along the beach serve seafood dishes from between $3.50-$8. Try a *camarones a la plancha* (a shrimp specialty served with salad, *tortillas* and *salsa*) for about $8. Right before the main road to the Cóbanos, there is a dirt road to the right. It leads to a quieter beach called **Salinitas**.

Buses to Sonsonate **(259)** run on the hour until 5pm and take about one hour. A taxi to the city costs about $11 midday during the week, but the price will be much higher during rush hour and on weekends. Be sure to set a price in advance.

😁 😁 😁 😁 😁

# Acajutla
Nahuat, "Place of Tortoises and Sugar Cane"
81km from San Salvador
16km from Sonsonate

Acajutla is really only good as a jumping-off and supply point for travel to nearby beaches. The sea breeze usually keeps the city cool, but can't seem to blow away the atmosphere of sleaziness that pervades the streets of one of Central America's busiest and most modern ports.

Acajutla isn't very pretty, and is more prone to bars and prostitutes than restaurants and hotels. The neighboring docks, the huge ships passing just offshore and the throngs of tourists that fill this place on weekends just add to the grimy feel of the town. The only thing worth doing here is to stroll down to the local fisherman's pier called the *muelle artisinal,* about two kilometers west of the main cargo terminal. The American utility Duke Energy is building one of the largest electrical generation plants in Central America in Acajutla which should bring many jobs and progress to this port city.

## ACCOMMODATIONS

**Hotel Miramar** The only decent place to stay right in town, with a small pool and a seafood restaurant overlooking the beach. However, even this place is frequented by prostitutes. *(3 blocks from bus station, tel 542-3183, 12 rooms $12.50, all with private bath; laundry; 10am checkout; pool; restaurant)*

**Hotel Santimoni** Just out of town at Kilometer 2 this is the best place to stay. The rooms are large, clean and comfortable and not surprisingly most visitors to the port stay here. *(Located on the main highway to town next to the "Gasolinera Esso"; tel 452-3192, fax 452-4074; 21D $17.20, all with private bath, AC; for another $2.70/day they will throw in cable TV)*

## FOOD & DRINK

**Restaurante Acajutla** Located on a high rock with a spectacular view of the ocean. Prices are moderate from $6 to $10 for the seafood specials. *(Av Miramar, Barrio Las Penas; tel 452-3709; 9am-10pm)*

**Restaurant Viña del Mar** Named after the famous Chilean beach resort the "Vineyard by the Sea" has great food and views. Plus, the waves hitting the rocks below as you dine makes for a very impressive dining experience. Prices on the varied menu start around $6 while all the shrimp plates are about $10 and well worth it. *(Next to Restaurante Acajutla; Tue-Sun 11am-9pm)*

## DETAILS

■ **BUSES: Sonsonate (207)**, every 10 min until 8pm, 16km, 35min.

■ **FESTIVALS: October 23-24 (24)** San Rafael Archangel. During a special nighttime ceremony, an image of San Rafael is placed in a special *panga* ("canoe") and decorated with flowers and lights. A procession of local fishermen follows the image from the new dock to the old dock, where mass is held.

# Beaches West of Acajutla

The beaches at Metalío and Barra de Santiago lie along the undeveloped plains bordering the Coastal Highway as it heads towards the Guatemalan border. The area is known at the Costa Azul ("Blue Coast") and the shores here are less cluttered with private homes than usual, since Metalío and Santiago are less accessible and exotic than other beaches further east. Both beaches are perfect for lazing around in a hammock and doing…nothing.

The Coastal Highway to the Guatemalan border begins 15 kilometers south of Sonsonate, about three kilometers south of where the Coastal Highway leaves to the east toward La Libertad. The newly improved road hosts a constant stream of tractor trailers carrying goods from the western border. One muddy river after another flows south towards the ocean under rough concrete bridges.

The improvement of the road has brought a lot of new private beach homes and there has been talk of developing a mega-tourism project call Bola de Monte in the area, but this part of the country remains quiet and pleasant.

# Playa de Metalío

Metalío is a quiet, narrow beach close to Acajutla. The gray sand here is a mixture of the black sand you find near the city and whiter sand from the other direction. The beach is lined with palm trees and continues off into the mist to the west. To the east you can see Acajutla—about as close as you'd want to be—which accounts for the trash that washes up on shore. Some of the lots along the shore are owned by fishermen who string out their nets between palm trees to dry, and drink stands line the road to the beach. Metalío isn't as fancy as other Salvadoran beaches, but it's a good day trip from Acajutla or Sonsonate.

To get there, turn left off the Coastal Highway ten kilometers from the Sonsonate-Acajutla road at the little town of Metalío (the first real cluster of buildings you'll pass). From there hop a microbus, hitch a ride or walk the two kilometers to the beach.

# Barra de Santiago

Playa Barra de Santiago is the closest easily accessible beach to the border with Guatemala. The long way there is, well, long, but if you don't have your own car there's an enjoyable little boat ride that can shorten your trip.

The beach at Barra de Santiago is fairly wide and completely empty from end to end, making it nicer than Metalío and worth the extra kilometers. You can string up a hammock between palm trees for the night and sack out; just be careful of your things (and yourself) out in the middle of nowhere. The best spots are at least a kilometer away from the small, run-down fishing village of Barra de Santiago. There are a few *comedores* in town, along with places to store your things while you're at the beach. Hire a fishing boat to explore the placid waters of the estuary for an afternoon, and take one back across to the Coastal Highway if that's how you arrived.

The entire area in the process of being declared an ecological reserve. Many endangered species like sea turtles and sea falcons make this place home. There have also been some prehispanic ceramics found at low tides.

There are two ways to approach Barra de Santiago, depending upon how you're traveling. If you are driving, take a left off the Coastal Highway 24 kilometers past the turnoff for Metalío, right in front of the bridge across the street from a yellow sign for "Las Villas de Shasca." This takes you to "La Barra," as locals call it.

The dirt road to the beach is lined with thick vegetation and filled with some impressive potholes. After a few kilometers it turns to the right while an even rougher road leads straight ahead to the ocean. Head to the right, and before long you'll pass the Villas de Shasca on the left with a huge yellow wall and gate. Further on are lots filled with evenly-spaced palm trees. The road ends after about ten kilometers at the village of Barra de Santiago in between the ocean and the El Zapote estuary.

If you're not driving, on the other hand, go further down the Coastal Highway until you reach the sign for "Barra de Santiago," near a sharp turn-off back to the left and a big Coke emblem on a *pupusería*. This is the road to the estuary's boat launching area.

Pay a couple of *colones* and ride in the pickup that serves as public transportation for the seven or so kilometers to the estuary where you can catch a small fishing boat across to the town of Barra de Santiago. The slow, pleasant ride in a dugout canoe takes 15 minutes and costs about $1 per person. The schedule for the pickup truck is irregular so you may wish to make arrangements for a time to come back with the driver.

## ACCOMMODATIONS

**AMAR (Asociación de Amigos del Arbol)** This NGO (Friends of the Trees Association) has worked to protect the mangroves and turtles here. They have a few rustic cabins that are often used by their ecologists, but can be reserved by tourists when available. *(Call 225-1413 to make reservations or to get involved with their important work; $15)*

**Reserva Natural de Barra de Santiago** Ximena's Guest House in San Salvador runs this more modern *rancho*. The beach house has a refrigerator, modern bathroom, stove, and BBQ area. There are three rooms and the house has both beach and estuary access. *($30 per room with private bath, make reservations at Ximena's Guest House in San Salvador, tel 260-2481)*

## DETAILS

■ **BUSES: La Hachadura/Guatemalan border (259)**, every 10 min until 7:30pm, 23km, 30min. **Sonsonate (285)**, infrequently, 65km, 1hr 30min. The 259 bus goes from Sonsonate to the border and doesn't go into Barra de Santiago, but stops by the bridge along the highway. From there it is not too difficult to find a ride in a pickup.

# Sonsonate

Nahuat, "400 Waters"
Pop. 85,000
65km from San Salvador

## SONSONATE THEN

Sonsonate sits near El Salvador's humid, fertile western coast with the Río Grande de Sonsonate passing through its center and continuing on to the ocean. The area was densely populated by the Izalco Indians before the Spanish arrived. According to legend, Pedro de Alvarado founded the city in 1524 as he rolled into Cuscatlán from the west.

The region's importance during the 18th and 19th centuries hinged on its prosperous cacao and balsam plantations and its proximity to the port of Acajutla. In 1833, Sonsonate served as the seat of the congress of the Central American Federation.

## SONSONATE NOW

Sonsonate is, according to the sign at the southern entrance, the "*Heroic y trabajador*" ("Heroic and Hardworking") city. It is also known as The City of Palms and Coconuts due to the great quantity of these crops growing in the surrounding countryside.

Sonsonate has a busy market and the surrounding villages are known for their baskets, mats and other types of woven products. Also of note are the numerous colonial buildings. Trains still run from the city to the port and other towns and a train museum is planned.

The muggy coastal climate means many people just use Sonsonate as a point of transit to El Salvador's western beaches and to the pleasant mountain towns of Apaneca and Juayúa to the north. A problem with the local water supply leaves the town dry from time to time.

## ACCOMMODATIONS

Sonsonate has many small *hospedajes* and hotels, but most owners will give you a strange look if you ask to rent a room for the whole night (hint, hint).

**Hotel Plaza** One of the best and newest hotels in the city with all the services a traveler could need such as a swimming pool, laundry service, bar and restaurant with especially good breakfasts. *(Tel 451-6626, 451-3610; 33 rooms, S $25, D $36, T $42, all with private bath, hot water, AC, cable TV, telephone; pool; laundry; bar restaurant)*

**Hotel Agape** This entire complex, which includes a convention center and hotel, belongs to the Asociación Agape, a project run by a famous American priest from Boston who has started various social and self-help projects over the past 25 years. The rooms are very comfortable and the service can't be beat. *(Located at km 63 of the highway to San Salvador; tel 451-1456, 451-2626, fax 451-4899, e-mail ramon@intradec.com; 25 rooms, S $16, D $22, 4-person suite $34, 5-person suite $40, all with private bath, hot water, AC, cable TV, telephone; 2pm checkout)*

### Melons and Chocolate

**I**n the late 16th century historian Juan López de Velasco wrote, "Sonsonate has many good vegetable and melon gardens, and good houses made of tile and adobe. The land is very fertile, especially for cacao, which is exported from the port of Acajutla three leagues hence."

**Hotel Orbe** One of oldest hotels in the city, but it still offers clean rooms and basic services. During the week it is usually booked solid since it is close to the city's commercial center. *(Tel 451-1416, fax 451-1517; 36 rooms, S $8 D $14 with fan, S $11.50 D $16 with fan and TV, S $17 D $22 with AC and TV, all with private bath; parking; 11am checkout; restaurant)*

**Hotel Sagitario** A hotel with very basic, but acceptable service. This is the best of the cheapies around the bus station but this area can be a little dodgy at night. *(Tel 451-1174; 10S $5.75, 4D $11.50, all with private bath)*

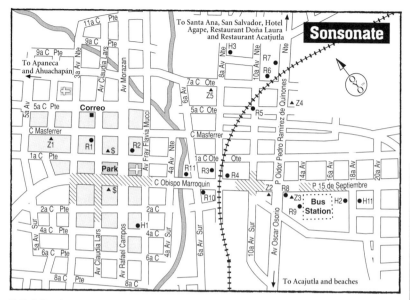

## FOOD & DRINK

**Burger House Plaza** A comfortable Burger King-like place inside with some seats outside on a patio. Hamburgers go for around $1 and they also serve complete fried chicken platters with salad and potatoes for around $3. This is very popular adolescent hangout. *(9am-8pm)*

**Burger House El Centro** Another branch of the Burger House Plaza with basically the same menu, prices and set up.

**Restaurant La Terraza** A well decorated place with very good air conditioning, which at noon in Sonsonate makes the food taste even better. The menu includes dishes like barbecued steaks for $5.75 or their famous house special surf and turf for $8.50. *(11:30am-10pm)*

**Restaurant Acajutla** Easily the best seafood place in the city. This is the same chain found in San Salvador and Acajutla but the prices here are lower. You can get a 1/2 lobster for $8, or a lobster stuffed with shrimp for $12.50. The famous Acajutla seafood soups go for $5.75 to $9. *(Km 63 on the highway from San Salvador at Quinta San Julian; tel 451-2322; 8:30am-10:30pm)*

**Restaurant Doña Laura** Located in the Hotel Agape this restaurant is the best in town for the price. The menu is full service and starts with complete breakfasts for $2.50.

● **ACCOMMODATIONS**
H1  Hotel Orbe
H2  *Hotel Florida*
H3  Hotel Plaza

● **FOOD & DRINK**
R1  Burger House El Centro
R2  *Pops Ice Cream/Pasteleria*
R3  *Pasteleria*
R4  *Pasteleria*
R5  *Panaderia El Angel*
R6  Restaurant La Terraza
R7  Burger House Plaza
R8  *Pollo Campero*
R9  *Atto's Pizza*
R10 Supermercado La Despensa de Don Juan
R11 *Señor Pollo*

▲ **OTHER**
Z1  Hospital
Z2  Shell Station
Z3  Texaco Station
Z4  Shell Station
Z5  Craft Store

TO THE WEST

They also serve a good variety of lunch and dinner plates such as the Typical Rural Menu (beef, beans, cheese and fried plantains) for $4.35 or a giant plate of shrimp prepared anyway you like for $9. *(7:30am-9pm)*

**Atto's Pizza** Popular with the locals they sell all kinds of pizzas from a personal for $2.50 to a giant for $11. *(11am 9pm)*

**Supermercado de Don Juan** Known as "la Despensa" this supermarket has a cafeteria where they serve breakfasts and lunches from $1.60 to $2.50. A great option for those on a budget.

## SIGHTS

**Cathedral of the Holy Spirit** This interesting colonial temple dates to the 19th century. Inside you can see two of the religious art floats used during the Holy Week processions. One is the biblical scene where Jesus was arrested and the other the mortuary scene after the crucifixion of Jesus.

**Church of the Pillar** A true colonial treasure. Highlights are the white facade which is characteristic of the 18th century. The church has conserved several unique old religious paintings and sculptures of the saints. Many have indigenous features that are not often seen in the religious art of this period.

## DETAILS

■ **BUSES: Acajutla (252)**, every 10 min until 8pm, 16km, 35min, the bus stop is in front of las Casas de Credito. **Ahuachapán (249)**, every 10-15 min until 7pm, 36km, 2 hr. A very scenic route which passes through the towns of Nahuizalco, Salcoatitán, Juayúa, Apaneca and Concepción de Ataco. **Barra de Santiago (285)**, although this is direct route, the service is irregular, so you are better off to take the 259 bus and walk a little to the beach. **La Hachadura/Guatemalan border (259)**, every 10-15min until 6:30pm, 60km, 2hrs. **La Libertad (281, 287)**, 6:15am, 3:45pm, 76km, 2hr. **Los Cóbanos (259)**, every hour on the hour until 5pm, 25km, 1hr. **Nahuizalco (205a)**, every hour until 3:45pm, 9km, 15min, although this is a direct route you are better off taking the 249. **San Salvador (205)**, every 5 min until 6:20pm, 65km, 1hr. Wait for a *directo* or the bus will stop at every chicken crossing. **Santa Ana (216)**, every 30 min until 5:40pm, 40km, 1hr 40min.

■ **FESTIVALS: January 19-20 (19)** San Sebastián Mártir. **January 25-February 5 (Feb 4)** Virgen de Candelaría. Highlights include the Cabalgata Artística de Candelaría, a horse show in Rafael Campo Park. **Semana Santa**. Sonsonate has some of the best parties in the country during Easter. A play about the tragedy of Golgotha is shown in the local theater and colorful rugs decorate the streets during the procession of the Santo Entierro. **June 12-13** San Antonio. **July 29-30 (29)** Santa Marta. **October 3-4** San Francisco. **December 24-31** Nacimiento del Niño Jesús. On the last day of the year the Vela de la Vara ("Vigil of the Staff") is held, a ritual in which a "staff of authority" was originally presented to the mayor of Sonsonate. Today the staff is presented to a "mayor" specially chosen for the night's festivities. Once located, the mayor is given ceremonial power to rule the city for a night. The new mayor's first order of business is always a command to capture everyone in town. Once captured, the citizens must *pasayuba bosu*, Nahuat for "pay the fine." Any money collected goes to charity. Citizens who refuse to pay the fine are threatened with being forced to smell a cow skull or a piece of cow manure.

# San Antonio del Monte

Pop. 12,000
68km from San Salvador
3km from Sonsonate

## SAN ANTONIO DEL MONTE THEN

In 1733 the Dominican friars of the convent of Santo Domingo built a hermitage just west of Sonsonate. Soon indigenous people and *mulattos*, attracted by the convent, built a small village around it. More and more people settled nearby, including many drawn by rumors that an image of San Antonio inside the church could perform miracles.

## SAN ANTONIO DEL MONTE NOW

The church that dominates the center of this small town is the most interesting thing about San Antonio del Monte. Vendors sell souvenirs and religious icons outside, giving the place the feel of a miniature holy Graceland. Sonsonate is almost within walking distance, so stop by if you're interested in colonial churches. Or just spend an afternoon at one of the *comedores* facing the church, watching people come and go. If you do stop here you'd still be better of staying in Sonsonate since walking around at night is not recommended.

## ACCOMMODATIONS

**Mini-Hotel El Socorro** It's the best of the town's hotels, but that's not saying much. The rooms are simple and clean, but not much of a bargain. *(Tel 451-2755; 6S $9.50, 4D $14, 3T $16.50, all with private bath and fans; laundry; parking)*

## FOOD & DRINK

**Comedor Daisy** Strike up a conversation with Toña, the feisty owner of this small eatery—it's hard not to. She'll tell you all about her town as she makes you a grilled chicken plate for $1.70.

**Comedor Alicia** The chicken plates at this small spot next to the church are good—and at $1.50, so is the price. Alicia does all the shopping herself in the market so you know the food is fresh.

**Taqueria Mexico Lindo** Bus drivers and locals insist this is the best place in town to eat. Rabbit tacos are the specialty of the house and will only set you back $3 an order.

● **ACCOMMODATIONS**
H1  Mini Hotel El Socorro

● **FOOD & DRINK**
R1  Pupuserias
R2  Comedor Daisy
R3  Comedor Alicia
R4  Taqueria Mexico Lindo

▲ **OTHER**
Z1  Artesania de Dona
     Amintia Quinteros

## SIGHTS

**Iglesia San Antonio del Monte** This colonial monolith was begun in 1841 and was funded by contributions left by faithful pilgrims. It took two decades to complete and replaced the original 16th-century church that had stood in the same spot. An overhead mural of Saint Anthony shows him in his deathbed surrounded by his disciples as angels wait to carry his soul away. Near the back of the church are hundreds of icons left by devotees. Worshippers leave these objects on top of the altar to ask the Saint for help or a favor, or to give thanks for a favor that has already been granted.

## DETAILS

■ **BUSES: Sonsonate (53)**, every 30 min, until 5:30pm, 3km, 15min.

■ **FESTIVALS: June 13** San Antonio del Monte. **Third week in August** Commercial Fiesta. During the traditional Baile de los Puros ("Dance of the Cigars"), two young women are selected to be the *madrinas*. Each dancer carries a tray full of cigars. In exchange for a cigar, spectators must dance with the *madrina* and put money into a little sack she carries in her blouse.

■ **SHOPPING: Artesania de Doña Amintia Quinteros** is a small arts and crafts store near the church.

# Izalco

Nahuat, "Houses Like Obsidian"
Pop. 45,000
59 km from San Salvador
5 km from Sonsonate

## IZALCO THEN

The Pipil chief Topilzin Acxtil founded this town in the middle of the 11th century and it eventually became an important trading center. One year before *La Matanza* Izalco experienced a chilling preview of what was to come. The authorities responded to an indigenous uprising in the town by tying the thumbs of suspected rebels together and leading them in groups of fifty to the back wall of the Asunción Church where they were gunned down by government firing squads. Others rebel sympathizers were forced to dig their own mass graves in front of the *commandancia* before being shot. Many women and children who refused to leave their men to die were also massacred. Many consider these events in Izalco as the beginning of the Salvadoran peasant revolution movement.

## IZALCO NOW

A 19th century visitor to Izalco wrote about the town that "In all the city, there's something—I don't know what—that brings to mind memories that date back many centuries." This is a feeling present day visitors will still sense, especially while watching butterflies and hummingbirds float from flower to flower in the wide-open main plaza (if only there were some benches!).

Izalco is the most indigenous town in El Salvador, and an Indian mayor, distinct from the official municipal government mayor, also serves its inhabitants. Locals proudly practice *Las Cofradias*, elaborate cultural traditions that mix the Catholic religion with pre-colonial beliefs; these are most evident during the Semana Santa celebrations. An impressive church and one of the country's best *turicentros* round out the Izalco experience.

## FOOD & DRINK
Your best bet for a meal is at the Turicentro Atecozol, though in town there are a number of simple *comedores* around the Iglesia de Dolores

## SIGHTS
**Iglesia de Dolores** Some of the sections of this masterpiece of colonial architecture date back to the 16th century. Also known as the Church of the Suffering the interior is rich in paintings and silver relief artwork. Restoration work is currently underway on the lacquered wood ceiling.

**Iglesia de Asunción** Not as spectacular as the Iglesia de Dolores, but still worth a quick visit if you are already here. It replaced another church destroyed by an earthquake in 1773. The bells in the tower were donated by the Emperor Carlos V and are still in use.

**Turicentro Atecozol** A statue of Atonatl (see "A Good Four Fingers") overlooks a giant waterslide and six swimming pools made of volcanic rock and filled with clean spring water. Hiking trails lead through the dense vegetation surrounding this recently renovated *turicentro*. Many small *comedores* serve snacks and drinks. If you don't want to use the free changing room, a small cabin where you can change and store your clothes runs $4 per day. Bus 205 between Sonsonate and San Salvador can drop you off nearby. *(From town take the road to the east of the Iglesia Dolores for about six blocks, from the highway to Sonsonate look for the large Atecozol sign 2 km north of Caluco; 8am-5pm, $0.80 per person)*

## DETAILS
■ **BUSES: Sonsonate (53A, 205)**, every 10-15 min until 6pm, 5 km, 15 min. **San Salvador (205)**, every 10-15 min until 6pm, 59 km, 50 min.

■ **FESTIVALS: January 19-20 (19)** San Sebastian Martir. **August 12-16 (14)** Virgin de la Asuncion. **December 3-8 (7)** Virgin de La Concepción.

# Near Izalco

**San Julian** In this interesting village 11 kilometers east of Izalco you can try some of the best cheeses made in Central America at the San Julian Dairy. The late Max Fernandez built this family business and his sons continue to run it. Their products

# The Witches of Izalco

Izalco has a tradition of witches (*"brujas"*) which dates back many centuries. Ancient medicinal and magical secrets have been preserved by the current generation of witches who learned their secret potions and chants from their ancestors. Like they do with Catholicism, many people mix the ancient traditions with the superstitious beliefs brought to El Salvador during the Spanish conquest. People from all parts of the country still come to Izalco to have spells cast and to learn about their future.

are for sale in stores all over the country, but here you can taste before you buy. Tours of the plant are also available, but need to be arranged in advance. *(Tel 273-5688)*

# Caluco

Nahuat, "City of Parrots and Hawks"
Pop. 10,000
65km from San Salvador
7km from Sonsonate

The road to this town, about two kilometers off the road between San Salvador and Sonsonate, is lined with banana and coconut trees. In colonial days Caluco was one of El Salvador's most important cities due to its vast cacao plantations. A sleepiness pervades Caluco, as residents doze in hammocks in bamboo houses. Frankly the town itself isn't all that interesting, but a picnic at the church ruins is a pleasant way to spend a few hours and it can easily be combined with a visit to Izalco.

## SIGHTS

**Colonial Church Ruins** Dominican monks built this brick church in the 17th century on what was believed to have been an Indian worshipping site. The church was destroyed in the Santa Marta earthquake of 1773 when the Izalco Volcano erupted. Now the site is overgrown with weeds and surrounded by local shacks, but it still maintains an air of imposing dignity. Some decorations on the outside have survived the years. The view across fields and mountains from the far end of the church is beautiful, and makes this a great place to stop for lunch—bring your own. *(500 meters south of Caluco, look for the path up to the left by the archeological work sign)*

## DETAILS

■ **BUSES: Sonsonate (205)**, every 10-15 min until 5:30pm, 7km, 20min. **San Salvador (205)**, every 10-15 min until 6pm, 65km, 90min.
■ **FESTIVALS: June 23-29 (29)** San Pedro Apóstol.

# Nahuizalco

Nahuat, "Four Izalcos"
Pop. 50,000
65km from San Salvador
9km from Sonsonate

## NAHUIZALCO THEN

Nahuizalco began as one of the strongest Pipil population centers in El Salvador. Two local legends relate how the town may have earned its name. First, a Franciscan priest reported in 1586 that the town had four times as many indigenous inhabitants as the town of Izalco. Also, four families from Izalco were said to have resettled here after Spanish forces swept through. Izalco remained predominantly indigenous well into the 20th century, although much of the population was decimated by government forces during *La Matanza*.

## NAHUIZALCO NOW

Nahuizalco has one of the largest indigenous populations in the country and the traditional Pipil culture is still quite strong here. Many of the older women still wear the traditional *güipil*, a colorful, sleeveless shirt as well as shawls and multicolored waistcloths wrapped around long dresses, as they have for centuries. The festivals here are especially colorful and are a great chance to see the native dances and customs and taste the local foods. If you find yourself here in the early evening be sure to take a stroll through the market which is lit by dozens of candles and lanterns.

The town's wicker crafts and furniture are the main reason to make a trip from Sonsonate. Nahuizalco was famous for the beauty and durability of its woven goods as far back as the 19th century and the industry is still going strong. Nahuizalco's carpenters, though overshadowed by its weavers, are also highly respected. A large number of shops in town sell a countless variety of the high quality furniture, household items, baskets, and decorative items. Many of the artisans learned their trade in the Arte Crecer

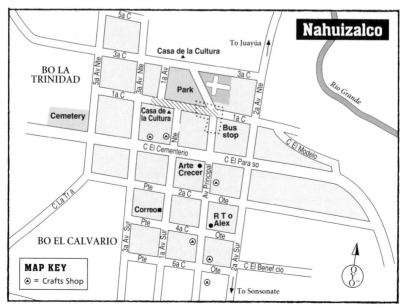

("To Grow Art") School which aims to preserve and promote this unique craft. Show someone a picture of a design you like it can probably be custom-made for you.

## FOOD & DRINK

**Restaurante Tío Alex** Carlos Calderón, a Los Angeles native, opened this place in 1994 and named it after his uncle. It is a family-style, outdoor restaurant with good music and no competition. Breakfast here is $1.70 and a plate of *tortillas* costs $4. *(9am-10pm)*

## SIGHTS

**Casa de la Cultura** You can watch craftspeople weave baskets and mats here. Tiny baskets cost $0.25 and small mats are $4.60. *(Across the street from park on the north edge of town; tel 453-0129; Mon-Fri 8am-12pm)*

**St. John the Baptist Church** (Parroquia de Juan Bapista) Built in 1859 on the site of an earlier temple that was destroyed by an earthquake. The exterior is in the colonial style and the interior is filled with religious art.

**Las Cascadas Papalhuate** About four kilometers down the dirt road that leads southwest out of town you will find this lovely 60-meter waterfall which is trisected by two ledges.

## DETAILS

■ **BUSES: San Salvador (205)**, every 10-15 min until 6pm, 65km, 90 min. **Sonsonate (249)**, every 30 min until 5:30pm, 9km, 30 min.

■ **FESTIVALS: March or April (Thursday and Holy Friday)** Semana Santa. **June 20-25 (24)** San Juan Baptista. **November 2** Día de los Difuntos ("Day of the Dead"). Participants offer food to the dead in a candlelight procession that leads to the cemetery. **December 22-29 and January 3-7** Niño Jesús y los Reyes Magos.

# Juayúa

Nahuat, "River of Purple Orchids"
Pop. 35,000
78km from San Salvador
17km from Sonsonate

Juayúa (pronounced why-you-a) is an enchanting mountain village with plenty of fresh air and a church that is worth a visit. The town plaza, church and homes, some dating back to the early 1800s, reflect the wealth generated by coffee during the last century. Throughout the year a kaleidoscope of flowers decorate a fountain in the central park, kept tidy by an active local government.

The town sits at 1000 meters above sea level in the midst of some of the best coffee farms in the country and has a lovely climate year-round. The road to Juayúa winds past the coffee plantations up into the hills of the Cordillera de las Apanecas ("Apaneca

Range") that surrounds the town and offer good hiking and camping opportunities.

## ACCOMMODATIONS

**Hostal de Doña Mercedes** Señora Mercedes has five double rooms to offer and if she likes you she may even throw in breakfast, but ask to be sure. *(Tel 452-2207; S $15, D $20, all have private bath, hot water, cable TV)*

## You've Been Warned

**W**hoever maintains the Parque Unión in the center of town evidently means business. Sign warnings are sharp and to the point: "Don't throw trash," "Don't stand on the benches," "Don't cut the flowers," "Don't enter the garden," and most importantly, "Don't mistreat the plants."

## FOOD & DRINK

**La Colina Restaurant** This pleasant place serves a good variety of Salvadoran and International dishes. They specialize in homemade jams, jellies and candies. The bottle of homemade hot chili sauce on each of the tables is also worth a try. You can relax or siesta in one of the hammocks on the porch with a view of the adjacent park. *(Located at the entrance to the city from the neighboring town of Salcoatitán; tel 452-2916; 12pm-2:30pm, 6-9pm)*

**Pastelería Festival** If you feel like sweets or coffee and desert stop by this place and try some of the traditional Spanish pastries like three milks ("*tres leches*") Gypsy arms ("*brazo gitano*"), and 1000 leaf pastries ("*mil hojas*"). *(9am-5pm)*

**Pollo Rico** Three dining rooms with high ceilings surround an airy courtyard garden, like a homey KFC. Chicken is $0.60 per piece and platters with all the fixings run $2.30. *(11am-8:30pm)*

## SIGHTS

**Templo del Señor de Juayúa** Red arches and crosses decorate the front of this mysterious looking church, built in 1957. An impressive nave is flanked by dark marble columns and the works or colonial art

● **ACCOMMODATIONS**
H1  Hostal de Doña Mercedes

● **FOOD & DRINK**
R1  Pasteleria "Festival"
R2  Restaurant Juayúa Hot
R3  Pollo Rico

▲ **OTHER**
Z1  Casa de la Cultura

Map labels:
Juayúa
To Ahuachapán
3a C
1a C
9a Av
7a Av
Av Daniel Cordón
2a Av
To Los Chorros de La Calera
Correo ■
C Mercedes Cáceres
Bus Stop
5a Av
3a Av
1a Av
R3 ●
$
Z1 ▲
Park
R2 ●
2a C
To Apaneca & La Colina
R1 ●
4a C
H1 ●
6a C
BO EL CARMEN
COL LA PROVIDENCIA

surround the altar. Look behind the altar for the famous icon of the Black Christ of Juayúa, made in the late 15th century by the renown sculptor Quiro Catano who also carved the world-famous Black Christ of Esquipulas, Guatemala towards the end of the 16th century. While a pilgrimage to Esquipulas is a must for many Central American Catholics you can see nearly the same thing here without the crowds.

**Casa de la Cultura** Stop by here to find out what is going on in town and maybe see some art displays. *(Tel 450-5070; Mon-Fri 8am-12pm, 1-4pm)*

## CLIMBING, HIKING & SWIMMING

There are some good hiking destinations in the mountains around Juayúa. The two most popular are the Cerro de Apaneca (1,800m) to the west and the Cerro de los Naranjos (1,950 m) to the northeast. Also, two mountain lakes are within a day's hike and are good places to swim and camp. Ask locals for detailed directions before heading off.

**Laguna de las Ranas** "Frog Lake" sits near the 2000-meter summit of Cerro Buenos Aires. It is about a three and half-hour hike or you can nearly reach the lagoon in a 4x4 vehicle *(Take 1a Av Sur out of town to the north.)*

**El Cerro de los Naranjos** Walk up a volcano covered with coffee farms for 2.5 hours and you reach the peak of "Orange Hill." The view is excellent and so are the breezes since the peak is nearly two thousand meters above sea level. The site maintains such steady winds that a monitoring station was placed here to study the potential for wind energy turbines.

**Laguna Verde** The road towards Ahuachapán passes near Laguna Verde, which rests on the slopes of an extinct volcano of the same name. You can drive by 4x4 or take the two-hour walk to the intensely green lake.

**Los Chorros de La Calera** Swimming holes were created here when the power company dammed up the natural springs. They make a good half-day hike and picnic spot as butterflies of every imaginable size and color fill the air. On the way there, notice the coffee fields on the facing hillside, with their characteristic line of bushes planted to break up the wind over the hillsides and to shade the coffee plants from the sun. The first waterfall off to the right (watch your step!) is the highest but also the dirtiest, since women from town wash clothes in the river upstream. If you keep going the trail soon becomes slippery and narrow, so be careful. The second set of falls, with the Pollo Rico ad painted on the rock, comes into sight 50 meters later. The third set, further down the path, is similar to the second. Finally, if you want to be totally secluded, the last set are the shallowest

and prettiest and are a great place to kick off your shoes and relax. You'll feel like you are playing in a Tarzan movie set. *(Take the dirt road east out of town and turn right where the road splits near the house. A few hundred meters after the split fol-*

*low a short, steep, gully that leads 100m down off to the right. At the end, you'll
arrive at a dirt road and a footbridge off to the right. If you're driving, the road winds
around until it reaches the bridge. Take the path across the bridge through the white
painted stone gate, then head for the sound of the falls)*

## DETAILS

■ **BUSES: Ahuachapán (249)**, every 30 min until 5:30pm, 24km, 1hr. **Sonsonate
(249)**, every 30 min until 5:30pm, 17km, 90min.

■ **FESTIVALS: Jan 6-15 (15) Cristo Negro**. During the second week of January there
are processions, floats, food and gastronomical events as well as the traditional celebration of the patron saint of the town. This is a good time to see the Dance of the
Historians. Try, if you dare, the *elote loco* ("crazy corn") sold during this festival. It's a
local specialty made of tender corn with a stick through the middle, and is covered with
mayonnaise, ketchup, mustard and cheese.

# Salcoatitán

Nahuat, "City of the Serpent Bird"
2km from Juayúa

Just beyond Juayúa, along a road lined by lovely flowerbeds and coffee farms, is the
pleasant town of Salcoatitán. The town plaza, which dates to 1824, sits in the midst of
colonial and rustic old wood homes. Like Juayúa it has a refreshing climate year-round
and like Nahuizalco it specializes in the fabrication of rattan furniture.

## ACCOMMODATIONS

**La Posada de Salcoatitán** This small but exceedingly pleasant hotel has five unique
rooms; each with a different décor. In the yard you'll find a pool, lovely gardens and
some great places to hang a hammock. The owner/manager Sonia de Salaveria
ensures you have a pleasant stay. Reservations are often required on weekends. *(Just a
few steps off the central plaza; tel 452-2550, 452-2454; 5D $12 per person, all with pri-
vate bath, hot water; pool; restaurant, bar)*

## FOOD & DRINK

**Los Girasoles** This great restaurant in La Posada de Salcoatitán has fine Central
American dishes from around $9. The decoration features lovely flower arrange-
ments and designs with, of course, the *girasol* ("sunflower") predominating.
*(Weekends only)*

**Cafeteria and Ice Cream Shop "Kevin"** If you are homesick, stop by this clean and
economical place for a hamburger or dessert. Meals are $1 and up. *(Weekends only)*

## SIGHTS

**San Miguel Archangel Church** Located near the central park this early 19th century
structure was rebuilt in 1921. The original wall was constructed with mortar made

from egg whites and lime, a concoction called *calicanto*. The flat supporting structure for the roof is an old colonial style known as *azotea*.

## DETAILS
▪ **BUSES: Sonsonate (249)**, every 30 min until 5:30pm, 15km, 75min.
▪ **FESTIVALS: January 5-6** Los Tres Reyes ("Three Kings"). Features a big folk dance. **June 9-14** St. Michael the Archangel.

# Apaneca

Nahuat, "River of the Wind"
Pop. 15,000
91km from San Salvador
20km from Sonsonate

Situated in the rolling hills of one of El Salvador's most important coffee-growing regions, Apaneca is clean and comfortable—the epitome of a quaint mountain town—and shouldn't be missed. Tiled-roof houses line the streets, and the large white church (which dou-

bles as a seminary) has an enticing view of the countryside. Besides the coffee, the town is known for the peaches and apples that thrive in the fresh local climate and the unique furniture made from pruned coffee tree branches.

Hiking and horseback riding near town are excellent with most of the higher elevations overlooking the famous patchwork shade coffee groves and river valleys. There are knowledgeable local guides that can show you some great trails through the coffee farms to the lagoons, mountain peaks and river valleys. Some of the trails cross private lands so if you go on your own you should know enough Spanish to be able to ask permission to cross. Camping is sometimes allowed in local *haciendas;* just ask beforehand for permission to *acampar*. And remember, many of the trails are at 1500 meters above sea level so you should bring some warm clothes if you plan to spend the night.

With Las Cabañas de Apaneca, La Cocina de Mi Abuela and so many surrounding sights within easy reach Apaneca is ideal for a short mountain getaway. The town's attractions are well known, though, so both the "Cabins" and "Grandmother's Kitchen" could easily be filled with wealthy Salvadoran tourists on weekends.

## ACCOMMODATIONS

**Las Cabañas de Apaneca** An architect built this hotel/restaurant, and it shows. The entire complex, which houses a flower garden, is spotless and meticulously landscaped. Sturdy wood cabins straight out of the Swiss Alps, complete with bunk beds, have stunning views down the valley from individual porches.

Six- and eight-person cabins are available in addition to the regular rooms. The restaurant serves traditional food under carved wood pillars. Breakfast with coffee is $2.85, while a grilled veal dinner costs $5.75. It's a great place to spend the weekend if there's space, but reservations are usually necessary a week in advance. *(Tel 479-0099; 4D $40, 1 quad $46, 7 cabins, all with private bath and hot water; 1pm checkout; restaurant Mon-Fri 11am-5pm, Sat 11am-9pm, Sun 8am-6pm)*

**El Paraiso Mini-Convention Center** This new villa-type compound recently opened on the south side of the highway (called "la via") leading into the town. The rooms are all quite, clean and comfortable. *(Tel 433-0025; 3 rooms D $28, group discounts available; all with private bath, hot water; pool; laundry)*

**Hostal Las Orquidias** This 4-room family home has recently opened as a bed and breakfast. It is pleasant and a good value. *(Tel 433-0061; S $5, D $10; all with private bath; pool)*

**Hostal Las Ninfas** A 2-room family home where the owners are glad to tell you all about the local folklore, traditions and culture. If you are looking to learn about the town of Apaneca with a touch of personal service and hospitality, this is the place. *(Tel 433-0059, 433-0089; S $6, D $10; all with private bath and hot water; pool)*

## FOOD & DRINK

**La Cocina de Mi Abuela** A national legend, La Cocina de Mi Abuela (Grandmother's Kitchen) has been going strong for nearly 10 years. This large gourmet restaurant is a shrine to another age decorated with antique photographs, plates, railings and stained-glass windows. Thirty wooden tables are inside on a tiled floor, while a gorgeous flower garden with a fountain sits outside beside a cage full of monkeys. More tables wait outside, where the veranda is patrolled by troops of short-tempered ducks. For $6 to $15 you can have a gourmet meal in this charming setting with lovely views of the patch work coffee groves in the background. Specials include an "Indian chicken plate" and chicken soaked in *chicha*. This is usually the busiest place in town so reser-

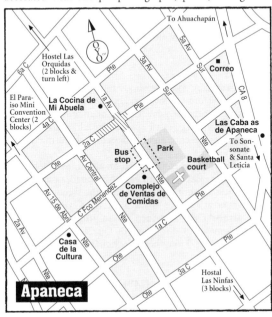

vations are advisable. There is a branch restaurant by the same name in San Salvador, but if you want Grandma's real home cooking you must travel to Apaneca. *(Tel 428-0809; Sat-Sun 11am-7pm)*

**Complejo de Ventas de Comidas** These informal market eateries near the bus stop serve a good variety of local, inexpensive foods such as soups, chicken and beef dishes and *pupusas*. *(Dawn until about 6pm)*

## SIGHTS

**Church of San Andres the Apostle** This interesting 17th century church next to the central park has some unique religious art and images.

**Casa de la Cultura** The House of Culture has arts and crafts displays and can provide you with information on hikes and sights in the area. *(Tel 433-0163; Mon-Fri 8am-4pm)*

**Horseback Riding** Look for the *alquilar de caballos* ("horses for rent") sign at the farm near Las Cabañas de Apaneca. Some of the saddles are more like thick blankets with a cushion, so you may want to see what you will be riding on before deciding on the duration of your trip.

**Santa Leticia Archeological Site** A 10-minute hike through the Santa Leticia coffee groves will bring you to this archaeological site. The entire site is about 15 hectares (37 acres) but the most interesting and unusual archeological objects are on the main path. Here you can view, on a ceremonial platform, three giant head figures called "Gordinflones" which roughly translates to "archeological fatsoes." The largest is estimated to weigh 24,000 lbs. and the smallest is about 14,000 lbs. According to archeologists they are over 2,600 years old.

There are many other objects at this site but nothing as spectacular as the giant heads has been unearthed yet. The entrance is well marked close to the main highway from Salcoatitán near Las Cabañas de Apaneca.

## HIKING

**Laguna Verde** A good two-hour hike to the northeast of Apaneca, four kilometers through the forest to the lake. The path up the mountain to the lagoon has some great backdrops of the Guatemalan mountain ranges and views of the white buildings with tile roofs in the colonial city of Ahuachapán. The lake receives many visitors and bathers on weekends and holidays though during the week you will probably have it all to yourself.

**Laguna las Ninfas** Another lagoon about two kilometers (1 hour) to the north near Cerro las Ninfas (1,756m), which is smaller than Laguna Verde and slightly closer. The forest is more spectacular than the lagoon itself. From the peaks along the trail you get great views of Apaneca and the town of Juayúa in the distance.

**Cerro Grande de Apaneca** A beautiful nearby hike and climb. Head south about one kilometer to the village of Quezalapa to find this mountain, also known as Chichicastepec. From there it's about two hours to the peak at 1,816 meters.

## DETAILS

■ **BUSES: Ahuachapán (249)**, every 15 min until 6:30pm, 14km, 40min. **San Salvador (206a)**, irregularly until 4:30pm, 91km, 2hr 30min. **Sonsonate (249)**, every 15 min until 6:30pm, 20km, 1hr 20min.

■ **CRAFTS: Artesanías Madre Tierra**, 800 meters east of Las Cabañas de Apaneca on the road to Sonsonate, sell ceramics and rough wood furniture.

■ **FESTIVALS: November 29-30 (29)** San Andrés Apóstol. **December 24-25 (24)** Nacimiento del Niño Jesús. Features the Baile de la Garza ("Dance of the Garza"). The cast of characters includes three policemen, a mayor, a bride, a groom, a "rascal," an Indian and the *garza*, a child dressed in a wooden frame covered with a white sheet. Each character wears a specific wooden mask according to the character he or she represents, and they all dance accompanied by string instrumental music.

■ **MARKET:** Peaches are sold in September and October.

■ **VISITOR'S INFORMATION:** Pick up a copy of the green and black brochure *Ecotour por la Cordillera de Apaneca* ("Nature tour through the Apaneca Range") in town, which describes nearby towns and natural attractions.

# Ahuachapán

Pok'omáme, "City of Oak Houses"
Pop. 95,000
100km from San Salvador

## AHUACHAPÁN THEN

Ahuachapán sits in the geothermally active western reaches of El Salvador, where hot springs, fumaroles and geysers fill the air with the smell of sulfur. It's El Salvador's western-most city and is one of the oldest and most densely populated in the country. The city's location at nearly 800 meters above sea level gives it an ideal climate year round.

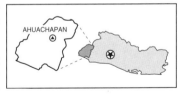

Pok'omáme Indians founded the city around the 5th century, evidenced by the many ceramic artifacts found nearby. At the end of the 15th century, the Pipil Indians conquered Ahuachapán but the Pok'omáme culture survived. A Spanish visitor noted in 1549 that while the male inhabitants spoke the "rich, sweet, harmonious tongue" of their Pipil conquerors, the women still communicated in their native Pok'omáme language. The Pok'omáme name, which describes the huge oak trees that once covered the area, has survived through the ages.

In 1821, the Battle of Espino erupted two kilometers north of town and resulted in the first victory for the young Republic of El Salvador in its fight for independence from Spain. In 1860 and again in 1937, earthquakes devastated Ahuachapán. By the early 20th century, the city had established a reputation as a center for coffee production.

During the 1980s, the owners of enormous local estates struggled to oppose any measure of land reform. When the government moved to confiscate any land holdings over 1,200 acres as required by law, some local landowners responded by forming their own private armies to defend their turf. Many of these private armies were better equipped than the government's forces.

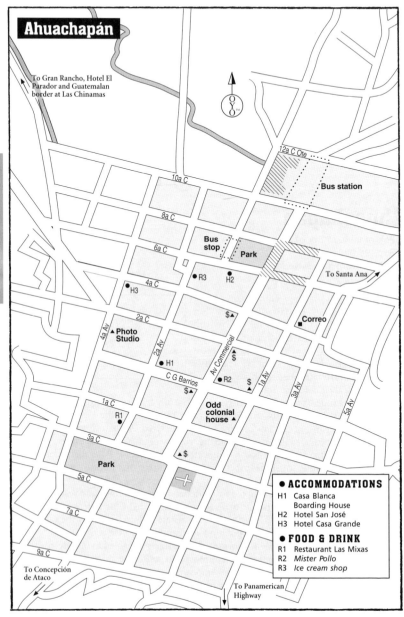

**Ahuachapán**

To Gran Rancho, Hotel El
Parador and Guatemalan
border at Las Chinamas

OYO™

12a C Ote

**Bus station**

10a C

8a C

6a C

**Bus stop**

**Park**

To Santa Ana

4a C

● R3   H2

● H3

2a C

$▲

**Correo**

4a Av   ▲ **Photo Studio**

2a Av

Av Commercial

● H1

$▲
$

C G Barrios

● R2   $

1a Av

3a Av

5a Av

$▲

**Odd colonial house** ▲

1a C

● R1

3a C

▲ $

**Park**

5a C

7a C

9a C

To Concepción
de Ataco

To Panamerican
Highway

● **ACCOMMODATIONS**
H1 Casa Blanca
    Boarding House
H2 Hotel San José
H3 Hotel Casa Grande

● **FOOD & DRINK**
R1 Restaurant Las Mixas
R2 *Mister Pollo*
R3 *Ice cream shop*

## AHUACHAPÁN NOW

A clock tower overlooks the kiosk in the middle of the plaza near the beautiful white Iglesia Asunción. The palm-lined road north to the Guatemalan border at Las Chinamas passes a lush middle-class neighborhood full of gardens. A modern highway to the border is currently under construction. The kiosk in the main park serves drinks and snacks.

For those entering El Salvador from the west, Ahuachapán is the best place to spend a few days getting accustomed to the country. It is more relaxed than Santa Ana (except around the bus station) and has some good, inexpensive hotels. It's also within reach of a few secluded beaches to the south.

There isn't a whole lot to see or do in town, but the Asunción church located in front of the city's Condordia Park is well worth a visit. The Iglesia El Calvario is another classic, well preserved colonial church with some interesting architecture.

For years, Central America's largest and most modern geothermal electric generating plant was nearby. While there are now more modern plants, the Ahuachapán plant is still the largest. The steam fields called *infiernos* ("little Hells") in Spanish are also known by their name in Nahuat "*ausoles*" which means boiling water. A visit to the fields or the plant let you see the power of nature up close.

# The Flower Route

**H**ighway CA-8 between Sonsonate and Ahuachapán winds through one of the most interesting and beautiful parts of El Salvador. This area earned its name, La Ruta de las Flores in Spanish, because of the millions of coffee flowers painting the landscape white between October and February, but it is a fascinating journey throughout the year.

The majestic peaks of the Cordillera de las Apanecas ("Apaneca Range") cut their path across the horizon with the distinctive triple peaks of Cerro Verde and the Izalco and Santa Ana Volcanoes always looming to the west. A patchwork of coffee farms climb the rolling green hills and line the winding river valleys. If you get out and hike your time and effort will be well rewarded by crisp mountain lakes, towering waterfalls, spectacular vistas and a unique archaeological site.

The five colonial, mountain towns you pass along the way are as wonderful as the countryside they are set in. Just nine kilometers north of Sonsonate is Nahuizalco, one of the most traditionally indigenous towns in the country. A quick detour from the highway takes you to the quiet village of Salcoatitán and the tidy and attractive town of Juayúa. Next comes quaint Apaneca, one of the loveliest villages in the country. Finally, just five kilometers south of the city of Ahuachapán is Concepción de Ataco known primarily for its unique wooden masks. You will not be lacking for great food or accommodation along the way and the town's skilled artisans make a variety of handicrafts.

The route could be covered in a day if you rush. Ideally, budget a few leisurely days to fully appreciate the beauty and variety found in this unique little corner of the world.

## ACCOMMODATIONS

**Casa Blanca Boarding House** Built in traditional Spanish style, this hotel is a great place to spend a few days outside of San Salvador. A grand entrance leads into a colorful interior decorated with antiques and an attractive wooden ceiling. Flowers and plants fill a center courtyard that encloses a small fountain. The attached restaurant serves breakfast, lunch and dinner. *(Tel 443-1505, fax 443-1503; 8 rooms, S $16 D $26 with fan, S $23, D $31.50 with AC, all with private bath and hot water; a TV will be brought to your room for $2.50; laundry; 24hr checkout; restaurant)*

**Hotel San José** This is one of the oldest hotels in the area, at least as old as the friendly man who maintains the high level of service and cleanliness. The gate is locked at 10pm; after that, ring the bell. *(Tel 443-1820; 20 rooms, S $7, D $13.75, all with private bath, fan; laundry; 11am checkout)*

**Hotel El Parador** While Casa Blanca has to be Ahuachapán's sentimental favorite, only El Parador offers a crocodile in a cage on the premises. It is brand-new, colonial style and has a swimming pool. The restaurant serves all meals, and a seafood plate will cost you $4-$7. Any bus or pickup to Chinamas passes by here. *(Km 102.5 on the highway to Guatemala; tel 443-0331; 10 rooms, S $26, D $32.50, all with private bath, hot water, cable TV, AC; laundry; 1pm checkout; restaurant, bar)*

**Hotel Casa Grande.** This pleasant and economical hotel is situated in an old colonial house. *(Tel 443-1697, 413-1697; 8 rooms, S $11, D $17, all with private bath, fan, TV; restaurant)*

## FOOD & DRINK

The hotels are good places for formal sit down meals, particularly the pleasant Hotel Casa Grande, while for cheap eats the cafeterias in the supermarkets are good options.

**Hotel Casa Grande** The restaurant here serves a wide variety of entrees between $3.50 and $9. *(12pm-11pm)*

**Las Mixtas** A lively place that is packed at lunch. Pizzas and sandwiches start at $1 and you can get a complete lunch for $1.75. Fruit juice choices are listed on the wall. *(12-2:30pm, 5:30-8pm)*

## DETAILS

▪ **BUSES: San Salvador (204)**, every 10 min until 5pm, 100km, 3hr 30min. **Santa Ana (202, 210)**, every 10 min until 7pm, 34km, 1hr. **Sonsonate (249)**, every 10-15 min until 7pm, 55km, 2hr. **Las Chinamas/Guatemalan border**, microbuses leave from the market every 10 minutes until 5:30pm, 14km, 30 min.

▪ **FESTIVALS: March 5-14 (13)** Dulce Nombre de Jesús. Almost a mini-Olympics, with bicycle races, soccer matches, marathons, swimming, basketball, motocross and Ping-Pong.

# Near Ahuachapán

**Concepción de Ataco and the Cruz de Ataco** A walk to this nearby town and mountain cross, five kilometers south of Ahuachapán, takes about two hours in each direction. Along the way, you can take a dip in the rivers. The town, founded by the Pipil, is known for the carved wooden masks its inhabitants have made since colonial times.

Top: View from Hotel de la Montaña, Cerro Verde
Bottom Left: Laguna Verde, near Apaneca
Bottom Right: Volcanic cone near San Salvador

Top: Izalco, Cerro Verde, and Santa Ana Volcanoes
Bottom Left: El Chingo Volcano
Bottom Right: San Miguel Volcano

# Parque Nacional El Imposible

40km from Sonsonate
115km from San Salvador

El Salvador's newest national park is a remarkable place–not just for what is there, but for the very fact that it is there at all. With over 95% of El Salvador's native forests cleared, El Imposible represents one of few remaining stands of rainforest in the country and one of the last remnants of Mesoamerican Pacific coastal rainforests anywhere. Not only is the park a vital refuge for many rare plants and animals but it is the source of eight rivers that supply drinking water to surrounding communities. These waters also feed the environmentally sensitive mangroves around Barra de Santiago.

Though it is relatively small El Imposible is the largest and most diverse wilderness in El Salvador. Logging was difficult in this rough mountainous terrain–elevations range from 300 to 1,400 meters–so most of the roughly 12,000-acre park still possesses primary forest.

The government began surveys of the flora and fauna in this area in 1976 and found many species that they had previously thought were extinct in El Salvador. Shortly after that they acquired large chunks of land, but this didn't actually become a park until 1989. And though only about 70 percent of the land is publicly owned, logging is banned on all areas within the park's boundaries, public and private.

Since 1991 El Imposible National Park has been managed by the private environmental organization SalvaNATURA who, working in conjunction with the National Park and Wildlife Service, have done an admirable job. Before setting out to see the park with one of their expertly trained guides you can get information about the forest and its inhabitants in the Mixtepe Environmental Interpretation Center.

In order to visit the park on your own you must obtain a permit ($2.86 per Salvadoran, $5.71 per foreigner) in advance from SalvaNATURA's offices in San Salvador (33 Av Sur #640, Col Flor Blanca; tel 279-1515; e-mail salnatura@saltel.net; www.salvanatura.org). Though you should have little problem getting a permit on short notice,

## Tacuba

This mountain village, 16 kilometers from El Imposible National Park, is best known for its strong and enduring traditions. Colorful dances, historic arts and crafts, and folkloric music played with traditional instruments are all still widely practiced.

The town also is surrounded by fantastic scenery. The Santa Ana, Cerro Verde, and Izalco volcanoes rise to the east while the Pacaya, Agua and Fuego volcanoes can be seen in Guatemala. Looming much closer are the majestic green slopes of El Imposible while to the south you can see the waves breaking on the Pacific coast. Closer to town there are some amazing waterfalls and thermal springs. Be sure to ask someone to show you the 500-year-old ceiba tree where thousands of parrots perch for the night.

A few simple hospedajes are spread around town, but most visitors head for the excellent Hotel La Cabaña *(Tel 883-1967, 417-4332, fax 260-2627, e-mail hoteltacuba@yahoo.com)* which has a huge garden, airy mountain views, and arranges transportation and guides for El Imposible. The eight rooms with private bath, hot water, fan, and cable TV cost $30 for a double.

## What's In a Name

**E**l Imposible, as you likely guessed, means The Impossible in English. At the turn of the century, farmers, particularly coffee growers, loaded their crops on to the backs of mules and sent them through the mountains to the port of Acajutla. Along the way the muleteers had to cross the treacherous Impossible Pass. Many constructed crude log bridges to avoid the long, difficult journey through the deep ravine. These bridges often broke under the weight of the passengers sending man and mule to a grisly death. In 1968 the Salvadoran government built a bridge to make the journey easier and less dangerous. The sign they erected upon completion read "Year of 1968, this is no longer impossible."

it is advisable to contact them a least a week in advance. Several tour agencies in the capital, notably Amor Tours, Salvador Tours and SET de El Salvador (contact details are in the Basics chapter), will arrange everything for you for around $30 per person. The Hotel La Cabaña in Tacuba is another good place to arrange tours.

### FLORA & FAUNA

The forests of El Imposible shelter more species of plant and wildlife than any other place in the country. An amazing 279 of El Salvador's 513 migratory and resident bird species have been recorded in the park. The rare crested curassow and black hawk eagle are just holding on. Birdwatchers can also add the groove-billed ani, orange-chinned parakeet and tropical peewee to their life lists. Another 500 species of butterfly flutter through the trees. The luckiest visitors might spot a collared anteater or one of the endangered species of felines–mountain lion, ocelot, margay, and jaguarundi–though squirrel, rabbit, weasel, and armadillo are more common.

There are three principal types of forest within the park. Midland semi-deciduous forest is found at the highest elevations, coastal plain evergreen forest at the lowest and lowland deciduous in between. The forest is composed of some 400 species of tree, 120 species of rattan and a high diversity of ferns and mushrooms.

## Eco-Tourism Isn't Just for the Birds

**I**llegal logging and poaching can bring a poor campesino quick cash—and lots of it. And in a country with a population density as great as El Salvador's every acre of farmland is significant. So locals in El Salvador, and around the world, are often understandably hesitant about conservation projects in their back yards. Environmentalists realize that for any conservation program to succeed the surrounding communities need to benefit so it is as important to look after the people who live near parks as it is the plants and wildlife.

Towards that goal SalvaNATURA not only hires as many locals as possible to work at El Imposible, but provides micro-loans to the people of San Miguelito village to help them start restaurants, handicraft shops, hotels, and similar businesses. Your support of these new enterprises, several of which are located just outside the park gate, can play an important part in protecting this important habitat.

## HIKING

Several hiking trails begin at the San Benito Visitor Center. Those looking to enjoy the park at a relaxed pace will appreciate the Interpretive Trail which leads to the El Mulo Lookout just over one kilometer away. Signs discussing the life of the forest line the path. A 3.5-kilometer trail to Los Enganches, a scenic spot where the Venada River merges with the Guayapa River, passes several vista points, countless waterfalls and the Piedra Sellada ("Sealed Rock") petroglyphs. The four-kilometer trail to Cerro León descends for a kilometer to the Ixcanal River and then climbs to the highest part of the park. From here a 360-degree vista lets you see the entire park, and well beyond.

The latter two trails cover some rugged terrain and are strenuous at points so plan on at least four hours for each. If you are looking for something more adventurous you can also arrange off-trail hikes through other parts of the park, but this must be arranged with SalvaNATURA in advance. All hikers must be accompanied by one of the reserve's knowledgeable guides who deserve a big tip. Binoculars are available for rent at the park office and food and water can be purchased in San Miguelito. You can use the showers to clean up after your hike.

## ACCOMMODATIONS

If you have your own tent and gear you can spend the night in one of the two camp-grounds ($2.85 per Salvadoran, $5.75 per foreigner), each with showers and bathrooms, situated near the San Benito Visitor Center. Also, local families in San Miguelito, just outside the entrance to the park, rent out very cheap rooms, but don't expect luxuries like running water and electricity. Many visitors to the park choose to stay in Tacuba.

## GETTING THERE

The main entrance, where the San Benito Visitor Center is located and where the main hiking trails start, is reached from Ahuachapán. Take bus 212 to Tacuba which makes the 27-kilometer journey every 30 minutes until 6:30pm. From Tacuba you can catch a pickup truck for the bumpy 16-kilometer run to the park entrance at San Miguelito. If you are coming in your own vehicle you will need four-wheel drive since most of the road beyond Tacuba is in poor shape, especially during the rainy season.

# Lago de Coatepeque

Nahuat, "Snake Hill"
58km from San Salvador
20km from Santa Ana

The enormous (nearly four miles wide and over 500 feet deep), peaceful crater Lake of Coatepeque sits east of Cerro Verde and the Santa Ana and Izalco Volcanoes. This is where El Salvador's aristocrats come to chill out and play, either in private homes which monopolize the shoreline or at one of the two luxury hotels. The three huge mountains and the achingly blue water of the lake add up to one beautiful scene.

The road from the Panamerican Highway splits at the edge of the lake and turns to

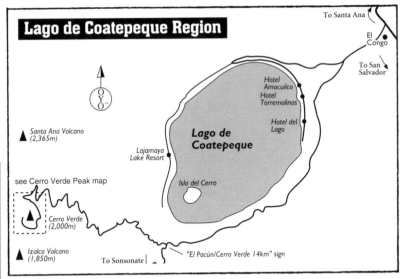

**Lago de Coatepeque Region**

To Santa Ana

El Congo

To San Salvador

Hotel Amacuilco
Hotel Torremolinos

Hotel del Lago

*Lago de Coatepeque*

Santa Ana Volcano (2,365m)

Lajamaya Lake Resort

Isla del Cerro

see Cerro Verde Peak map

Cerro Verde (2,000m)

Izalco Volcano (1,850m)

To Sonsonate

"El Pacún/Cerro Verde 14km" sign

dirt. A few *balnearios públicos* (semi-public beaches) near the Hotel Torremolinos have access to the lake, and charge next to nothing for admission and parking.

Coatepeque is beautiful, but suffers from its popularity. The large, private houses make access to the lake almost too difficult to be worthwhile. There are places to swim for everybody else, but with crowds, buses and garbage to battle, the experience can be less than relaxing. To really enjoy Coatepeque, come during the week…or buy a house on the shore.

## RECREATION

**Boat Trips** If you didn't happen to bring your own jet-ski, you can still hire a boat for a tour of the lake. Find a captain at any of the hotels who will bring you to an isolated spot, but make sure that if he drops you off he'll return for you later. Short trips of an hour or so start at $14 per boat and the larger boats can carry as many as 15 people. The route that passes by the crater dive peninsula of Los Anteojos ("The Eyeglasses") and some of the fancier home along the shores is a good choice. With a little more time take a ride to Isla del Cerro where you'll find hot springs just beneath the surface of the lake that turn the place into a stone-age hot tub.

**Crater Diving** A number of San Salvador dive shops specialize in taking divers to see the unique volcanic formations at the depths of this lake. Agua Caliente, where you can observe 95 degrees F thermal waters emerge, is one of the main attractions.

**Kayaking** Kayaks are available for rent at the hotels. Rates are variable but during the week expect to pay $4.50 per hour.

## ACCOMMODATIONS

**Hotel Torremolinos** This white colonial building offers patios, a clean pool and a large grassy area fronting the beach. The rooms are big, but far from cheap. The restaurant

# El Congo

**T**his small town sits along the Panamerican Highway between San Salvador and Santa Ana at the turn-off for the Lago de Coatepeque and Cerro Verde. Fruit and vegetables from all over El Salvador and other Central American countries are sold here at restaurants that double as impressive produce stands.

Many people stop here to pick up a snack and some great fruit on their journey along CA-1. A favorite stand is Merendero Paraíso Tropical, the last stop on the right side going toward Santa Ana. Try a fruit shake with milk and say hello to Martha Isabel Serrano, the lady who has run this place with her sons for years. She claims to have started the "fruit shake trend" back in the 1970s.

Remember that this is the main highway from Guatemala to San Salvador and thus is very busy. You need to be careful entering and leaving the stands since the vehicles coming up from behind are usually speeding past at over 100km per hour. Car accidents are not uncommon.

The actual town of El Congo is located on the old highway to Santa Ana about three kilometers behind the fruit stands. There is not much there today since the new highway has displaced most of the traffic that passed by the old town. El Congo and its glory days as a train stop are written about in Sandra Benitez's novel *Bitter Grounds*, a semi-fictional history of El Salvador. The heroine of the novel made frequent visits back to El Congo. The interesting day to day life leading up to the Salvadoran civil war of the 1980s is well portrayed in the book. *(Panamerican Highway, 50km west of San Salvador and 12km east of Santa Ana)*

has a great view of the lake and live Latin music on weekends. A main dish such as chicken goes for just $4.50 while an exquisite lobster will set you back $17.50. Breakfast is a good value at $3.50. *(Tel 441-6037, 447, 9515; 15 rooms, D $28, Family room (3-5 people) $40, some with AC, all with private bath and fan; pool; laundry; restaurant 8am-8pm)*

**Hotel del Lago** The 115-year-old Hotel del Lago is the oldest hotel in the country and once served as a quiet lakeside retreat for harried Salvadoran presidents. Until remodeling plans are carried out the architectural gem will remain one of the most charming. Older parts of the hotel have big wooden doors and colorful tile floors. While a more modern wing houses most guests you can (and should) stay in the old section. The restaurant is straight out of an old movie, with high ceilings and *merengue* music on Sunday afternoons. Try the *sorbete con merengue* (the dessert, not the music) for $1.60 or a bowl of *sopa de cangrejos* ("crab soup") for $5. Other dishes, including fresh fish, average $7 while breakfast starts at $3. A seat on the pier will cost you an additional $1.15 per person. *(Tel 446-9511; new section 18D $37 with private bath, AC, cable TV; old section 8D $23 with private bath and fan; laundry; 2 pools; restaurant 7am-8pm)*

**Hotel Amacuilco (Aka Guest House Amacuilco)** Amacuilco is very well maintained but it feels weird and spooky, with an occult atmosphere and creepy decor. Also, for some strange reason, the owners only welcome foreigners here. The eating area, which looks out over the lake, has meals ranging from a $3 breakfast to a full course lunch or dinner for about $7. This has become a budding art center with live jazz, blues, or rock concerts on many Sundays and occasionally a Spanish language school operates here. The pool sits next to a small grassy area and a small outdoor library. *(Tel 887-7409, 441-0608; 3D $15, 2 larger rooms $17.50; pool; laundry; restaurant 7am-9pm)*

**Lajamaya Lake Resort** The newest place on the lake was recently opened by a 200-family strong farmer's cooperative whose more traditional pursuits include coffee, dairy and fruit. If you are just here for the day they have lakeside cabañas (called "*glorietas*") for rent starting at $3. Hiking trails will entertain those who aren't interested in aquatic pursuits. One of the advantages of staying here is that they will arrange roundtrip transportation for guests from San Salvador for $2.50. *(Tel 871-5687; 8 rooms and a cabin ranging from $8.50-$18 per person; private bath; restaurant 7-9am, 12-3pm, 5-8pm)*

## DETAILS

■ **BUSES: Santa Ana (220)** via El Congo (this bus takes you right past the hotels on the eastern shore), every half hour until 6pm, 20km, 1hr.

😄 😄 😄 😄 😄

# Parque Nacional Cerro Verde

### 70 km from San Salvador

Cerro Verde is El Salvador at its best—forests, mountains, volcanoes and clean, crisp air. The 1250-acre park is one of the country's most impressive natural attractions, with commanding views of the countryside, hiking, camping, and a comfortable hotel. This orchid-studded retreat was opened in 1958 to take advantage of the views of the erupting Izalco Volcano, but as fate would have it the volcano went to sleep soon after.

Half of the beauty of Cerro Verde is the 2,000-meter ascent of the mountain of the same name. The road up, red with volcanic soil, was finished only in 1990 after six years of effort. The project was supposed to have been completed in the early 1970s, but construction funds were repeatedly embezzled.

The first half of the climb reveals the panorama of the Lago de Coatepeque to the northeast. Soon the air grows chilly and you can see the huge Santa Ana Volcano to the north. By the time you've put on your sweater near the top of the road, the famous black cone of the Izalco Volcano comes into view, followed by the Hotel de la Montaña.

The hotel and a parking lot sit atop the thickly forested Cerro Verde, with various hiking paths leading off in all directions. Izalco looms just off the hotel's balcony, almost close enough to touch, and views of the Lago de Coatepeque and the Santa Ana Volcano are only a short hike away. You can climb either volcano in a reasonably strenuous day hike. An orchid garden near the hotel is usually open, there's a playground with a tree house for children, an arts and crafts pavilion and a few small *comedores* sell snacks. The air is clean and cool—even cold at night—and the views are unbeatable. *($0.80 per person, seniors free)*

## FLORA & FAUNA

The high-altitude forests of Cerro Verde are filled with squirrels, weasels, rabbits, porcupines, moles and armadillos, and an occasional mountain lion has been known to visit. There are many species of birds at Cerro Verde as well, including toucans, 14 varieties of hummingbirds (one as light as three grams), the guardabarranco (known for its beautiful chirping) and xaras, with black heads and iridescent blue bodies and wings. You will certainly notice the impressive number of songbirds in the upper reaches of the park.

One of the most interesting types of high-altitude plant are the epiphytes which are common to Cerro Verde. Orchids are the most famous, but also look for plants that resemble the tops of pineapples perched on the limbs and trunks of trees. Instead of drawing nutrients the soil epiphytes can live off the water and organic debris that accumulate in the crevices between their leaves or draw enough moisture to survive from the clouds that roll through the forest.

## HIKING & CAMPING

From the parking lot a short, easy path leads through the woods to lookouts over the Lago de Coatepeque and the Santa Ana Volcano. There have been some robberies of tourists that have wandered off on a few of the less traveled paths. The National Police (PNC) have a station here and you can ask them for advice and even request a police guide to accompany you if you contact them in advance. Guides can also be hired in San Salvador for serious exploration around the park. Camping was allowed in the past, but changes are underway so you should confirm this is still true. You can also ask for permission at the private Finca San Blas along the trail to Santa Ana Volcano.

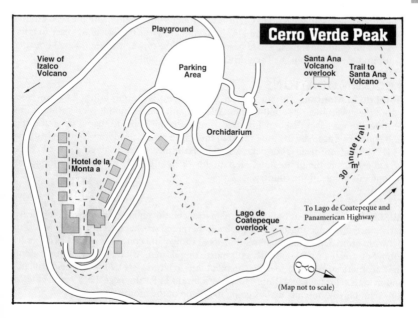

**Santa Ana Volcano** Halfway around the lookout path, another trail leads north towards the Santa Ana Volcano. Santa Ana, also known as Ilamatepec ("The Mountain of the Old Woman" in Nahuat) and "Father Hill," is El Salvador's tallest volcano (2,365m). At the top are four small craters superimposed on a larger, older crater, and a green lagoon filled with sulfuric water. The volcano erupted three times in the early part of this century—always at the same time as Izalco—and is considered active. Lava from Ilamatepec has been found 10 kilometers away. A moderately strenuous three-hour hike will bring you to the top. The trail passes by the Finca San Blas, a private farm where you can camp if you get permission.

**Izalco Volcano** Izalco is a geological oddity, one of the youngest volcanoes in the world. In 1770, a smoking hole in the middle of a farmer's field slowly began to burp out volcanic rocks. Over the next two centuries, Izalco grew continuously and spewed enough lava to be named the "Lighthouse of the Pacific" by sailors who navigated by its glow. Native tribes, on the other hand, called Izalco the "Inferno of the Spanish." The eruptions stopped in 1966—just as construction on the Hotel de la Montaña was finished.

Today, the perfectly shaped cone is 1,900 meters high without a speck of green on its barren slopes. The trail to the top begins 200 meters down the road from the hotel, and is a difficult climb over volcanic rocks. You can reach the rim in about four hours and wave at everybody back at the hotel. It is a difficult, and potentially dangerous, climb to the summit because of the loose ash.

**Lago de Coatepeque** A ten-kilometer hike leads to Lago de Coatepeque, the blue jewel visible from the trail around the hotel. The trailhead is called El Jicote and is four kilometers up the road to Cerro Verde from its intersection with the road around the lake from El Congo. The trail leads downhill towards the lake and is easy to miss. Look for it on the right if you're heading toward the top, a little less than a kilometer around the bend from the Lago de Coatepeque viewpoint.

## ACCOMMODATIONS

**Hotel de la Montaña** The fancy Hotel de la Montaña is the only hotel on Cerro Verde, but the government has put it up for sale and only the restaurant is operating at this time. Rumor has it that a major international chain is going to snap it up so it could be operating again by the time you read this–check with Salvadoran Tourism Institute (ISTU) in San Salvador for details. In the meantime, you can still get a cup of coffee and a snack in the in the hotel's restaurant which offers one of the most spectacular look out points in the country.

## DETAILS

**BUSES:** If the bus is your only option, plan to spend the night on the mountain or leave early since a connecting bus will probably be necessary–be sure not to get stuck in between. From Santa Ana, bus **348** transits El Congo and continues on to Cerro Verde. From Sonsonate or the south, it's a bit more complicated. Ask the driver of buses along the Panamerican Highway to drop you off at Puerto Negras, six kilometers past Armenia and next to a Texaco gas station. Then take a bus to El Pacún, near the "Cerro Verde 14 km" sign. Finally, hop on any bus going to the top of the mountain.

# Santa Ana

Pop. 240,000
63km from San Salvador

## SANTA ANA THEN

El Salvador's second-largest city sits in the valley of Sihuatehuacán on the northeast edge of the slopes of the Santa Ana Volcano. This temperate, fertile area at 650 meters above sea level has been inhabited for a long time. Pok'omáme tribes first settled here around the 5th or 6th century. Pipils arrived from the north five centuries later, absorbing some elements of the Pok'omáme culture and erasing others, including the language.

Just as the independence movement was gaining momentum in the early 19th century, Santa Ana was beginning to prosper through its burgeoning coffee industry. When forced to choose sides in the fight for independence, many of the local gentry were content with the status quo and swore loyalty to the king of Spain.

In 1811, however, citizens of Santa Ana joined with other nearby towns to battle royal troops and called for the abolition of taxes on tobacco and *aguardiente*, a popular sugarcane liquor. On September 21, 1821, the people of Santa Ana learned, via mail, that the movement for independence had succeeded. When the good news reached the crowd that was waiting in the main plaza, celebrations erupted that lasted for days.

The 19th century was hard on the city, although the population continued to increase. In 1822, Guatemalan forces occupied Santa Ana in an effort to force El Salvador into the new Mexican empire. José Arce eventually succeeded in recapturing the city. Revolutions were suppressed in 1837 and 1839. In 1863, Rafael Carrera, president of Guatemala, occupied Santa Ana with a force of 6,000 soldiers and used the city as a base to attack Salvadoran fortifications at Coatepeque. In spite of all this, Santa Ana continued to grow and thrive. By the turn of the century, the city counted 30,000 inhabitants.

Santa Ana wasn't terrorized with guerrilla attacks during the early part of the civil war, but it did suffer other problems. Unemployment hovered around 50 percent in the city for much of the 1980s and was as high as 70 percent in the countryside.

## SANTA ANA NOW

The *Segunda Ciudad* ("Second City") is second only in size with 250,000 inhabitants. It features open streets, a neo-Gothic cathedral, a lavish national theater and an abundance of stylish restaurants. Sharp green hills surround the city, with the cones of Cerro Verde and the Izalco and Santa Ana Volcanoes further to the South. It's still a coffee town, surrounded by many plantations where workers till the rich volcanic soil. Sugarcane plantations can also be seen in the surrounding areas.

Also known as *Ciudad Heróica* ("Heroic City") and *Ciudad Morena* ("Brown Skinned City") Santa Ana's

### Let's Make a Deal

A series of strong earthquakes and chicken pox epidemics in the early 18th century wrought havoc on the population of Santa Ana. In a desperate cry for relief, the town fathers invoked the Virgen del Rosario, promising her a great festival every year in exchange for her protection. Over the years, the festival has expanded from nine to fifteen days.

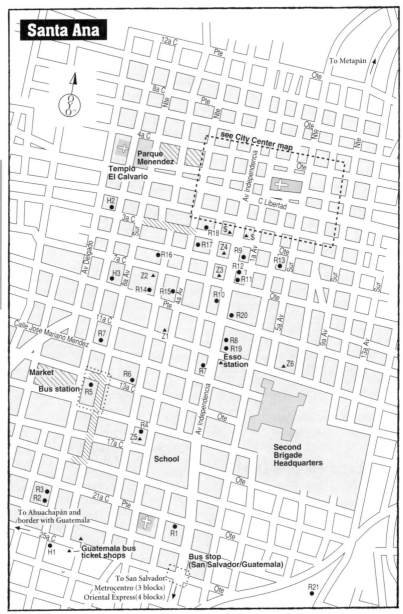

Santa Ana

architecture is unmatched anywhere else in the country. Not only is this degree of colonial heritage unusual for a city of this size, but it makes Santa Ana much more pleasant than the country's choking capital. Wide, clean streets pass between old buildings in surprisingly good condition; most are under two stories high and painted in pastel colors. The low buildings leave lots of blue sky that give the city a spacious feel.

A given on any itinerary west of San Salvador, Santa Ana enjoys a cool climate and an impressively large fruit market. Come here to relax, enjoy the city and maybe even have dinner at a fancy restaurant. The hiking, camping and boating to the south are among the best in the country, and both the Lago de Coatepeque and the Guatemalan border are within easy reach. You could while away an entire afternoon admiring the colonial houses—in particular those around 4a C between 6a and 10a Av—peeking through the grillwork into the gardens and enormous courtyards.

## ACCOMMODATIONS

**Hotel Sahara** The is the top of the line for Santa Ana. Clean but a little cramped, it was built by ex-president José Napoleón Duarte in 1952. *(Tel 447-8865, e-mail hotel_sahara@yahoo.com; 10S $48, 7D $65, 3T $76, all with private bath, most with AC and cable TV; parking; laundry; restaurant Mon-Sat 6:30am-10pm, Sun 6:30am-12pm)*

**Internacional Hotel-Inn** A cramped but clean and friendly place. Ana Rivas is the pleasant owner and she runs a tight ship. You can hop a bus on its way from Ahuachapán to San Salvador right out front. *(Tel 440-0810; 8S $19, 4D $26, 2T $38, all with private bath and cable TV; laundry; restaurant 7am-8pm; noon checkout)*

**Hotel Libertad** (City Center map) José Valmoré García, the owner, will show you to your spacious room. There's a nice view of the cathedral bell tower from the stairs, but the rest of this hotel could use thorough scrubbing and new fixtures. You can put your own locks on the doors, which is probably a good idea. *(Tel 441-2358; 6S $11, 6D $18, 6T $24, most with private bath and TV; laundry; noon checkout)*

**Hotel Livingston** The concrete rooms are run-down but at least the sheets are clean. Adequate for the budget traveler. *(Tel 441-1801; 7S $14, 12D $16, all with private bath and cable TV; parking; 24 hr checkout)*

**Hotel Posada Real** A cozy, familiar environment located in a residential area near the city's new commercial zone to the south. *(Urb Loma Linda # 43; tel 440-4767; 12 rooms S $23, D $46; most with private bath, AC and cable TV; parking; laundry; home cooked meals upon request, from $1.75 - $3)*

## FOOD & DRINK

**Ban Ban** The local's favorite place for fine pastry. Established in 1975 it has several locations around the city, all nicely decorated. Perfect for quiet moments with a bite over coffee or fresh tropical fruit juices. *(8am-6:30pm)*

**Carymar** A place for all sort of traditional snacks and dishes. You can get a full meal for $2.40 or *pupusas* for $0.50 each. *(8am-9pm)*

**Kiko's Pizza/Rosti Pollo** Sixteen-inch pizzas and a chicken dinner for $3.45. *(Tue-Fri 10:30am-2pm, 4-8pm, Sat-Sun 10:30am-8:15pm)*

**Ky Jau** (City Center map) Many locals swear this is the best chow mein in town, and it's just $4. Daily specials are available that will get you a full meal with a soda for $2.30 *(7am-8pm)*

**La Tertulia Bar & Restaurante** Located near the city's stadium this fine place is often visited by the local soccer team's directors, players and journalists. You can either chat while having some drinks in the cozy bar or enjoy delicious international and Salvadoran dishes from $4-$15. There is live music on weekends. *(Av Fray Felipe de Jesús Moraga and 33a C Pte; 12-9:30pm)*

**Los Horcones** (City Center map) Hanging banana plants and bamboo columns give Los Horcones a definite jungle atmosphere true to its name ("The Tree Trunks"). Food is served on clay plates at interesting wooden tables with odd shaped benches. A delicious onion soup is $1.75, and a *carne asada* costs $3.75. Top it all off with a fruit shake for $1.15. Vegetarian dishes are also available. Try to eat upstairs on the terrace where there are more tables and a great view of the main plaza. *(10:30am-10pm)*

**Lover's Steak House** An unpretentious place with a traditional look serving local and international dishes at moderate prices. A typical meal of meat, rice, avocado, sausage and salad costs $6.50. *(11am-10pm)*

**Metrocentro Food Court** Located on the second floor of Santa Ana's large shopping center, it offers a variety of options from typical food (El Guapinol, Ay Caray and Folklóricos) and fried chicken (Pollo Campero) to international chains (McDonald's, Pizza Hut, Wendy's and Domino's Pizza). *(10am-8:30pm)*

**Oriental Express** Good Chinese food for eat-in, take-out or delivery. Have *wonton* soup for $2.35 or a main dish from $4. Daily combo specials available. *(Tel 440-0846; Mon-Fri 9am-3pm, 5pm-8pm, Sat-Sun 9am-8:15pm)*

**Regis Restaurant** This high-quality *cafetería* has been around since 1972. Steak plates range from $4 to $6 and there are daily soup and seafood specials. *(8am-11pm)*

**Restaurante Acajutla** A real delight for seafood lovers. Try anything from the traditional *mariscada* (seafood soup) to the exquisite stuffed lobster. Prices from $5 to $16. *(Tel 440-3517; 10am-9pm)*

**Restaurante El Tucán** El Tucán was born during the war when the owner and cook,

## Tehuas

Centuries ago Santa Ana was known as the "City of Priestesses." The area's early residents tried to influence nature and the spirits through *tehuas* or mystic mediators. *Tehuas* occupied an important place in pre-Columbian society. Sometimes they cast beneficial spells to help and protect people; other times they interpreted signs to predict the future.

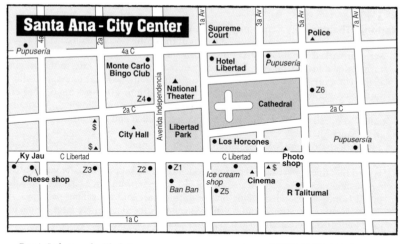

Santa Ana - City Center

| | | |
|---|---|---|
| Z1 | Western Regional Museum | |
| Z2 | *Café Cappuchino* | |
| Z3 | Cafeteria Sananeco | |
| Z4 | Super Selectos | |
| Z5 | R. Mayerling | |
| Z6 | *Pastelería Roxana* | |

René Lobato, decided to open a restaurant where Salvadorans could go to enjoy the food rather than just fill up or get drunk. René is a charming fellow willing to answer hard questions about his country. His restaurant is formal and decorated with Salvadoran paintings. The second floor has romantic lighting, hanging plants and a balcony. Main dishes are $5-$11.50 and the onion soup is excellent. *(Tel 441-1071; Fri-Wed 11:30am-3pm, 5:30-10pm)*

**Restaurante El Patio** The entrance to Santa Ana's classiest restaurant is a large, semi-circular wooden door that opens into a shaded interior courtyard decorated with hanging plants, a fountain and a stone garden. This stylish, laid-back place has over 200 seats at 50 tables and golden walls. Don't be confused by all the colonial styling–they take credit cards here. Entrees on the international menu start at $5 and climb to $15. This place is ideal for prime meat. *(Tel 440-4221; Tue-Sun 11am-3pm, 5-10pm; live marimba during Sunday lunch)*

**Restaurant Talitumal** (City Center map) Edwin Maldonado is a surgeon who opened Talitumal (Nahuat for "Sun and Land") after becoming a vegetarian for health reasons. He gave up traditional "chemical" medicine in–of all places–medical school, came up with a recipe for a vegetarian hamburger and opened this little haunt back in the 1980s. The soybean hamburgers are chewy, but the natural bread for $1.80 can't be beat. The menu is mainly vegetarian and changes every day. Every healthy goodie you could ever desire is for sale here, including medicinal plants, honey and natural pastas. Some not-so-healthy but delectable pastries are also very inexpensive. *(Tel 447-7549; 9am-7pm)*

**Taquería Manolito's** The well-known *tacos, tortas and burritos* among other Mexican delicacies are served in a small but cozy room with just eight tables. Prices range from $1-$4. Add a seasonal fruit juice for just $1. *(Fri-Wed 11:30am-3pm, 5:30-9pm)*

## SIGHTS

**National Theater** (City Center map) Santa Ana's gorgeous theater was begun in 1902 and still recalls the city's heyday at the turn of the century, when coffee export taxes were earmarked for its construction. When the national theater in San Salvador burned down in 1910, all the theater companies moved to Santa Ana, to the delight of the city's art lovers. Things soon took a turn for the worse, though, and during the economic crisis of the 1930s it was turned into a (gasp!) movie theater, which it remained until 1978 when serious repairs were begun. Following a Mexican-funded restoration project the theater reopened in 2000 and is again the pride and joy of Santa Ana.

Inside a set of grand wooden staircase leads to the inside of the theater which is an impressive example of what can be done with quality woods and a whole lot of taste. Stylized tiles line a foyer with maroon wooden columns supporting a ceiling painted in pastel blue and rose. The theater itself is also maroon, with three terraces and balconies. Notice the wooden railing on the third terrace and the ceiling paintings of Mozart, Beethoven, Strauss and Tchaikovsky. Below the stage, three large basins of water were used to create an echo that allowed actors' voices to resonate. Currently the sound and lightning system is being modernized by the Japanese International Cooperation Agency.

During town festivals, the theater usually hosts art exhibitions. Performances and cultural events are also held regularly; either check with the desk for a schedule or call 441-2193 or 441-6268.

**Cathedral** (City Center map) The center of Santa Ana is dominated by its cathedral, the most famous church in El Salvador. Construction began in 1905 in a mixture of neo-Gothic and Byzantine architecture. Its interior has 13 naves decorated with images dating back to the 16th-century conquest. The pink and gray columns look like marble, but they are actually painted concrete. The imposing white facade is currently undergoing restoration.

**City Hall** (City Center map) Construction of the massive new City Hall began in May 1874 to replace the old one which was destroyed by an earthquake four years earlier. It wasn't finished until 1927 but the six decades of construction resulted in one of the most beautiful buildings in the country.

**Templo El Calvario** A figure of Jesus in purple robes carrying the cross stands inside this church in Parque Menéndez. The walls are lined with detailed sculptures, and the image of Jesus on the door is repeated above the altar.

**Western Regional Museum** (City Center map) This new regional historical museum will be open by the time you read this. We expect it will be pretty good. *(Tel 441-1215)*

## SHOPPING

**Luís Pedro Leather Shop** A small boutique with leather shoes and bags made in Santa Ana. Dress shoes run about $25, belts $30 and purses $115. Everything is high quality. *(9am-12pm and 2:30-5pm)*

**Artesanías de El Salvador** This souvenir shop in the city center offers a good variety of local and regional arts and crafts. *(Tel 441-3762; Mon-Sat 8am-5pm)*

**Metrocentro** The newest (and only) shopping mall in town where you can find almost anything you might need including a supermarket, travel agency, souvenir shop, pet shop, music stores, camera studio and a hair salon. SIMAN, one of the largest department stores in the country, is also here. Or just come to enjoy one of the latest movies.

## DETAILS

■ **DOMESTIC BUSES:** Make sure you get your ticket at the correct kiosk since there are three and each sells tickets to different destinations. You can also pay the driver when getting on the bus. **Ahuachapán (210)**, every 10 min until 7:30pm, 34km, 1hr. **Cerro Verde (248)**, every 15 min until 6pm, 47km, 2hr. **Chalchuapa/Tazumal (218)**, every 15 min until 7pm, 15km, 35min. **Lago Coatepeque (220)**, every 30 min until 6pm, 28km, 75min. **Metapán (235)**, every 15 min until 6:40pm, 45km, 90min. **San Cristóbal (236)**, via Candelaria de la Frontera, every 15 min until 6pm, 32km, 70min. **San Salvador (201)**, every 5 min until 8pm, 63km, 2hr. Direct every 7 min, 90min. **Sonsonate (216)**, every 15 min until 6pm, 40km, 70min.

■ **DRUGSTORES/PHARMACIES:** While there are pharmacies spread throughout the city if you need one late at night go to 25a C where you can always find at least one open.

■ **ENTERTAINMENT:** Feel like shaking your body in a local dance club? Try it at **Titanic**, Santa Ana's largest discotheque. It is usually filled with a young crowd following the rhythms of tropical and American pop music inside its modern facilities *(Thur-Sat 8pm-2am; $3.45 cover)*. Another popular option is **Casa Vieja**, inside a big, old house, where people of all ages have snacks, eat dinner (from $4) and dance to the live tropical music. *(Tel 440-1814; Fri-Sat 8pm-2am, Sun 3pm-7pm; $3 cover)*. If you're feeling lucky you could check the newly opened **Monte Carlo Bingo Club** which offers blackjack, roulette, poker, slot machines and free drinks *(6pm-4am)*

■ **FESTIVALS: July 18-26 (25)** Señora Santa Ana.

■ **INTERNATIONAL BUSES:** Six different companies originating in San Salvador run buses to Guatemala. A round trip to Guatemala City (4 hours) costs $14 for regular buses; every hour from 5am to 4pm; tel 271-1361, 243-1300. Special buses with AC, bathroom, TV and snacks cost $45; 7am and 4pm; tel 440-1608.

■ **SPORTS:** Soccer games are played in the *Oscar Quiteño* local stadium most Sundays.

■ **TAXIS:** Unlike other large cities of the world, you'll seldom spot a cab wandering around Santa Ana's streets. Call any of the following numbers: 447-1962, 447-2026 or 871-8876.

# Near Santa Ana

**Turicentro Sihuatehuacán** Six and a half kilometers east of Santa Ana you'll find three pools, including one Olympic and one kiddie-size, along with tennis courts, restaurants, picnic areas, sports fields and an outdoor theater. Admission gives you access to changing rooms and lockers. *(Catch bus 51a or 51b between 25a C Pte and 10a Av Nte, or in the Central Park in front of the Cathedral; 8am-6pm; $1 per person; parking $1)*

# Chalchuapa/Tazumal

78km from San Salvador
15km from Santa Ana

## Chalchuapa

Chalchuapa was the center of El Salvador's early Pok'omáme civilization. In the 15th century, Pipils moved into the area and forced the Pok'omámes to leave for Guatemala. The city is on the road to Guatemala and was repeatedly fought over in the 19th century. Federal armies occupied the main plaza three times in the 1820s, and in 1851 Guatemalan troops stormed the town.

Today Chalchuapa is best known as the home of one of the principal archeological sights in El Salvador. To reach Tazumal get off the bus at the Chalchuapa Cemetery and walk about two football fields along the graveyard wall. Since there is no hotel, sleep in Santa Ana and come here for the day.

### SIGHTS
**Church of Santiago Apostle** This church is one of the best-preserved colonial churches in El Salvador. Some researchers think the famous architect Diego de Porres built this church. In the church's cupola is the image of Santiago the Apostle and a watchtower that is similar to the designs of some of de Porre's works in Antigua, Guatemala.

### FOOD & DRINK
**Restaurante El Bosque** This restaurant on the outskirts of town is known for their steaks and beef dishes. Try the *churrasco del bosque* for $6 or the surf and turf (*churrasco mixto con camarones*) for $8.70. *(Km 70 on the highway from Santa Ana; Tue-Sun noon-close)*

**Restaurante Los Anojitos** An interesting place specializing in beef and shellfish. The menu has a wide variety of *antojitos* ("appetizers") all priced in the $4-6 range. *(Calle Ramon Flores #6; 9am-close)*

## Tazumal Ruins

The ruins of Tazumal are the most famous and best-studied ruins in El Salvador. They won't blow you away, but the view from the top of the surrounding countryside is worth the climb.

**History** The Pacific coastal belt between Tapachula, Mexico and the Río Lempa in El Salvador was the cradle of the oldest civilization in Mesoamerica. Tazumal ("place of many lakes" in Nahuat) is an ancient site which, according to estimates, has been populated for the past 3,200 years, although the earliest phases of construction didn't begin until around 500 BC.

The site changed hands more than once and was linked through trade to other civilizations throughout Central America. Ceramic remains found at Tazumal indicate a possible link with the Mexican civilization of Teotihuacán. Mayan objects have been found which date to the 7th and 10th centuries AD, and other artifacts show a

Pipil influence.

Researchers believe that Tazumal controlled much of the Mayan Obsidian trade and produced some of the most famous Mayan ceramics. The people who lived at Tazumal appear to have had writing systems and calendars similar to those of the Olmecs in the Southern Mayan region of Mexico.

**The Site** The site is divided into five zones: Tazumal, the best known, along with Casablanca, Las Victorias, Pampe and El Trapiche. Recently some important finds have been unearthed by Japanese and Salvadorans archaeologists at the nearby Casablanca site. This zone has not been opened to the public yet but you may get permission to see the work in progress.

Excavations carried out between 1942 and 1954 revealed two different building complexes. The older one, known as mound number one, is sometimes compared to the main mound of the ruins of San Andrés. It consists of a rectangular terraced platform nearly 25 meters high, crowned by a pyramidal temple. The structure probably served as both a sanctuary and as an astronomical observatory, and archaeological evidence indicates that it endured as many as 14 phases of construction. Excavations of the tombs have yielded some important finds of jade jewelry and ceramics brought to Tazumal from Guatemalan sites.

The recently discovered mound number two, situated immediately to the west of mound number one, is similar. Though the mounds appear to be united, they are actually separate structures. Archeologists have also unearthed part of a court once used to play *tatchi*, a pre-Columbian ball game. This court, most of which is covered by the cemetery next door, is difficult to distinguish.

A small museum next to the excavation is well organized, with many ceramics on display as well as a model of the entire site. English and Spanish captions describe both the objects and the laborious process of excavations and preservation. Cheap ceramics are sold at the entrance, but don't believe anyone who tells you they have "original" artifacts, since everything is either in a museum or covered in concrete.

A well-known stela called the "Queen of Tazumal," now housed in the new David J. Guzmán National Museum in San Salvador, was found here. The three-meter high image bears both male and female features and has the head of an animal, probably a monkey. The museum, which also contains many other Tazumal artifacts, can conveniently be visited before your trip to the ruins if you are coming from the capital.

In spite of its reputation, the site is disappointing, especially if you've just been to Guatemala or Honduras. Although excavation is still underway, what little that has been uncovered is encased in concrete. At sunset, though, when you can still see the structure's shape but the concrete fades and the crowds are gone, the ruins take on the glow of another century. (*11a Av Sur, a 10-minute walk east of town; Tue-Sun 9-5; admission $0.50 locals and $2.50 for visitors*)

## DETAILS

■ **BUSES: Ahuachapán (202, 406)**, every 7 min until 8pm, 18km, 15min. **San Salvador (202)**, every 7 min until 5:30pm, 78km, 90min. **Santa Ana (218)**, every 15 min until 7pm, 15km, 35min.

■ **FESTIVALS: August 10-16** Santiago the Apostle.

# Atiquizaya

Nahuat, "Place of Spring Water"
90km from San Salvador

Atiquizaya is a small, seldom-visited town, but it is worth a stop if you are in the area. The town's rich colonial architecture has remained largely untouched throughout the years and at times walking down the streets is like taking a stroll through the past. Be sure to spend some time in the Parque 5 de Noviembre admiring the decorative metal work on the buildings which surround it. You might also take a look at the Iglesia de Concepción which has a decent display of 19th century religious art.

The large statue (a tribute to Don Quixote de la Mancha) that greets you as you arrive in town exemplifies Atiquizaya's metal working renown. It was sculpted by Don Alfredo Melara, a very well known tinsmith who has been shaping metal here for over 70 years, and he is still going strong. Alberto Flores, another well-known tinsmith, creates mobile amusement park like figures. You can visit their workshops, as well as many others.

If you appreciate fine woodworking you may just want to head down the road to the small artisan village of Turin just 3km west of Atiquizaya where guitars and many carved goods are made.

## SIGHTS

**Salto de Malacatiupan** Here you will find four beautiful waterfalls and several natural pools fed by the Río Agua Caliente ("Hot Water River"). You can bathe in the upper pond where the water temperature is about 40 degrees C. Extraordinarily, considering the water temperature, some fish manage to live in the river. Before making a trip out here you may want to get in touch with the Fundación Malacatiupan (tel 444-1607). They can arrange guides, offer camping permission, and provide detailed information about the area.

If you ask locals about the various legends surrounding this place you will here some fantastic stories. The most famous story is about a golden crab that lives in these ponds. A golden crab is now Atiquizaya's symbol and is found in the town's coat of arms. (*Located 7 km from town on the road to San Lorenzo; take the dirt road one street down from the church to the west where it joins up with the paved road*)

## HIKING

**Cerro El Cachio** This extinct volcano, in the Apaneca Range south of town, rises around 1900 meters above sea level. Climbing it requires skill, determination, and about three hours, but the reward is worth the effort for the impressive views at the summit and along the way. You should talk to locals before making the climb for information.

## DETAILS

■ **BUSES: San Salvador (202)**, every 10min until 6pm, 90km, 3hr. **Santa Ana (210)**, every 15min until 6pm, 22km, 75min

■ **FESTIVALS: January 7-15** A host of celebrations are held to honor the Black Christ.

😄 😄 😄 😄 😄

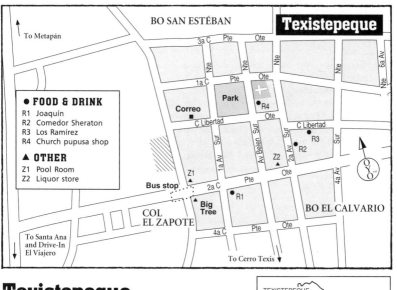

# Texistepeque

Nahuat, "Place of Snails"
Pop. 26,000
80km from San Salvador
16km from Santa Ana

## TEXISTEPEQUE THEN

Like many early Pok'omáme cities in El Salvador, Texistepeque was taken over by the Pipils in the late 13th century. By the beginning of the 18th century, the town was still purely indigenous without a single *mestizo* family (much less any pure Spanish) in residence.

## TEXISTEPEQUE NOW

The approach to Texistepeque from Santa Ana to the south isn't too attractive, except for the volcanic cones that jut out of the surrounding plains like huge earth pyramids. The road passes a terrible landfill on the way to the town's ramshackle dirt-road entrance that is decorated with political graffiti.

Everyone seems to know everyone else in Texistepeque. The atmosphere is very familiar—many of the restaurants aren't even marked as restaurants—but the town is anything but closed. Residents, including many who have lived in the United States, are eager to talk to the infrequent traveler who passes this way. If you're looking for a place off the beaten track to meet everyday Salvadorans and hear about their lives, stop off here on your way north to the Bosque Montecristo, the Lago de Güija and the Honduran border at Anguiatú. There still aren't any hotels or boarding houses so don't plan to visit late in the day.

## FOOD & DRINK

**Drive-In El Viajero** Fast food in the Shell gas station at the entrance to town, with sandwiches for $1.50. *(7am-6pm)*

**Joaquín** Typical and fast food in the $2 range. Set in a small house—you can peek inside it and the others attached to the same courtyard. *(4:30-9pm)*

**Comedor Sheraton** This place has a terrace but no sign so look next to the blue house. *Pupusas* for $0.10, or a beefsteak for $1.15. *(Open a few hours off and on in the morning and afternoon)*

**Church Pupusa Shop** Serves *pupusas*, milk tapioca and bread cake on weekends. Belinda and Isela Dalila, the two bubbling girls who work here, love to talk about their town.

**Los Ramírez** Recommended by locals for home cooking (*"comida casera"*) from $2. Daily specials vary with what is in season and how the cook feels—as do the hours.

## HIKING

**Cerro Texis** A.k.a. Cerro Huevo, a.k.a. Cerro Piedra, this hill goes by many names but you can't miss it three blocks southeast of Texistepeque.

## DETAILS

■ **BUSES: Metapán (235),** every 15 min until 6:30pm, 25km, 50min. **Santa Ana (235, 235a),** every 15 min until 6:30pm, 16km, 40min.

■ **FESTIVALS: December 25-27 (26)** San Estéban and the Virgen of Belén de Güija. **Semana Santa (Holy Thursday and Friday)** On Holy Monday the town presents a skit known as the "Talciguines." According to tradition, the Talciguines are seven devils dressed in colored tunics with handkerchiefs around their heads, who run around the town and pretend to beat everyone they meet with a whip. At one point during the day, another character representing Jesus shows up wearing a purple tunic and carrying a cross and a bell. When the Talciguines meet Jesus, they try to whip him, but when He shows them the cross they fall to the ground in defeat.

# Metapán

Nahuat, "River of Agava"
Pop. 75,000
111km from San Salvador
40km from Santa Ana

## METAPÁN THEN

A lovely ride on the winding but modern CA-12 highway will take you from Santa Ana to Metapán, an ancient town that has adapted well to the 20th century. Descendants of the Maya-Chortí have inhabited the area since the 13th century. By the time the Spanish arrived in the 16th century, Pipils had come to dominate Metapán, though locals spoke a dialect that included some Maya-Chortí words. The town was nearly destroyed by fire and invaded by Guatemalan troops in the 1800s. Another of the city's claims to fame stems from being among the first cities to follow the lead of Father Delgado as he led the fight for independence from Spain in November 1811. At the time, the people of Metapán rioted against the government, stoned the house of the Spanish mayor and threatened to lynch anyone who didn't support their cause.

## METAPÁN NOW
Today, the second-largest city in the department of Santa Ana prospers from its mining, ranching and cement industries while eco-tourism is becoming increasingly important because this is the best jumping off point for Bosque Montecristo. The city has a great setting on one end of the Alotepeque-Metapán range and there are some lovely views of Lago de Güija and the Ostua River that forms the border with Guatemala. Tall palm trees surround the main plaza and you'll hear music and see cowboy hats everywhere.

Metapán has a few more restaurants than most cities of its size and one very good hotel. This along with its proximity to Bosque Montecristo, the Lago de Güija and the Honduran border make Metapán a convenient stop, either on your way out of the country or just to explore the area.

● **ACCOMMODATIONS**
H1   Hotel San José

● **FOOD & DRINK**
R1   *Ice Cream Shop*
R2   *Pastry store*
R3   Multidelicias
R4   Pollo Kentucky
R5   *Sorbetería El Polar*
R6   *Pastry shop*

▲ **OTHER**
Z1   Supermarket
Z2   Supermarket
Z3   Supermarket
Z4   Gas Station

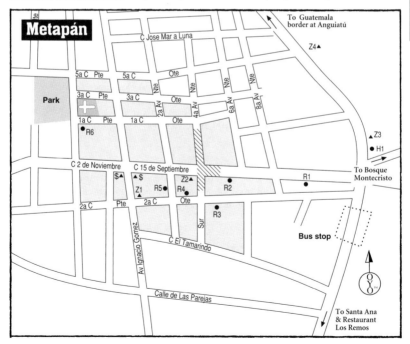

## ACCOMMODATIONS

**Hotel San José** One of the area's better hotels, with good service in an agreeable atmosphere. The hotel has a good restaurant and carnivores will love the *Corazón de Lomito al Carbón*, 12 oz of grilled steak for $9. Breakfast is $3.50 and lunches are $6. *(Tel 442-0556, 442-0320; 28 rooms S $23, D $29, T $43, all with private bath, TV, AC; restaurant 9am-9pm)*

## FOOD & DRINK

**Pollo Kentucky** Not to be confused with the Colonel's franchise, here you will find the Salvadoran version of fried chicken in Central American spices. A three-piece meal costs less than $3. *(8am to 8pm)*

**Multidelicias** A pizzeria and pastry store with clean white tables, green chairs and a friendly atmosphere. Pizza costs just $6, and pastries are $0.20 or less. *(10am-9pm)*

**Sorbetería El Polar** Serves ice cream, breakfast or lunch (or ice cream *for* breakfast or lunch). *(7:30am-8:30pm)*

**Restaurante Los Remos** ("The Oars") A new place situated on the banks of the Metapán lagoon. The menu is mostly seafood and you might try some of the lake fish called *mojarra*. Meals run from $8.50 to $10.50 *(Km 109.5 on the highway to Metapán; 11am-9pm)*

## SIGHTS

**Church of San Pedro** This white colonial church with beautiful red doors, which vaguely resembles a dollhouse, dates from 1740. It is one of the best preserved of El Salvador's colonial churches. The organ hasn't worked for ages though, and today is home to several bats. Inside the church's dome you'll find excellent paintings, the traditional local silversmiths work with silver taken from the nearby mines and other religious artwork. Also inside are images of saints who gaze down from above and stand vigil from within glass cases decorated with gold-painted wood. Below the church are catacombs which can be entered through a trap door in the floor of the main nave. Locals often hid here during the civil war.

## HIKING

A number of hiking opportunities, compliments of the area's overactive geology, lie directly south of Metapán along the road to Texistepeque and Santa Ana.

**Cerro Metapán** Directly southwest of Metapán, this 640-meter hill overlooks the Laguna Metapán, a small companion lake to the Lago de Güija in a valley formed by ancient lava flows.

**San Diego Volcano** (790 m) A few kilometers south of Metapán on the shores of the Lago de Güija, San Diego has a well-formed crater at its summit. **Cerro El Desagüe** (460 m) South of the San Diego Volcano, El Desagüe also overlooks the lake. It's smaller but closer to the road, near kilometer 102.

## DETAILS
■ **BUSES: Anguiatú/Guatemalan border (211a)**, every 30 min, 12km, 30min. **Santa Ana (235)**, every 15 min, 40km, 1hr 30min.

■ **FESTIVALS: June 25-29 (28)** San Pedro. **October 25-November 5** Todos los Santos. **December 16-26** Virgen de Perpetuo Socorro. Fifteen masses, called *misas juradas*, are celebrated in this ten-day festival. By tradition, each mass is sponsored by a particular local family, as long as family members survive. According to legend, an ancestor of each of the families promised the Virgen that they would observe these masses in exchange for protection from cholera.

# Bosque Montecristo

Almost lost in the clouds of the Central American highlands, Montecristo is one of El Salvador's last remaining regions of unspoiled wilderness beauty and was established in 1986 with funding from the European Union, U.S. AID and the United Nations. The park is El Salvador's slice of the larger international biosphere known as El Trifinio which straddles El Salvador, Honduras and Guatemala and is jointly administered by the three countries.

Montecristo has escaped the deforestation that has ravaged so much of the rest of El Salvador's surface, and it's reassuring to see that it is so well-maintained—maybe it's because the three countries meet here and are competing for the nicest section of forest, or maybe it's just too hard to reach. Regardless, Montecristo is by far the best place in El Salvador to experience the outdoors, with unequaled hiking and camping and an endless supply of cool, fresh air.

Making the journey from Metapán to here is emerging from a night of urban bustle and commotion to a day of cool breezes and dripping trees. Montecristo is hard to get to, but well worth the effort. So worth it, in fact, that you might want to spend a night or two here exploring the gorgeous topography.

Montecristo sits in the most humid area of El Salvador, a corner of the country drenched with over two meters of rainfall per year. Clouds scud through the hills and keep the humidity high even at night. It can get cold at this altitude, especially at night, so bring at least one warm layer, and preferably a waterproof one too. Within the park you'll find the Cerros Miramundo (2,394m), Brujo (2,410m) and Montecristo (2,418m). The last one gives the park its name and includes on its peak the exact point where the three countries converge, called El Trifinio.

At about 2,000 meters, the normal lowland forest gives way to the dripping *bosque*

## Animals Courting, Please Do Not Disturb

**M**ontecristo is one of a handful of places left in Central America where it is possible to conduct ecological studies in a tropical cloud forest, with its rich but threatened abundance of plant and animal life. El Trifinio is closed from May to the end of October to allow the animals a chance to breed in peace.

*nuboso* ("cloud forest") for which the park is famous. Cypresses, pines and oaks, some up to 30 meters high, crowd close enough together to block out most of the sunlight in spots. Unfortunately, the lower limit of the cloud forest used to be closer to 1,800 meters, but encroaching small farms have pushed it higher in recent years.

While most of the trails are well marked if you plan to hike you should pick up a map at the park gate or take a guide. If you don't, you won't be the first visitor to get lost.

To visit Montecristo, you need permission in advance from the Agricultural Ministry in Soyapango or Santa Tecla. Call 228-4443 or 295-0328, fax 294-0575 for a reservation or to arrange for camping. The park limits the amount of people who may enter on any one day so during holidays and on weekends, you should reserve your place in advance if at all possible.

## FLORA & FAUNA

The Park is home to a wide variety of plant and animal life. Orchids, mosses, fungi and lichens hide in the shadows, and some types of ferns tower over a meter and a half tall. If you're lucky you might spot porcupines, foxes, anteaters, white-tailed deer, monkeys and maybe even a jaguar. Birdwatchers can expect to see hummingbirds, striped owls, and the spectacular quetzal. Beautiful butterflies are everywhere, even in the higher elevations.

## LOS PLANES

Los Planes, a lovely recreation area perched at 1900 meters within Montecristo, is one of the few public areas in the country with garbage cans that people actually use. It has a soccer field, picnic tables, bathrooms, cooking grills and camping space beneath tall cypresses. There is also a small food stand, but you should bring all your own provisions since it is not always open

From Los Planes a number of hiking trails lead off into the wilds. At the far end of the camping area is a well-marked path that leads down to a river. A five-minute hike will bring you past an orchid garden to a small, crystal-clear waterfall. The spectacular garden has been the work of many local and international botanists and biologists over the years.

Another path leaves from behind the soccer field. It's much less distinct, so look for signs of heavy travel. After about 50 meters through constant birdcalls and insects noises, the path becomes clearer and begins to go downhill, with natural tree-root steps. Walking another five minutes brings you to a hanging bridge. Go left at a fork in the road, then left at the next, smaller fork and uphill. Twenty meters past the barbed wire fence is a beautiful panoramic view straight out of the Sound of Music. To the right in the distance you can glimpse the Lago de Güija.

If you're up for a more serious trek you may try to tackle El Trifinio, visible four kilometers away from the soccer field. There are other well-traveled paths in the area, so if you decide to take one—and why not?—just make sure you can find your way back. Always hike prepared, too, with warm clothes, a waterproof layer, a water supply and a realistic estimate of your own limits.

## GETTING THERE

Montecristo's beauty is due in large part to its inaccessibility, so expect that getting there will be difficult. No buses reach the top and you can't enter on foot. You have the choice of bringing your own car, hiring a taxi or catching a pickup from the market in Metapán ($1.25 per person) to Majadita, a village partway up the mountain. Unfortunately the latter service does not run on a regular schedule. If getting there on your own is too much work any tour operator can organize a trip to the park either from San Salvador, Santa Ana or Metapán. Prices are reasonable, and like you would expect, drop with an increase in group size.

The park's gate is five kilometers northeast of Metapán. The dirt road into the park turns into a rough concrete track more suitable for a 4x4 than anything else. Four kilometers from the gate is the San José administrative area with offices and a huge colonial house decorated with hanging baskets, orchids and wild ferns. The next stop on the road up is a nice spot called Majadita, and at the 18 kilometer marker is Los Planes. Hiking to Los Planes from San José will take you more than three hours. From Majadita the hike is a little shorter. To catch a round-trip taxi from Metapán to the camping area should cost about $40, but you might be able to talk your way into a better deal. *(6am-5pm; $2 per Salvadoran, $5.75 per foreigner)*

# Lago de Güija

12km from Metapán
52km from Santa Ana

Just over ten kilometers south of Metapán, the beautiful Lago de Güija straddles the border between El Salvador and Guatemala. Large and small volcanic cones, including San Diego, Igualtepeque and El Tule, dot the lake's Salvadoran shoreline. Some ruins on the islands have yielded museum pieces that were buried during volcanic eruptions. Cerro Negro, a rough jumble of boulders used by fishermen for shelter in emergencies, is nearby.

## Isla Tipa

Isla Tipa, the largest island in the lake, once had a Pipil sanctuary, called Teotipa, that was used to worship the divine couple Quetzalcoatl and Izqueye. According to legend, the sanctuary was created when the two gods appeared out of the waters of the lagoon.

The Güija hydroelectric plant, about 12km from Metapán, is the first dam on the Lempa River and plant tours can sometimes be arranged through the electrical utility CEL (222-7444 or 222-9576). More interesting, however, are *las figuras*, ornate Mayan hieroglyphics and stone carvings, just a short distance downstream from the plant. They are said to date back to the late Mayan Post-Classic period. You can also still see many of the locals fishing or collecting shellfish here.

While at the lake you can hire a boat to visit some of the islands like La Tipa or you can climb one of the surrounding hills for a great panorama of the lake all the way across to Guatemala. *(Take bus 235 from Metapán towards Santa Ana and get off at the small village of Desagüe just 15 minutes away, take the unpaved road to the right for about 100 m and cross the bridge to the town, Ask for directions to the lake in town, it is about half an hour's walk)*

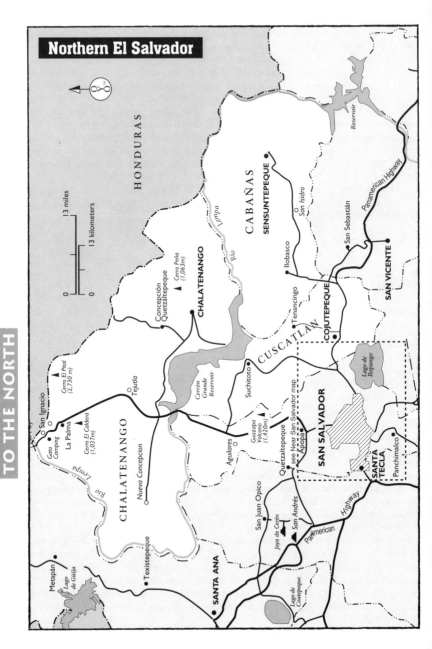

# Northern El Salvador

**TO THE NORTH**

# TO THE NORTH

E l Salvador buckles and rises as it heads north into Honduras and Guatemala. Timber is the major industry in this hilly territory near the border, while grain fields and pastures fill much of Cabañas and Cuscatlán departments. The main attractions up here are the crafts made in a handful of small towns, like La Palma's painted wood boxes, Concepción Quetzaltepeque's hammocks and Ilobasco's pottery. Other cities, like Chalatenango, Suchitoto and Ilobasco, are worth a visit just in themselves. In between are kilometers of secluded mountains that are perfect for time away from the city.

It's not that easy to get around in the north. Cities are widely spaced and buses are infrequent. The mountain roads in Chalatenango are especially bad, and the weather can get downright chilly up this high. It's beautiful country, though, and many of the small cities are worth the extra effort to get there. You can enter Honduras at El Poy in Chalatenango, north of La Palma.

■ **EMERGENCY POLICE NUMBERS (PNC): Cabañas department**: 382-0121, 382-0122, 382-0801. **Chalatenango department:** 301-0323, 301-0330, 301-1602. **Cuscatlán department**: 372-0156, 372-2533, 372-2537, 372-2976.

## Cojutepeque
Nahuat, "Mountain of Turkeys"
Pop. 46,000
32km from San Salvador

### COJUTEPEQUE THEN
One of the first Christians to travel through Cojutepeque, the priest Don Ravo Medina, reported in 1650 that the city's original Pipil inhabitants waded naked in the nearby rivers together "without fear of God." In the 17th century, a group of Spanish monks on

a mission from San Salvador tried to remedy the situation by building the town a church.

The local Indians and European Christians, most with little or nothing in common except the land they shared, fought side-by-side during El Salvador's drive toward independence, rallying under the cry "Death to the newly arrived Europeans!" When Spanish government forces arrived to quell the independence movement, the city's main plaza, a windmill and most of the town had already been destroyed by rebel sympathizers.

Cojutepeque's proximity to San Salvador made it known as the country's "reserve capital." The government relocated here repeatedly, first after earthquakes which devastated the capital in 1839 and 1854, and later during periods of civil unrest.

During the civil war, rebel influence in the area created some interesting political problems. In an attempt to convince locals to support the Salvadoran government, the US government increased aid to the city, pouring thousands of dollars into the local economy. The aid often arrived in the form of food and weapons, and was sometimes used to rebuild schools and other buildings destroyed during the war. Although the FMLN objected to the source of these funds, they quickly realized that attacks on these buildings turned public sentiment against them. As a result, the rebels allowed construction to proceed, and in exchange were occasionally permitted to teach classes about leftist politics in the same buildings.

## COJUTEPEQUE NOW

Cojutepeque is a bustling commercial city without much to interest the traveler besides daily Salvadoran life. The streets are filled with people selling the usual range of products and vegetables, and the few nearby sights aren't anything special.

The town is famous for some of the best sausage and citrus fruit in Central America. All along the Panamerican highway you will see dozens of stands selling all types, shapes and flavors of sausages called *chorizos* and a local favorite called *butifaras*. These are best washed down with either a beer or orange juice depending on your preference and the time of day. If you stop to eat here make sure the stand you pick has at least a chance at the good housekeeping seal. There is also a large cottage industry that makes a wide variety of very inexpensive clay vases, pots and planters.

Cojutepeque has three *hospedajes*, but we can't recommend any of them.

## FOOD & DRINK

**La Familiar** This eatery is a combination mini supermarket and fast food shop. You can have a variety of sandwiches for about $1 or the small *comida a la vista* ("buffet") for $2. *(8am-8pm)*

**Comedor La Cancha** A tiny place with five tables. The *encebollados* (beef and onions) are the specialty of the house for $3.20. This is a popular spot for the locals to stop, have a beer and watch life go by. You might as well join them. *(9am-8pm)*

**Restaurante El Panoramico** Just outside the city you can dine with a spectacular view of Lake Ilopango, Chichontepec

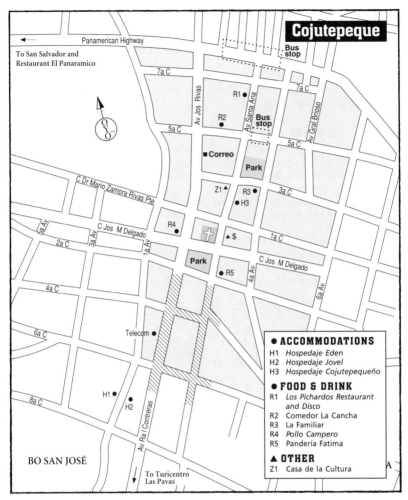

Cojutepeque

● **ACCOMMODATIONS**
H1  *Hospedaje Eden*
H2  *Hospedaje Jovel*
H3  *Hospedaje Cojutepequeño*

● **FOOD & DRINK**
R1  *Los Pichardos Restaurant and Disco*
R2  Comedor La Cancha
R3  La Familiar
R4  *Pollo Campero*
R5  *Panadería Fatima*

▲ **OTHER**
Z1  Casa de la Cultura

volcano and the surrounding mountains. The menu is a la carte with steak and seafood from $4.50 to $7.50. *(Km. 30.5 on the Panamerican Highway; 11am-5:30pm)*

**Panadería Fatima** One of the most traditional bakeries in Cojutepeque, they make a wide variety of fresh goods at very low prices.

## DETAILS

■ **BUSES:** Getting to and from Cojutepeque is easy because all buses to many eastern and northern towns, such as San Vicente, La Union, San Miguel, and Sensuntepeque leaving from or heading to San Salvador's Eastern Bus Terminal stop here. Buses pass through every few minutes until 7:30pm. Note that all buses except the 113 from San Salvador drop passengers along the Panamerican Highway, about two blocks down the hill from the park.

■ **FESTIVALS: January 12-21 (20)** San Sebastián and La Inmaculada Virgen de Concepción. Vendors sell carved wood objects, modern ceramics and famous sausages. **August 28-31** San Juan Degollado.

## Near Cojutepeque

**Turicentro Las Pavas** An easy half-hour hike brings you to the top of this hill, the geographic center of El Salvador, overlooking Cojutepeque and the Lago de Ilopango. The air is always cooler up here and the ocean is visible on a clear day. A shrine to the Virgen de Fátima at the summit attracts pilgrims from far away; many of whom believe miracles have taken place here. Near the summit are several food and crafts stands. Walk down Av Raúl Contreras to find the road to the top. *(1.2 km south of town)*

**Parque Ecologico de Café** The government and Procafe have just opened the country's first coffee park in the nearby village of Santa Cruz Analquito. The mix of educational and recreational areas make this a nice place to relax and learn about the coffee farms and crops. *(Four km north of the town; tel 372-4149; Tue-Sun 9-5; $0.60 per person)*

# Suchitoto

Nahuat, "Place of Birds and Flowers"
Pop. 52,000
44km from San Salvador

### SUCHITOTO THEN

Suchitoto, founded over 1000 years ago, was one of the most densely populated pre-Columbian Pipil cities. In 1528, when repeated Indian attacks forced the nearby villa of San Salvador to temporarily relocate to Suchitoto, local tribes resisted for 15 years. Following the destruction of the capital by the 1853 earthquake, affluent San Salvador society surged into Suchitoto bringing a great deal of wealth (13 grand pianos made the trip up to the mountains with them).

### SUCHITOTO NOW

A bustling commercial center before the civil war "Suchi," as the locals call it, saw heavy fighting during the war. Today the colonial streets are busy again but peaceful. Narrow cobblestone roads wind between the wrought iron window gratings of houses freshly painted in different pastel colors. Suchitoto has many side streets which are perfect for

## Home of the Painter

**V**ictor Manuel Sanabri has been painting in Suchitoto since he was a child, so it's no surprise that many of his paintings depict the town's streets and surrounding countryside. Today, much of his work-all with his characteristic signature "Shanay"-hangs in galleries in San Salvador and the rest of the world. If he has a finished piece sitting around, though, he might be willing to part with it. Prices run between $200 and $800. Sr. Sanabri doesn't speak any English but will be glad to show you around. His house is behind the church on 3a Av Nte, a white building with black window gratings and a large brown door with the number 8 on top and 721 on the side.

afternoon wandering. You might find yourself sitting on one of the tree-trunk benches in San Martin Park admiring the view out over the lake.

Suchitoto has been undergoing a revival for the past several years and there are many new restaurants plus regular theatrical and musical performances. While this is one of the best day trips from the capital you may want to stay much longer.

## ACCOMMODATIONS

**Hotel La Posada de Suchitlán** This restored colonial hacienda, surrounded by lovely gardens, offers a fantastic view of the bend of the Lempa River as it opens into Lake Suchitlán. The European couple who run it will meet your every need. Reservations are recommended on weekends. *(4a C Pte, Barrio San José; tel 335-1064; 6D $57 including breakfast, all with private bath, hot water, cable TV, AC; pool; restaurant, bar)*

## FOOD & DRINK

**El Obraje** Good food and good value makes this restaurant the busiest in town. A vari-

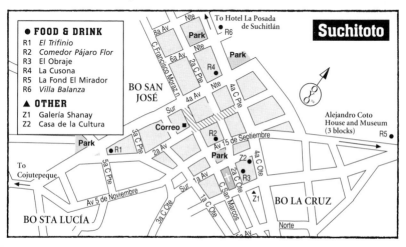

**● FOOD & DRINK**
R1  El Trifinio
R2  Comedor Pájaro Flor
R3  El Obraje
R4  La Cusona
R5  La Fond El Mirador
R6  Villa Balanza

**▲ OTHER**
Z1  Galería Shanay
Z2  Casa de la Cultura

**Suchitoto**

ety of typical Salvadoran dishes run between $3 and $6.75. *(12-2pm, 6-9pm)*

**La Casona** This moderately priced cafeteria is located in a grand old colonial house, which also houses a small coin museum. Entrees start at $2.50. *(12-3pm, 6-9pm)*

**La Fonda El Mirador** An informal eatery with a good variety of typical Salvadoran dishes. The seafood dishes with the daily catch from the nearby Lake Suchitlán are the house specialty, but the local chicken soup and steak are also good. A meal here will set you back between $5 and $9.50. *(8am-6pm)*

**La Posada de Suchitlán** Even if you're not staying here you should consider splurging on at least one meal. Most dishes are Salvadoran with a Spanish flare. The *gallo en chicha* is a cultural experience you will surely remember. A meal will set you back at least $8, but the price includes the spectacular views. A marimba band provides the atmosphere during Sunday lunch. *(12-3pm, 6-9pm)*

## SIGHTS

**Church of Santa Lucía** The original church, built in 1858, was destroyed by fire. It features lovely mosaics, religious art and a unique old roof that from a distance looks like it was built with hubcaps. The Spanish government is currently funding a complete restoration. Some of the buildings surrounding the church and the plaza it faces date to the 18th century.

**Alejandro Coto House and Museum** Señor Coto himself will show you around the eclectic collection contained in this fantastic, fountain-filled house. Works of art from many of the country's best painters and some unusual antiques are displayed throughout the halls and rooms. Don't miss the splendid views from the exotic, tropical garden. *(8 blocks east of the church at the end of Av 15 de Septiembre; 9-5pm; admission $3.50)*

## DETAILS

■ **BUSES: San Salvador (129)**, every 15 min until 5pm, 44km, 1hr 30min.

■ **FESTIVALS: Second Sunday in November** Grand November Fair. A huge event with abundant food, music, crafts and a parade. **December 6-13** Virgen de Santa Lucía and Virgen de Concepción. Candies called *colaciones*, made in the nearby Aguacayo canyon out of refined sugar, are sold.

# Near Suchitoto

**Los Tercios Waterfall** Two and a half kilometers east of the city is this 25-meter cascade. It is surrounded by strange cubic rock formations and has an inviting pool at the bottom. It is best seen between May and December since the water flow is reduced dramatically during the dry season.

**Chinnapa Caves** "Las Cuevas" is a place for serious cave explorers. Chinnapa, just a few minutes drive east of town, has never been totally mapped. Local folklore says there is a lost treasure hidden deep in the cave but it hasn't been found because a magnetic force distorts true north on a compass disorienting treasure hunters.

**Cerrón Grande Reservoir** Suchitoto sits on the shore of this artificial lake, also known as Lake Suchitlán, which was formed in 1976 by the construction of the Cerrón

Top: National Theater, Santa Ana
Bottom Left: San Vicente
Bottom Right: Family, Apaneca

Top: Gulf of Fonseca
Bottom Left: El Tamarindo Beach
Bottom Right: Mizata Beach

Grande Dam and Hydroelectric Center. The Lempa River is one of the world's most efficiently used rivers for hydroelectric power. If you call CEL in advance (tel 222-9576) you can get a tour of the dam.

Many people come here to bathe and fish near the mouths of the various rivers that empty into it. The lake is also home to a great variety of birds and other wildlife. Between November and February the many migratory birds add to the beauty. Paths down to the lake start at the north end of town; ask for directions.

If you want to take a trip on the lake follow Av. 15 de Septiembre for half a kilometer until it dead-ends at the ugly boat dock. A ferry takes cars and people across the lake to the villages of San Francisco Lempa and Los Naranjos de San Luis del Carmen ("The Orange Groves of San Luis del Carmen") for $.75 per person and $3.50 per car. Both towns offer a glimpse of tranquil village life and in the rainy season waterfalls and natural pools emerge near the latter. The ferry schedule varies with the season and traffic.

You will also find numerous boatmen who will take you pretty much wherever you want to go for between $3.50 and $8 per person depending on the length of the trip. Isla de los Pájaros ("Bird Island") and Ermilaño Island are just a short distance away and make good excursions.

# Ilobasco

Nahuat, "Place of the Tortillas"
Pop. 80,000
54km from San Salvador
27km from Sensuntepeque

## ILOBASCO THEN

The mountain village of Ilobasco, like the rest of Cabañas department, was originally occupied by the Lencas. Pipil tribes moved in toward the end of the 15th century, absorbing the culture of the Lencas and renaming the town Hilotaxca, which means "place of *elote* [soft corn] tortillas."

The population of Ilobasco remained almost completely indigenous until well into the 18th century when the town was relocated under strange circumstances. It seems that Ilobasco originally sat northwest of its present location in an area now known as Sitio Viejo ("Old Place"). One day an icon of San Miguel, patron saint of the town, disappeared from its shrine in the church and was discovered sitting on a stump six kilometers away. The priest of the town, who probably felt that a new church was in order anyway, persuaded the entire town that this event was a sign from God and that the town should be moved. Before long, everyone agreed and a new town was constructed near where the stump stood.

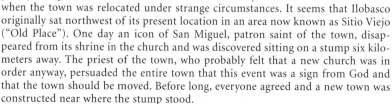

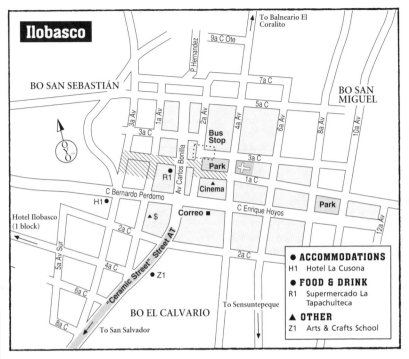

**Ilobasco**

To Balneario El Coralito

BO SAN SEBASTIÁN

BO SAN MIGUEL

9a C Ôte

P. Hernandez

7a C

5a C

3a Av

1a Av

2a Av

4a Av

6a Av

8a Av

10a Av

3a C

Bus Stop

Park

3a C

R1

Av Carlos Bonilla

Cinema

1a C

Hotel Ilobasco (1 block)

C Bernardo Perdomo

H1

$

Correo

C Enrique Hoyos

Park

12a Av

2a C

"Ceramic Street" Street AT

4a C

2a C

5a Av Sur

6a C

Z1

8a C

BO EL CALVARIO

To San Salvador

To Sensuntepeque

● **ACCOMMODATIONS**
H1   Hotel La Cusona
● **FOOD & DRINK**
R1   Supermercado La
     Tapachulteca
▲ **OTHER**
Z1   Arts & Crafts School

## ILOBASCO NOW

The road to Ilobasco winds uphill past buses belching diesel fumes and women carrying baskets of mangos on their heads. The town's meandering cobblestone streets follow the gentle slopes of the surrounding hills.

Ilobasco is well known for its artisans, who produce painted ceramics. The tradition dates back to the 1940s, when a few families began to sculpt plain figurines out of fine-grained clay. A talented local artist soon gained national recognition for his painted ceramics, and other local artists copied the technique. Today, Ilobasco's ornate ceramics are one of the most distinct Salvadoran crafts and have gained international recognition. This local art form has evolved to the point where it is the town's principal economic activity.

You can observe the design and production process in the town's many shops or at the local school for ceramic arts ("la Escuela de Artisanos"). The school was supported by the European Union and has been home to many famous ceramics teachers.

Most of the ceramic shops are located on the main street into town, which is appropriately known as Ceramic Street ("Calle de la Ceramica"). Painted mugs, jars, plates, vases, dolls, nativity figurines and countless others variations are for sale at prices far lower than in San Salvador. Also, look for the *sorpresas* ("surprises") which conceal tiny, detailed scenes inside a clay shell. Some *sorpresas* are real surprises, and conceal a sexual scene inside a painted egg or house.

## ACCOMMODATIONS

**Hotel Ilobasco** Not just the best hotel in town, but the entire Cabañas department. The rooms are clean, cheap, and some come with great views. The small restaurant on the second floor serves typical local foods for less than $2 a plate. *(4 C Pte, aka Hospital Street; tel 332-2563; 13 rooms; $6 per person with shared bath, $11.50 with private bath, $14 with cable TV; restaurant)*

**Hotel La Casona** Not quite as pleasant as the Hotel Ilobasco, however it is still a good choice if the Hotel Ilobasco is full or you just want to be a few blocks closer to the center. *(Tel 332-2388; 7 rooms, S $6 D $10 with shared bath, S $12 D $18 with private bath and cable TV)*

## FOOD & DRINK

Ceramic Street and the streets around the central park have many small and economical food stands, pastry shops and of course *pupuserías.*

**Supermercado La Tapachulteca** A popular option for locals and visitors alike is to buy some take-out food at this supermarket and have your meal in the central park, just a block away. *(8am-7pm)*

**Mariscos Doña Virginia** Though far from the Pacific, Mrs. Virginia's Shellfish is known throughout the land. If you tell a Salvadoran you are heading to Ilobasco they will likely encourage you to try the *mariscada* ("seafood soup"). This traditional Salvadoran meal costs $9 and includes lobster, shrimp, crab and fish. *(Located 10 kilometers from town on the main highway, 5 blocks off the Panamerican Highway; 11:30am-6pm)*

## SIGHTS

**Iglesia de los Desamparados** This 18th century renaissance style church, white inside and out, sits next to a small garden with a cave housing the famous icon of the Virgin of the Abandoned Ones. It is a place of great devotion for the townsfolk, but generally you can only get a look inside on weekends.

**Central Park Enrique Hoyas** Following a major reconstruction this central park is a good place to while away the time watching life go by, particularly at the end of the day. When the streetlights are illuminated local residents meet here for conversation and the evening stroll.

## DETAILS

■ **BUSES: San Salvador (111)**, every 15 min until 5pm, 54km, 1hr 40min.

■ **FESTIVALS: January 27-28** Romería del Señor de las Misericordias. **May 10** Virgen de los Desamparados ("Virgin of the Helpless or Abandoned"). **May 13** La Fruta. **September 26-29** (28) San Miguel.

## Near Ilobasco

**Balneario El Coralito** Señora López owns this private man-made pool, which is surrounded by a few benches and tables. There are changing rooms nearby and food is sold on the weekends—pack a lunch during the week. To get there, take 4a Ave Nte to its end, go right one block and then left on the road that leads to the village Las Huertas, where the balneario is situated. The one and a half-kilometer trip should take you under half an hour on foot. It has recently turned into a bit of a hangout for gang members so you may want to ask around in town whether or not it is still worth a visit. (*Admission $0.80 per person*)

😕 😕 😕 😕 😕

# Sensuntepeque

Nahuat, "Four Hundred Hills"
Pop. 67,500
84km from San Salvador

### SENSUNTEPEQUE THEN

Pipil Indians overran this pre-Columbian Lenca village in the 1400s. A century later, Sensuntepeque was turned into an evangelical village by the Dominican friars of San Salvador, who erected a church in honor of Santa Barbara.

By the beginning of the 19th century, the city's residents rose up in support of Salvadoran independence and clashed with federal troops in the main plaza. The insurgents were quickly outmanned and defeated; men were thrown in jail and women were each given 25 lashes in public.

### SENSUNTEPEQUE NOW

The capital of Cabañas department is quite isolated, but worth a visit if only for its ambiance. The road to the city rises and falls in the hills and valleys of the surrounding countryside eventually depositing you in this interesting town. Sensuntepeque doesn't have any fancy restaurants and only one very simple hotel, but it does have a large, thriving market which you will notice immediately. There has been a major animal market here since colonial times and you may want to plan your visit for a Thursday morning when horses and cattle are sold.

The colonial architecture also adds to the town's charm. As you walk the steep street you will see an abundance of buildings adorned with neoclassical columns, balconies and windows protected by ornamental wrought iron. You can get an excellent view of the town and the main church from 6a Av.

The city makes up for its lack of facilities with a subtle but definitely positive vibe and a slight tinge of lawlessness. That, along with the fantastic market, is enough reason to drop by.

## San Antonio Is Standing On His Head

**M**any years ago I noticed that the owner of a pharmacy had an image of San Antonio placed upside down. When asked about it the lady replied, "I have a single daughter who is at the age that she should be married. By turning this image of San Antonio upside down I am asking San Antonio to help my daughter find a husband." I later discovered that throughout El Salvador many mothers of single daughters have San Antonio standing on his head.

The story came to a happy ending. The lady from the pharmacy is now my mother-in-law and the good San Antonio has been standing upright for over ten years now.

—*Hank Weiss*

## FOOD & DRINK

**Acuarius Restaurant** This clean and friendly restaurant—really only a glorified *comedor*—*looks* like the set of an old Western movie. Sandwiches and trimmings are $2.50. There isn't any sign outside, so look for the building with the red and white painted walls. *(8am-6pm)*

**Restaurant La Familia** This new place serves up typical Salvadoran dishes buffet style. A complete lunch will cost from $1.50 to $3. *(8am-8pm)*

**Restaurant and Turicentro Valle Encantado** The "Enchanted Valley" is definitely the best place to eat in the area. The menu ranges from sandwiches and hamburgers for $2.50 to the specialty of the house, known as *delicias del mar* ("delights of the sea") which includes shrimp, lobster, fish, potatoes and salad for $11.50. After dinner you can take a dip in one of the well-maintained pools. *(Located at km 81 of the highway that leads to Sensuntepeque. Follow the dirt road 800 meters, turn right and continue for one block; Tue-Sun 9am-9pm; $0.60 to use the pool)*

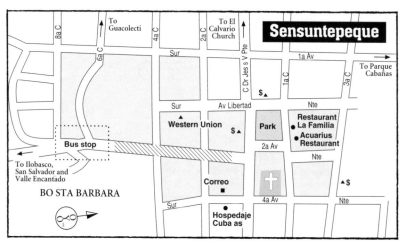

## SIGHTS

**Iglesia de Santa Barbara** This simple church covers an entire block. The interior of the church houses some interesting altars and altarpieces from the 18th and 19th centuries. The image of San Antonio, the town's patron saint, has several metallic human statuettes in the hands. The Salvadorans have great devotion to this saint, especially those wishing to get married (see San Antonio is Standing on his Head).

**Iglesia El Calvario** This interesting church is located at the summit of the hill seen from the Central Park. Inside are some good paintings that represent Dante's scenes of the great tribulation, Hell, purgatory and the sky.

**Parque Cabañas** Located on a hill called El Pelón ("The Hairless One") the park offers impressive views. From the peak you can get a panoramic view of Sensuntepeque, mountains in neighboring Honduras to the east, and two nearly perfectly cone-shaped volcanoes in the distance, the Volcán Chaparrastique to the southeast and Volcán Chichontepec to the southwest.

## DETAILS

■ **Buses: San Salvador (112)**, every 15 min until 4:30pm, 84km, 2hr.

■ **Festivals: September 15** Virgen de Asunción. **December 1-6 (4)** Santa Bárbara. The processions are accompanied by a group of dancers called *los viejos* ("the old ones") who are disguised with masks to make them look older.

# Near Sensuntepeque

**Guacotecti** The only attraction of the town next to Sensuntepeque is the small church where the "Señor de Salome" is worshiped with devotion. El Señor's feast days are January 21 and 22 and are said to be very colorful so if you are passing by during this time you may want to stop. A wide variety of rosaries made of *aguacayo*, a traditional Salvadoran white candy, are sold here.

**San Isidro** This is a very traditional farming town located near km 75 of the highway to Sensuntepeque. You will usually see ox carts hauling a wide variety of agricultural products. The town's new church is also worth a visit to see an interesting mural with scenes of the typical Salvadoran countryside.

⊜ ⊜ ⊜ ⊜ ⊜

# Chalatenango

Nahuat, "Valley of Water and Sand"
69km from San Salvador

## CHALATENANGO THEN

The provincial capital and largest city in the northern region of El Salvador, Chalatenango began as a pre-Columbian Lenca village that was eventually absorbed by the Pipils. During the civil war, the army and guerrillas each struggled for control of the city, and battles raged in the streets. An FMLN stronghold throughout

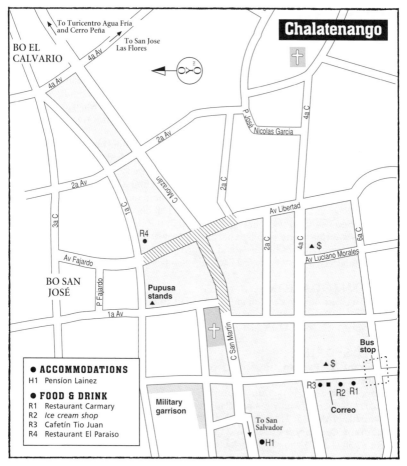

Chalatenango

BO EL CALVARIO

To Turicentro Agua Fria and Cerro Peña

To San Jose Las Flores

4a Av
4a Av
2a Av
2a Av
2a Av
3a C
1a C
C Morazán

P José
Nicolas Garcia
4a C
2a C

Av Libertad

R4

Av Fajardo

BO SAN JOSÉ

P Fajardo
1a Av

Pupusa stands

2a C
4a C
6a C

▲ $
Av Luciano Morales

C San Martin

Bus stop

▲ $

R3 ●■  ■   ●
        │  R2  R1

Military garrison

To San Salvador
●H1

Correo

**● ACCOMMODATIONS**
H1   Pensión Lainez
**● FOOD & DRINK**
R1   Restaurant Carmary
R2   Ice cream shop
R3   Cafetín Tio Juan
R4   Restaurant El Paraiso

TO THE NORTH

much of the early part of the war, Chalatenango was later occupied by government forces who turned the city into a virtual fortress and built the huge military garrison.

As a pivotal city in El Salvador's hotly contested northern region, all funds allotted to run the city were diverted to the military. For most of the 1980s, 310 police officers had to share only nine cars and each car was allotted three gallons of gas per day.

Even with the garrison in place, the rebels didn't give up; they attacked Chalatenango in early 1989 in an effort to disrupt local elections. At one point in 1990, the guerrillas advanced to within one block of the military garrison.

During the 1994 presidential elections, the ruling ARENA party was supported in the city of Chalatenango while the FMLN was more popular in the countryside. The government tried too hard to change the vote, though, and the FMLN later uncovered the

names of 17 long-deceased "supporters" of ARENA on the voting lists.

## CHALATENANGO NOW

Today the former military fortress is a comfortable city filled with typically Salvadoran one-story buildings with red tile roofs. Tall green mountains surround Chalatenango, providing a backdrop for a view of the Lago de Suchitlán, the artificial reservoir formed by the Cerro Grande hydroelectric project to the west.

The city is full of interesting old colonial architecture including over 200 colonial arch and column structures. Central America's largest stretch of arched walkways ("*portales*") covers nearly four city blocks and has been declared a national monument. Chalatenango also has a famous regional rodeo and auction where horses and cattle are bought and sold. Many unique types of horses have been raised here for generations.

Many people in Chalatenango have lighter skin, hair and eyes than most Salvadorans and are descended from the Spanish who settled in the area in the 16th century. You'll see women wearing shorts and men sporting cowboy hats brought in from Cojutepeque and Tenancingo. The cowboy hats and shaded porch shop fronts, held up by large wooden banisters, make the city feel like a town straight out of the old frontier.

## ACCOMMODATIONS

**Pensión Lainez** Your only option in town is a dark, run-down place, but it's clean and at these prices you can't really go wrong. No restaurant here, but they'll make you food if you ask—plates run about $1.75. *(Tel 335-2085; 7 rooms, $6 per bed; laundry; 24hr checkout)*

## FOOD & DRINK

**Restaurant El Paraíso** Great, tacky velvet chairs and friendly waiters add to the ambiance at El Paraíso, the fanciest place in town. The owner lived in the US for five years, which explains the American movies they show from time to time. *Lomo de auja* (grilled meat with rice and salad) costs $2.85, but seafood dishes go for about twice that. *(Mon-Sat 11am-11pm, Sun 11am-10pm)*

**Restaurant Carmary** If El Paraíso is the fanciest, then Carmary is the most pleasant. For $2.50 to $3.75 you can get a good meal in this clean colonial setting with a variety of entries. Breakfast is about $1 and there is a good-looking lunch buffet. *(Mon-Sat 7am-5pm, occasionally open Sun)*

**Cafetín Tío Juan** A modest little place for a bite, popular with bus drivers and passengers. Plates start around $1.15. (7am-9pm)

## SIGHTS

**Iglesia de Chalatenango** This colonial church was built in the 18th century and has undergone repeated repairs following earthquakes. The exterior has an interesting shape and the clock hands on the bell tower are missing.

**Iglesia de San Antonio** From this small church east of the center you get a panoramic view of the city and surrounding areas. As you walk around the churchyard you can observe much of the lovely colonial architecture of the city.

### HIKING

**Cerro La Peña** A three-hour hike up "Crag Mountain" brings you to a view over much of Chalatenango department, including the capital. Santa Ana is barely visible in the distance. A clear path up the hill leaves from the Agua Fría *turicentro*. Ask for directions there or in town. The path is popular and well known among the townspeople—almost everyone seems to have been there at least once.

### DETAILS

■ **BUSES: San Salvador (125),** every 10 min until 5:30pm, 69km, 2hr 20min.
■ **FESTIVALS: November 1-2** Feria de los Santos ("All Saint's Day Fair"). **June 24** San Juan Bautista. **December 18-25** (24) Nacimiento del Niño Jesús.
■ **SHOPPING:** The town market sells everything a cowboy/girl could possibly want, including spurs and saddles. Hammocks from Concepción Quetzaltepeque are also sold on the streets.

## Near Chalatenango

Many of the small towns around the city were badly affected by the civil war. The street leading out of the city towards the River Sumpul will take you to several of them. You will pass the villages of Guarila, San Jose Las Flores and San Isidro Labrador before reaching the Río Sumpul, one of the largest rivers in the country. If you speak with the locals on your way you will get a fascinating history lesson as they tell you about the results of 12 years of civil conflict.

**Turicentro Agua Fría** These pools are filled by the river which can be seen from the far end of the complex. Currently the complex is a little run down and the Olympic-sized pool is a bit dirty, but a major renovation is underway and once finished this should be a nice place to visit. *(Three blocks from town on C Principal; $0.80 per person, children and seniors free; cafetería)*

**El Paraiso** On your return to San Salvador you might stop awhile at the small town of El Paraiso, 19 kilometers from Chalatenango along the highway back to the Capital. There is a relaxing and picturesque site by the Río Grande for bathing or just watching the water flow by. During the winter you will spot flocks of migratory birds.

😊 😊 😊 😊 😊

# Concepción Quetzaltepeque

Pop. 8,500
69km from San Salvador
12km from Chalatenango

### CONCEPCIÓN QUETZALTEPEQUE THEN

Lencas were the first inhabitants of Quetzaltepeque ("Mountain of Quetzalcoatl"), as the town was called before the arrival of the Spanish. Over time the town has been influenced by the Chorti, Pipil and Ulúa tribes.

This area was claimed by the FMLN in the early 1980s. In fact, the guerrillas "celebrated" Christmas in 1984 with an attack on Concepción Quetzaltepeque, breaking a year-end truce.

## CONCEPCIÓN QUETZALTEPEQUE NOW

The northern Salvadoran foothills surround "Quetzalte," as the town is also known, near Chalatenango and the Cerrón Grande Reservoir. The road there is rocky but passable, flanked by odd-shaped hills and cornfields. Concepción Quetzaltepeque is a small, unassuming town known for its high-quality handmade hammocks and crocheted curtains. The streets are quiet; children hum soap operas themes and cowboys ride horses out in the fields.

Inside, however, entire families are busy weaving the hammocks for which the town is famous. These hammocks have been woven by generation after generation, and their quality and price vary widely depending upon the materials used and the ability of the weaver. Generally, the thicker the hammock, the better the quality.

The best nylon hammocks are made out of the same nylon used in fishing nets, usually imported Korean or Taiwanese twine. A cheaper type of nylon used comes from Honduras. A good, thick nylon hammock sells for $37.50 in San Salvador, but costs about $20 here.

Cotton hammocks, which are harder to find but softer and prettier, can be custom-sewn with any words you want. A thin, narrow cotton hammock will cost around $8 ($14 in San Salvador), while thicker, wider cotton hammocks with wooden frames cost up to $30. Hammocks made of a natural fiber called *mezcal* are also available, but the material is a little rough.

Most weavers leave their doors wide open and are happy to invite you into their homes; just ask first. The house of José Ernesto Silva is a good place to stop by, chat and see weaving firsthand. His nylon hammocks are beautifully detailed, with carved handles.

The six children of María Teodora Sanches de Pérez help her weave *mezcal* hammocks. Each hammock takes one person about half a day to make. In the Pérez household, and in many others, you can see the entire process: first the fiber is finger-combed, then strung, dyed and woven.

## DETAILS
■ **BUSES: Chalatenango (300b)**, every 30 min until 4pm, 12km, 30min. **San Salvador (125)**, every 15 min until 5pm, 69km, 2hr 30min.
■ **FESTIVALS: January 19-20 (19)** San Sebastián Mártir. **December 6-8 (7)** Virgen de Concepción.

# La Palma
Pop. 20,000
81km from San Salvador

## LA PALMA THEN
The tiny village of La Palma sits eight kilometers south of the Honduran border, just off the main road north from San Salvador. In the early 1980s the army tried to organize a civilian defense militia in La Palma to protect the town from guerrilla attacks. Few people joined, though, because until that point the town had not been attacked and people feared that a militia would just invite problems.

In 1984, President Duarte met here with rebel leaders at the Iglesia Dulce Nombre de María in an attempt to end the civil war. The peace talks were held under tight security and with high hopes among supporters of both sides. In the end, Duarte and guerrilla leaders reached an impasse that ultimately undermined Duarte's ability to govern and contributed to the escalation of the war.

## LA PALMA NOW
At first glance, La Palma seems an unimpressive mountain hamlet. People ride horses and donkeys down the streets, past a church painted by Fernando Llort. Llort's influence on La Palma doesn't stop there, though. The artisans of La Palma labor in 110 different shops to produce the painted ceramics, leather, wood, seeds and cloth goods for which the town is famous.

Over 200,000 of these pieces are made each month, painted in the wide-eyed, colorful style popularized by Llort. You can peek behind some of the gift shops to view the artists at work. Ask politely, though; since this town is more isolated than other craft villages, the artists may be a little bit uncomfortable at first, especially if you can't speak Spanish. La Palma is a little out of the way, but the craft shops, hiking trails and the Hotel La Palma make the town a worthwhile stop, either on the way to the northern border or for a day's side trip from the capital.

## ACCOMMODATIONS

**Hotel de la Montaña Paseo al Pital** All the facilities in this unique country hotel complex are brand new since it was destroyed during the war and only reopened in early 1994. It has spacious rooms and a lovely pool and playground. Each room can be equipped with three beds and prices are negotiable. Paths nearby lead down to the La Palma River. *(Tel 335-9258; 6 rooms, $40-70 depending on which room, all with private bath, hot water, cable TV; pool)*

**Hotel Entre Pinos** Set on 150 acres just three kilometers outside of La Palma is one of the best country hotels in El Salvador. Amidst the wooded grounds you will find a pool, small zoo, and an artificial lake. You can hike to the helicopter pad for great views or take a horseback ride for about $7 an hour. In the main dining room *a la carte* meals start at about $4 for breakfast and $7 for lunch and dinner and are served amidst lovely murals with typical scenes of the countryside. In the small café you can enjoy snacks and drinks from the comfort of your hammock. *(Tel 335-9382, 335-9370, fax 335-9322; 40 rooms, S $58, D $77, suites $94, all with private bath, hot water, cable TV; pool; restaurants)*

**Hotel Posada Real** A brand new hotel run by the same owners as the Paseo Pital. It's a bit more economical than the city's other hotels, but rooms still aren't cheap. The restaurant, however, serves up typical dishes for about two dollars. *(Tel 335-9002; 12 rooms, S $28, D or T $35, all with private bath, hot water; restaurant)*

## FOOD & DRINK

**Restaurant La Estancia** A friendly restaurant with a visitors' book to browse through and local artwork decorating the walls. Simple chicken and beef dishes are around $3 each. *(8am-7pm)*

## SIGHTS

**Gallery of Alfredo Linares** The gallery sells high-quality paintings of typical La Palma scenes by Sr. Linares, who studied in Italy and is now a local legend. Prices for origi-

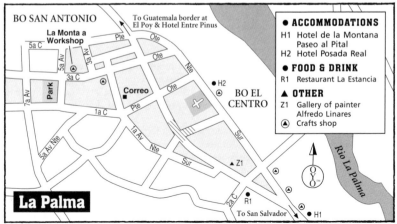

## San Ignacio

**F**our kilometers north of La Palma is the arts and crafts village of San Ignacio. The town's famous woodwork has a trademark pastel floral motif on a coffee-colored wood background. You'll find a lot of jewelry and ceramics for sale too, and the Central Park has a lovely old church that is worth a quick look.

You'll also notice that most of the locals have very light complexions. Many of the town's families claim to be direct descendants of the Spanish colonists who founded this village in the 18th century.

nals run from $10-$600. Reprints are around $13 and colorful postcards cost $1. *(9am-12pm, 1-5pm)*

### HIKING & CAMPING

The surrounding Alotepeque-Metapán Range is the highest in the country and the views from some of the trails which crisscross it allow you to see all the way to the Montecristo National Park.

**Cerro El Pital** (2,750m) Cloud forests wait on top of El Salvador's tallest mountain, which sits on the Salvadoran side of the border to the northeast. The three and one half-hour hike to the peak begins down the road leaving San Ignacio to the west at the small Río Chiquito. The view is impressive and not only can you see La Palma and San Ignacio but at night you can see glow of San Salvador far away. If you camp during December or January come prepared for temperatures below freezing.

**Cerro Miramundo** (2140m) Another nearby peak known for its excellent view—hence the name which means "View of the World" in Spanish. A hike to the top, best begun in the village of Las Pilas, is an all day excursion.

**Gato Camping** This little campground is in the middle of nowhere, a few kilometers north of La Palma on the road to San Ignacio and the border. It's set up like a summer camp, with a volleyball court, lots of wooden signs and trailheads leading into the nearby countryside. If you want to go hiking, plan ahead and buy a map from the Instituto Geográfico Nacional in San Salvador (see San Salvador). Otherwise, you may get lost since even the owner doesn't seem to know the trails very well. Bring food for your stay here. *(About 10km north of La Palma; open every day, $1.70 per person)*

### DETAILS

■ **BUSES: El Poy (119)**, every 30 min until 4pm, 11km, 30min. **San Salvador (119)** every 30 min until 4pm, 81km, 4hr.

■ **FESTIVALS: February 10-18 (17)** Dulce Nombre de María.

# Near La Palma

**Las Pilas** This famous village three kilometers north of La Palma produces peaches and organic vegetables. Part of their success over the years has come from their use of new scientific production techniques. The Cooperative League of the USA (CLUSA) has done a lot to promote healthy crops and agriculture in this area.

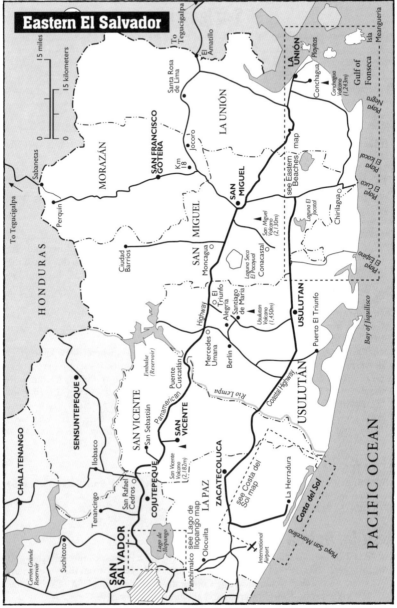

# TO THE EAST

Past the Lempa River, El Salvador's terrain quickly becomes rougher and wilder. Although this region saw the hottest fighting of the civil war, it remains beautiful. It's a little less user-friendly than the west, but offers some hidden gems to travelers willing to do a little exploring. Eastern El Salvador runs from the rolling hills of Morazán and northern La Unión department, through the hot plains of central La Unión and San Miguel, over the volcanic coastal mountain range and down into the Pacific. Many of El Salvador's exports are grown on the rich coffee, sugar and cotton plantations in San Vicente department, while Usulután's fertile valleys produce cattle, cotton, coffee, grains and fruit.

San Miguel is the busy commercial hub of the east, and the port city of La Unión sits on the sweaty shore of the Gulf of Fonseca, just around the corner from outstanding beaches. San Francisco Gotera and Perquín are nestled in the damp mountains to the northeast. Whether you feel like climbing a volcano or lazing away the afternoon on an island in the Gulf of Fonseca, you can find it in the east. Have an unforgettable meal at Restaurante Doña Pema in San Miguel, learn about the history of the rebel movement at the FMLN museum in Perquín or stroll down the best beach in the country at El Espino. Take your pick.

The San Vicente region has always been one of the most prosperous parts of El Salvador. Add this to the underdevelopment and poverty of the rest of the east and you have a recipe for turmoil. As a result, the northeast became a guerrilla stronghold during the civil war and saw intense and frequent battles. FMLN guerrillas stationed on the Usulután Volcano launched raids on government troops in the city of Usulután. The department's economic importance led US advisors to say that the war "would be won or lost in Usulután."

Peasant migration away from the region emptied much of San Vicente department and bloated refugee camps in the capital. When US aid was funneled to rebel-controlled towns in the department, the FMLN allowed schools to reopen—provided that teachers would step aside for one class period each day and allow a rebel instructor to "teach" the students.

"El Oriente" as the eastern region is referred to has largely overcome the toll of the war. In spite of the turmoil that it has recently endured, this is still one of the most interesting

and surprisingly welcoming regions of the country to visit. The coastal highway has been completely rebuilt along with the two main bridges over the Lempa River. Modern buses and telecommunications now serve the region making it easier to plan a trip here. Since the east is hot and dry in the center, muggy near La Unión and dripping to the north, come prepared for almost any weather.

Cities are more spread out than they are in other regions, which sometimes makes it harder to get where you want to go, but buses eventually reach even the farthest towns. You often have to switch buses at intersections to get to out-of-the-way cities like San Francisco Gotera.

The Panamerican Highway links San Vicente to San Salvador and Usulután, running onward to the Honduran border at El Amatillo. Cross into Honduras there or at Sabanetas. Or hop a boat across the Gulf of Fonseca to Honduras or Nicaragua—just make sure your papers are in order.

■ **EMERGENCY POLICE NUMBERS (PNC): La Paz department:** 334-4016, 334-1690, 334-4919. **La Unión department:** 664-4140, 664-3516. **Morazán department:** 654-0084, 654-0003, 654-1315. **San Miguel department:** 661-0424, 661-0381, 661-1677. **San Vicente department:** 393-4181, 393-0415, 393-4182. **Santa Rosa de Lima:** 664-2007, 664-2072, 664-2129. **Usulután department:** 662-1337, 662-1333.

# Olocuilta

Nahuat, "Place of the Worm"
16km from San Salvador

Olocuilta is a pleasant hill town known throughout the country for *pupusas* made of rice rather than corn. Rice *pupusas* taste a bit lighter than the typical ones and are usually cooked without lard. These *pupusas* are now frozen and exported to many cities in the US and Canada. The entrepreneurial "*pupusa* ladies" will kid around with you pointing out that to eat these same *pupusas* in the USA would cost you $2 each, not the roughly 30 cents each you pay in Olocuilta.

Strangely, despite its proximity to the capital and easy bus access, few foreign tourists stop in Olocuilta. It is certainly worth a quick visit, however, even if you aren't a *pupusa* fan. Olocuilta has a comfortable climate and an active arts and crafts industry. From the bell tower of the colonial San Juan Batista Church in front of the Central Plaza and from most of the nearby hilltops you can see the ocean and the valleys formed by Chichontepec and the San Salvador volcanoes.

## ACCOMMODATIONS

**Til Til Coffee Farm Bed & Breakfast** Til Til's two cabins offer a lovely escape from the hustle and pollution of San Salvador. There are some great hikes in surrounding hills and valleys and Don Mauricio and the other old-timers who have been at this coffee and fruit farm for years will gladly give you a tour. Afterwards you can lounge in the swimming pool. Even though it is often empty during the week reservations are required. *(Located on the old highway ("la via tejera") about 2 km north of town, you can't miss the large, stone Til Til sign at the gate; tel 263-6713; 4 rooms, $12 per person with shared bath, $20 per person with private bath)*

## FOOD & DRINK

**Las Pupusarias** At the entrance to town you will find over 50 little, family-run *pupusa* stands selling every conceivable variety of this Salvadoran mainstay. The baskets of fruit candies that the women sell are another popular local treat and Salvadoran crafts are also available here. The tradition here for locals is to eat your *pupusas* with a drink of hot chocolate in the evening.

**El Pupusodromo** Along the old highway from Santo Tomas to Zacatecoluca, at the exit for Olocuilta, is a new *pupusa* center with dozens of clean, friendly and inexpensive stands. Several women here grill their *pupusas* over wood fires, a method that some locals swear by.

**Los Antojitos** The friendly owner/chef worked in the USA before returning here. He offers a varied menu of typical Salvadoran dishes ($2.50-$5), appetizers ("*antojitos*"), desserts, and fresh juices. *(Located between the town's two churches, in front of the bank; 8am-6pm)*

## SIGHTS

**Casa de la Cultura** Local craftmaking techniques are taught here and you can often buy the finished baskets, pottery or unique hammocks. They will also know of any upcoming events in town. *(Located next to the municipal government building; tel 330-6588)*

**Glass Blowers** Vases, jars, pitchers and drinking glasses of all shapes and colors are sold along the highway. Each piece is unique and the prices are excellent. Even if you aren't going to buy anything the speed and flare these skilled artisans demonstrate is worth a look. *(Located next to the school on the north side of the Comalapa Highway, 6km north of town)*

**The Roof-Tile Route (La Via Tejera)** Along the old highway between Olocuilta and Santo Tomas you will come across numerous brick and tile kilns. This craft has not changed since colonial times. The road winds through some tight hairpin turns so drive carefully.

## DETAILS

■ **BUSES:** Urban bus **A1** leaves every 10 minutes from the "Hula Hula" bus stop in front of the National Palace in the center of San Salvador. Or, from San Salvador's Terminal del Sur, the **Costa del Sol (494)**, **Zacatecoluca (133)**, **Usulután (302)** and **La Herradura (134)** buses also stop in Olocuilta. There is a departure as often as every 5 minutes until 10pm.

■ **FESTIVALS: September 30-October 9** Virgen del Rosario.

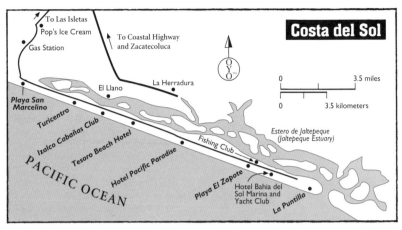

# Costa del Sol

### 60km from San Salvador

Sun-soaked and wave-stroked, this 15-kilometer stretch of sand in the center of El Salvador's Pacific coast is one of the country's most famous and popular beach destinations. As a result, everything here tends to be more expensive—many parts of the "Sun Coast" are crowded with mansions, imported cars and expensive hotels. If you have the cash to spare, splurge and treat yourself to a luxury hotel. With a little legwork, though, you can leave the development behind

and spend the day on your own special slice of empty sand, with warm waves and palm trees thrown in for free.

There aren't many cheap hotels on the Costa del Sol, but they can be found. Keep in mind that some of the better hotels will negotiate prices for non-holiday weekdays and if you are in a group you can save a lot by sharing costs. Camping out isn't easy since there aren't many deserted stretches of coast with shade like there are in other parts of the country. If you haven't managed to find a hotel you can afford you can always come here on a day trip. No matter how you arrange it, this is a great little peninsula with plenty to see and do.

If you want to come out here without a reservation you can try looking around La Puntilla where there are a number of budget places that go for about $8 to $15 a night. None are listed here since the confusing nature of the titles. to the "public" tip of land causes places to open, close, and change hands frequently.

The road to Costa del Sol branches off the road to La Herradura 11 kilometers south of the Coastal Highway and runs the length of the peninsula. The brackish Jaltepeque estuary, on your left as you drive out along the peninsula, is often less than one kilometer from the ocean and in a few places near the tip you can see both the estuary and the ocean at the same time. A number of boats ply the estuary and you can arrange the same trips from here as you can in La Herradura. Ask at your hotel for details.

■ **BUSES: San Salvador (494, 513)**, every 30 min until 5pm, 60km, 2hr. **Zacateco-luca (193)**, every 20 min until 6:40pm, 27km, 90 min.

# Playa San Marcelino

Large waves caress two kilometers of this so-so beach at the beginning of the Costa del Sol. Facing the ocean, the best beaches are to the left; to the right is the mouth of the polluted Jiboa River. Local fishermen launch their boats to go fishing in the late afternoon, usually around 5pm. If you're around when they leave, you can try to talk your way into a short ride into the waves—forget about amusement parks, this is the real thing. It's also interesting to watch the fishermen unload their catch in the early morning and late evening.

If you are out here for the day there's a *turicentro* (cabañas are $3 for the day) with entrances to the beach and the estuary on opposite sides of the road, but it's not very clean and usually jam packed on the weekends. A better option are the two restaurants listed below which both have pools and good beaches for just $3 a day.

## ACCOMMODATIONS

**Kennymar** On the beach, the Kennymar has simple rooms (the ocean is your shower) next to a seafood restaurant. It's quiet on weekdays, but be ready for a crowd of people and a few drunken fishermen on weekends. *(5D $9.50 plus deposit for fan and TV)*

**Costa del Sol Club** A plush place two blocks from the beach with sports facilities, pool, miniature golf, a Jacuzzi and a disco. The club's beach area hides another pool, a restaurant and gazebos. They have lowered their prices considerably over the past few years with no drop off in service. Reservations are necessary through Condominios Cuscatlán in San Salvador (25a Av Sur and 4a C Pte; tel 281-2674, 271-1698). *(58 rooms S $55, D $67, suites $82; laundry; pools; restaurant)*

**Izalco Cabaña Club** Actually a hotel, the Izalco Cabaña Club has clean but run-down facilities. Somebody should set that poor monkey free, too. An attached restaurant serves seafood soup for $6.75 and fish plates for $5.50-$8. *(Next to the turicentro; tel 224-0387, 264-1170; 13S $60, 17D $77 in back $86 by beach, all with private bath, AC, huts $23; laundry; 11am checkout; restaurant 6am-9pm)*

## FOOD & DRINK

When choosing from one of the many cheap seafood stands here or elsewhere along the peninsula you may want to take a look at the kitchen since they can range from spotless to filthy.

**Bar de Ostras** The friendly Señora Salazar runs this rustic place with her daughters. A good seafood dinner goes for about $9. They also serve chicken and seafood rice combos for $4.50 to $6. *(Km 62; 12-2:30pm, 6-9pm)*

**Martin Fierro** This is a gourmet restaurant with very spacious grounds. Meals here run from $8.50 to about $16 for a wide variety of seafood, beef and chicken entrees. *(Km 62.5; 12-3pm, 6-10pm)*

# Playa Los Blancos

The trashy entrance to the public part of Playa Los Blancos is crammed with *comedores* that give way to empty expanses of sand and shallow waves. The best part of the beach is near the Tesoro Beach Hotel, where it's as wide and flat as a football field. This is about as good as El Salvador's "popular" beaches get—which is pretty good.

## ACCOMMODATIONS

**Tesoro Beach Hotel** If you can afford it, this is the classiest hotel on the Coast. The tiled-floor rooms have all the amenities, including hot (albeit brackish) water, and many look directly out over the ocean. When the place is full, which occurs less and less often lately, the indoor restaurant is open. Otherwise, eat outside by the ring-shaped pool, have a drink at the bar or wander off into the distance on the seemingly endless beach out front. Bands play outside on weekends. *(Tel 338-0111; 120 rooms $79 per person, all with TV, AC, hot water; laundry; 2pm checkout; pool; 2 restaurants; parking)*

**Suites Jaltepeque** This is a beachfront condominium development next to the Tesoro Beach Hotel. They rent 1, 2 or 3 bedroom condos by the day, week or month. Most come fully furnished with a great view of the Pacific. They offer horseback riding as well as a beachfront restaurant. Prices vary and can sometimes be negotiated directly with the condo owner. *(Tel 223-1984, 245-4530; 1 bedroom $90 to $105, 2 bedrooms $147.75 to $185.50)*

**Hotel Pacific Paradise** An older Swiss couple moved here for health reasons in the 70s and built up the this lovely hotel over many years. They returned to Europe in the 1980s and left the place abandoned. New owners have completely remodeled and brought it back to its old charm. It is located on a great beachfront and has a dock, pool, tennis courts and rooms across the road on the estuary side. *(Tel 260-3366, 271-2606; $65 per person, all with private bath, TV, AC; laundry; 4pm checkout; restaurant)*

**Hotel Bahia del Sol Marina and Yacht Club**. The last of the posh resort hotels before you reach La Puntilla. As you would guess from the name this is a luxury resort with all the amenities. The modern two-story townhouse layout has a great beachfront setting. On the estuary side there is also a full service marina, another restaurant and pool, and more rooms. *(Tel 298-7186, 278-6661; $125 per person, all with private bath, TV, AC; pool; restaurant)*

😊 😊 😊 😊 😊

# La Herradura

### 60km from San Salvador

This small fishing town, with nets under repair at every turn, isn't too impressive at first glance. La Herradura's saving graces are fresh seafood for sale and the tranquil Jaltepeque Estuary, where green trees overlook muddy waters branching out in every direction towards the Pacific Ocean. There is a new seafood pier where a number of places offer all the usual seafood dishes plus raw clam cocktails and chicken plates for $2.75-$3.50. If your tastes run to sushi instead, raw fish is also available to go.

Even better than the fish, though, is hopping a boat to explore the estuary and nearby islands. Prices will be outrageous (over $20) if you're not ready to bargain. The cheapest way to go is with locals, who use the boats as transport to outlying points. Boats are designed to hold at least ten people, so that's one way to split costs. Be sure that the boatman understands how long you want to be out on the water, where you want to go, and that the price includes a return trip ("*ida y vuelta*"), or you may find yourself playing Robinson Crusoe. Prices for locals are under $1.50 each way, so you can see how much a little bargaining can save you. The most visited islands are: La Tasajera (25km, 30min), La Calzada (10km, 20min) and Isla Colorada (35km, 1hr).

Tasajera Island has a popular seafood restaurant and the rustic **Oasis de Tasajera** hotel. A two-day stay with transport, a boat trip through the estuary and all meals costs about $70 for two people. Call 263-8572 or 223-9265 for reservations or information.

■ **BUSES: Costa del Sol (495, 193)** 20km, 30min. **San Salvador (495)**, every 15 min until 6pm, 60km, 2hr 10min. **San Vicente (193)**, every 30 min until 5:30pm, 66km, 2hr 15min. **Zacatecoluca (193)**, every 30 min until 5:30pm, 42km, 1hr 30min.

# Zacatecoluca
Nahuat, "Place of Owls and Herbs"
Pop. 75,000
55km from San Salvador

## ZACATECOLUCA THEN
Before the city became a major battleground during the war, Zacatecoluca was El Salvador's fifth largest city–today it no longer even makes that top ten. Storekeepers frisked shoppers as they entered, people refused to replace broken windows knowing they would be broken again soon, and patients had to be moved to the local seminary after the hospital suffered much damage following fighting on the top floor. When fighting got especially intense the army forcibly conscripted people into the army.

## ZACATECOLUCA NOW
The coastal highway drops you to the long, narrow city of Zacate, as the locals call it. Though the Pacific Ocean is over 20 kilometers away you can see it from almost every street in town while the San Vicente Volcano rises to the north. At the entrance stands a monument to the hero of independence and the city's most famous son José Simeón Cañas.

There isn't really much to do here, but if you are passing through it is worth a stop to take a quick stroll through the large and colorful market and to see daily life in a non-touristed town. The city is known for its jewelry and if you come here you might want to stop by a shop to admire the patience, precision and skill of the jewelers. Many still use processes which haven't changed since colonial days.

## FOOD & DRINK
**Pollo Campero** Of course the country's biggest fast food chain, which specializes in roasted chicken, has a branch here. (*7am-8pm*)
**Golden Gate** Good, cheap Chinese food. (*12-8pm*)

## SIGHTS

**Iglesia de Santa Lucia** Though built in the colonial era there have been several renovations to this church, leaving very little of the original construction. However, some of the original 18th century artwork remains inside and is worth a peek.

**Turicentro de Ichanmichen** This recreational and bathing center has something for everyone such as: swimming pools of various sizes (cabin rental is $2.50), botanical garden, crafts market, tropical forest, and restaurants. *(Located 1.5 km south of Zacatecoluca, take urban bus #92; 8am-6pm; $1.25 per person and $1.25 for parking; 8am to 6pm)*

## DETAILS

■ **BUSES:** The bus terminal is hidden behind storefronts at Avenues Villacorta/Delgado and Calle 7.

**Costa del Sol (193)**, every 30 min until 5:30pm, 27km, 90min. **La Libertad (540)**; every 30 min until 4pm, 51km, 2hr. **San Salvador (133)**, every 8 min until 6pm, 55km, 1hr. **San Vicente (177)**, every 15 min until 6pm, 23km, 1hr. **Usulután (131)**, leaves from one block below the terminal at 5, 5:40, and 11am, 55km, 90min.

■ **FESTIVALS: January 6** Niño de Atocha. **February 1-2 (1)** Virgen de Calendaria. **August 14-15** Virgen del Transito. **December 10-13 (12)** Santa Lucia.

# Usulután

Nahuat, "City of the Ocelots"
Pop. 90,000
112km from San Salvador

## USULUTÁN THEN

Usulután's original Lenca inhabitants were pushed aside in the 15th century by immigrating Pipil tribes. In 1529, the Usulutecos battled Spanish forces under the command of Diego de Rojas. Although Rojas was captured, the native armies were only able to hold off his forces for a short while. Usulután was sacked and burned by English pirates near the end of the next century, and in the early 19th century El Salvador's first coffee bush was planted nearby.

During the civil war, guerrillas repeatedly attacked the military garrison in the center of town, and houses were occasionally damaged in street fighting. A 1988 attack on the garrison was timed to coincide with a meeting of Central American foreign ministers, who were trying to implement a regional peace plan engineered by Costa Rican President and Nobel Prize winner Oscar Arias.

## USULUTÁN NOW

The capital of Usulután department sits off the Coastal Highway at the foot of the coastal mountains, to the south of the volcano of the same name. A colorful pastel cemetery at the western entrance gives way to a city that bustles with business all day long. Usulután isn't large, but it has the feel of a big city. Shops line streets that bristle with signs and are packed with constantly moving crowds of people. Vendors sell huge baskets of shrimp in a thriving central market.

Usulután has changed from a war torn city to a bustling state capital with a very large agricultural market filled with produce from the surrounding hill towns. There are plenty of places to eat here and a few good hotels make it a good place to stop on your way along the coast to the east or as a jumping-off point for area beaches.

## ACCOMMODATIONS

**Hotel España** This old place is fairly well maintained but time has taken its toll. It's still the best place right in town though. A grand entrance with a world map, old wood furniture and high ceilings give it a relaxed, tired atmosphere. A *plato del día* at the restaurant usually includes chicken and rice, and costs $2.50. The front desk closes early so get a room before dark. (*Tel 662-0358; 4S $11.50, 2D $14, all with private bath, fan; laundry; 3pm checkout; restaurant*)

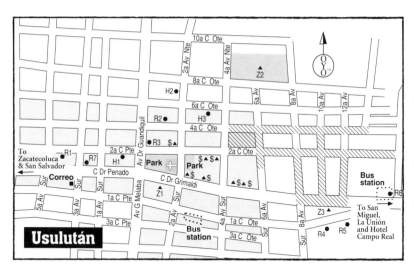

**Posada del Viajero** Modest rooms surround a small court-yard in this cozy place that is larger than it looks. If you really want air-conditioning check that it works before taking a room. *(Tel 662-0217; 20 rooms, S $11.50, D $14.25 with private bath, all with fan, some with AC; 24hr checkout)*

**Hotel Campo Real** A compromise—the best hotel in Usulután is also outside of town. Clean and a good value with a swimming pool and a pleasant poolside cafe. A taxi there should cost about $1.70 and a plate in the attached restaurant starts at $3.50. *(2.5km east of Usulután on Coastal Highway, take bus 89 from next to Pollo Campero to the Universidad Gerardo Barrios next to hotel; tel 662-0161; 29S $12.25, 25D $18; all with private bath, AC, cable TV; laundry; pool; noon checkout; restaurant)*

● **ACCOMMODATIONS**
H1   Hotel España
H2   *Boarding House
       El Principal*
H3   Posada del Viajero

● **FOOD & DRINK**
R1   *Mi Pandería*
R2   Café Terraza
R3   Lathyno's Restaurant
R4   *Pollo Campero*
R5   Pollo Pamper
R6   Toro Pampero
R7   El Ranchón

▲ **OTHER**
Z1   Town hall
Z2   Military compound
Z3   Esso gas station

## FOOD & DRINK

**Pollo Pamper** Broasted chicken plates served on the leafy patio run between $2.25 and $4.75. *(11am-8pm)*

**Supermarket La Dispensa de Don Juan** Located in the new Plaza Oriente shopping mall on the Coastal Highway this is a popular option for locals and visitors alike. *(7am-7pm)*

**Toro Pampero** The locals say this is the place to go for a steak and the best food in town. It has the feel of a cattleman's rest house but good service in a typical local ambience. The menu includes a wide variety of seafood (lobster is $14) but everyone recommended the beef dishes which start at $6.50. *(11:30am-9pm)*

**El Ranchón** Popular with students, locals, and travelers on a budget since meals range from $2 to $3.25. While it is highly recommended for lunch, for some reason it has a reputation for bad service during dinner. *(10am-10pm)*

**Lathyno's Restaurant** One of the classier places in town with light music, an open courtyard with a fountain and…tablecloths! Seafood and pasta from $5.25 to $11.50, with weekly specials. *(10:30am-10pm)*

**Café Terraza** Popular with students, with lots of tables and bright colors. School kids gossip and sip Cokes in a friendly atmosphere (in spite of the red and green-checkered floor). A typical chicken plate is about $4. *(9am-9pm)*

### DETAILS

■ **BUSES: Berlín (349)**, every 20 min until 4pm, 22km, 1hr 15min. **Jucuarán (358)**, 4 buses until 4pm, 40km, 2hr. **Playa El Espino (351)**, 5, 7am, 2pm, 33km, 2hr. **Puerto El Triunfo (363)**, every 15 min until 5:30pm, 8km, 30min. **San Miguel (301, 335, 373)**, every 10 min until 5:30pm, 65km, 1hr 40min. 335 is an express bus via the Panamerican Highway. **San Salvador (302)**, every 10 min until 4:15pm, 112km, 2hr 30min. Express buses leave at 7am and 3pm take just 90min. **San Vicente (417)**, every hour until 2:30pm, 78km, 2hr 30min. **Santiago de María (349)**, every 20 min until 4pm, 22km, 1hr 15min. **Zacatecoluca (171)**, at 3, 5:40, and 11am, 55km, 90min.

■ **FESTIVALS: November 18-25 (24)** Santa Caterina de Alejandra.

## Near Usulután

**Laguna Olomega** Ask around in the pleasant little village of Olomega, on the shore of this scenic, 4km wide volcanic lake, about renting a boat for a brief tour. During your ride you will see plenty of birds and, if very luck, even an alligator. There is nowhere to spend the night so come here in the morning. *(Located about 20km from Usulután, buses run from both Usulután and San Miguel, but service is infrequent)*

# Puerto El Triunfo

Pop. 18,000
107km from San Salvador
20km from Usulután

### PUERTO EL TRIUNFO NOW

The road south from the Coastal Highway almost peters out in the dusty town of Jiquilisco. At the south end of town, the road grudgingly becomes paved again and continues on to Puerto El Triunfo, a clean and quiet fishing village with a small, shady central market. There is more than enough to do here to warrant a day trip from Usulután.

The new *terminal turistica* is a Canadian-funded dockside project that was inaugurated in early 2000. There are six little

## The Hammock Maker

**M**arroquín Aguilar Cruz is a wizened old fisherman who lives on the outskirts of Puerto El Triunfo. You might spot him outside his house twisting nylon on an old machine for the finely-woven hammocks he weaves. He learned his craft from Mexican seamen he worked with for 22 years. His hammocks are very soft and fine, take two weeks to make and require eleven pounds of nylon each. A medium-sized one will run you upwards of $100. *(4a C Ote. and Av Jorge Guirola/1a Av, at the north end of town across from the huge tree)*

seafood places and a dozen or so more that sell typical Salvadoran food, arts and crafts, and the catch of the day brought in by the many fishing boats. It offers a great view of the Jiquilisco Bay and is a real improvement over the grubby old fishing pier.

## ACCOMMODATIONS
A new hotel will be opening on the Punta San Juan.

## FOOD & DRINK
**El Jardin** The best place in town has an astoundingly varied seafood menu. The a la carte menu ranges from $6 to $11.75 and the grilled shrimp *a la plancha* is wonderful at $8.25. *(7am-7pm)*

## SIGHTS
**Boat Trips** Renting one of the small, colorful fishing boats with an outboard motor from the dock to explore the bay and islands is a pleasant way to spend a day. The best places to visit are Punta San Juan, Isla La Parilla, Isla Coral de Mula and Isla de Menéndez. Isla Coral de Mula is the only one with regular passenger service ($0.60 one way). For any of the others, you have to rent a boat yourself.

It's easiest (and cheapest) to rent a boat for a whole day, rather than by the hour. The prices for day trips vary quite a bit depending on the boat and the destination. This is one place where some Spanish negotiation skills can be very useful. Make sure the boatman understands how many hours you intend to be out and what destinations you want to see. Isla La Parilla has a place to buy beverages, but you'd better carry your own food and drinks.

**Cooperativa de Cocos** The local coconut cooperative gives tours of a coconut farm on the Isla El Jobal. If you have never seen one, it's an interesting place to visit. Just watch out for falling coconuts–a hard hat or football helmet might not be a bad idea. Contact CORSATUR (243-7835) or Barillas Marina (632-1802, 263-3650, e-mail info@barillasmarina.com) to arrange a visit. Chartering a boat to the island will cost about $28.

## DETAILS
■ **BUSES: San Miguel (377)**, every 40 min until 8:30am, then 11am, 3pm, 75km, 2hr 40min. **San Salvador (185)**, every 30 min until 2:30pm, 107km, 2hr 30min. **Usulután (366, 366a)**, every 10 min until 5:30pm, 20km, 50min.
■ **FESTIVALS: May 1-2 (1)** Día de La Cruz. **May 10-13 (12)** Virgen de Fátima.

# Berlín

Pop. 37,000
109km from San Salvador
35km from Usulután

## BERLÍN THEN

This traditional coffee-growing city was built in 1885 in the fertile Valle Agua Caliente ("Hot Water Valley") overlooking the Lempa River. Farms around Berlín grow much of the country's coffee. Because the FMLN established many camps on the slopes of the nearby Tecapa Volcano, Berlín was fiercely contested up to the very end of the civil war. Guerrillas warned local coffee pickers against going to work in the fields in an effort to destabilize the country's coffee-dependent economy.

Seven hundred guerrillas seized Berlín in 1983 after local government forces were diverted to fight another battle in a remote part of the country. The Salvadoran Air Force proceeded to strafe the city plaza with US-supplied jets, and reduced an eight-block section of the town to rubble. Even though the army retook Berlín in three days, the guerrillas considered the battle a victory. Enormous coffee warehouses were set ablaze as the guerrillas retreated.

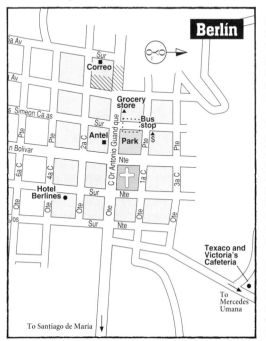

Berlín received more US economic aid than any other rural Salvadoran city and was often called a "US propaganda village." When guerrilla forces took control of as many as 25 percent of El Salvador's cities in the early 1980s, the US diverted military aid money to reconstruct schools and hospitals that had been damaged by the war and to plant crops in fields long abandoned by war-ravaged farmers. Some schools in Berlín still bear the name of the US congressman, Clarence Long, who initiated the program.

## BERLÍN NOW

One of the best things about Berlín is the road there, which slowly winds and twists its way upward from Mercedes Umana into the mountains.

TO THE EAST

## And I'll Need That By Tomorrow

**D**uring their temporary "liberation" of Berlín, guerrillas looted the bank, pharmacies and stores. Soon the biggest spending spree in the city's history was underway. FMLN commanders ordered hundreds of pairs of shoes and new uniforms; tailored quickly enough so that they would be ready before the army could retake the city.

Make sure to sit on the right hand side to see the hills folding down into the Lempa river valley, which lies on one side of the far-off department of San Vicente. Also on the right, the Tronador Geyser has been developed into the most modern geothermal electrical generation plant in Central America. It is owned by CEL, the national electrical utility, and if you call in advance (tel 222-9576) you can arrange a tour. The air cools as the road climbs until it arrives at the Texaco station at the entrance to Berlín.

Berlín is dirty and still bears the scars of fighting. Many of the buildings, especially the church bell tower, are peppered with bullet holes. There are a couple of good places to eat and some hiking paths in the hills around the city, but otherwise there isn't much to Berlín.

## ACCOMMODATIONS

**Hotel Berlines** This new hotel is your only option to stay in town. The rooms are very basic and a bit dark, but acceptable. *(Tel 663-2053; $4.50 per person all with private bath, fan, $13.75 double with cable TV)*

## FOOD & DRINK

**Victoria's Cafetería** An outdoor restaurant with the nicest bathroom you're likely to find in these mountains. Ten big plastic lawn tables, plenty of chairs and a big Coke refrigerator are set inside. A meat dish with rice, salad, tomato and onions is $3.20. *(6am-10pm)*

## DETAILS

■ **BUSES:** Mercedes Umana sits at the intersection of the road to Berlín and the Panamerican Highway, so many buses to cities along the highway can be caught there. Buses that pass by Mercedes Umana include **301** (San Salvador-San Miguel), **304** (San Salvador-La Unión), **306** (San Salvador-Santa Rose de Lima) and **309** (San Salvador-Santiago de María). **Mercedes Umana (304)**, every 45 min until 5pm, 8km, 30min. **San Salvador (303)**, infrequently until 2:30pm, 109km, 3hr. **Santiago de María (322, 348)**, every hour until 5pm, 30km, 40min **Usulután (369)**, every 2 hours until 3:30pm, 35km, 90min.

■ **FESTIVALS: March 15-20 (18)** San José. Tricycle and motorcycle races (separately, of course), theatrical presentations and musical concerts. **December 11-12 (11)** Virgen de Guadalupe. During the Procession of the Indians, participants wearing Indian costumes parade accompanied by band music and firecrackers. **December 24-25** Nacimiento del Niño Díos. Images of San José and the Virgin are brought to each house in search of donations. Songs and fireworks on the 24th are followed by a Misa de Gallo ("Rooster's Mass") late at night.

## Near Berlín

**Cerro Pelón** The two to three-hour hike up this hill (1,400m) to the east of Berlín offers a good view of the city and the beautiful hills and mountains of the coastal range. The hike is about five kilometers each way.

# Alegría

125km from San Salvador

Often called the flower nursery of El Salvador because of the abundant plants grown in small home gardens, Alegría is one the country's most beautiful towns. The cool climate and peaceful streets combine to make this a refreshing destination and one befitting of its name, which in English means Happiness. The locals take pride in the colonial heritage exhibited in the houses, paved streets, and graceful church.

Alegría is also proud to be the hometown of two Salvadoran celebrities: the writer, Alberto Masferrer, known for his philosophical book *Minimum Vital* that was inspired by the 1932 revolution, and ex-president Dr. Manuel Enrique Araujo.

There is no hotel, but you can camp at the Laguna de Alegría or make a day trip from Santiago de María or Berlín along a rough, but scenic road. Whether you want to enjoy the colonial architecture, hike in the surrounding mountains, or just get off the beaten path Alegría is a fantastic place to visit

### FOOD & DRINK

**Mi Pueblito Restaurant** Doña Margarita, the friendly owner dishes out tasty, low-priced food right next to the Central Park. A typical Salvadoran lunch shouldn't set you back more than $2 and breakfast is as little as half that. *(12-2pm, 6-9pm)*

### HIKING

**Laguna de Alegría** Just two kilometers from town this crater lake sits at the top of Volcán Tecapa. It was christened "La Esmeralda de América" ("America's Emerald") by the famous Chilean writer Gabriela Mistral, who was impressed by its dark green water. The mahogany and oak forest surrounding the lake may be unusual for this area, but it certainly adds to the beauty. Many legends surround the lake including one about a mermaid living in its depths. The sulfuric fumes it gives off are also said to be medicinal—they may be good for you, but they make the place too smelly for swimming. The walk from town to the lake takes about an hour and passes through coffee and orange plantations. If you want to camp here you need to get authorization at the Town Hall and pay $0.25.

### DETAILS

■ **BUSES**: Rattletrap public buses run from Berlín or Santiago de María about every 15 minutes.

■ **FESTIVALS: September 26-29 (29)** San Miguel Archangel.

# Santiago de María

Pop. 23,500
118km from San Salvador

## SANTIAGO DE MARÍA THEN

The first of the many successful coffee plantations around
Santiago de María was owned by General Gerardo Barrios.
An earthquake and the eruption of Cerro El Tigre to the
east in 1878 caused part of the mountain to collapse and
buried more than a dozen peasants in their homes on the
skirt of the volcano.

During the 1980s local coffee owners ignored rebel
threats and refused to raise worker wages from $3 to $4.50,
as required by law. Rebels occupied the town in 1983 long enough to harvest a crop's
worth of coffee. The FMLN also attacked an enormous coffee storage compound in the
area owned by then-president Cristiani in order to draw attention to their struggle.

## SANTIAGO DE MARÍA NOW

The second-largest town in Usulután department is surrounded by mountains and is
enveloped in clouds which roll up and down its steep streets. Kids in their school uni-

To Laguna de Alegría
To El Triunfo and the Panamerican Highway

**● ACCOMMODATIONS**
H1  Hospedaje El Quetzal
H2  Hotel Villahermosa

**● FOOD & DRINK**
R1  Pastelería
R2  Restaurant La Cumbre
R3  Pastelería Lorena
R4  Chalet El Paso

**▲ OTHER**
Z1  Basketball court
Z2  Monument
Z3  Shell gas station

5a C  Pte        5a C    Ote
3a C  Pte
7a Av Nte   5a Av Nte   3a Av Nte   1a Av Nte   2a Av Nte   4a Av Nte
R1●   Z1 ▲
1a C  Pte
● H1
● H2
C Masferrer
Av Mariscal Gonzalez
R2 ●
R3 ●    Park
C Bol var
To Cerro El Tigre
2a C  Pte    2a C  Ote
7a Av Sur   5a Av Sur   3a Av Sur   2a Av Sur   4a Av Sur   6a Av Sur   8a Av Sur
▲$    ● R4
4a C  Pte    Av 15 de Septiembre    4a C  Ote
10a Av
Correo    ■ Z2
Bus Stop.
To Usulután    Z3

**Santiago de María**

SANTIAGO DE MARÍA
USULUTAN

## "Cuidado con el ciclista, podría ser su hermano."

("Be careful of the cyclist, he could be your brother.")

**A**s you travel around El Salvador, you'll notice a series of road signs with personal messages imploring drivers to watch out for cyclists alongside the road. These precautionary signs are the brainchild of one Dr. Ayalla, known throughout the country for his efforts to make the roads safer for everyone. Shocked by how many Salvadoran cyclists were being hit by cars, Ayalla secured permission from the government to erect signs throughout the country with messages designed to remind motorists of the danger. "La familia del ciclista le agradese." ("The cyclist's family thanks you.")

forms crowd the clean central park during their mid-day lunch break. The surrounding countryside is spectacular, and you can go for a mountain hike in just about any direction out of town.

The town is at its most lively during the coffee harvest. The cutting (as they call it locally) of coffee takes place between the months of October and March. To arrange a visit to one of the coffee mills or coops near town inquire at the *alcaldia* ("mayor's office").

## ACCOMMODATIONS

You should call ahead if you plan to stay the night since both hotels shut down for long periods in the off season.

**Hotel Villahermosa** Looks like someone's living room turned inside out, with plants, music and couches. Clean, spacious rooms and bathrooms are complemented by a friendly atmosphere. *(Tel 660-0146; 5S/D $5.75/$9.20, 2T $13.80, all with private bath, fan; 24hr checkout; parking; restaurant 7:30am-6pm)*

**Hospedaje El Quetzal** The owner complains he's had no business since the Villahermosa opened next door. No surprise.

## FOOD & DRINK

**Restaurant La Cumbre** You can't go wrong here. This comfortable place serves good food at low prices. A full breakfast costs just $1.50 while a complete lunch or dinner of meat, rice and salad costs $2.30. *(8am to 8pm)*

**Pastelería Lorena** This is a branch of the large San Miguel bakery.

## HIKING

**Cerro El Tigre** A few kilometers to the east of town, this monster is the most impressive climb within easy distance. A hike to the summit leads you 1,500 meters up through coffee plantations. There's a great view of Santiago de María and the entire valley from the top. You need at least a day to get up and back. Go prepared since the path isn't too clear, even though the mountain itself is visible from the town.

**Cerro Oromontique** This smaller hill is less than a kilo-

TO THE EAST

meter directly south of Santiago de María. A few hours' hike brings you to the top, for a view of the town and the much larger mountains in every other direction. The flat peak is a great place for a picnic.

### DETAILS
■ **BUSES: Berlín (322, 348)**, every hour until 4:30pm, 30km, 40min. The bus that passes Mercedes Umana instead of Alegría takes 90min. **San Miguel (355)**, every 30 min until 5:30pm, 24km, 1hr 15min. **San Salvador (310)**, every 20 min until 4pm, 118km, 2hr 30min. **Usulután (337, 362, 370)**, every 15 min until 6pm, 14km, 1hr.
■ **FESTIVALS: February 19-25 (24)** Santiago Apóstol.

# San Vicente
Pop. 80,000
58km from San Salvador

### SAN VICENTE THEN
San Vicente was founded in 1635, when 50 Spanish families gathered under a shady tree on the banks of the Río Acahuapán to create a new town that would be safe from the increasingly hostile Indian population nearby. The town was named after San Vicente Abad, a famous Spanish martyr.

SAN VICENTE

San Vicente emerged as a seat of power in the 19th century. During the brief existence of the Central American Federation in the 1830s, San Vicente served as El Salvador's capital for a few years. The

## The Legend of Pilar

**A**ccording to a traditional story, a couple named José Marino and Manuela Arce lived together in San Vicente in the middle of the 18th century. One night Arce, crazy with jealousy over her husband's constant philandering, plotted to kill him. When she approached, murder in her eyes and knife in her hand, a framed image of the Virgin of Pilar on the wall of the room began to shake violently. Arce fled in terror.

The Virgin's warning wasn't sufficient to hold off Arce's fury for long, though, and soon she went after her husband again. But once again, just before she attacked, the picture shook wildly and Arce fled in fear. After this happened a third time Arce became convinced that a higher spirit was involved and, trembling with remorse, she gave up her plot to kill her husband.

Marino, meanwhile, began construction on a small chapel on the western side of the plaza of Pilar where he planned to house the lifesaving image of the Virgin. Although Marino died without completing the chapel, the site was set aside as a tribute to the Virgin of Pilar. It was later replaced by the larger Church of Pilar which stands there today.

TO THE EAST

Top: Craftsman carving wood
Bottom Left: *Pupusa* vendor, Olocuilta
Bottom Right: Crafts shop, La Palma

  Top: Try to attend at least one of El Salvador's colorful festivals
Bottom Left: *Frijoles* for sale, Chalatenango
Bottom Right: *Campesino,* San Juan Opico

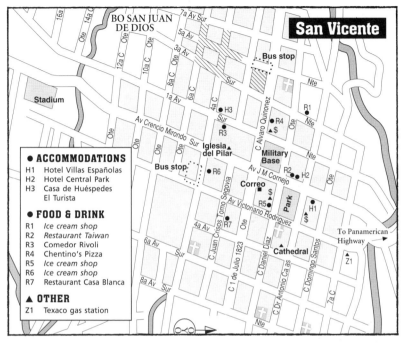

### San Vicente

**BO SAN JUAN DE DIOS**

Stadium

**● ACCOMMODATIONS**
H1    Hotel Villas Españolas
H2    Hotel Central Park
H3    Casa de Huéspedes
       El Turista

**● FOOD & DRINK**
R1    *Ice cream shop*
R2    *Restaurant Taiwan*
R3    *Comedor Rivoli*
R4    *Chentino's Pizza*
R5    *Ice cream shop*
R6    *Ice cream shop*
R7    *Restaurant Casa Blanca*

**▲ OTHER**
Z1    Texaco gas station

Iglesia del Pilar
Military Base
Correo
Park
Cathedral
Bus stop
To Panamerican Highway

town has suffered through many serious earthquakes, including an especially destructive one in the 1930s. During the civil war the area endured heavy fighting as FMLN troops moved south through the region and battled with the army. A strong army presence settled over the town, with a huge military compound at its center.

## SAN VICENTE NOW

The capital of San Vicente department is nestled in the Jiboa Valley, one of the most beautiful valleys in El Salvador, at the foot of the San Vicente Volcano. Rolling hills and fields of sugar cane surround San Vicente, which in spite of its rocky history is one of the most pleasant, relaxed cities in the country. From the Panamerican Highway to the west you can get a spectacular view of the city, with its white church, clock tower and the twin peaks of the volcano in the background. A plantation owned by former President Cristiani is visible on the slopes of the volcano.

## Strategic Location

In 1774, a mudslide near the peak of the San Vicente Volcano released a raging torrent of water down its side. San Vicente itself was spared only because the hill of San Antonio, which sits between the town and the volcano, diverted the water around San Vicente into two streams. The gully carved by the torrent can still be seen as a scar down the side of the volcano.

TO THE EAST

Women stand at the entrance to San Vicente selling red, white and black beans by the pound. The city is an archetypal colonial town with cobblestone streets and a prominent clock tower that overlooks the central plaza. The volcano is reachable in a day's hike and you can cool off in the nearby Apastepeque *turicentro*. The Peace Corp trains many of its volunteers here so there is a good chance you will meet some if you stick around a little while. This calm, quiet city has a number of quality restaurants, making it a good place to stop off the Panamerican Highway as you head east.

## ACCOMMODATIONS

**Hotel Villas Españolas** Built in a traditional Spanish style but modern on the inside. Rooms are all well kept and the pleasant patio is a nice bonus. Singles and doubles are the same size. *(Tel 393-0322; 11S $9.20, 4D $12.60, all with private bath, cable TV; noon checkout)*

**Casa de Huéspedes El Turista** An old but very clean and very friendly place with good beds. It's a good second choice if the Villas Españolas is full. Prices may be negotiable. *(Tel 333-0323; 18 rooms from $6.75 to $9, all with fan, most with private bath, hammock, cable TV; noon checkout)*

**Hotel Central Park** Although it isn't as nice as the Villas Españolas, the Hotel Central Park is still a good value. You can enjoy the view of the main square from the porch and it's also a good place to meet people in town. The restaurant is good and moderately priced. *(Tel 333-0383; 18 rooms, S $7.50, D $11.40 with fan, S $11.40, D $14.50 with AC, all with private bath, TV, phone; laundry; restaurant 6:30pm-9pm)*

## FOOD & DRINK

**Restaurant Casa Blanca** Very comfortable setting in a pleasant hanging garden with trees and a clean little pool. Steak and seafood dishes average $6. *(11am-9pm)*

**Comedor Rivoli** Like no other *comedor* in town, the Rivoli is a spic and span, traditional cafeteria with plenty of orange and white tables and chairs. Plates are in the $2 range. *(7am-8pm)*

**Chentino's Pizza** These friendly guys have their act together; they've been here for seven years and have another shop in San Miguel. Come here for pizza and natural fruit shakes—nectar of the gods. A large plain is $7 and shakes are $1. *(10am-9:30pm)*

### Bones in the Plaza

On his way to church one day in the late 18th century, a visiting curate noticed human bones scattered around San Vicente's main plaza. When he inquired, the clergyman learned that certain people in the area practiced a strange ritual; they exhumed dead bodies to obtain particular bones, which they used in a magic ritual that they believed made them impossible to capture or confine. Those covered by the spell were even supposed to be able to escape effortlessly from jail. The rest of the bones were simply discarded in the plaza.

## SIGHTS

**Iglesia del Pilar** The church was ordered built in 1762 by Francisco de Quintanilla. He died in Guatemala, but his son completed the construction. Today this beautiful

## Aquino's Folly

In 1831 rebel forces under indigenous leader Anastasio Aquino spread out from Santiago Nonualco and eventually gained control of the entire coastal region between the Comalapa and Lempa rivers. The town of San Vicente sent two forces to subdue the rebels, but both were defeated. Aquino advanced towards San Vicente and, in 1833, occupied the town's central plaza.

When Aquino's troops took San Vicente, they sacked the town and robbed the Church of Pilar of much of its valuable jewel collection. Drunk with alcohol and success, Aquino crowned himself "Emperor of the Nonualcos" with the Crown of San José, still on display in the Iglesia del Pilar.

As he prepared to return home, Aquino abducted Lucilla Marín, a beautiful young local woman, and left with her in hasty retreat. Marín's uncle Escolástico chased after Aquino with an army of 150 Vicenteños determined to rescue his niece and to teach Aquino a lesson. Escolástico caught up with Aquino in Santiago Nonualco, soon defeated him and freed Lucilla. As both sides counted their losses, Escolástico captured Aquino and returned with him to San Vicente, where the rebel leader was tried and executed.

As you travel from San Salvador to the airport, about eight kilometers south of the Olocuilta exit, you will pass a mountain seven kilometers to the north of the highway that is now known as El Cerro del Indio Aquino. If you look closely at the outline of the mountain against the sky you will see the profile of a male Indian face.

church, which survived Aquino's ransacking, is decorated with benches, an altar made of dark wood and intricate designs on white walls.

**La Torre Vicentina** The St. Vincent Tower rising from the main plaza was inspired by the famous Parisian tower. You can enjoy great views of the Jiboa Valley and the truly impressive Volcán Chichontepec from the top. To visit you need to stop by the *alcaldía* ("mayor's office") and get a permit which is a unique chance to witness Salvadoran democracy at work.

## DETAILS

■ **BUSES:** There are two bus stations in San Vicente. **Station #1: San Salvador (116)**, every 10 min until 6:30pm, 58km, 1hr 30min. **Zacatecoluca (177)**, every 15 min until 6pm, 23km, 1hr. **Station #2: Turicentro Amapulapa (171)**, every 15min until 2pm, 9km, 1hr. **Apastepeque (156)**, every 30 min until 6pm, 12km, 1hr. There are a handful of direct buses each day to Costa del Sol and Usulután from Station #1, but it is generally quicker to go to Zacatecoluca and catch the appropriate bus there. There are also a few direct routes to San

Sebastián and Ilobasco from Station #2 though for these towns your best bet is to take a San Salvador bus down the Panamerican Highway to the appropriate intersection and wait for a passing bus.

■ **FESTIVALS:** Crafts made in the penitentiary of San Vicente, including wooden toys, decorations and stringed instruments, are sold during the town's festivals. **January 1-30 (5)** Romería del Señor de Esquipulas. A masquerade ridicules local figures during this pilgrimage, and processions wind through town on January 14 and 30. **October 1-15 (14)** Nuestra Señora del Rosario. **October 16-November 16** La Feria de Los Santos. Originally centered around the indigo trade, this fair has become the most popular *fiesta* in San Vicente. It's a more commercial festival than some, with many different products brought in from neighboring towns for sale. **December 15-31 (26)** San Vicente. **December 24-25 (24)** Nacimiento del Niño Jesús. A group of young people called Los Pastores dress as shepherds—complete with robes, hats and shepherd's hook—and visit the church and various houses as they sing songs about the birth of Christ.

# Near San Vicente

**San Vicente Volcano** "Chinchontepec," the Nahuat name for this huge dormant volcano, means "Mountain of Two Breasts." A flat peak and a cone-shaped peak each rise to about 2,200 meters, with a depression in between that used to be a crater. The panoramic view from the top is one of the best in the country. The volcano hasn't erupted recently, but hot springs at its base known as Los Infernillos make you wonder if it really is dead, or just sleeping.

The climb to the top follows a long, steep trail that starts just past the Turicentro Amapulapa. If you walk the whole 14 kilometers from San Vicente, it should take you at least six hours each way. It's quicker and easier, though, to catch one of the regular buses around the base of the volcano to the small town of Guadalupe. From there it's about five kilometers to the top, or a three-hour hike.

**Los Infernillos** ("The Little Hells") These natural hot springs, in the sugar fields on the southern side of the base of Chichontepec, are bathed in strong sulfuric fumes and smoke. For years, people with health problems came here to be cured by the water. During the war the area was mined by the FMLN so few people showed up. Now that the area has been de-mined life is returning to normal.

**Turicentro Apastepeque** Relive summer-camp memories at this crater lake, the smallest turicentro in the country but one of the cleanest and most pleasant. A section of the lake is separated for use by families, which is probably best since it plunges to over 100 meters deep in the middle, a reminder of its volcanic origins. Be careful swimming out alone—there aren't any lifeguards. String up your hammock between a couple of shady trees and hang out. Take bus 156 or 156a from San Vicente and ask the driver to let you off at the sign for the *turicentro*. From there it's about a kilometer and a half to the lake. *(8am-5pm; $0.90 per person and $0.70 per car, cabins $4)*

**Turicentro Amapulapa** Cleaned up considerably in recent years, this is a good place to relax. The largest of the four pools has a small waterfall. A statue of San Cristóbal, the patron saint of motorists, gazes down on everything. A few huts serve food and drinks for reasonable prices. Take bus 176 from San Vicente or catch a pickup, it is just three kilometers away so you could walk too. *(8am-6pm; $0.90 per person and $0.70 per car, cabins $4)*

# San Sebastián

Pop. 26,000
50km from San Salvador
15km from San Vicente

## SAN SEBASTIÁN THEN

In September 1988, ten peasants near San Sebastián were killed by government troops, continuing a pattern of rural massacres that had become common through the early part of the war. Information about the case was both shocking and predictable. Ballistics evidence showed that all been shot at close range. Witnesses described how army troops had surrounded their hamlet, herded residents into a school and separated a group of "rebel collaborators." As the accused

were being led away for questioning, they were gunned down at close range.

The army had a different story to tell. After first claiming that the peasants were guerrillas killed in combat, the army changed its account to say that they had been caught in the crossfire of a guerrilla ambush. The guerrillas, they said, had returned later and shot up the bodies at close range to make the army look guilty.

At first, the army's claim of rebel crossfire was accepted and the case appeared closed. It was reopened, however, when US Vice President Dan Quayle visited El Salvador and threatened to withhold the $1.5 million that El Salvador was receiving daily unless the military demonstrated a commitment to improving human rights. Quayle declared that the incident at San Sebastián would be a test case.

With the US pressing the military for results, the media reported that a high army figure would soon be jailed. US officials were quick to portray the reports as a sign that the army had reversed course and would now answer to Salvadoran law.

Just as quickly, though, events took another turn. In 1990, charges against 11 of the 12 army officers indicted in the San Sebastián massacre were suddenly dropped. US policy makers and Ambassador Walker, who had personally encouraged progress in the case, were stunned and embarrassed. Nonetheless, US military aid continued.

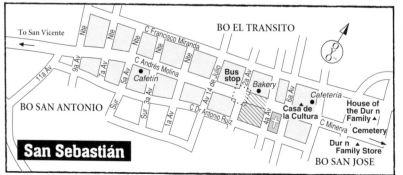

TO THE EAST

During a soccer game near San Sebastián towards the end of the war, rebel troops surrounded the field and herded 200 people, including players and food vendors, off into the hills. Within ten days, everyone had escaped or been freed from the rebel camp, returning with tales of endless propaganda speeches and lousy food. Players, still wearing only their thin soccer uniforms, complained that they had almost frozen. In the end, the operation turned into a public relations nightmare for the FMLN, and soccer games in the area were suspended indefinitely.

## SAN SEBASTIÁN NOW

The road to San Sebastián passes through the quiet town of Santo Domingo. Recently paved, it's a pleasant detour past small farms, swaying cornfields and wandering cows. Although most of San Sebastián itself is downright drab, some scenes are almost painfully picturesque, with yards of brilliantly colored yarn left to dry outside red-tiled houses.

The town has regained its fame for its unique, brightly-colored weavings which are often still done on traditional looms. Synthetic materials and cheap Asian imports have diluted the craft to some degree, nevertheless the technique is interesting and they still make good souvenirs. Weavers use foot pedals to manipulate pairs of sticks to create the designs. More complex designs must be planned in advance. The larger the weaving, the more pairs of sticks are needed. The town's artisans are usually delighted to show you how everything works, and they may even let you pass the shuttle a few times. Ask politely before taking photographs, however.

## FOOD & DRINK

There are only a few simple cafes in town and all are pretty much the same. A typical Salvadoran meal will be under $2. For a snack or a coffee break there is also a bakery in front of the market.

## SIGHTS

**Iglesia de San Sebastian** This late 18th century church has suffered much earthquake damage over the years. The main altar area conserves many of the original features and is worth a peek if you are in town.

## CRAFTS

Numerous shops line the main street selling local woven products at prices well below what you would pay in the shops in the capital.

**Casa de la Cultura** This is a good place to appreciate the painstaking labor that goes into each weaving. A few looms inside surround a pretty little enclosed garden. Knock if they look closed. *(Mon-Sat 8am-4pm, occasionally open on Sundays)*

**House of the Durán Family** This family has been weaving for generations. Sr. Durán employs a full brigade of weavers who labor away on some ancient looms inside this combination funeral home/weaving studio. Locals buy blankets here and resell them in San Salvador. They have a store on Minerva Street, but to see the productions process visit their house on Buena Ventura St.

## DETAILS

■ **BUSES: San Salvador (110)**, every 30 min until 5pm, 50km, 1hr 30min. **San Vicente (176)**, 6:30am, 1:30pm, 15km, 1hr.

■ **FESTIVALS: January 23-28 (27)** San Sebastián Mártir. **December 11-12 (11)** Virgen de Guadalupe. **December 24-25 (24)** Nacimiento del Niño Díos.

# San Miguel

Pop. 250,000
136km from San Salvador

## SAN MIGUEL THEN

Barely seven years after the Spanish founded the city in 1530, San Miguel was almost wiped out by an indigenous insurrection that shook many parts of Central America. The native population, enraged by their treatment at the hands of the Spanish, seized San Miguel and other cities.

When the city government came under attack, it sent out a desperate call for help to the capital, which soon dispatched reinforcements. As churches in San Salvador rang their bells in support of the Spanish in San Miguel and government troops rushed to the city, the insurrection grew more fierce. Troops battled for six months before the rebellion was eventually suppressed.

Toward the end of the 17th century, English pirates appeared off the coast and sacked undefended indigenous villages along the shore. When San Miguel and San Salvador prepared their armies for a full-scale invasion, the pirates decided to flee rather than fight. As they fled back to their ships, they left behind an image of the Virgin Mary in the port of Amapala. Soon the icon, which came to be known as "The Miraculous Patron," was brought to San Miguel where an elaborate procession was held in honor of all who survived.

During the early years of the civil war, the army stationed some of its best forces near the city in an attempt to neutralize the guerrillas next door in the department of Morazán and on the slopes of the San Miguel Volcano. From the volcano, rebel troops periodically launched raids on the city's electrical installations and were able to black out eastern El Salvador. For over 10 years the FMLN attacked the roads around San Miguel choking trade and travel. The Deliro Bridge, five kilometers to the south, was repeatedly attacked by the rebels in an attempt to knock out transit between San Miguel and the capital. The bustling commerce San Miguel was always known for nearly ground to a halt and the city center was left deserted at night.

## SAN MIGUEL NOW

El Salvador's eastern hub sprawls alongside the Panamerican Highway on its way toward La Unión, in the shadow of the San Miguel Volcano. The sticky heat can't suppress this bustling commercial center where streets are practically bursting with business and trade.

TO THE EAST

Those who saw San Miguel during the war and return to visit now call the post-war change remarkable. The economic boom gripping San Miguel today shows why the city's citizens are known for their work ethic. It is also a remarkable display of the power of peace in the economic well being of a community and nation.

Some of the richest coffee fields in El Salvador lie on the slopes of the enormous volcano which overlooks the city. San Miguel is the country's center for the production of cotton and henequen, a natural fiber used to make bags, ropes and hammocks.

Two recent highway projects, the Ruta Militar and connecting highway to the Southwestern Honduran border as well as the Coastal Highway through eastern El Salvador have helped the city's commerce. These excellent highways have led to urban sprawl and some of the highest land prices in the country. This is also due to the fact that many of the "Miguelenos" who migrated during the war, now have money to send back home or are returning themselves to buy real estate.

San Miguel, the east's only really large city, is a place to enjoy crowds, eat well, visit a thriving market and watch a soccer game, but it's not a place to relax. Prices are higher here than in the west and the sun beats down on the low-lying countryside without mercy. The market is a crazy clutter of wooden tables where you can browse through heaps of inexpensive plastic watches, hand-hammered pots, imitation jewelry, live lizards and hand-rolled cigars.

| ● ACCOMMODATIONS | |
|---|---|
| H1 | Hotel China House |
| H2 | Hotel Oasis |
| H3 | Casa de Huéspedes El Viajero |
| H4 | Hotel El Mandarin |
| H5 | Hotel La Terminal |
| H6 | Hotel Trópico Inn |
| H7 | Hotel Posada Real |

| ● FOOD & DRINK | |
|---|---|
| R1 | Pop's Ice Cream |
| R2 | Pollo Campestre |
| R3 | Pollo Campestre |
| R4 | Ice cream |
| R5 | Restaurant Acajutla |
| R6 | Pollo Campero |
| R7 | Pupesería Los Gorritos |
| R8 | Restaurant La Pradera |
| R9 | Restaurant La Ronda |
| R10 | Pastelería Lorena |

| ▲ OTHER | |
|---|---|
| Z1 | Iglesia Capilla Medalla Milagrosa |
| Z2 | Music cassette shop |
| Z3 | Supermarket |
| Z4 | Supermarket |
| Z5 | Cinema Barrios |
| Z6 | El Sarape |
| Z7 | Post Office |
| Z8 | Supermarket |
| Z9 | Marquis Supermarket |
| Z10 | L.A. Disco |
| Z11 | Iglesia El Calvario |
| Z12 | Mercado de Artesanías |

## ACCOMMODATIONS

**Hotel Trópico Inn** This classic hotel, once the only quality stop in San Miguel, suffered repeated guerrillas attacks during the late 1980s. In 1989, a celebration during the Miss San Miguel pageant was interrupted by a guerrilla assault on the city. The Salvadoran vice president was attending the ceremonies, conveniently enough, and became trapped. The next day he was evacuated by helicopter.

The Trópico is the most traditional hotel in San Miguel and has undergone a complete renovation making it the best once again. The pool, restaurant and convention area are very pleasant and very tropical. For the high quality you get the prices are pretty good. *(Tel 661-1800, fax 661-1399; 105 rooms, S $45, D $57, all with private bath, hot water, TV, telephones, AC, some have internet access; laundry; business center; restaurant 6:30am to 11pm)*

**Hotel del Centro** (City Center map) A completely remodeled father-and-son establishment with a friendly staff and very clean rooms. It is a great option in the city center and perhaps the best thing is that the prices are negotiable. Lunch at the restaurant costs about $4 and is very tasty. *(Tel 661-6913, 661-5473; 34 rooms, S $11.50, D $14.30 with fan, S $20, D $26 with AC, all have private bath and cable TV; noon checkout; restaurant 6am-9pm)*

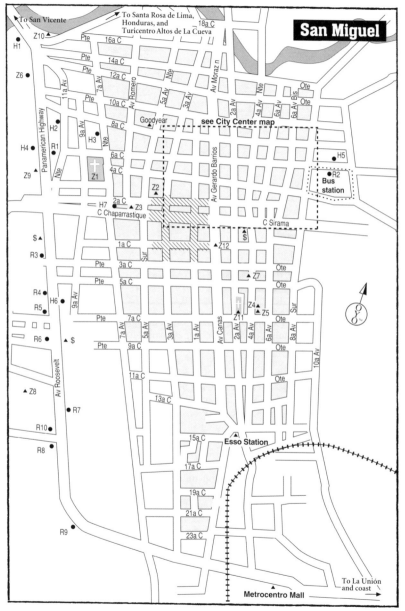

San Miguel

To San Vicente
To Santa Rosa de Lima, Honduras, and Turicentro Altos de La Cueva
18a C
Z10
H1
Pte
16a C
Pte
14a C
Z6
Pte
12a C
11a Av
7a Av
Av Romero
Nte
Av Moraz n
2a Av
Nte
4a Av
6a Av
6a Av Bis
Ote
Ote
Pte
10a C
5a Av
3a Av
Panamerican Highway
9a Av
Pte
8a C
Goodyear
see City Center map
H2
R1
H3
6a C
Av Gerardo Barrios
H5
H4
Nte
Z1
4a C
R2
Z9
Bus station
2a C
Z2
H7
Z3
C Chaparrastique
Sur
C Sirama
$
1a C
$
R3
3a C
Sur
Z12
Pte
5a C
Ote
R4
9a Av
Z7
Ote
R5
H6
Pte
7a C
7a Av
5a Av
3a Av
1a Av
Av Canas
2a Av
Z4
Ote
4a Av
6a Av
8a Av
Sur
Z5
Z11
R6
$
Pte
9a C
Ote
Av Roosevelt
11a C
Ote
Z8
10a Av
R7
13a C
R10
15a C
Esso Station
R8
17a C
19a C
21a C
R9
23a C

To La Unión and coast
Metrocentro Mall

TO THE EAST

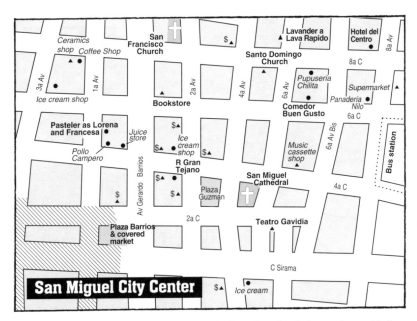

San Miguel City Center

**Casa de Huéspedes El Viajero** Reasonably clean, though a little run-down, this is a good option for the budget traveler. For over 20 years the same little old manager has been running the place and he has his tales. Small rooms with a courtyard that serves as a parking lot. *(12 rooms, S $5.75 with shared bath, $7 with private bath, rooms with AC $11.50; 24hr checkout; parking)*

**Hotel Oasis** This spacious yet simple hotel is bustling with salesmen during the week. It won't pass the white glove test, but it is fairly clean. Because they are usually full the service isn't always the best. Reservations recommended. The cafeteria will cook up whatever they have on hand for about $4. *(Tel 661-2126; 7S $10, 15D $16, all with private bath, AC; cafeteria)*

**Hotel China House** This clean hotel has hammocks in the center of a courtyard attached to a restaurant that serves Chinese, American and Salvadoran plates from $2.85 to $3.50. The China House Combination for $3.45 includes chop suey, chicken, salad, potatoes and fried rice. Jaime Quan, the very personable owner, speaks English. His grandfather came to San Miguel and opened China House after emigrating to Mexico from Canton, China. *(Tel 669-5029; 19 rooms, S $12.50, D $20, T $23, all with private bath, AC; laundry; noon checkout; restaurant)*

**Hotel El Mandarín** One of San Miguel's best hotels. It isn't inexpensive, but it's new and well managed, on par with a rural Holiday Inn back home. The restaurant serves Chinese food for $3.50 to $8 a dish, including a great big bowl of wonton soup for $3.50. The owner, a Chinese immigrant who has lived in El Salvador his entire life, ran a Chinese restaurant in town for many years. *(Tel 669-6969; 32 rooms, S $38, D $45, all with private bath, AC, cable TV; laundry; pool; parking; 2pm checkout; restaurant)*

TO THE EAST

**Hotel La Terminal** A pleasant enough place with clean, comfy rooms in front of the bus station. *(Tel 660-6353; 38 rooms, D $14.50, all with private bath, AC, cable TV; 24hr checkout; parking; cafetín)*

**Hotel Posada Real** This pleasant mid-range hotel has good service and a good location. *(Tel 661-7174, 661-7177; 18 rooms S $21, D $25, T $34, all with private bath, AC, cable TV)*

## FOOD & DRINK

**Restaurante Doña Pema** Without a doubt this is one of the most famous restaurants in Central America. The old gal and her daughters learned their trade secrets in the dusty highway town of Santa Rosa de Lima and so broad was her reputation that even during the war years her place was always full. The year after the war she opened shop in San Miguel. And the reputation is worth the hype, as many ambassadors and other foreign dignitaries can attest.

Her cooking is now world famous and not to be missed. The seafood and soup platter *La Pema* is a unique and tasty experience and the *mariscada* ($10) is world-class. The tortillas and cheese are meals in themselves so save room for your proper meal. *(Located about 2 km south of San Miguel at Carretera Playa El Cuco; 10:30am-4pm)*

**Pastelería Lorena** (City Center map) Plenty of space inside to enjoy Lorena's wide variety of pastries. This is the biggest bakery in San Miguel with eight local branches. Pastries and bread start at $0.10 and juices are $0.70. They also serve good low-budget luncheon specials for $1.75. *(8am-6pm)*

**Pastelería Francesa** (City Center map) This is Lorena's main rival in San Miguel. Not to be outdone they also serve good low-budget luncheon specials for $1.75 in AC rooms and have just as wide a selection of pastry. *(8am-5:30pm)*

**Restaurant Gran Tejano** (City Center map) Dark inside and decorated like a ranch, with wooden tables and animal hides on the wall. Kind of smells like a ranch, too. Not

## Abracadabra, Royal Flush

Judging by the comments of an 18th-century traveler who passed through the city, San Miguel has seen its share of action. In his diary, the traveler noted how the city was set in the panoramic foothills of the San Miguel Volcano and how the Spanish, mestizo and indigenous populations generally lived together peacefully.

But, he added, San Miguel was "a hell of dissidence and gangs" where "the dominant vice is gambling." "This vice is so extreme," he continued, "that gamblers steal everything from their wives, even their dresses, and leave them naked as the day they were born just to be able to play."

Apparently, some gamblers even resorted to witchcraft. The traveler wrote that gamblers would first grind human bones into a powder, use the powder to form a candle and burn it wherever they played. The magic smoke that was released made everyone sleepy and was supposed to help the gambler win more easily

surprisingly, steak is the specialty of the house. The *BBQ Carne a la Parrilla* is another good choice. Prices run from $10-$15. *(11am-10pm)*

**Restaurant La Pradera** This white open-air building, set off from the road, is a father and son run business where many of the young men in town like to drink beer. Dishes are on the expensive side; a plate of shrimp costs $12.60. *(11:30am-9:30pm)*

**Pupusería Los Gorritos** A good place to have this Salvadoran staple, *pupusas* here run $0.35 and are made with vegetable oil. Do not be surprised if the *curtido* (pickled veggies) has mayonnaise, that's the way they make it in San Miguel. *(4-9pm)*

**Restaurante Don Beto** A good choice for Mexican food. Don Beto has a varied menu of burritos, tacos, churrascos and the like from $3.50. *(Open noon-close)*

**Restaurante Los Panchos** Another pleasant place for Mexican is located at the Metrocentro Mall. Tacos start at $1 while a full spread with BBQ beef is $8. *(11am-10pm)*

**Restaurante Bar Armando's** This place north of town is popular with locals, for their beef, chicken and seafood cocktails usually washed down with plenty of beer. Menu prices run from $5 to $11. *(Final 4 Av Nte y Ruta Militar; Tue-Sat 10:30am-11pm)*

**Restaurante Mama Gallina** Relaxed and informal. The blue plate special is the traditional chicken soup ("*Sopa de Gallina*") for $4. Don't leave Central America without giving it a try. *(10:30am-9pm)*

## ENTERTAINMENT

San Miguel is packed with nightlife options, but many are not very safe. Remember this was the center of a 12-year-long civil war and many local people remain armed. You can dance the night away at any of the following without having to worry, but if you want to go anywhere else you should ask about it first.

**L.A. Disco** A favorite with the younger crowd, they play all the latest music and some tropical tunes. The cover charge is $2.50 per person.

**El Sarape** A new spot where you can dance to live music, mostly local tropical bands. The Mexican menu is quite diverse with good quality food.

**Marquis Discotec** This place plays all kinds of music and draws all ages of dancers. The cover charge is $2.50 per person.

## SIGHTS

**Iglesia Capilla Medalla Milagrosa** A hospital compound used to surround this beautiful little white church that was designed by the French nuns who worked there. The hospital is now gone and the church windows display some of the finest stained glass in El Salvador. The church is enclosed by a black steel gate and a forest of trees.

**Teatro Gavidia** (City Center map) Built at the turn of the century, with fine neoclas-

## Jocoro

This small town in the southern foothills of Morazán department, 22 kilometers from San Miguel, saw a lot of fighting during the war. Today, it's a quiet, pretty stop-off on the road between San Miguel and Santa Rosa de Lima. There aren't any hotels or restaurants in Jocoro, but there's some good hiking in the hills just to the south.

sic structural details, this is one of San Miguel's historical and architectural treasures. The theater was opened in 1909 after eight years of construction. Besides musical and theatrical performances there are also regular art, painting and photography expositions held here. *(Mon-Fri 8am-12pm, 2pm-4pm)*

**San Miguel Cathedral** This majestic church in the center of the city has lovely murals and other religious art. Unfortunately much of it was damaged during the war. The main altar is dedicated to the Virgin of the Peace (*Virgen de La Paz*) who is, ironically, the patron saint of El Salvador. Many of the locals hold deep devotion for and strictly follow the Catholic traditions associated with the *Santa Patrona*.

**Other Colonial Churches** There are several other historic colonial churches in the center of town that are worth a quick look. Among the most interesting are San Francisco, El Calvario and Santo Domingo all of which date back to the 18th century.

## DETAILS

■ **BUSES:** From San Salvador you have a choice of two routes to get to San Miguel, the Coastal or the Panamerican. The Coastal route leaves from the Terminal de Sur and involves taking an express bus or else the Usulután 302 bus and then getting another bus to San Miguel from Usulután. The Panamerican route is more scenic if you like volcanoes and coffee farms, but a bit slower and windier. The Panamerican route leaves from the Terminal de Oriente and involves taking the 301 or an express bus to San Miguel or the 304 to La Unión. You can call the San Miguel bus station (tel 661-3784) for the most current schedule information. **Ciudad Barrios (316)**, irregular service until 5pm, 48km, 2hr. **El Cuco (320)**, every 30 min until 4pm, 40km, 1hr 30min. **El Amatillo/Honduran border**, some of the 330 buses for Santa Rosa de Lima continue on to the border. **El Tamarindo (385)**, every 30min until 4pm, 75km, 2hr 15min. **La Unión (324)**, every 8 min until 6pm, 42km, 1hr 20min. **Moncagua (316, 317)**, every 20 min until 5pm, 13km, 40min. **Olomega (384)** infrequently, 30km, 45min. **Perquín (332b)**, infrequently, 85km, 3hr. **Puerto El Triunfo (377)**, every 40 min until 8:30am, then 11am, 3pm, 75km, 2hr 40min. **San Francisco Gotera (328)**, every 10 min until 6:30pm, 35km, 50min. **San Salvador (301)**, every 5 min until 4:30pm, 136km, 3hr; ask about express buses at the terminal as the schedule is highly variable depending on the day and season. **San Vicente (301)**, every 5 min until 4:30pm, 96km, 2hr. **Santa Rosa de Lima (330)**, every 10 min until 6pm, 49km, 1hr. **Usulután (373)**, every 15 min until 5:30pm, 60km, 1hr 30min.

■ **FESTIVALS: November 14-30 (20, 21)** Nuestra Señora de la Paz. Hot-air balloons, go-kart, bicycle and motorcycle races. **Late November** Carnival Noviembrino. A well-known carnival that attracts visitors from all over.

■ **LAUNDRY: Lavandería Lava Rápido** One of the few do-it-yourself laundromats outside the capital. $2 per load for eight pieces, $1.40 to dry, no ironing. *(8am-5pm)*

■ **SHOPPING: Metrocentro San Miguel** This fancy new shopping mall has department stores, hardware, fashion shops, arts and crafts, two movie theaters and a food court with franchise eateries like Pizza Hut, Pollo Campero, and Wendy's. **Mercado de Artesanías** At San Miguel's arts and crafts market you can find a wide variety of items from across Central America. *(8am-5pm)*

# Near San Miguel

**Turicentro Altos de La Cueva** "The Cave on High" is one of the best *turicentros* in the country and a real oasis during a hot day in San Miguel. *(Located on La Ruta Militar Highway, 8am-4pm; $0.80 per person, seniors free)*

**San Miguel Volcano** This granddaddy of a mountain, largely isolated from the rest of the Chinameca range, juts 2,140 meters out of the southern coastal plain. This perfectly shaped cone looks especially impressive from the Coastal Highway, and as you drive away in any direction it remains visible for kilometers.

Chaparrastique, as it is traditionally known, is good for a serious climb. Be careful, though, since it occasionally comes to life—it last erupted in 1976. The climb to the top winds through some enormous coffee plantations. In fact, you're not likely to see much on the way up except coffee plantations, bushes and pickers. If that sounds interesting, and you can handle sulfur fumes at the top, then you'll get a world-class view down into the crater. Portions of the climb are along a 70-degree slope with very loose volcanic stones so unless you know what you are doing you should consider hiring a guide. A dirt road leads to the top. Bring your own food and drink.

You can either drive or catch a couple buses to get to the mountain village of Conacastal. From there, there's a path that leads to the top of the volcano. If you're going by bus, catch one that's heading to San Vicente and ask to be dropped off six kilometers west of San Miguel on the road to the left that leads toward San Jorge. At that point, the Laguna Seca ("Dry Lagoon") El Pacayual is to the right and the San Miguel Volcano is to the left. From the intersection, get a lift up into the mountains and hop off in tiny Conacastal. The entrance to the Finca Miracielo is pretty clear—there's a red door with two white pillars and a sign outside that reads, "Recibidero Prieto." If you're coming by car, be out by 6pm or they'll lock you in. Sr. Ricardo Men holds the gate keys, so you'll want to speak with him before leaving your car behind.

**Laguna El Jocotal** Get a taste of the rough beginnings of Salvadoran eco-tourism at this bird sanctuary/wetlands preserve. Unfortunately, things still have a ways to go. Women wash clothing and men fish at the lagoon. The area is rich with wildlife and this is one of Central America's key migratory bird refuges–over 250 species stop by between November and April–but passing through the small village and crossing the muddy estuary to reach it isn't the most inviting prospect. You have to take a boat out into the lagoon to truly appreciate the surroundings. A one-hour ride with one of the local fishermen should run about $3.50. A slightly longer trip will allow you to visit one of the four islands in the lagoon; La Monca is the best.

Look for the turnoff for the Cantón Borabollón off the Coastal Highway between San Miguel and Usulután, near a light blue church at km 132. Bus drivers should know where it is. The concrete road leads away from the San Miguel Volcano towards the village. The government was supposed to pave this road to increase tourism, but it looks like they ran out of steam after the first 80 or so meters—from there on in it's all mud. The lagoon is about one kilometer from the small cluster of houses that comprise the village. Notice that the walls and building foundations are built with rock from the San Miguel Volcano.

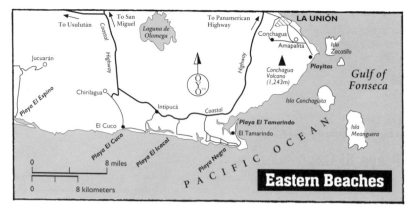

# Eastern Beaches

Some of El Salvador's best beaches are located between Usulután and La Unión along the Coastal Highway. Set against the coastal mountain range, a few have clean, white sand and are hundreds of meters wide.

## Playa El Espino

Playa El Espino is, hands down, both the best beach in the country and the most difficult to get to. But rest assured, the rocky approach over mountains and through small rivers is worth enduring. There are even those who say it is one of the best beaches on Central America's Pacific coast. El Salvador's coastal Shangri-La is a beach connoisseur's dream that will make you want to ride a horse naked down the sand, like in some B-movie dream sequence.

The beach is big enough for a boardwalk, two Club Meds and crowds of thousands, but it's absolutely silent, clean and devoid of gaudy houses. The lazy Pacific waves lap the sand in slow motion, while the beach itself (like any good beach) is lined with palm trees and continues out of sight in either direction. A few *comedores* are near the end of the road, and serve seafood dishes for about $3 on the weekends. Come here to get away from absolutely everything: walk for hours, swing in a hammock, pretend you're a million kilometers from anywhere. You won't be disappointed.

### Good News, Bad News

Getting to Playa El Espino is going to get easier since the 11-kilometer road is currently being paved. After the project is completed (estimates are for August 2001) a hotel will likely open up here. While the chance to spend the night in the palm-fringed paradise is exciting, who knows what else the improved transportation will bring? Club Med just might make it here after all. Major changes won't come overnight, though, so you've still got plenty of time to enjoy this fantastic beach at its best.

El Espino's seclusion has its downside, however. Because of the risk of crime you should not stick around at night and it would be advisable to come in a group during the week.

If you're driving, turn off the Coastal Highway at the sign for Playa El Espino and Jucuarán, 11 kilometers east of Usulután. Follow the road up and over the mountains and stay right at the large tree near the turn-off for Jucuarán at the top of the mountains. After you pass over the crest of the mountains, the ocean never looked so welcoming.

Another option is to come here by boat from Puerto El Triunfo. The round trip will set you back about $100, but you can enjoy the beauty of the bay with its mangroves and desert islets along the way.

## DETAILS
■ **BUSES: Usulután (351)**, 5, 7am, 2pm, 33km, 2hr.

# Playa El Cuco

The road to El Cuco twists its way up and over the coastal mountain range, with a great view of the San Miguel Volcano to the right. The beach itself—once you get away from the little town at the end of the road—is another one of El Salvador's hidden coastal gems. Wide, white sand stretches off into the distance, and everything is yours during the week. The gorgeous vista is completed by palm trees, red tile roofs and mountains in the distance.

Most of the area is privately owned, and consequently some hotels may want to charge you to enter the beach through their property. Get off somewhere along the dirt road that runs parallel to the beach, think inconspicuous thoughts, cross over quietly and you can probably get in for free. Or just ask permission to enter through someone's private lot. You can catch a ride on a pickup running up and down the road along the beach, and shower in one of the local shops for next to nothing. The town is filled with little *comedores* that sell seafood plates for $3.50-$6.75.

## ACCOMMODATIONS

There are a handful of budget choices, but they are all very basic and not especially inviting–you can't even count on them to have blankets. They charge about $6 per person, but you should be able to get that price down during the week.

**Hotel Leones Marinos** A large, walled-in coconut grove that has shaped up considerably in recent years. The rooms are large and have hammocks, but it's still not a good value. *(150m from El Cuco; tel 619-9015; 20D, $29 with fan, $40 with AC and phone, all with private bath, add $5 on weekends; 24hr checkout)*

**El Tropi-Club Cabañas** The club has a grassy area flanked by palm trees good for relaxing. The rooms, with two beds, thatched roofs, brick floors and big fans are clean but not much for the price. A restaurant operates on weekends, serving up shrimp dishes and the like for $6-$11, but they might cook you something during the week if you ask. There are discounted all-inclusive packages if you book in advance *(1km from El Cuco along the road parallel to the beach; tel 619-9006; 12 cabins D $40 with fan, 3 suites $65, all with private bath, AC; laundry; restaurant)*

## DETAILS
■ **BUSES: San Miguel (320)**, every 30 min until 4pm, 37km, 90min.

## Intipucá

**A**t first glance, the unassuming little town of Intipucá near Playa Icacal seems like any other seaside village. Spend some time there, though, and you'll notice that the streets are a little cleaner, the pastel colors a little brighter and the iron gates a little newer in Intipucá than in most towns, and for good reason. Intipucá receives more money from relatives in the US than any other town its size in El Salvador—more, even, than many large cities. Fifteen thousand Intipuqueños live in Washington DC and its suburbs, and send nearly $100,000 back to Intipucá per month.

Such a huge cash flow has had interesting consequences. Five courier services bring packages and letters to this town with a population of just 12,500. More phones calls are made from Intipucá to the US than from almost any other city in the country. During holidays, the national airline offers special deals to residents of Intipucá.

# Playa El Icacal

The clean shores of Icacal stretch for 13 kilometers from end to end, with a great combination of unspoiled beauty and relatively easy access. The soft, white sand is more than 100 meters wide at low tide, and the ocean is only knee-deep even far from the beach. Locals say that this is the safest beach along the estuary that connects to Playa El Cuco. There aren't any places to spend the night, just plenty of palm trees waiting for a hammock. There are a few *comedores*, but come prepared with food and drink just to be sure.

The beach seems wide enough to land a plane on, and it is; during the war, guerrilla contraband and arms were brought in here at night by boat and plane from Nicaragua. Every once in a while a Cessna still lands here.

## GETTING THERE

The turnoff from the Coastal Highway is 25 kilometers southwest of La Unión. Acres of spiky, gray-green maguey (henequen) cover the surrounding fields. The shady dirt track is barely passable by regular car. Four kilometers in, you may have to bribe the gatekeeper with a few *colones* to let you enter this "private" stretch of beach.

## DETAILS

■ **BUSES: San Miguel (385)**, infrequently, 39km, 90min.

# El Tamarindo

This dusty fishing town at the end of the road south of La Unión isn't worth a trip all the way out here just in itself. But a few small openings to the water outside of town lead to cleaner and quieter sections of beach with a great panorama of the nearby volcanoes and islands. El Tamarindo doesn't feel as exotic as Espino or Icacal, but these hidden spots are more easily accessible and more pleasant than any other beaches nearby. Several small *comedores* in town serve delicious cocktails of scallops, oysters, and crabs.

To find a good part of El Tamarindo beach, stop about one kilometer before the town at the first or second dirt road after La Mariscada. From there, take a side passage to the beach past one of the big, well-maintained houses. Even though it's lined with houses and boats, the beach is quiet on weekends; the volcanoes and gently curving shore can almost convince you you're on a tropical island. The bodies of land visible in the bay, from left to right, are the Conchagua Volcano near Usulután, the islands of Conchagüita and Meanguera and the northwest edge of Nicaragua.

## ACCOMMODATIONS

**Hotel Tropitamarindo** Generally decent rooms and a swimming pool for when you aren't in the ocean. The restaurant has fish from $7 and lobsters and shrimp from $13.50. *(Located on the highway to El Tamarindo; tel 649-5082; 5D $65, all with private bath, AC, TV; restaurant 7am-8pm)*

## DETAILS

■ **BUSES: La Unión (383)**, every 90 min until 5pm, 44km, 1hr 30min. **San Miguel (385)**, every 30 min until 4pm, 55km, 2hr 30min.

# La Unión

Pop. 62,000
183km from San Salvador

## LA UNIÓN THEN

La Unión became eastern El Salvador's largest port near the end of the 17th century, replacing the older port of Amapala to the south near Playa El Tamarindo. La Unión was repeatedly attacked by Spanish forces during battles for Central American independence. In 1856, troops from El Salvador and Guatemala set sail

from here to battle William Walker in Nicaragua. In the last two centuries the city has been repeatedly jolted by earthquakes, though none have hit since the late 1940s.

## LA UNIÓN NOW

Just before it reaches La Unión, the Panamerican Highway heads off to the north for the Honduran border at El Amatillo, and the Coastal Highway heads south and west for the eastern beaches. The port city of La Unión is set along the western shore of the Bay of La Unión off of the Gulf of Fonseca, bordered on the south by mountains that fold and slip quietly into the sea. The city went downhill since the port closed in the mid-80s, but the resumption of ferry service to Nicaragua should commence a reversal of fortunes. The city itself is still run-down and dirty with nothing specifically worth seeing, but with all that there is nearby many tourists still find themselves staying here. This is the best place to embark on a trip to one of the islands in the Gulf of Fonseca. You can also use La Unión as a base to explore some of the better beaches to the south by day, and relax at Gallo's Restaurant at night.

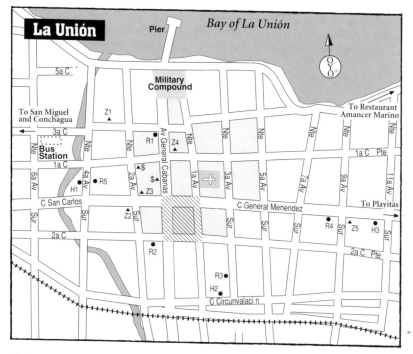

## ACCOMMODATIONS

**Hotel Portobello La Unión** The best hotel deal in La Unión is three stories tall with a parking area, large rooms, clean showers and hammocks in every room. The owner Luís opened the hotel in 1994, and he and his family will help you out around town. He also has some interesting stories to tell about his life in this war-ravaged region, and his rocky road from selling cattle to opening a hotel. *(Tel 604-4113; 20 rooms, $9.20 per room with shared bath and fan, $20 with private bath, AC, cable TV; laundry; 24hr checkout; parking)*

**Hotel San Francisco** Large metal doors off the street mark the entrance to this old but passable hotel. *(Tel 604-4159; 30D, $9.20 with fan, $16 with AC, all with private bath; 24hr checkout; parking)*

**Hotel Centroamericano** Improved in recent years, but still not a great value. Located in a fenced-in yard with the look and feel of a military compound. A big, dated lobby and old bathrooms complete the picture. *(Tel 604-4029; 20 rooms S $14.50, D $21.70 with fan, S $21.70 D $26 with AC, all with private bath; noon checkout; parking)*

● **ACCOMMODATIONS**
H1 Hotel Portobello
    La Unión
H2 Hotel Centroamericano
H3 Hotel San Francisco

● **FOOD & DRINK**
R1 *Cafetín El Marinero*
R2 *Pollo Rico*
R3 *Gallo's Restaurant*
R4 *Snack bar*
R5 *Cafetín El Asador*

▲ **OTHER**
Z1 Office of Immigration
Z2 Basketball Court
Z3 Police Station
Z4 Music Hall
Z5 Hospital

TO THE EAST

## FOOD & DRINK

**Gallo's Restaurant** This classy restaurant is a great deal and one of La Unión's saving graces, with the some of the tastiest food in the area. Waitresses serve steaming plates of real Mexican food that sizzle for a minute after they're set down in front of you. Plates of corn tortillas, burritos, tacos and enchiladas cost $3.50-$5.75.

Owner Alex Gallo worked in a Mexican restaurant in Washington DC for 14 years and then returned to El Salvador to open his own. He wanted to keep prices low so locals could enjoy his restaurant too. There was a problem with the quality of local tortillas, so he buys his Mexican-style tortillas directly from San Salvador. *(8am-midnight)*

**Cafetín El Asador** With a wide variety of tasty Salvadoran food this is a good choice for any meal. Chicken dishes start at $3.50 and fish goes from $4.50 *(7am-8pm)*

**Restaurant Amanecer Marino** A wide variety of seafood served with an outstanding sea view. Dishes start around $5.50. *(12-9pm)*

## DETAILS

■ **BUSES:** To get to the Honduran border at El Amatillo, you must first go to Santa Rosa de Lima. **Conchagua (382)**, every 15 min until 6pm, 4km, 20min. **El Tamarindo (283)**, every 90 min until 5pm, 30km, 1hr 30min. **Playitas (418)**, every hour until 4pm, 13km, 1hr. **San Miguel (324)**, every 8 min until 6pm, 42km, 1hr 20min. **San Salvador (304)**, every 40 min until 4pm, 183km, 4hr. **Santa Rosa de Lima (342)**, every 10 min until 5pm, 48km, 1hr 30min.

■ **FESTIVALS: December 3-31 (7)** Virgen de Concepción.

### A Lasting Legacy

Some of La Unión's inhabitants are descended from English pirates who raped and pillaged their way through indigenous populations in the 17th century. Their distinctive light hair, fair skin and blue eyes serve as a reminder of what El Salvador has endured over the centuries.

# Near La Unión

**Conchagua Volcano** Of all the volcanoes in El Salvador, few have such a choice location; from the top you can see all the islands of the Gulf of Fonseca, Honduras to the east, Nicaragua to the southeast and the Pacific Ocean to the south. The four-hour hike to the peak from the village of Amapalita on the road to Playitas passes coffee plantations and only takes three hours coming back. Head for the antenna at the top of the mountain. *(Take the bus to Playitas and get off at Amapalita)*

**Playitas** Eight kilometers from La Unión, Playitas is a 100-meter black sand beach in front of a fishing village. This is the real thing: wooden fishing boats are rolled up onto the beach on logs, and in the afternoon fishermen repair their nets in the fading light. Some places in town serve drinks and fresh fish. The islands of Conchagüita and Meanguera loom just off the beach. Around the corner to the left are the smaller islands of Martín Pérez and Zacatillo. Zacatillo has the remarkable Playa Carey on its southern end and both are sparsely populated so you will have tranquility and privacy to go along with the scenery. You can hire a boat to reach these islands in Playitas or La Unión–or if you are a strong swimmer you could reach Zacatillo under your own power, but we don't recommend it. Playitas itself isn't the most inviting place to hang out, and the beach itself doesn't justify a trip, but if you like fishing villages you might enjoy a stop here—you'll almost certainly be the only tourist.

☺ ☺ ☺ ☺ ☺

# Isla Meanguera

The island-studded Gulf of Fonseca, where Honduras, Nicaragua and El Salvador meet, is a stunning area of coastal mountains and tranquil fishing hamlets. Because they are so isolated from noisy civilization the islands are home to a great variety of birds, especially aquatic species and the North American winter brings many additional migratory species.

Spanish navigator Andrés Niño sailed here in 1522 becoming the first European to see this part of the world. He was followed by a succession of English pirates who made this their haven throughout the 16th to 18th centuries. Settlements on the islands were frequently plundered and burnt so the inhabitants fled. The islands weren't repopulated until the beginning of the 20th century.

Until a recent border resolution Honduras maintained claims on the gulf's major islands, including Meanguera and Conchagüita. El Salvador cemented their hold by running underwater electrical cables to the islands. Locals, however, still drink their Pilsner and eat their *pupusas* while watching TV from their neighboring nation since antenna TV transmissions from El Salvador don't quite make it this far.

Peaceful Meanguera is truly one of the hidden gems of El Salvador. The largest of El Salvador's islands in the gulf, also has the largest *pueblo* and only hotel. You can pass the time on the spectacular beaches, watch the fishing boats come in to the port or take in spectacular views from the miles of hiking trails. Better yet, spend a few days and do it all. Most of the island's 5000 residents are engaged in fishing and if you ask around you can usually find someone willing to let you accompany them on a fishing trip.

## ACCOMMODATIONS

**Hotel El Mirador** This hotel is the best on the island for one reason—it is the only hotel on the island. The basic rooms all have a double bed, hammock, and fan. It's passable, but the monopoly means the price is a bit high for what you get. The owner, Don Julio César Ramos, can tell you whatever you need to know to enjoy your stay on the island and can arrange transportation if you call ahead. *(Tel 648-0072; 14 rooms with shared bath, $11.50 per room; 10pm curfew; 2pm checkout; restaurant)*

## FOOD & DRINK

At last count the village has three *pupusa* stands, all located just up the road from the fishing port.

**Restaurant El Mirador** Not surprisingly the island's only proper restaurant is attached to the hotel. The good news is that they serve great seafood at reasonable prices. A huge plateful of fish will run you $4 and you can add three jumbo shrimp for a buck. Breakfast comes in at $1.50.

### HIKING

The Island's only road is the one that runs through town so a well established series of hiking trails lead to points throughout the rest of the four-by-two mile island. If the views of the Gulf of Fonseca are not spectacular enough from the hotel, head up for higher ground. Cerro Evararisto rises 512 meters above sea level so needless to say, it offers a spectacular panoramic view of the Gulf. Be sure you take plenty of water because once you leave the village you will not be able to find any.

### BEACHES

Mahujhula, an overwhelmingly huge black sand beach, is one of the country's best. The gradual sloping beach has plenty of palm tree shade, but rarely any people. To walk there just head south out of town and when the road ends take the hiking trail, you will know it when you see it. The hike takes about an hour. You could also hire a boat from the fishing dock for a ten-minute ride–just be sure to arrange a time to be picked up.

### DETAILS

■ **GETTING THERE:** Meanguera and Conchagüita are served by a regular ferry service. The boat leaves La Unión at around 10am and returns from Meanguera at about 5pm. It costs $1.75 each way and you should try to reserve a space the day before if you can. This service is very prone to changes so you may want to call the Hotel El Mirador to see what the current schedule is.

If you ask around the pier you can also hire a boat on your own. You might be able to get a boat to Meanguera for as little as $12-15 but coming back can run as high as $25–bargain hard. Offer half payment up front and the rest when you're picked up (as the song says, "Don't pay the ferryman/ 'til he gets you to the other side…"). Private boats can also be arranged in the village of Playitas, but don't expect a much lower price even though it is closer.

■ **FESTIVALS: March 15-19** San José.

# Conchagua

Potón, "Flying Jaguar"
Pop. 32,500
5km from La Unión

## CONCHAGUA THEN

The original inhabitants of Conchagua lived on the islands of the Gulf of Fonseca, just off-shore from La Unión. The name Conchagua originally belonged to one of the Lenca towns on the island of Conchagüita.

In the late 17th century English pirates raided the islands and pillaged the towns, leaving the indigenous populations with little or nothing. When the townspeople decided to

## Isla Conchagüita

**U**nlike Meanguera, Conchagüita lacks a restaurant, hotel and black sand beach, so it gets very few visitors. However, since the population is minimal it is easier to hike about the island and because it is closer to the port a private boat will be cheaper. You can get fresh water, drinks and pupusas in the tiny village of the same name.

emigrate to the mainland, they petitioned the Spanish king for land and were granted a site on the edge of the Conchagua Volcano. Ten years after founding the new Conchagua, villagers began construction of the church that still survives (with a few new coats of paint).

## CONCHAGUA NOW

This small town is nestled partway up the slopes of the 1,245-meter Conchagua Volcano to the south of La Unión. The church is well maintained and local choirs sometimes perform inside.

Conchagua is charming for what it doesn't have: heat, trash, traffic and crowds. It's a place to come after a day at the beach to breathe in some cool mountain air, sit in on a church service and talk to residents around the *pupusa* stands about their relatives in the US. If you come early enough, you might even be able to join a game of basketball.

Conchagua was one of the places hit hardest by Hurricane Mitch and nearly the entire town was destroyed. The Salvadoran and US Armies did joint community service operations to totally rebuild the town on higher and safer ground. In just a matter of months new roads, water, drains, electric lines and housing were built for the relocated citizens. Though the town has been rebuilt evidence of the strength of nature still abounds. There are rocks the size of 2 and 3 story buildings that were moved around like pebbles during the strongest floods.

If you're driving, take the Panamerican Highway out of La Unión and turn left 20 meters before the Esso gas station, across the road from the cemetery. Soon you'll pass railroad tracks and the cobblestone road becomes paved for the rest of the four kilometers to Conchagua. If you stay until the early evening after the last bus leaves (and you should), you can catch a taxi back to La Unión from here for about $3.50. A ride in the other direction, though, costs about $5.

## FOOD & DRINK

Of the many simple dining rooms and coffee shops in town the Cafetín Villa Central is probably the best. They serve breakfast, lunch, and dinner for $1.25 to $2.25.

## SIGHTS

**Iglesia Colonial de Conchagua** This pretty, cream-colored church, one of the oldest in El Salvador, is decorated with light blue trim. The church was first built in 1693 and still has its original facade. Images inside date back to the 17th century. It suffered a great deal of damage during Hurricane Mitch, but has been carefully restored.

### HIKING

**La Glorieta** If the views from Conchagua aren't enough, the lookout called La Glorieta offers a view out over the city of La Unión, the Gulf of Fonseca and all the way to Honduras. Start on the opposite side of the church and continue uphill on foot for about half an hour.

### DETAILS

▪ **BUSES:** The bus stop is next to the church. **La Unión (382)**, every 15 min until 6pm, 5km, 20min.

▪ **FESTIVALS: January 18-21 (19)** San Sebastián. **July 24-25 (24)** Santiago Apóstol.

# Santa Rosa de Lima

Pop. 37,500
176km from San Salvador
44km from La Unión

### SANTA ROSA DE LIMA THEN

Manuel Días, a rich Spaniard from Peru, bought land in northeastern El Salvador in 1743 and erected an enormous *hacienda* which he named Santa Rosa de Lima in honor of Peru's patron saint. In the 19th-century, a traveler described the town as a "pretty and progressive city with stone streets."

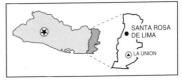

In 1983, El Salvador's eastern border trade with Honduras almost collapsed when rebel troops blew up six bridges connecting the two countries, including the bridge at the El Amatillo border crossing just east of Santa Rosa de Lima. Honduran troops opened fire on the guerrillas but were unable to stop the destruction, which the FMLN claimed was in response to a speech by President Reagan calling for a renewed battle against them.

### SANTA ROSA DE LIMA NOW

The second largest city in La Unión is surrounded by the low mountains that fill northern La Unión and Morazán departments and run to the El Amatillo border crossing to Honduras. Santa Rosa de Lima is a bustling place with lots of buildings under construction. The L-shaped church seems almost too large for the town, but the interior is clean and well kept and has a fresh coat of paint. Because of its proximity to the border the town has more banks than you would expect for a city of this size. There are also several dealers who buy gold which is still extracted from the surrounding hills, though the largest mines have closed.

Many Salvadorans heading for the border spend the night here to get an early start. With the famous La Pema restaurant no longer operating, this is now pretty much the only reason for travelers to stop too.

TO THE EAST

● **ACCOMMODATIONS**
H1   *Hotel Florida*
H2   *Hotel El Recréo*
H3   *Hotel El Tejano*

● **FOOD & DRINK**
R1   *Comedor Charito*
R2   *Pollo Campestre*

▲ **OTHER**
Z1   *El Presidio*
Z2   *Biblioteca Municipal*

Santa Rosa de Lima

## ACCOMMODATIONS

**Hotel El Recreo** Best lounge area in town, complete with couches and chairs. This is the best option in town, but that's not saying much. The concrete rooms are small and stuffy. Despite all this the constant stream of border traffic means you should make a reservation. *(Tel 664-2126; 10S $7, 7D $11, all with private bath, fan, a double with AC costs $20; 11am checkout; free laundry; parking)*

## FOOD & DRINK

**Pollo Campestre** It's a far cry from La Pema, but this Salvadoran chicken chain will do if you need a meal while passing through. Fried and roasted chicken platters start at $1.40 *(10am-8pm)*

## DETAILS

■ **BUSES: El Amatillo (346)**, every 20 min until 5pm, 30km, 1hr 30min. **La Unión (304, 342)**, every 10 min until 5pm, 44km, 1hr 30min. **San Miguel (330)**, every 10 min until 6pm, 40km, 1hr. **San Salvador (306)**, every 30 min until 3pm, 176km, 4hr
■ **FESTIVALS: August 22-31 (30)** Santa Rosa. Includes a famous rodeo.

# San Francisco Gotera

Potón, "High Hill"
Pop. 17,000
170km from San Salvador

## SAN FRANCISCO GOTERA THEN

The ruins of ancient San Francisco Gotera are now no more than two rectangular buildings set atop the Cerro de Corobán, four kilometers to the northeast of the town's pre-

TO THE EAST

sent location. It is uncertain when the town relocated, but the townsfolk were probably motivated by the difficulty of finding drinking water nearby and the strong mountain winds, which made fires difficult to control.

A visitor to the new and improved Gotera in 1811 noted that its indigenous inhabitants spoke a unique dialect of the Lenca Potón language, incomprehensible even to other native speakers. The Goterans, on the other hand, could understand other Potón speakers without a problem.

During the civil war, Gotera had the misfortune to serve as a military stronghold smack in the center of a guerrilla-dominated department. At one point in 1981, urban gun battles left the city's streets filled with bodies.

For most of the war, though, life in the city remained at least superficially normal. San Francisco Gotera was one of the few places in the region that had a consistent supply of electricity. Soldiers filled the streets and the army occupied the central plaza, which didn't leave much room for locals to socialize. Although life in Gotera during the war was difficult, it was simply unbearable in many other towns in the province. The capital became a center of refuge for up to 15,000 people who left towns north of the Río Torola in the early and mid 1980s.

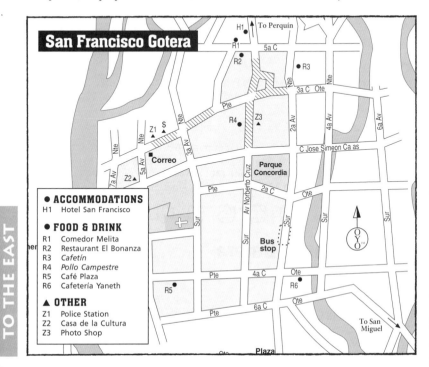

**San Francisco Gotera**

**● ACCOMMODATIONS**
H1    Hotel San Francisco

**● FOOD & DRINK**
R1    Comedor Melita
R2    Restaurant El Bonanza
R3    Cafetín
R4    Pollo Campestre
R5    Café Plaza
R6    Cafetería Yaneth

**▲ OTHER**
Z1    Police Station
Z2    Casa de la Cultura
Z3    Photo Shop

To Perquín

5a C

Nte
3a C Ote
Nte
2a Av
4a Av
6a Av

Pte
R4 ●
Z3 ▲

Z1 ▲   $
Nte
3a Av

Correo

C Jose Simeon Ca as

5a Av
7a Av
Z2 ▲

Av Norberto Cruz

Parque
Concordia

2a C

Pte
Ote

Sur

Sur
Sur
Sur

Bus
stop

R5 ●
Pte
4a C
Ote
R6 ●

Pte
6a C
Ote

To San
Miguel

Plaza

**TO THE EAST**

## SAN FRANCISCO GOTERA NOW

San Francisco Gotera hugs the hills of central Morazán, which give it one of the more beautiful settings in the eastern part of the country. Barefoot children play soccer up and down the city's gently rolling streets. The military compound that once loomed over the town is gone and Gotera has come a long way since the days of the bombs and bullets. After living the most intense and sudden attacks of the war, the town has returned to be the peaceful place that it was before the war years. This is a pleasant place to combine with a visit to Perquín.

## ACCOMMODATIONS

**Hotel San Francisco** A relaxed place with a small courtyard around a garden. Rooms are clean with hanging light bulbs, hammocks and tile roofs. *(Tel 664-0066; 18 rooms, $4.50 per person with shared bath and fan, S $17, D $23 with private bath, cable TV, AC; noon checkout)*

## FOOD & DRINK

**Restaurant El Bonanza** In this big, plain joint you can eat upstairs on the open-air terrace. The prices for seafood are steep, though, and the food is greasy. Shrimp plates are $8 though chicken and beef dishes cost just $3.50. *(9am-10pm)*

**Comedor Melita** Across the street from Bonanza, with cheaper food. *(Mon-Sat 6:30am-7:30pm, Sun 6:30am-1pm)*

**Café Plaza** Set back in a little courtyard with Salvadoran crafts on the walls. Good for a leisurely hamburger and a dish of ice cream. *(6:30am-10pm)*

**Cafetería Yaneth** Grab a coffee and pastry here in the morning, or fast food throughout the rest of the day. Sweetbreads are inexpensive, and a cheeseburger with fries goes for $1.50. *(6am-9pm)*

## SIGHTS

**Iglesia de San Francisco Gotera** This beautiful yellow and white colonial church, built in 1888, is usually locked, but you can get in through a side door to see the interesting tile mosaic in the shape of a huge sun above the altar. At one point during the war, the army was going to tear down this church because it blocked their view of the town from the barracks next door. Fortunately, they didn't.

**Parque Concordia** A small park with a few concrete gazebos sits on top of a hill in the center of the city. From here you can see the entire town below and the surrounding hills that meander off into the distance like a herd of green camels. Climb the wall behind the bust of Francisco Morazán for the best view, but be careful of the drop on the other side. At night, the park isn't safe.

## HIKING

Ask at the Casa de la Cultura—they're very helpful and will point you in the right direction for hiking in the area.

**Cerro Corobán** A foot trail up this mountain near the pueblo of Lolotiquillo (northeast of San Francisco Gotera) has great views all the way to La Unión. The seven-kilometer hike up should take about three hours, less coming down. *(Take bus 337 to Lolotiquillo, head east)*

## DETAILS
■ **BUSES: Lolotiquillo (337)**, service is irregular so check at the bus station in advance, 7km, 1hr. **Perquín (332a)**, infrequently, 33km, 1hr 30min. Goes on to the Honduran border at Sabanetas. **San Miguel (328)**, every 15 min until 6pm, 40km, 1hr. **San Salvador (305)**, this direct service is slow and irregular, 170km, 3hr 30min. You are much better off taking a bus to San Miguel and transferring there.
■ **FESTIVALS: October 1-5 (4)** San Francisco. **November 8-14 (13)** Virgen de Candelaría.

## Near San Francisco Gotera
**"Kilometer 18" Bus Stop** Many people switch buses here at the intersection of the road between San Miguel and Santa Rosa de Lima and the road north to Gotera. Buses pass here heading for Perquín, Gotera, San Miguel, Santa Rosa de Lima and the Honduran border at El Amatillo and Sabanetas.

# Perquín
Potón, "On the Road of Coals"
Pop. 5,400
203km from San Salvador
33km from San Francisco Gotera

### PERQUÍN THEN
If the FMLN had a capital, the northern city of Perquín was it. The city's location was strategically important; Morazán is one of the poorest depart- ments in the country, so residents were more likely to sympathize with the revolutionaries. Also, Perquín sits near an important intersection of three roads that link northern and southern Morazán.

When the army moved through Perquín, rebels retreated into the hills and waited. Government forces never stayed very long in Perquín, since troop deployments into northern Morazán required so many soldiers and because of the constant threat of guer- rilla ambushes. Radio Venceremos, the radio station of the FMLN, remained undetected in its hidden underground bunkers near here for the duration of the war.

Once-prosperous Perquín was abandoned by almost everyone except rebel sympa- thizers during the war, leaving many buildings empty toward the end of the 1980s. By that time, many residents had acquired the ability to identify an airplane by the roar of its engines and could tell where a bomb would drop by the angle of an airplane's flight.

### PERQUÍN NOW
The road from San Francisco Gotera goes up into steep mountains, past slopes filled with henequen, farms with lava rock fences and evergreen trees in the distance.

# The Peace Route

**D**uring the war most of Morazán Department was a living hell for its residents and off limits for travelers. Peace has brought a complete turnaround to the small villages set in the rolling hills of El Salvador's northeast corner. Each of these villages spread out along the roads has something special for the intrepid visitor. Most rewarding, however, is a chat with the residents of these tranquil pueblos. Their stories about the war, village history and the local folklore will be enlightening and entertaining.

Along the "Ruta de la Paz" you will see plantations of henequen, which has been used in El Salvador for thousands of years to produce a soft fiber for making rope and hammocks. You can reach these villages by public transport from San Francisco Gotera and Perquín, but service is irregular so you are best off going with your own wheels.

**CACAOPERA** Nine kilometers north of San Francisco Gotera, is the "Chocolate Orchard," as the name means in Nahuat, whose inhabitants are descendants of the Ulua and Lenca tribes. Many interesting festivals are held throughout the year. On February 5th locals wash the clothes of the Holy Virgin where the Torola and Chiquito rivers merge. The day and the place, located two kilometers north of the village, is called Los Encuentros ("The Encounters"). From the 14th to the 17th of January the Baile de los Emplumadas ("Feather Dance") takes place in the 18th century La Asunción church whose walls are up to five meters thick.

The Guinakirika Museum (Tel 651-0251); open on Saturday afternoons and all day Sunday is worth a visit. Local resident Miguel Amaya has opened his impressive collection of local historical, artistic and cultural artifacts to the public. The name means "From Our Pueblo" in the Lenca language. During the week you can stop by the Casa de la Cultura to see crafts being made. The town is known for its hammocks, made of cotton and henequen; pottery; and sugarcane sweets.

**GUATAJIAGUA** This small Lenca village, 14 kilometers west of San Francisco Gotera, is famous for a unique style of pottery which is colored black using a natural dye made from nacascol shells. As you walk through the streets you will likely see women making the beautiful comales ("frying pans"). The name in the local language means "Valley with Tobacco Fields," but these days it is mostly beans and coffee blanketing the hills.

**CORINTO** Just south of Honduras, along the deep and thickly wooded Río Torola valley, is this bustling market town which thrives on cross-border trade. Locals also produce dairy products and sugarcane sweets. Most visitors come here to see the famous La Gruta del Espíritu Santo (open Tue-Sun 10am-4pm; admission $1; guides are available) which has been declared a national monument. Inside are a series of petroglyphs known as the *arte rupestre* which specialists like Wolfgang Haberland have estimated date to sometime around 1000 AD. You can also ask at the Casa de la Cultura (Tel 658-1217) for information about hikes around town.

The town is most interesting on Wednesdays and Sundays, which are market days, and June 29 when St. Peter, the town's patron saint, is honored. Corinto is 11 kilometers east of Perquín via the same road that leads to Cacaopera.

Halfway there you cross a creaky wooden one-lane bridge over the Río Torola. Keep your eyes peeled for the occasional waterfall and FMLN graffiti.

**Perquín**

To FMLN Museum
1a Av Nte
2a Av Nte
4a Av Sur
6a Av Sur
1a C
3a C
Comedor PADECOMSM
To SF Gotera, Casa de Huéspedes, El Gigante and Hotel Perquín Lenca
8a Av Sur

Perquín is at the end of the road, although at that point it is an exaggeration to call the final few kilometers of the route to Perquín "paved" (or even a road). Though another road heads north to the Honduran border, traveling to Perquín still makes you feel like you're reaching the end of something, as if you could turn around and see the entire country spread out below you.

In town, the bombed out buildings are being repaired and the outside of the church has a large mural of Archbishop Romero. The sun rises and falls behind cone-shaped peaks of the pine-tree-studded mountains surrounding the town. Perquín's climate is cool due to its altitude, and its rocky streets are unbelievably steep. It's difficult getting around in a pick-up truck, and almost impossible in a regular car.

Following the war Perquín became one of the country's most popular tourist destinations, but the FMLN museum, which along makes the long, tough trip here worthwhile, is no longer the only reason people come here. The exodus of Salvadorans from the

## El Mozote

A few crumbling adobe buildings scarred with bullet holes are all that's left of this small town southeast of Perquín. Yet tourists still brave the road up here to snap pictures under the disinterested gaze of a handful of National Police stationed nearby because this quiet spot was the site of one of the worst massacres in Latin American history.

The Salvadoran Army's 800-member Atlacatl Battalion, fresh from training in the US, arrived near El Mozote in December 1981 under the command of the notorious Domingo Monterrosa. The soldiers left the area three days later. Soon after, a chilling story emerged: the battalion had killed as many as 1,000 people in El Mozote and nearby villages and had left the victims, mostly women and children, jumbled together in mass graves or simply buried under the ruins of houses that the soldiers had set on fire before leaving.

The story was told by Rufina Amaya, the sole survivor of El Mozote, who was found lost and hysterical in the woods near her village six days after the army moved out. Later, Amaya described how the soldiers had arrived in El Mozote on the night of December 11 and ordered everyone inside their homes. The next morning they ordered the villagers outside and led them off in groups to be killed—first the men, then the women, then the children. Although some soldiers were initially hesitant to carry out their instructions, they eventually followed orders and systematically proceeded to execute everyone in the town.

region during the war had the unintentional result of protecting the environment and the surrounding forests have some of the richest biodiversity in the entire country. The hiking and birdwatching are fantastic here and the organization PRODETUR (Barrio El Centro, Av Reconstrucción; tel 680-4086, e-mail prodetur@navegante.com.sv) can offer information and advice. Several new eco-tourism projects are planned or already under way in the area including the Río Sapo Ecological Reserve detailed below.

With so much history and potential Perquín is a place you should not miss while you're in El Salvador.

## ACCOMMODATIONS

**Hotel Perquín Lenca** Not just the best place to stay in Perquín, but one of the best mountain lodges in the country. Your room is a well-constructed log cabin decorated with beautiful textiles and other Salvadoran *artesania* set in a pristine natural environment which you can admire from your porch. Their restaurant, La Cocina de Ma'Anita, has a great international menu with steaks and other platters averaging $10. (*Located at Km 205 on the main road to Perquín; tel 661-5077, ext 246 in Perquín, 225-9627 and 226-2094 in San Salvador, e-mail perquin@netcomsa.com, small log cabin with 2 beds $63, 3 beds $72, big log cabin with 4 beds $120, 5 beds $129, 6 beds $137, all with private bath, hot water*)

**Casa de Huéspedes El Gigante** Once the only place to stay in Perquín, and still the town's only budget lodging. This is really just a warehouse partitioned into separate rooms with bunk beds and thin mattresses; you'll think you're in the army. Light sleepers beware, you will hear all the goings on of your neighbors through the thin walls. They also have a cafeteria and even room service of sorts, where you can get breakfast

As soldiers prepared to kill Amaya and a group of other women, she knelt to pray as the others struggled. In the midst of the commotion, Amaya managed to crawl away into the woods. She hid near enough to the town that she could still hear the killings, which went on for hours.

When the press first published Amaya's account and evidence was collected that supported her claims, the Salvadoran government said nothing. For years, government investigations made little progress, and in time the incident became a symbol of how the Salvadoran military operated outside the law, even under the worst circumstances.

The US government, after an investigation by its embassy, claimed that no evidence pointed to a systematic massacre. Behind the scenes, the Reagan administration worked to ease Congressional concerns and to continue military aid.

El Mozote was finally investigated in the early 1990s under pressure from the Salvadoran Truth Commission. In late 1992, the first skeletons were exhumed, followed by hundreds more. Dozens of bodies were found grouped inside buildings where soldiers had shot them from the doorways.

Today, El Mozote is enveloped in a quiet, eerie light during the late afternoon. A few families have moved back into town, but most buildings remain deserted. In the clearing stands a metal sculpture of a family—father, mother, son and daughter—holding hands in silhouette. On the front is an inscription: "They did not die. They are with us, with you and will all humanity."

## Into The Light

**P**erquín is home to the first new electrical cooperative in Central America in decades. Following the war the power companies had more pressing problems than providing electricity to these poor hill communities. So, Myk Manon and Bob Dalton, a couple of dedicated Americans from the Rural Electric Co-op Association (NRECA), with the help of USAID and the locals citizens led by a young women named Sandra Medrano, got the Rural Electrical Co-op of Morazán Department (ACAEM) going on their own. The locals, including many former guerillas, helped build the power lines and today most of the town's people have electricity. If you want to hear a heart-warming story of local development visit Sandra at the co-op when in Perquín.

or dinner for less than $2. (*2 blocks before town on the main road; tel 680-4037; 15 rooms hold 4 people each, $5.75 per person, shared bathrooms, laundry; 24hr checkout; cafeteria*)

## FOOD & DRINK

If you don't want to eat at the Hotel Perquín Lenca (though if you can afford it you should) you have numerous small restaurants and cafeterias in town to choose from, though few stand out. Three kilometers south of town near Segundo Montes is a former guerilla training center that has a simple *cafetería* notable more for the spectacular views of the countryside than the food. Not only do they not have a menu but they don't keep regular hours.

**Comedor PADECOMSM** This simple, rustic joint overlooking the plaza is popular with locals. Food is served on communal picnic tables under naked hanging light bulbs. There's no menu, so the selection just depends on what's in season and in the cook's mind. Most plates are $1.15-$2.20, and chicken soup is $0.80. (*6am-6pm*)

## FMLN MUSEUM

This sobering museum is the place to come face-to-face with the guerrillas and learn one version of the civil war. Numerous exhibits are housed in a series of simple concrete buildings laid out along a dirt road just north of town. The little museum yard is filled with lime trees, rose bushes, a mammoth bomb crater and the remains of military jets and rusted artillery.

The idea for the museum came from Martín Vigil, a wizened, sharp ex-guerrilla. Sr. Vigil scoured the country for museum pieces, photos and memories. The ex-guerrillas who work along with Sr. Vigil give tours daily. No smoking or picture taking is allowed inside, and a small gift shop sells T-shirts and posters.

■ **BUILDING 1: Sala de los Héroes y Mártires** (Room of the Heroes and Martyrs). These photographs provide some background on the famous and not-so-famous who influenced the cause of the FMLN, including Martí, Sandino, Miguel Mármol (a survivor of *La Matanza* and founder of the Salvadoran Communist Party), the victims of El Mozote, assassinated human rights workers and those killed at Romero's funeral. Museum curators traveled to many small *pueblos* to visit the families of those killed and to collect these relics. On the outside back wall are German posters supporting the FMLN.

■ **El Mozote Memorial.** A symbolic grave in memory of victims of the massacre at El Mozote.

■ **Grave of Alvaro Rodriguez Cifuentes Carmona.** Carmona was a Chilean Special Forces soldier who came to El Salvador in the early 1980s to help train the guerrillas. He was killed in Usulután in 1982 when his mortar misfired, and his remains were eventually laid to rest here.

■ **Model Guerrilla Camp.** This mock-up of a temporary guerrilla camp shows the amazingly crude conditions the rebels lived under while in the field. The simpler huts were used until 1981, when plastic huts replaced them. Rebels walked one foot in front of the other to disguise their tracks as they entered and exited campsites.

■ **Bomb Crater.** A 500-pound bomb fell here in 1981. Next to the crater is a disarmed example of this type of bomb, which explodes only after entering the ground, leaving holes the size of houses and hurling shrapnel up to 100 meters.

■ **BUILDING 2, ROOM 1: Causas Que Originaron la Guerra** (Origins of the War). This room presents the cases of those who suffered under military rule. Your guide will explain that they were helpless to change the circumstances of their misery in any way except through violent struggle. Inside are displays of people who suffered and were repressed for complaining, others who organized resistance to the government, US troops deployed in El Salvador and Salvadoran government leaders. There's a seat from an airplane that was shot down by the FMLN, an unintentionally ironic quote from ex-president Reagan ("The time has come for the United States to take the initiative in other parts of the world.") and an intense photo of a man with a pistol looking out onto the Plaza Barrios from the Metropolitan Cathedral in San Salvador.

■ **ROOM 2: Países Solidarnos con la Lucha Revolucionaria** (Countries in Solidarity with the Revolutionary Struggle). The FMLN considered these countries friendly to their revolution and claimed that all except Nicaragua provided only non-combative aid (although Cuba and the USSR funneled arms through Nicaragua).

■ **ROOM 3: Vida de Campamientos** (Camp Life). This display of arms used during the war includes guns confiscated from government troops and homemade rebel bombs. Notice the detonator and instructions for assembling it. On the wall are attack plans used in 1983 to destroy the once grand Cuscatlán Bridge and energy plants. The FMLN motto ("Resist, Grow, Advance") is displayed proudly on the wall, above uniforms captured from government troops. (The "END" label stands for the Salvadoran National Democratic Army.) The far wall has maps showing areas that were controlled by the FMLN.

■ **ROOM 4: Armas Convencionales** (Conventional Armaments). The surface-to-air missile launcher and guns used in war were disabled in accordance with the 1992 peace accord. Notice that the metal on the guns is sliced through the trigger area and that the larger armaments, including a 120mm gun, are disabled at other points.

Behind the building are the remains of helicopters shot down by the FMLN, including one that carried Domingo Monterrosa, the notorious commander of the Atlacatl

# WFMLN: Guerrilla Radio

**H**idden deep in underground bunkers, working with sadly substandard equipment and always on the move to escape detection by the army, the FMLN's Radio Venceremos shared the hardships that many of its listeners had to endure during the civil war. Through it all, Radio Venceremos kept the country informed, connected and entertained.

Radio Venceremos ("We Will Overcome"), whose broadcasts could be heard throughout the country, was the guerrillas' most powerful political and ideological weapon. The station, along with a handful of other clandestine rebel stations, competed with government broadcasts for audience and credibility. But the rebel disc jockeys had more in mind than just advertising revenue, and they mixed news and songs with military reports and political opinions.

Radio Venceremos broadcast continually despite repeated government bombing runs and jamming attempts. Sound rooms were dug into the hillsides, camouflaged and reinforced with concrete. Disc jockeys (including one named Elvis) used repeater stations—boxes placed throughout the country to rebroadcast the signal even further—to reach FMLN troops and anybody else who would listen, especially the rural poor. With a team of three to 15 people, the station broadcast every day at 6pm on FM and short wave, usually from its bunker but sometimes in the field under fire from government troops. Broadcasts were made on three frequencies simultaneously, and disc jockeys instructed listeners to switch from one to the other if the program was jammed.

When the peace accords were signed in 1992, the first song Radio Venceremos played was John Lennon's "Give Peace a Chance." In August of that year Radio Venceremos finally became a licensed station and moved into new headquarters in a middle-class neighborhood in San Salvador (as a unique example of the new San Salvador, some of the station's office space is rented from a member of the right wing ARENA party) and the new pop-heavy play schedule mixes Latin American sounds with European and US rock. The cheap sound mixer, car battery and old auto antenna that once carried the station's signal were replaced with state-of-the-art equipment.

Under the new slogan "Venceremos: Revolutionizing Radio to Unite El Salvador," Radio Venceremos has changed its tune somewhat. Commercials now cost money and they accept ads from all political parties. The station has assumed a moderate political stance and now interviews people it once railed against, such as Salvadoran generals and US ambassadors. As a result, some Salvadorans believe that Radio Venceremos has begun to betray its original audience. The station says they are just giving the people what they want.

Battalion, to his death. The destruction of Monterrosa's helicopter was a major triumph for the guerrillas.

■ **BUILDING 3, ROOM 1: Vida de la Radio Venceremos Durante la Guerra** (Life of Radio Venceremos During the War). On the green table to the right are pieces of a radio transmitter similar to the one used to blow up General Monterrosa's helicopter. The generator was used to power the radio during the war. The drawings on the wall were created in 1983 by Salvadoran schoolchildren in exile in Honduras.

On the middle table are hand-held transmitters and recorders used by Radio Venceremos reporters to report from all parts of the country. Guerrilla reporters amazed listeners with their ability to roam to even the most tightly controlled parts of El Salvador and report on events under the nose of the military. The Casio laptop computers were used to keep track of the number of lives and armaments gained and lost in battles. On the wall to the left are photos of underground tunnels used to hide radio transmitters, protecting them from detection and making it possible to broadcast throughout the country.

■ **ROOM 2: Centro de Memoria Historica.** The green antenna was used to transmit radio signals from northern Morazán.

■ **ROOM 3: Cabina de Transmisión de la Radio Venceremos** (Radio Venceremos Transmitting Room). This mockup of Radio Venceremos' transmission room shows how the original room used cardboard egg holders to minimize noise. Notice the FM and AM transmission signals painted in red. (Take 3a C Pte out of town to the west; tel 680-4053; Tue-Sun 8:30am-4:30pm; $1.15 per Salvadoran, $1.75 per foreigner)

## DETAILS

■ **BUSES: San Miguel (332a)**, infrequently, 85km, 3hr. More frequent departures are available by pick-up trucks which run between Perquín and San Francisco Gotera. They run from about 5am to 5pm and stop at all the towns along the way.

■ **FESTIVALS: January 21-22** San Sebastián. **August 2-8** Winterfest. A celebration of Lenca and Ulúa folklore where you can see traditional dances and crafts. **August 13-15 (14)** Virgen del Tránsito. **December 7** Day of the Bonfires ("Día de los Fogones"). A magical evening of bonfires that goes back to days of the Lenca. **December 9** A vigil is held to commemorate the massacre at El Mozote.

■ **GAS STATION:** If you are coming here (or anywhere in the region) with your own vehicle fill up when and where ever you can as there are no gas stations in Perquín. The nearest one is 20 minutes before town and closes at 5pm.

# Near Perquín

**Llano del Muerto** The Plain of Death is a popular area for hiking. Throughout the pine-tree forest you will find several crystal-clear, spring-fed rivers including the Río Guapo ("Handsome River") which has a beautiful, 30-meter high waterfall known as El Perol. You can walk here from Perquín in about an hour or drive if you have a 4X4; follow the road that leads to Bolsón Nahuaterique in Honduras. A bus, known as Las Marcalenas, runs irregularly from San Miguel to the Honduran border and passes Llano del Muerto along the way.

**Río Sapo Ecological Reserve** The Río Sapo ("Toad River"), so named because of its green waters, is one of the cleanest and most biologically rich rivers in the country.

It is also the sight of one of the most ambitious eco-tourism projects in the country and the first to be created by the private sector.

Though still in its infancy, the goal is to protect over 6000 hectares. Phase 1, a 200-hectare pilot project, designed to win the confidence of the surrounding communities, has just been completed. The success of eco-tourism is vital to the region since, unlike the volcanic soil across most of the country, the ground in this northern region is rocky and not suited to agriculture. If successful this initiative will give many of the poor villagers an alternative source of income.

More than 70 species of birds have been recorded here including toucans, hummingbirds, roadrunners, and the large White King Vulture. You might also be lucky enough to spot an otter, coyote, ocelot or panther–all severely threatened in El Salvador.

Hiking, mountain biking, horseback riding, rock climbing and canoeing are all fantastic here and as the project moves forward trails will be developed. The Eco Albergue Rio Sapo campground ($3.50 per night, get permission to use it at PRODE-TUR or the FMLN museum in Perquín) has space for about 10 tents plus toilets, showers, picnic tables, and cooking and laundry facilities. Tents can be rented. If you don't want to cook for yourself the park rangers and their families will provide you with meals for a few dollars.

To get there go to Arambala and then take the paved road towards Joateca for five kilometers to Cumaro. For more information contact PRODETUR in Perquín or CORSATUR in San Salvador.

😃 😃 😃 😃 😃

# Ciudad Barrios

Pop. 27,000
159km from San Salvador
48km from San Miguel

## CIUDAD BARRIOS THEN

The original Potón name for this town was Cacahuatique, meaning "Hill of the Cocoa Gardens," but it was changed in 1913 in memory of a prominent local coffee farmer. Although this small northern town was the army's strongest outpost in the northern part

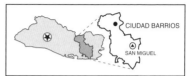

of San Miguel during the civil war, the city suffered repeated street battles. The nearby coffee cooperative was occasionally the focus of guerrilla attacks.

Guerrillas positioned themselves on the slopes of Cerro Cacahuatique, five kilometers to the east, and launched periodic raids on the town. When the FMLN became entrenched in Ciudad Barrios, the government sent in paratroopers and chased the guerrillas back into the hills with helicopters.

In 1982, rebel troops burned down all the public buildings in Ciudad Barrios. In November of the following year, a force of 500 guerrillas occupied the town, forced 87 government soldiers to surrender, and executed all of them.

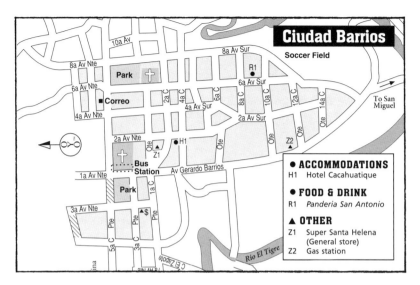

## CIUDAD BARRIOS NOW

The road to Ciudad Barrios from the Panamerican Highway passes through Moncagua and Chapeltique. The 15-kilometer drive heads up a beautiful valley with steep green hills rising on either side. Streams cascade down the hillside to the left and run under the road. The fields to either side look too steep to stand in, let alone cultivate, but cultivated they are. Sit on the right of the bus if you can bear being so close to the steep drop-off.

The road emerges from the high end of the valley into the lush, rolling hills of the Cacahuatique mountain range as it reaches Ciudad Barrios. In the city, kids on horseback ride up and down steep cobblestone roads which leave first-floor windows suddenly three meters above the street. Many residents work in the coffee plantations just outside of town The huge Iglesia Roma looks like a warehouse complete with corrugated metal roof. A bust out front commemorates Archbishop Romero, who was born in Ciudad Barrios.

If you're really looking to get away from it all, Ciudad Barrios is a good escape. Come here to enjoy the cool mountain air and to talk with the residents—that is, if you can get past the curious stares. There aren't many tourists who make it this far off the beaten track, so you'll really feel like a visitor here. From October to February you have the added bonus of being able to observe the coffee harvest and the milling of sugarcane juice. There's some good hiking in the nearby mountains; ask around for details.

## ACCOMMODATIONS

**Hotel Cacahuatique** Lucky for you the only place in town is well kept. Clean rooms and…(drum roll)…hot showers! To find it, head for the din of the arcade next door. *(Tel 665-9160; 17 rooms, $8.60 per person, all with private bath, hot water; laundry; noon checkout; cafetín)*

## A Helping Hand

Enrique Ayala is a good person to know in Ciudad Barrios. After ten years in the US, Enrique came back to his childhood home and discovered that Ciudad Barrios needed him. For the last 15 years he has taught English in an academy for poor local students. He welcomes visitors to drop by with any questions about the area, or just to chat. Ask for him in town or call him at 665-9003. You can also e-mail him at super-hierro@yahoo.com.

## FOOD & DRINK

Don't come here expecting fine dining. Your only options are simple coffee shops, *comedores* and *pupuserías* spread around town where you can pick up tacos, tamales and other local foods for about $1.50 per plate. **Las Gemelas**, the most popular *pupusería*, is in the center. The **Santa Helena Shop** is a good place to pick up trail food for hikes.

## SIGHTS

**El Amaton Ecological Park** This park, recently opened by the Coffee Grower's Association of Ciudad Barrios is a hit with the locals. After admiring what remains of the farm that used to be here, including coffee plants and the deer yard, you can enjoy the swimming pool and basketball and tennis court. There is also, of course, a coffee shop. (*Located on the main road, 1 km south of town; 9am-6pm; admission $0.60*)

## HIKING

**Cacahuatique Hill** This extraordinarily beautiful place has been declared an ecological reserve due to the area's biological diversity. There are fantastic views from the summit of this extinct volcano (1663 meters) as well as from many points on the surrounding trails. Plan on nearly two hours to make the five-kilometer hike to the top. If you have the time and skill you can make several long treks from Ciudad Barrios, but if you plan to get far off the beaten path take a good map and know how to use it or hire a guide.

## DETAILS

■ **BUSES: San Miguel (316, 317)**, irregular service, usually one trip in the morning and one in the afternoon at around 4:30pm, 48km, 2hr.

■ **FESTIVALS: January 10-11** Señor de la Roma. **February 6-14 (13)** Jesús del Rescate. **March 19** San José. **March 24** The assassination of Archbishop Romero is remembered with a mix of local and religious celebrations by large crowds. **June 26-29 (28)** San Pedro. **December 11-12 (11)** Virgen de Guadalupe. Features the Procession of the Virgin, with people in indigenous dress accompanied by bands and fireworks.

# SPANISH PHRASEBOOK 😄 😄 😄

## Pronunciation

a – like f*a*ther (just remember *Adiós*)
e – in between g*e*t and th*e*y
i – like pol*i*ce
o – like ph*o*ne
u – like b*oo*t except when it follows c g
   or h then like w and when it
   follows a q it is silent.

c – like *c*at except before e and I then
   like *s*it
h – silent
j – like *h*ope
ll – like *y*es
ñ – like ca*ny*on
v – like *b*oy
y – like wh*y*, except when it is alone,
   then like b*e*
z – like *s*afe

## Numbers

0 – *cero*
1 – *uno(a)*
2 – *dos*
3 – *tres*
4 – *cuatro*
5 – *cinco*
6 – *seis*
7 – *siete*
8 – *ocho*
9 – *nueve*
10 – *diez*
11 – *once*
12 – *doce*
13 – *trece*
14 – *catorce*
15 – *quince*
16 – *dieciséis*
17 – *diecisiete*
18 – *dieciocho*
19 – *diecinueve*
20 – *veintiuno*

21 – *veinte y uno*
30 – *treinta*
40 – *cuarenta*
50 – *cincuenta*
60 – *sesenta*
70 – *setenta*
80 – *ochenta*
90 – *noventa*
100 – *cien*
101 – *ciento uno*
200 – *doscientos*
1,000 – *mil*
2,000 – *dos mil*

## Greetings and Civilities

Hello. – *Hola.*
Good morning. – *Buenos días.*
Good afternoon. – *Buenas tardes.*
Good evening. – *Buenas noches.*
How are you? – *¿Cómo está?*
Good bye. – *Adiós.*
See you later. – *Hasta luego.*
Thank you. – *Gracias.*
Thank you very much. – *Muchas gracias.*
You're welcome. – *De nada.*
Excuse me. – *Perdóneme.*
I'm sorry. – *Lo siento.*
please – *por favor*

## Accommodation

Can I see a room? –*¿Puedo ver una habitación?*
single room – *habitación sencilla*
double room – *habitación doble*
bathroom – *baño*
shower – *ducha*
hot water – *agua caliente*
towel – *toalla*
fan – *ventilador*
air conditioner – *aire acondicionado*
blanket – *manta*
key – *llave*

## Food & Drink

menu – *menú, lista*
breakfast – *desayuno*
lunch – *almuerzo*
dinner – *cena*
fork – *tenedor*
spoon – *cuchara*
knife – *cuchillo*
napkin – *servilleta*
salt – *sal*
pepper – *pimienta*
bread – *pan*
fruit – *fruta*
water – *agua*
carbonated water – *agua gaseosa*
non-carbonated water – *agua natural*
bottled non-carbonated water – *agua cristal* or *agua purificada*
coffee – *café*
tea – *té*
juice – *jugo*
beer – *cerveza*
I am a vegetarian. – *Soy vegetariano(a)*
I can not eat meat, chicken or fish. – *No puedo comer carne, pollo o pescado.*
Check please. – *La cuneta por favor.*

## Getting Around

I want a ticket to…
                – *Necesito un tiquete a…*
I want to stop at…
                – *Necesito parar en…*
Stop! – *¡Pare!*
bus station – *terminal terrestre*
airport – *aeropuerto*
boat – *lancha*
street – *calle*
highway – *carretera*
left – *izquierda*
right – *derecho*
straight ahead – *adelante*
next – *próximo(a)*
first – *primero(a)*
last – *último(a)*
near – *cerca*

far – *lejos*

## Other Useful Words and Phrases

Do you speak English? – *¿Habla Inglés?*
I don't understand. – *No entiendo.*
Where is…? – *¿Dónde está…?*
I need… – *Necescito…*
How much does it cost? –
                *¿Cuanta cuesta?*
cheaper – *más barato*
too expensive – *muy caro*
large – *grande*
small – *pequeño(a)*
more – *más*
less – *menos*
today – *hoy*
tomorrow – *mañana*
yesterday – *ayer*
yes – *sí*
no – *no*
bank – *banco*
telephone – *teléfono*
condoms – *condónes*
tampons – *tapónes*
aspirin – *aspirina*
I'm sick. – *Estoy enfermo.*
doctor – *doctor*
hospital – *hospital*
Help! – *¡Ayuda!* or *¡Auxilio!*
Police! – *¡Policia!*

# INDEX

NOTES

NOTES